THE GROWTH OF ENGLISH SCHOOLING
1340-1548

THE GROWTH OF
ENGLISH SCHOOLING
1340-1548

*Learning, Literacy, and Laicization
in Pre-Reformation York Diocese*

Jo Ann Hoeppner Moran

PRINCETON UNIVERSITY PRESS
PRINCETON, NEW JERSEY

Copyright © 1985 by Princeton University Press
Published by Princeton University Press, 41 William Street,
Princeton, New Jersey 08540
In the United Kingdom:
Princeton University Press, Guildford, Surrey

All Rights Reserved

Library of Congress Cataloging in Publication Data will be
found on the last printed page of this book

ISBN 0-691-05430-4

Publication of this book has been aided by
a grant from The Andrew W. Mellon Foundation

This book has been composed in Linotron Caslon

Clothbound editions of Princeton University Press books
are printed on acid-free paper, and binding materials are
chosen for strength and durability

Printed in the United States of America
by Princeton University Press, Princeton, New Jersey

TO MY FAMILY
ESPECIALLY MY HUSBAND TED
AND TO THE
MEMORY OF DAVID S. BERKOWITZ

CONTENTS

CHARTS AND MAP

TABLES

PREFACE

This study investigates the causes, course, and consequences of educational growth in pre-Reformation northern England. It goes beyond prior research on the subject in the development of quantitative data, the use of wills as a source for educational history, and the investigation of the impact that educational change had. The results, in numbers of grammar and especially of elementary schools, have led me to argue that opportunities in elementary and secondary education before 1548 were much greater and expanding more rapidly than previous historians have supposed. By concentrating on a specific but fairly comprehensive data base, the records of York diocese, not only does this study present a detailed picture of the educational resources of the time, but it also offers a more extensive analysis of their impact upon both the clergy and the laity than has hitherto been available.

The choice of York diocese for such an investigation was originally inspired by A. F. Leach's two-volume collection on *Early Yorkshire Schools*. Although Leach chose to print documents for only a select number of schools, the wealth of information he uncovered suggested, at an early stage in my research, that this was a rich field of inquiry. York diocese was also attractive because, geographically, it was the largest of seventeen medieval dioceses, composed of some seven hundred parishes, twenty-four deaneries, and five large archdeaconries. It included all of Yorkshire and Nottinghamshire, the northern half of Lancashire, and small parts of Westmorland and Cumberland. Although York was not the most populous of the dioceses, it nonetheless contained approximately 10 percent of the nation's people. Topographically they were distributed over a tremendous variety of terrain, from the isolated mountain valleys of the Pennines to the wild moorlands of the North Riding and the "champion" country of the vales of York, Cleveland, and Trent. With its southernmost boundary located barely 100 miles north of London and its northernmost boundary only 20 miles from the Scottish border, York diocese served as the link between southern England and the wilder northern border regions. Thus the results of a study of this diocese, large and diverse as it was, cannot be explained away as idiosyncratic or isolated from the rest of England.

The question that initiated my research over ten years ago was: What was the relationship between education, literacy, and the English Reformation? In pursuit of an answer to this question I had to address a wide range of issues. In order to document the educational changes and especially in order to investigate levels of literacy, it was first necessary to consider whether one could differentiate elementary from secondary education in the documents. While it is indeed possible, as well as methodologically desirable, to do so, medieval educational categories were relatively fluid, and separating levels of learning, which is both useful and justifiable, is also tentative. Once this task was completed, a number of other questions remained: How much evidence for schooling is there in the late medieval and early Tudor period? How does this evidence relate to the available sources, and what does it tell us about educational developments in the period between 1340 and 1548? Is there corroborative documentation for the growth in educational opportunities? What was the relationship between the Church and pre-university, pre-Reformation education? Or between the laity and education? How did an increase in available schooling affect clerical recruitment? lay literacy? or the relations between clergy and laity? In the end the answers to all these questions reinforce one another, and the picture that emerges—one of dramatic educational development in the two centuries before the Reformation—is consequently all the more convincing. In the final analysis, the results suggest a need to revise current interpretations of the English Reformation as catalyst for an educational revolution in the sixteenth century.

The book opens with a survey of the debate over medieval English elementary and secondary education. Chapter one begins by evaluating the contributions of A. F. Leach and, more recently, Nicholas Orme, both of whom argue that medieval education was expanding from at least the twelfth century on to the eve of the Reformation. It then attends to the counterarguments of Joan Simon and W. K. Jordan, who share a more negative view of pre-Reformation education, and to the picture presented by Lawrence Stone of an educational revolution not beginning in force until the second half of the sixteenth century. Recent studies in literacy contribute to the debate. Although the evaluation of medieval literacy is a complicated endeavor, current research suggests a growth in the numbers of literate laity from the twelfth century on. Thus far, however, sixteenth-century historians have not yet begun to integrate these more recent findings into their work.

This study is rooted in the tradition of Leach and Orme. Based upon new findings from York diocese, it details the increase in elementary and secondary education in the two centuries before the Reformation and stresses the significance of rising medieval literacy. Chapter two begins to introduce the evidence from York with a survey of the curricula of late medieval English schools drawn largely but not exclusively from York diocesan documents. While this chapter points out the flexibility of medieval schools in terms of curriculum, it also argues that contemporaries did differentiate between song, reading, writing, and grammar educations, and modern historians should try to do likewise. Chapter three develops a methodology for determining the types of schools mentioned, often fleetingly, in the documents. At the same time, the reader is cautioned not to interpret the institutional nature of these schools in an overly rigid sense. The flexible, transitory, and often indeterminate nature of medieval schools, especially at the elementary level, is at odds with the historian's need to analyze and therefore to categorize. The evidence is widely scattered and sometimes frustrating in its brevity. Only very infrequently is one fortunate enough to learn just which texts were being studied in a particular school or to discover the statutes that describe precisely its purpose. In order to try to overcome these limitations, it is helpful to develop further criteria based on the evidence with regard to age, gender, and number of scholars; level of learning displayed; subsequent careers of scholars; status and learning of the schoolmaster; and the physical circumstances of the school itself. The ensuing analysis reflects the difficulties inherent in research that depends on local sources which are neither comprehensive nor produced for the purpose of making educational data available. To a certain degree, therefore, our present understanding must remain problematic.

Even considering the source limitations, the evidence points to over 250 schools of one kind or another in York diocese in the two centuries prior to the Reformation, a number greater than the next best estimate for all of England. Some of these schools were longstanding; many were not. Some, especially at the elementary level, had little institutional basis and should be understood to be "schools" only in a qualified sense and for lack of another appropriate label. Overall, the references to schools, scholars, and schoolmasters increase markedly throughout the period and especially in the fifteenth and early sixteenth centuries. While part of the climb in numbers, especially of the elementary schools, is a function of the greater availability of sources, there are a variety of reasons, detailed in Appendix A, why the increasing references to education reflect a real, growing educational presence at all levels prior to 1548. Chapter four, which presents the tabulation of schools, argues that this impressive increase must still represent an underestimate. Since a complete body of educational data from the medieval and early Tudor periods can never be fully recovered, because so much of the educational process was ephemeral, and because many schools combined elementary reading, writing, song, and grammar functions, there are an unknown number of schools that will have escaped documentation. The study concludes that one can no longer talk about the educational revolution of the sixteenth century without taking into account the pre-Reformation developments in grammar, but especially in elementary education.

A further task of the study is an explanation of this late medieval, early Tudor growth in education. Chapter five argues that it was spurred, in part, by the Church in the wake of demands for better-educated clergy, and, after the bubonic plague struck in 1348, demands for more clergy to say masses for the dead. The result was an enormous increase in the ordinations of priests. The educational level of these clergy is a particular focus of this chapter. Chapters six and seven argue that the developing educational opportunities also promoted a rise in lay literacy and increasing lay involvement in education. By the turn of the sixteenth century laity were more and more likely to be founding and endowing schools, supporting scholars, sending sons to local schools, or maintaining a household school. The book concludes that lay concern with education owed much to traditional religious values, and that it began well before the impact of printing or humanism, or the emergence of Reformation sentiments. The origins of the "educational revolution" of the sixteenth century are clearly pre-Reformation. And in the end the trend toward large numbers of clergy, occurring simultaneously with increasing lay literacy and the laicization of education, prepared the way for the Reformation.

The dates in the title, 1340-1548, reflect the availability of data. The approximately 15,000 wills that I have examined are the best source for York diocesan elementary education in the fourteenth and fifteenth centuries, but they are available for the first time in any number only in the 1340s. Similarly, the ordination data, essential to the argument in chapter five, are only available from the 1340s on. The year 1548 marks the dissolution of the chantries and the compilation of the chantry certificates. These provide, by the mid-sixteenth century, better information on schools than do the wills, and it therefore seemed appropriate to extend the study to include them. At the same time, 1548 also seems an appropriate place to halt. Whether or not the chantry dissolutions disrupted English education (and it seems increasingly clear that any disruption was minimal), by 1548 the Reformation, and to a lesser degree the rise of humanism, had begun to make an impact on the legacy left by a more Catholic, less classically learned but nonetheless educationally motivated age.

Besides the wills, ordination lists, and chantry certificates, other manuscript sources used in this study include a range of materials from the ecclesiastical archives such as inventories, archbishops' registers, visitation records, chapter acts, churchwardens' accounts, and foundation statutes for schools; materials in the Public Record Office relating to specific schools; and town records from York and Hull. In addition, I have consulted much of the available printed primary sources for York diocese from 1300 to 1550, along with printed sources on schools and schooling in other parts of England.

The research and writing for this book have taken more than ten years to complete. Over the decade my debts to others have been multifold. I am primarily indebted to the staffs of the Borthwick Institute, the York Minster Library, and the Public Record Office, especially to D. M. Smith, William Sheils, and C.B.L. Barr. I would like to give particular credit to David Berkowitz of Brandeis University, who supervised the original dissertation. It is a great sadness to me that Professor Berkowitz, who continued to be an invaluable help as well as an excellent critic and friend, died before he could see the printed book. I would also like to express my appreciation to A. G. Dickens, who first encouraged me to use the York archives and whose supportive letters and conversations over the years have buoyed the spirit. The advice that R. B. Dobson and Claire Cross have given me at York has been crucial through the various stages of rethinking and rewriting the original dissertation, and I am particularly grateful for Barrie Dobson's reading of the final version. Nicholas Orme, at the University of Exeter, has also been most helpful, and my task would have been much more difficult without his various publications at hand. I want to thank William Courtenay, Joel Rosenthal, John McKenna, J. N. Miner (Br. Bonaventure), and John Thomas for their support and for reading various drafts of articles and chapters. Fellowships received from the Woodrow Wilson Foundation in 1970-1972, from the ACLS in the summer of 1977, and from Georgetown University in the summer of 1981 made it possible to do sustained archival research in England. These trips were supplemented by the resources of the Mormon Genealogical Library, which has filmed most of the diocesan probate records of England. Without its invaluable microfilm library, available through its branch libraries, such a study could never have been attempted from this side of the Atlantic. My colleagues, first at George Washington University and then, for the past five years, at Georgetown, have been wonderfully supportive. Mary Dyer has typed successive drafts of the manuscript with care and good cheer. Jim Todesca has carefully checked the footnotes and helped compile the bibliography. But most of all, I am indebted to my husband, Ted, and my children Robbie and Jamie, who have travelled with me to England or stayed at home without me, provided me the time to write, and convinced me that it was worth the sacrifices.

Georgetown University
January, 1984

ABBREVIATIONS

BI	Borthwick Institute of Historical Research, York
BJES	*British Journal of Educational Studies*
CPR	Calendar of Patent Rolls
D. & C.	Dean and Chapter
EETS	Early English Text Society
EHR	*English Historical Review*
Emden, *BRUC*	A. B. Emden, *A Biographical Register of the University of Cambridge to 1500* (Cambridge, 1963)
Emden, *BRUO*	A. B. Emden, *A Biographical Register of the University of Oxford to 1500*, 3 vols. (Oxford, 1957-1959)
Emden, *BRUO, 1501-1540*	A. B. Emden, *A Biographical Register of the University of Oxford 1501-1540* (Oxford, 1974)
EYS	*Early Yorkshire Schools*, ed. A. F. Leach, 2 vols., YAS rec. ser., nos. 27, 33 (Leeds, 1898-1903)
J. Eccl. Hist.	*The Journal of Ecclesiastical History*
Leach, *ESR*	A. F. Leach, *English Schools at the Reformation, 1546-8* (Westminster, 1896)
Leach, *SME*	A. F. Leach, *The Schools of Medieval England* (London, 1915)
L & P, Henry VIII	*Letters and Papers, Foreign and Domestic, of the Reign of Henry VIII*, ed. J. S. Brewer, J. H. Gairdner, and R. H. Brodie, 21 vols. (London, 1860-1920)
NCW	*North Country Wills: Abstracts of Wills at Somerset House and Lambeth Palace, 1383-1558*, ed. J. W. Clay, Surtees Society, no. 116 (Durham, 1908)
Orme, *ESMA*	Nicholas Orme, *English Schools in the Middle Ages* (London, 1973)
Power, *Med. Eng. Nunneries*	Eileen Power, *Medieval English Nunneries c. 1275 to 1535* (Cambridge, 1922)
PCC	Prerogative Court of Canterbury
Prob. Reg.	Probate Register
PMLA	*Proceedings of the Modern Language Association*
PRO	Public Record Office
Reg.	Archbishop's Register
Rot. Parl.	*Rotuli Parliamentorum*
STC	Short Title Catalogue

ABBREVIATIONS

Test. Ebor.	*Testamenta Eboracensia*, ed. James Raine et al., 6 vols., Surtees Society, nos. 4, 30, 45, 53, 79, 106 (Durham, 1836-1902)
TRHS	*Transactions of the Royal Historical Society*
VCH	*The Victoria History of the Counties of England*
York Civic Rec.	*York Civic Records*, ed. Angelo Raine, 5 vols., YAS rec. ser., nos. 98, 103, 106, 108, 110 (Leeds, 1939-1946)
YML	York Minster Library
YAJ	*Yorkshire Archaeological Journal*
YAS rec. ser.	Yorkshire Archaeological Society Record Series

THE GROWTH OF ENGLISH SCHOOLING
1340-1548

CHAPTER 1

Medieval and Early Tudor Education and Literacy: The Debates

Throughout most of this century the history of medieval and early Tudor English education has been shaped by the views of one man, Arthur Francis Leach, who argued, often passionately, that medieval education was dynamic and growing, while the policies of the Reformation, especially under Edward VI, were educationally destructive. Leach's interpretations, particularly of the Reformation, were not always sufficiently supported by his sources, and the value of his work has remained an issue among scholars ever since.

In 1884 Leach was appointed an assistant charity commissioner under the Endowed Schools Act. His first assignments were to look into the history of two schools, one at Chichester Cathedral and the other at Southwell Minster in York diocese. Subsequently he expanded his inquiries into the early histories of other collegiate, cathedral, and chantry schools. In 1914, in a paper read before the British Academy, Leach described the results of his thirty-year investigations. "My researches have led me first to doubt, then to deny, and finally to disprove the authorized version, and to revise, recast, or perhaps rather to create *de novo* the history of English education, through that of the schools in which it was given."[1]

In his revision of English educational history Leach engaged in a series of furious controversies—over the importance of medieval monastic schools (which he denied), the existence of girls' education (which he likewise denied), the availability of schools in the Middle Ages (greater in proportion to the population than the nineteenth-century schools), and the role of the government of Edward VI in the history of English education (destructive). His polemics were backed by an impressive amount of research. Leach was the first to explore systematically the evidence for medieval schools, and his two general studies (*English Schools at the Reformation*, 1896, and *The Schools of Medieval England*, 1915), in addition

---

[1] A. F. Leach, "Some Results of Research in the History of Education in England; with Suggestions for Its Continuance and Extension," *Proceedings of the British Academy* 6 (1913-1914):436.

to various editions of documents and numerous articles on schools in the *Victoria History of the Counties of England*,[2] formed the basis for all subsequent work on medieval and Reformation schooling until the publication of Nicholas Orme's *English Schools in the Middle Ages* in 1973. As a consequence of the importance of his publications and the ferocity of his arguments, Leach's work has continued to be a touchstone for historians of English educational history while at the same time remaining an object of ongoing, often bitter debate.

Leach was arguing against two entrenched views of nineteenth-century historians: first, that medieval education was mainly monastic, deteriorating with the decline of religious houses in the fourteenth and fifteenth centuries; and second, that the origins of the modern English grammar school lay in the Tudor foundations of the sixteenth century. Leach disagreed strongly with both of these assumptions, neither of which had much, except tradition, to recommend it. In his pioneering contributions, Leach attempted to trace the evolution of grammar schools in the cathedral, collegiate, and parish churches from the twelfth and thirteenth centuries onward, and in several cases from pre-Norman times. But Leach was not a professional historian, and his work has an antiquarian cast to it. Although his knowledge of the educational sources was unrivalled, in some ways Leach was an enthusiastic amateur who, as F. W. Maitland noted with regard to Leach's edition of Beverley town documents, sometimes "gives the rashest judgment about the most disputable matters."[3] Leach overstated his arguments, being unwilling to concede, for example, that monks or monasteries made *any* positive contribution to secular or even religious teaching. When evidence for the existence of a monastic school appeared incontrovertible, Leach downgraded the educational role of the monastery by stating that it held the school and lands endowed for the school in trust or maintained it out of appropriated rectories. He thereby proved, to his own satisfaction, that the monastic role was that of financial middleman and that the monasteries had no interest in education per se.[4]

Leach's contemporaries were well aware of problems in his work. In a letter of 16 November 1916 to the Reverend A. T. Fryer, R. L. Poole stated that, "He [Leach] may generally be depended upon for what he says about the late middle ages and the sixteenth century; but for early

[2] There is an incomplete bibliography of Leach's work at the beginning of Leach, *SME*. J. N. Miner (Br. Bonaventure) at the University of Windsor is currently preparing a book on Leach that will include a full bibliography of his writings.

[3] C.H.S. Fifoot, *Frederick William Maitland: A Life* (Cambridge, Mass., 1971), 242-43; see also Orme, *ESMA*, 3-7.

[4] Leach, ESR, i:16-19; Leach, SME, chaps. 3-7.

times he is not only highly prejudiced but also ill informed." And in a subsequent letter to Fryer, Poole added:

> Great as were Mr. Leach's merits as an explorer of a particular subject, he was apt to go astray when he went outside it. In particular, he had monks "on the brain" and would never believe that they contributed anything to the advance of letters and learning. Consequently if he found a monk doing anything which he approved, he at once attempted to prove that he was not a monk at all. . . . When any evidence did not suit Mr. Leach's views, it was straightway condemned as a forgery. This prejudice vitiates a great deal of what he has written about early times.[5]

In an oft-cited review of Leach's last book, A. G. Little noted that, "Mr. Leach is a pioneer, and, like most pioneers, is prone to exaggeration and prejudices." Little detailed Leach's anti-monachism, showing that Leach mistranslated and misunderstood several crucial Latin passages, and asserting that he was "reckless in disputing the authenticity of documents which did not suit his views." Although Leach was a safer guide from the twelfth century on, Little contended that he continued to underestimate the extent of monastic involvement in education and was overly enthusiastic with regard to the educational role of cathedral and collegiate churches. Arguing by analogy with the early schools found in some of the cathedral and collegiate churches, Leach went too far in concluding that "there can be no manner of doubt then that all the [eleventh and twelfth-century] cathedral and collegiate churches kept schools."[6]

Little's review did not cover all the problems, and he might well have noted cases where, from one or two recorded instances of a school, Leach would argue for its continued existence over several centuries. Although Leach was acutely aware of the problem of continuity, he tended to err on the optimistic side. As for parish chantry schools, Leach often dated them from the foundation of the chantry rather than from the first recorded date of the school. And he was prone to affirming the existence of a grammar school when the documents refer only to a school or to the teaching of young children. The result is to render Leach's estimate of

---

[5] Letters pasted to the inside of Rev. Fryer's copy of Leach, *ESR*, in Widener Library, Harvard University (Educ 806.16B).

[6] *EHR* 30 (1915):525-29; Leach, *SME*, 115. There is a rejoinder to Little's review by W. N. Chaplin, "A. F. Leach: A Re-appraisal," *BJES* 11 (1962-1963):99-124. Chaplin argues convincingly that Leach's statements only apply to the early collegiate foundations and not to the smaller fourteenth- and fifteenth-century colleges of priests. This does not obviate the problem that these earlier schools have not all been documented.

some three hundred grammar schools in England by the year 1535[7] useful only after careful confirmation and constant allowance for his biases.

Leach's second major assertion was the damaging, indeed disastrous, effect of the dissolution of the chantries (and, to a much lesser extent, the dissolution of the monasteries) upon the grammar schools. His sentiments on the roles of Henry VIII and Edward VI in the history of English education were strongly worded:

> The "true truth" about the matter, is that so far from Henry VIII or Edward VI being benevolent founders of schools, they were their spoilers, and instead of being the munificent creators of a system of endowed secondary education, they were its destroyers. In the most favourable cases, the Tudors were reviving, or restoring under new management, an old foundation with the same revenues which it had previously enjoyed before the suppression. . . . In these cases they can at the best only be said to have endowed schools in the sense that a police magistrate, who restores a stolen purse to a citizen who has had his pocket picked, endows the citizen.[8]

Leach's main contention was that the 1547 Chantry Act, while well-intentioned, was very badly executed. It allowed the chantry commissioners to release the endowments of the schools and to put the schoolmasters on a pension from the state. These endowments, he argued, were then reinstated piecemeal, as inadequacies became apparent and voices were raised in protest. Leach propounded his thesis with insufficient evidence, citing the complaints of Thomas Lever, Master of St. John's, Cambridge, in sermons before Edward VI and at Paul's Cross in 1550, and providing a few examples of schools that were refounded only after great difficulties.[9] Reasoned argument tended instead to give way to rhetoric. But Leach was launching a broadside attack on the received opinion of English historians which chiefly credited Edward VI with founding England's early grammar schools. This view, formulated by John Strype in his *Ecclesiastical Memorials* (1816), institutionalized by the Schools Inquiry Commission (1864-

[7] Leach, *ESR*, i:6.

[8] A. F. Leach, "Edward VI: Spoiler of Schools," *Contemporary Review* 62 (Sept. 1892):369. Four years later, when Leach's analysis of this process was published in the introduction to his edition of the chantry certificates, he had toned down his pugnacious style under pressure from his editors. Leach, *ESR*, i:1-7, where parts of the earlier essay are substantially rewritten. He also seems to have modified his stance, speaking more positively of Henry VIII's policies (despite the fact that the inclusion of colleges and hospitals in the monastic dissolutions was educationally destructive) and giving credit to Northumberland under Edward VI. Leach, *ESR*, i:58-59, 80-83. For a more positive assessment of Henry VIII's role, see also Leach, *SME*, chap. 13.

[9] E.g., Sedbergh, Sherborne, Macclesfield, Grantham, Louth, and Morpeth. Leach, *ESR*, i:71-83, 114-22. See also *EYS*, 2:358-64.

1868), and popularized by J. R. Green in his *Short History of the English People* (rev. ed., 1888),[10] had been accepted by schoolmasters and school-children throughout Great Britain. Leach therefore felt the need to express himself strongly, particularly in his earlier journal articles.[11] Much of his zeal stemmed from the fact that he was convinced of the revolutionary importance of the new materials he was bringing to bear on the history of education. No one before Leach had taken the time to examine in detail the documentary basis for ascribing medieval education to monasteries and an effective schools policy to Edward VI. And for years no one followed up on Leach's work. His zeal, biased as it was, combined with his un-rivalled but sometimes unreferenced command of the sources, meant that educational historians especially, while wary of the tone and many of the particulars of his books, were content to accept their general conclusions.[12]

It was not until 1955 that Leach's views were substantively challenged. Joan Simon, in a two-part article in the *British Journal of Educational Studies*, set out to reexamine the role of Edward VI (or Protector Somerset) in the history of education.[13] Her article attacked Leach for underrating the monastic contribution to medieval education, overestimating the num-bers of medieval collegiate schools, and not taking adequate account of the Tudor refoundations. It was a long-delayed and necessary reassessment, but it was too sweeping in its rejection of Leach. Simon found Leach's arguments for medieval schooling unconvincing in part because

> they rest on formal evidence and fail to take into account the decline
> of the church in the later Middle Ages. The fact that ecclesiastical
> legislators intended a grammar school to be kept is one thing; the fact
> that visitation records reveal neglect of obligations and statutory duties
> is another. Leach stressed the first, but ignored the second.[14]

Aside from the arguable decline of the Church, it is inaccurate to state that Leach's conclusions rest on formal evidence alone. Although he quoted the injunctions of the fourth Lateran Council of 1215 and others that all

---

[10] John Strype, *Ecclesiastical Memorials*, Vol. 3 (London, 1816), 221-23, 461-65; J. R. Green, *A Short History of the English People*, rev. ed. (London, 1888), chap. 6, sec. 4; chap. 7, sec. 1. The Schools Inquiry Commission attributed fifty-one schools to Edward VI. Leach, *ESR*, i:5. For Leach's own description of this tradition, see Leach, "Some Results of Research," 434-36; *ESR*, i:1-5.

[11] Leach, "Edward VI," 368-84; "School Supply in the Middle Ages," *The Contemporary Review* 66 (Nov. 1894):674-84.

[12] Among those historians who accepted the main outlines of Leach's work were Foster Watson, J. W. Adamson, Eileen Power, and A. Hamilton Thompson.

[13] Joan Simon, "A. F. Leach on the Reformation," *BJES* 3 (1954-1955):128-43; 4 (1955-1956):32-48.

[14] Ibid., 3, 134.

parish priests should teach the local sons of the poor and that cathedral churches and others should organize schools, he did not automatically assume that these orders were fulfilled, and his evidence frequently derived from the substantive material of visitations, bishops' registers, wills, account rolls, and legal documents. Because of the nature of these sources, mention of schools sometimes arises in connection with dereliction of duty; nonetheless, the evidence confirms that the schools (however poorly maintained) existed, which was Leach's primary contention.

Joan Simon also argued that Leach had overestimated the number of ecclesiastical (as opposed to monastic or lay) schools for the fifteenth and early sixteenth centuries. Although she pointed out effectively that many collegiate and chantry foundations did not hold schools (a conclusion Leach himself reached for the later medieval period), she did not thereby destroy Leach's basic contention that pre-Reformation grammar education was both substantial and ecclesiastically supported.[15]

Simon's attack on Leach made way for a very different interpretation of education on the eve of the Reformation which stressed the growth of lay involvement and the decline of ecclesiastical initiatives. "From the early fifteenth century, lay initiative in the founding of schools had been increasing, and the interest of the Church in sponsoring education had progressively declined. . . . The chantry certificates suggest that, whatever their earlier importance, ecclesiastical schools proper constituted an almost negligible proportion of the total provision for education at the Reformation."[16] Where Leach had tried to wrest the primary role in late me-

[15] Simon attacks Leach for claiming that there were 200 important collegiate schools at the Reformation and suggests that "Leach obscured the concrete information provided by the chantry certificates; these only refer to some twenty-two collegiate foundations that were either supporting a schoolmaster, contributing to or housing a school." Ibid., 139. But Leach was well aware of the varieties of schools. He did not claim that the chantry certificates documented primarily collegiate schools, and he considered the chantry schools (not the colleges) to have been the most abundant on the eve of the Reformation. Leach, *ESR*, i:5-58. Simon's assessment of the educational contribution of the chantries is ambivalent and somewhat contradictory. Simon, "A. F. Leach on the Reformation," 4, 35-36, 41, 47n. On the one hand she argues that "the prevailing idea that many, or all, chantry priests kept school, as a matter of course, throughout the later Middle Ages is mistaken. . . . It has been estimated that there may have been some 2,000 priests drawing pensions after 1548. But the surviving certificates record only some twenty-five teaching, as apart from those bound to keep school by foundation deed or doing so by agreement with their employers; and a number of these charged fees. The disappearance of chantries was not, then, in itself educationally disastrous, as has sometimes been assumed." On the other hand, later on in the same article she refers to the Chantries Act as "virtually a national survey of schools." In *Education and Society in Tudor England* (Cambridge, 1966), 235 n. 1, Simon estimates that approximately 10 percent of all chantries held schools, a figure Leach had previously suggested. Leach, "Edward VI," 375.

[16] Simon, "A. F. Leach on the Reformation," 3:143.

dieval education from the monasteries, Simon endeavored to do the same with regard to the secular ecclesiastical foundations. Neither view is convincing. Although significant changes did occur in the proportional relationship of these schools to one another, the changes were far too complex to be characterized generally as "the decline of monastic or secular ecclesiastical schools" or "the rise of lay education." In fact, the majority of schools continued to be under the auspices of the Church, even if they may not have been "ecclesiastical schools proper," a term that Simon uses without sufficient precision.

Simon's major criticism of Leach was well taken, however. "The claim that schooling suffered a severe setback after 1548 is . . . difficult to reconcile with the evidence of educational expansion and change in the post-Reformation period."[17] Although she admits Leach's argument that many of the schools were disendowed, she is nevertheless correct in saying that Leach overestimated the negative educational impact of the dissolution of the chantries. Her evidence that a substantial number of the ecclesiastical schools were reendowed, that new lay foundations helped fill the gap, and that there was a revitalization of the grammar school curriculum, has restored credibility to the educational pronouncements of Edward VI's government.[18]

Subsequently, in a series of articles in the *British Journal of Educational Studies* from 1962 to 1964, W. N. Chaplin and Joan Simon debated the value of Leach's work in greater detail. Chaplin argued that the usefulness of Leach's work had been greatly underestimated and generally ignored by medievalists. This unfortunate circumstance, as he saw it, derived from A. G. Little's influential and cautionary review. Chaplin therefore took issue with the way Little's review was received, pointing out that Little did not mean to warn scholars away from all of Leach's work and in fact generally endorsed his conclusions for the later medieval period. Chaplin then took even stronger exception to Simon's attack on Leach, accusing her of misrepresenting Leach's arguments and of unjustifiably using Leach's own work against himself. Simon, in turn, defended herself, citing sundry supporters, and arguing that Leach's work had been too uncritically accepted (and not ignored, as Chaplin would have it), that its very serious problems could not be dismissed, and that Leach's work should no longer remain the basis for any acceptable evaluation of medieval or, especially, Reformation schooling.[19] The effectiveness of her rebuttal, in which she

---

[17] Ibid., 130.

[18] These themes are further developed in her book, *Education and Society*.

[19] Chaplin, "Leach: Re-appraisal," 99-124; Simon, "A. F. Leach: A Reply," *BJES* 12 (1963-1964):41-50.

scarcely acknowledged the more detailed points broached by Chaplin, makes one suspect that Chaplin's summing up of the debate was shaped by a spirit of conciliation and not out of regard for Simon's argument. "The problem," he noted, "of the use of the work of A. F. Leach has been clarified by Mrs. Simon's *Reply*. Her aim seems to be the same as mine, that it should be used for an accepted history of English medieval schools."[20]

Simultaneous with Chaplin's enthusiastic reappraisal of Leach, additional assessments appeared which called for a reevaluation of the "Leach legend." W. E. Tate's 1963 monograph on "A. F. Leach as a Historian" detailed Leach's failings as a proofreader, topographer and historian of elementary education. Besides taking offense at Leach's often cavalier treatment of dates and place names, Tate was concerned with the gaps in Leach's compilation of Yorkshire schools and his "donnish approach to educational matters." These criticisms aside, however, it is clear that Tate had in mind using Leach's work as a steppingstone to a better, successor work, for he performed the useful service of indexing every reference to a Yorkshire school throughout Leach's works.[21] A more positive appreciation of Leach by J. N. Miner in 1962 argued that Leach was substantially correct in his treatment of the monastic contribution to education for those outside their ranks, while his emphasis on the educational role of the secular clergy in cathedrals and colleges, justified in part, could be supplemented (as Leach himself made clear) with more attention to chantry, gild, and hospital educational foundations. The proof of Leach's main point (that late medieval England was well supplied with schools) would, however,

> require a series of detailed regional studies in social history, involving, among other things, any significant changes in the proportion of the clerical to the non-clerical population. Moreover, a study of this nature would only be possible if evidence were forthcoming of the continuity of a number of these schools as distinct from their foundation or dissolution, an intricate problem of which Leach was well aware.[22]

P. J. Wallis summed up the medieval aspect of the debate: "a summary account of medieval schools is needed, . . . Such a co-operative effort would clearly be indebted to A. F. Leach, who showed that English

---

[20] W. N. Chaplin, "A. F. Leach: Agreement and Difference," *BJES* 12 (1963-1964):173.

[21] W. E. Tate, *A. F. Leach as a Historian of Yorkshire Education* (York, 1963).

[22] J. N. Miner, "Schools and Literacy in Later Medieval England," *BJES* 11 (1962-1963):27.

education did not begin with Edward VI, but would also show that the story is more complex than he suggested."[23]

While the debate went on about the value of Leach's contribution, Wallis and Tate were at work to revise it. By 1956 they had compiled a "Register of Old Yorkshire Grammar Schools." This preliminary list, while in no way definitive and in many ways defective, did support Simon's position that most of the grammar schools were not swept away with the Chantries Acts. But it also increased by one-third Leach's estimate of the number of schools for Yorkshire before 1536. This result, while rendering Leach's statistics outdated, simultaneously vindicated his thesis of the vitality of late medieval grammar education, at least within Yorkshire. Although the value of this list has not been such as to warrant the drawing of any secure quantitative conclusions, Wallis and Tate did point the way for future researchers, and Tate's call for a clearinghouse for educational information is an admirable goal which still awaits implementation.[24]

Within the last decade, Nicholas Orme has made the single greatest contribution to the study of medieval education since Leach. His first book, *English Schools in the Middle Ages* (1973), is a survey of medieval schools that sketches the literary needs, interests, and capabilities of the various social classes; describes the schools (their management and curricula); and traces their evolution from the twelfth century to the accession of Queen Elizabeth. Appended to it is a list of schools for the years 1066 to 1530. Orme argues that twelfth- through fourteenth-century England saw the first significant extension of public, secular schools (as opposed to private monastic or household schools). These schools, organized under the auspices of cathedrals, colleges, towns, or villages, were usually fee-paying but were also, increasingly, the focus of private benefactions and supportive ecclesiastical legislation. In all, Orme locates over sixty thirteenth-century schools, distributed evenly over the country, representing some unknown proportion of an unknowable total. The number of documented schools rises to 114 in the fifteenth century and to 124 by 1530, during which time endowments of the schools (both by laity and ecclesiastics) developed to such an extent that, Orme concludes, it is "here, not in the age of the Reformation, that the great movement really begins by which during five centuries hundreds of private benefactors founded

[23] P. J. Wallis, "Leach—Past, Present, and Future," *BJES* 12 (1963-1964):194.

[24] P. J. Wallis and W. E. Tate, "A Register of Old Yorkshire Grammar Schools," *The University of Leeds Institute of Education, Researches and Studies*, no. 13 (1956):64-104. Tate, *Leach as a Historian*. See also Wallis, *Histories of Old Schools: A Revised List for England and Wales* (Newcastle-upon-Tyne, 1966).

hundreds of endowed schools all over England, and thus effected one of the principal achievements of English civilization."[25]

Orme is free of Leach's bias against the monasteries; although, while reasserting their importance, he excludes monastic schools from his appended list of schools. He is far more careful in documenting schools than was Leach, and he takes a cautious reconciliatory position between Leach on one side and Simon on the other with reference to the dissolution of the chantries. Orme concludes that a gradual increase in the number of known schools took place throughout the Middle Ages and up to the Reformation, at which time losses to education were gradually made good by a somewhat tardy governmental response and by private gifts.

Subsequently Orme has published detailed local studies of education in six southwestern English counties and in Worcestershire, in which he reiterates and elaborates on his earlier conclusions.[26] Yet, some significant shifts in perspective are evident. The number of schools has increased. In his 1976 book on *Education in the West of England* Orme lists fully one-third more schools before 1530 from this region than were mentioned in his earlier book, and he adds another twenty schools for the previously unenumerated period from 1530 to 1548. Greater sensitivity to local conditions allows Orme to differentiate more clearly the relative educational importance of towns and villages, with the result that education in the west of England appears to be a largely urban phenomenon. The difficulty of delineating one school from another on the basis of curriculum is stressed for the first time, and more emphasis is placed on the fortuitous survival of educational references and the presumably greater availability of schools about which we may never be fully informed. In these regional studies Orme adheres less rigidly to his earlier position that schools must be documented every twenty-five years in order for the historian to assume continuity. In place of this, Orme argues for tenacity on the part of medieval peoples with regard to their educational resources and a more optimistic stance on the part of historians in allowing for continuity. In this respect, Orme has moved closer to the assumptions underlying Leach's original contribution.

Orme's careful attention to the period from 1530 through the 1550s in his most recent work allows him to enumerate the growing number of

[25] Orme, *ESMA*, 194.

[26] Nicholas Orme, *Education in the West of England 1066-1548* (Exeter, 1976); "The Medieval Schools of Worcestershire," *Transactions of the Worcestershire Archaeological Society*, 3rd ser., 6 (1978):43-51; "Evesham School before the Reformation," *Vale of Evesham Historical Society Research Papers* 6 (1977):95-100; "Education in the West of England, 1066-1548: Additions and Corrections," *Devon and Cornwall Notes & Queries* 34 (1978):22-25.

chantry schools in the 1530s and '40s and to evaluate in greater detail the impact of the Reformation. The effect of the chantry dissolutions on the Worcestershire schools, for example, was slight, and the losses sustained were made good throughout the 1550s. Despite some disruptions, the changes in organization, curriculum, and public importance probably produced an education superior to that which was available in the medieval period. Overall, however, in the west of England, Orme's assessment is that the Reformation gains and losses tended to cancel one another out. He concludes that, "it is difficult to ascribe either a significant expansion or recession of schooling to the Reformation alone."[27] In this respect, Orme's recent work does not support Leach's view. Nor is it entirely in agreement with Joan Simon's emphasis on the educational significance of the Reformation.[28]

The debate over schools has provoked another recent shift in perspectives. Leach described medieval educational opportunities in institutional terms. Although he rarely paused to analyze the term "schools," he clearly understood it to connote an organized grammar school governed by statutes, with master and pupils functioning in an organized and continuous fashion—all very much along the lines of a nineteenth-century English public school.[29] Nor was he particularly interested in the social and cultural context of schooling. Subsequent educational historians retained this bias toward institutional history.[30] Once again, Joan Simon, in her typically

[27] Orme, "Medieval Schools of Worcestershire," 49-50; *Education in the West of England*, 32.

[28] Although it is only fair to note that Simon's views seem also to have changed. In a 1968 study of Leicestershire schools she finds that "no local schools were reconstituted by royal charter after the dissolution of the monasteries and chantries" and characterizes Edward's reign as "short and stormy and in many smaller places problems, rather than being cleared up, accumulated." Joan Simon, "Town Estates and Schools in the Sixteenth and Early Seventeenth Centuries," in *Education in Leicestershire 1540-1940*, ed. Brian Simon (Leicester, 1968), 3, 6.

[29] ". . . they [London Schools] . . . were giving precisely the same kind of classical education as the great public schools gave in the sixteenth to the nineteenth centuries, and perhaps even more effectively." Leach, *SME*, 140. See also 181 and Leach, *ESR*, i:6. J. N. Miner, who is engaged in a full-scale study of Leach, contends, however, that "Leach became quite conscious of the need to clarify the meaning of *scole*. This is a central question and requires careful study, but Leach comes very close, I think, to capturing the 12th and 13th c. meaning, i.e., the *activity* involved in the teaching and learning process." Personal communication, March 1, 1983.

[30] Foster Watson, *The Old Grammar Schools* (Cambridge, 1916); Clara P. McMahon, *Education in Fifteenth-Century England* (Baltimore, 1947), esp. chap. 3; S. J. Curtis, *History of Education in Great Britain*, 7th ed. (London, 1967), chap. 1; John Lawson, *Medieval Education and the Reformation* (London, 1967). Among the older historians, J. W. Adamson's *A Short History of Education* (Cambridge, 1919) takes a societal view of education. The more recent editors of educational documents have shifted toward a social perspective. John Lawson and Harold Silver, eds., *A Social History of Education in England* (London, 1973); David Cressy, ed., *Education in Tudor and Stuart England* (New York, 1976).

iconoclastic fashion, was the first to criticize medieval educational accounts (again, primarily Leach's work) for developing too rigid distinctions in an era where "schooling" did not necessarily imply "schools."[31] The institutionalization of education, Simon argued, is largely the work of the Renaissance and Reformation. It is more properly the result of the laicization of education, particularly in urban areas, promoted by local needs, humanist concerns, and state policy. In contrast, medieval lay education can more fruitfully be analyzed in terms of informal social processes. Chivalric training, bureaucratic procedures, and gild practices were more significant factors than schools. In her 1972 study of social origins in English education, Simon's emphasis on informal modes of medieval education was expressed more radically. Primitive educational patterns based on kinship and community bonds, participation in the liturgy, as well as chivalric training and apprenticeship, persisted alongside schools, which remain, for Simon, only "one element, the more so since they are still relatively few and far between and restricted to instruction in Latin." It is only with the Reformation that "the foundations are laid of a system of education in the modern sense" and attitudes change as humanists recognize the importance of education. Medieval education therefore appears to be the result of unreflective ritual; self-conscious, constructive, organized education is a product of the humanist and the reformed.[32]

Simon's arguments—overstated though they sometimes are—bear close analysis precisely because of their provocative and pioneering quality. It is salutary to be reminded that education cannot be understood solely in terms of formal institutions. Nicholas Orme, whose first book followed Leach's use of the word "schools," has moved away from such an institutional approach toward a concern with what he calls "evidences of education."[33] The references we have to medieval education are not always clear-cut. Scholars and schoolmasters are mentioned more often than schools, and the effort to categorize educational resources often seems quixotic by reason of the paucity of evidence and the fluidity and flexibility of medieval society.

Given the shifting grounds upon which medieval educational historians try to stand, post-Reformation educational historians appear to be on terra firma. There is near universal agreement among them that the sixteenth century was a revolutionary age with regard to the growth of educational

---

[31] Simon, *Education and Society*, 3-4.

[32] Joan Simon, *The Social Origins of English Education* (London, 1972), 50-54.

[33] Personal communication, June 24, 1980.

facilities, particularly in contrast with the age that preceded it.[34] Between 1959 and 1961, W. K. Jordan, in a multivolume study of philanthropic bequests from 1480 to 1660, provided a bleak picture of medieval education. In ten counties in 1480 he discovered notices of only thirty-four functioning schools, few supported by endowments. For Yorkshire his sources revealed at most seven schools in 1480, and "probably no more than six, none of which can be described as a really strong or well-administered institution." The situation was even worse for Lancashire where Jordan found only three grammar schools surviving in 1480.[35] And between 1480 and 1540 Jordan discovered foundations for only nine more schools in Yorkshire. It was not until the two decades after the Reformation (where he documented nearly £5,000 in provisions for grammar school foundations) and the Elizabethan period (where he lists sixteen endowed and several unendowed schools) that Jordan finds the "almost feverish interest of Yorkshiremen . . . in the founding of a system of popular education which would offer opportunity to all aspiring youths. . . ."[36]

Jordan's work offered proof that the English Reformation produced a revolution in aspirations and a rise in charitable bequests, particularly in education. Jordan argued that an educational explosion, which depended in large part upon London merchants and English gentry, occurred in the wake of the Reformation and in marked contrast to "the meagre educational institutions . . . inherited from the Middle Ages."[37] Although

[34] See, in particular, the works of Joan Simon listed above; Lawrence Stone, "The Educational Revolution in England, 1560-1640," *Past and Present*, no. 28 (1964):44; T. W. Baldwin, *William Shakspere's Small Latine & Lesse Greeke*, 2 vols. (Urbana, Ill., 1944), ii; Kenneth Charlton, *Education in Renaissance England* (London, 1965), esp. chaps. 4-5; A. J. Fletcher, "The Expansion of Education in Berkshire and Oxfordshire, 1500-1670," *BJES* 15 (1967):51-59; Peter Clark, *English Provincial Society from the Reformation to the Revolution: Religion, Politics and Society in Kent, 1500-1640* (Hassocks, 1977), chap. 6; Jay P. Anglin, "The Expansion of Literacy: Opportunities for the Study of the Three Rs in the London Diocese of Elizabeth I," *Guildhall Studies in London History* 4 (1980):63-74; and Mark H. Curtis, *Oxford and Cambridge in Transition, 1558-1642* (Oxford, 1959). For a cautious view of this educational revolution in terms of its impact on social stratification and literacy levels, see David Cressy, "Educational Opportunity in Tudor and Stuart England," *History of Education Quarterly* 16 (1976):301-20, and *Literacy and the Social Order: Reading and Writing in Tudor and Stuart England* (Cambridge, 1980).

[35] W. K. Jordan, *Philanthropy in England, 1480-1660* (London, 1959), 287, 290; *The Charities of Rural England 1480-1660* (London, 1961), 301; *The Social Institutions of Lancashire, 1480-1660*, Chetham Society, 3rd ser., 11 (Manchester, 1962), 30.

[36] Jordan, *Charities of Rural England*, 304-27.

[37] Ibid., 299.

Jordan's methodology, especially his disregard for price inflation, was attacked by numerous reviewers, his educational thesis still stands.[38] If anything, it has been reinforced in subsequent studies by Tudor historians.

Lawrence Stone, whose name is most closely associated with the idea of a sixteenth-century educational revolution, was the first to give quantitative support to the generally accepted view among Tudor historians that English education expanded rapidly between 1560 and 1640. Taking entrance records to the Universities and the Inns of Court, Stone argued that the years 1560-1580 and, particularly, 1604-1640 were periods of enormous expansion.[39] He noted that the impressively large numbers of students matriculating in higher education correlated with Jordan's figures for endowed school growth and with other evidence for large numbers of fee-paying schools. The educational revolution was further confirmed by higher levels of literacy indicated by signatures to the 1642 loyalty oath and the large proportion of criminals (47 percent) successfully pleading benefit of clergy by reading a passage from the Bible. Educational incentives (such as benefit of clergy and access to the English Bible), growing demands for professional training, the impact of humanism, a new respect for children, and, especially, Puritan enthusiasm for education combined

[38] For criticisms of Jordan's failure to allow for monetary inflation, see the reviews by Lawrence Stone (*History* 44 [1959]:257-60), D. C. Coleman (*The Economic History Review*, 2nd ser., 13 [1960-1961]:113-15), G. R. Elton (*The Historical Journal* 3 [1960]:89-92), Charles Wilson (*EHR* 75 [1960]:686-87), and R. Ashton (*History* 46 [1961]:136-39). These reviews also suggest significant problems in Jordan's arguments linking merchants, Protestantism, and philanthropy. On this, see also Mordechai Feingold, "Jordan Revisited: Patterns of Charitable Giving in Sixteenth and Seventeenth Century England," *History of Education* 8 (1979):257-73. Feingold also raises questions with regard to Jordan's statistical handling of educational benefactions. For a further discussion of the impact of inflation on Jordan's data, see the analyses by W. G. Bittle and R. Todd Lane and responses by J. F. Hadwin, D. C. Coleman, and J. D. Gould in *The Economic History Review*, 2nd ser., 29 (1976):203-10; 31 (1978):105-28.

Most of the critical attention has been directed to Jordan's post-Reformation conclusions. For some criticisms of his medieval materials, see John A. F. Thomson, "Piety and Charity in Late Medieval London," *J. Eccl. Hist.* 16 (1965):178-95, and a few comments in the response by J. F. Hadwin, noted above, 112-13. Lawrence Stone, in his 1959 review of Jordan's work, agreed with Jordan's estimate of the meager medieval contribution to schools, and in his 1964 article "Educational Revolution" (p. 44) cited Jordan's 1480 figures without comment, although he had reservations about Jordan's conclusions for the later period. Joan Simon also used Jordan's conclusions on medieval schooling to buttress her thesis in *Education and Society*, 3. For more recent examples of Tudor historians who depend on Jordan's educational analysis, see Peter Clark, *English Provincial Society*, 189, 443 n 14-16 and Cressy, *Literacy and the Social Order*, 164-73.

[39] Stone, "Educational Revolution," 41-80. In a later essay, Stone's chronology for the years of expansion in student numbers at Oxford is slightly different—1550 to 1580 and 1615 to 1639. Stone, "The Size and Composition of the Oxford Student Body 1580-1909," in *The University in Society*, ed. L. Stone, 2 vols. (Princeton, 1974), 1:17.

to produce, in Stone's words, "a quantitative change of such magnitude that it can only be described as a revolution."[40]

In 1966, two years after Stone presented his ideas in *Past and Present*, Joan Simon's *Education and Society in Tudor England* was published. Although Simon's book was written originally in reaction to Leach,[41] she did not dwell on her longstanding debate with him but proceeded to survey anew the status and trends of education in sixteenth-century England. Her study, which looked back to the fifteenth century and forward to the early Stuart period, suggested growth, albeit uneven, in the availability of education throughout the period. This growth was spurred by a developing lay interest in education, by humanism, by state intervention, and by puritanism. Although Simon saw educational expansion starting in the fifteenth century (associated with the beginnings of lay involvement), the centerpiece of her book is the Edwardian Reformation. It was then that humanism, defined both as civilized learning and religious reform, began to effect changes in the curricula of grammar schools and universities. It was Edwardian initiatives, both governmental and private, that left England with a more substantial, institutionalized, and humanistic educational system than had existed before the dissolution of monasteries, chantries, hospitals, and gilds.

Although there are differences in emphasis, Jordan, Stone, and Simon agree that the history of sixteenth-century education is one of new and dramatic developments. Nor is this surprising. It would be uncharacteristic of Tudor historians to deny the revolutionary implications of their age. But if Orme's reconstruction of Leach is accurate, and significant educational developments do precede the Reformation, then the sixteenth century may be robbed of some of its luster as an educational takeoff point. More than that, Leach's view, as restated by Orme, undercuts the traditionally accepted views of English historians who see the Reformation and humanism as the sine qua non of the educational developments of early modern England.

The issues that separate historians in the history of education have their counterparts in the history of literacy, the study of which is closely linked to educational issues.[42] The history of literacy is a younger field of inquiry

[40] Stone, "Educational Revolution," 68.

[41] Simon, *Education and Society*, preface.

[42] The acquisition of literacy, especially in vernacular languages, cannot be strictly equated with schooling, although there is clearly a connection between the two. Latin learning in the Middle Ages was more difficult to acquire by self-education, although it was occasionally done. M. T. Clanchy, *From Memory to Written Record: England, 1066-1307* (Cambridge, Mass., 1979), 153, 189-92. As the fourteenth-century translator of the *Speculum Vitae* noted, "Latin as I trowe, can nane Bot þoe þat have it at Scole tane." Historical Manuscripts Commission, *Report on the Manuscripts of Lord Middleton Preserved at Wollaton Hall* (London, 1911), 239.

than the history of education, and it has no one person, such as A. F. Leach, whose influence has dominated the debates. It is also, for the medieval period, a highly problematic field of research. Medieval Englishmen were often at home in more than one language—English, French, Latin, and sometimes Hebrew.[43] Anyone specifically described as *literatus* was, however, not only capable of reading Latin but probably also able to express himself, both in writing and speech, in Latin.[44] This is especially the case prior to the fourteenth century. Thus literacy rates derived from such references may only include persons with some scholarly attainments or members of a learned latinate elite. A further problem is that traditional ways of determining literacy, by analyzing the evidence for signatures, have little relevance in medieval society where seals or the sign of the cross were employed instead of signatures.[45] And in a society where writing was a special skill, frequently taught apart from reading,[46] studies in literacy need to differentiate writing from reading literacy. The latter, which would appear to be the more widespread, is also the harder to discover. In addition, the medieval historian works with fewer extant documents, almost none of which are useful in developing quantitative evidence. Considering how varied the issues and how circumstantial the evidence, M. B. Parkes, in the best brief introduction to the problem, cautions that "the extent of literacy among the laity in the Middle Ages must always be a matter for debate."[47] Nonetheless Parkes goes on to

[43] Clanchy, *From Memory to Written Record*, chap. 6; J. Hoeppner Moran, "Literacy and Education in Northern England, 1350-1550: A Methodological Inquiry," *Northern History* 17 (1981):3-5.

[44] M. B. Parkes, "The Literacy of the Laity," in *Literature and Western Civilization: The Medieval World*, ed. D. Daiches and A. Thorlby (London, 1973), 555; Michael Richter, "A Socio-Linguistic Approach to the Latin Middle Ages," in *Studies in Church History*, vol. 11, ed. D. Baker (Oxford, 1975), 69-82; Clanchy, *From Memory to Written Record*, chap. 7; Brian Stock, *The Implications of Literacy: Written Language and Models of Interpretation in the Eleventh and Twelfth Centuries* (Princeton, 1983), 6, 26-27. Clanchy emphasizes oral expression; writing Latin was not always an essential ability for the *miles literatus*. This insistence on the spoken element is pointed to by Stock, who quotes the late thirteenth-century *Catholicon* of John Balbi of Genoa: "Literator uel literatus non dicitur ille qui habet multos libros et inspicit et reuoluit ut monachus qui proprie potest dici antiquarius, quia antiquas historias habet ad manum. Sed ille dicitur literator uel literatus qui ex arte de rude uoce scit formare literas in dicionibus et diciones in orationibus et orationes scit congrue proferre et accentuare." Ibid., 27 n 56.

[45] Clanchy, *From Memory to Written Record*, 184, 244-48; Moran, "Literacy and Education," 8-12.

[46] See Chapter two below, pp. 49-52. See also Clanchy, *From Memory to Written Record*, 88, 97, 183; Ralph V. Turner, "The *Miles Literatus* in Twelfth- and Thirteenth-Century England: How Rare a Phenomenon?" *American Historical Review* 83 (1978):929.

[47] Parkes, "Literacy of the Laity," 571.

argue that lay literacy (defined as the ability to read either Latin or the vernacular) was expanding from the twelfth century on, that a growing middle class was becoming literate for pragmatic reasons, and that, by the fourteenth and fifteenth centuries, middle-class reading was increasingly in the vernacular and increasingly sophisticated. "The general pattern of the evidence indicates that from the thirteenth century onward increasing reliance and importance was placed upon the written word. This was accompanied by the growth of the reading habit, checked only by the high price of a book or by the necessity to write it for oneself."[48]

Parkes's conclusions are supported, not only by the array of examples he offers of literate laity or manuscripts produced for such individuals, but also by a series of studies on literacy published in the 1930s and '40s,[49] and by the more recent contributions of M. T. Clanchy and Ralph V. Turner.[50] Clanchy and Turner agree that the literate (i.e. latinate) knight was not an isolated phenomenon in twelfth- and thirteenth-century England. They both characterize post-conquest England as a society that demanded a knowledge of Latin of its lay administrators and provided Latin instruction through aristocratic households and in scattered local elementary and secondary schools.[51] By the beginning of the fourteenth century knowledge of Latin may have extended sufficiently far down the social scale to include members of the peasant class.[52]

Based on the evidence for a widespread vernacular literature and for Bible-reading by Lollards of very humble origins, there is general agreement among late medieval historians that a further expansion of literacy took place among all classes in the fourteenth and fifteenth centuries.[53] Although any attempts to quantify the extent of a functional, reading literacy in the late Middle Ages are extremely tentative, F.R.H. Du

---

[48] Ibid., 572.

[49] John William Adamson, "The Extent of Literacy in England in the Fifteenth and Sixteenth Centuries: Notes and Conjectures," *The Library*, 4th ser., 10 (1929-1930):163-93; V. H. Galbraith, "The Literacy of the Medieval English Kings," *Proceedings of the British Academy*, 5th ser., 21 (1935):201-38; J. W. Thompson, *The Literacy of the Laity in the Middle Ages* (Berkeley, 1939); Lynn Thorndike, "Elementary and Secondary Education in the Middle Ages," *Speculum* 15 (1940):400-408.

[50] Clanchy, *From Memory to Written Record*; Turner, "The *Miles Literatus*."

[51] Clanchy, *From Memory to Written Record*, 197-201; Turner, "The *Miles Literatus*," passim.

[52] Clanchy, *From Memory to Written Record*, 188-96.

[53] Adamson, "Extent of Literacy," 165-70; Charles L. Kingsford, *English Historical Literature in the Fifteenth Century* (Oxford, 1913), esp. chap. 1; H. S. Bennett, "The Production and Dissemination of Vernacular Manuscripts in the Fifteenth Century," *The Library*, 5th ser., 1 (1947):167-78; V. J. Scattergood, *Politics and Poetry in the Fifteenth Century* (London, 1971), esp. chap. 2; Janet Coleman, *Medieval Readers and Writers 1350-1400* (New York, 1981), chap. 2; Margaret Aston, "Lollardy and Literacy," *History* 62 (1977):347-71.

Boulay has estimated that "perhaps 30% of the population could read in the fifteenth century, and about 40% by 1530, though rather fewer could also write," while Sylvia Thrupp suggests a reading literacy rate of perhaps 50 percent among London laymen by the 1470s. In contrast, David Cressy, assessing a literacy based on signatures, argues for a 90 percent illiteracy rate among Englishmen and 99 percent illiteracy among Englishwomen at the start of the sixteenth century.[54] The disparate assessments of literacy, based in part on different ways of defining and discovering literacy, help account for the widely diverse views put forward by medieval and Tudor historians. A measure of the gulf that separates them can be seen in the varying reactions to Sir Thomas More's famous assertion that England enjoyed a literacy rate in 1533 of between 50 and 60 percent. ". . . people farre more than four partes of all the whole dyuyded into tenne, could neuer rede englysche yet, and many now to olde to begynne to go to scole . . ."[55] Whereas David Cressy quotes More skeptically, arguing that the remarks of contemporaries on the extent of literacy are to be distrusted, and Lawrence Stone characterizes More's statement as "alarmist nonsense," medievalists such as M. B. Parkes and J. W. Adamson use More's estimate as evidence and quote it approvingly.[56]

I will address myself in this book to the debates delineated in this chapter. While the following chapters argue for the significance of medieval education and a rise in lay literacy prior to the Reformation, they also offer a bridge between contrasting views by suggesting that the "educational revolution" of the sixteenth century can be better understood given the prior developments, first in elementary education, and, by the beginning of the sixteenth century, in Latin grammar education. In addition, they seek to reconcile conflicting views on literacy by emphasizing the differences between the acquisition of reading and writing skills and by offering some rough, tentative estimates of medieval literacy which, because they are quantified, may provide common ground for discussing the history of literacy in medieval and early Tudor England.

[54] F.R.H. Du Boulay, *An Age of Ambition: English Society in the Late Middle Ages* (New York, 1970), 118; Sylvia Thrupp, *The Merchant Class of Medieval London, 1300-1500* (Ann Arbor, Mich., 1948), 156-58; Cressy, *Literacy and the Social Order*, 176.

[55] *The Complete Works of Sir Thomas More*, Vol. 9, ed. J. B. Trapp (New Haven, 1979), 13.

[56] Cressy, *Literacy and the Social Order*, 44-45; Stone, "Educational Revolution," 43; Parkes, "Literacy of the Laity," 571; Adamson, "Extent of Literacy," 171.

CHAPTER 2

Elementary and Grammar Education in Late Medieval England

Despite a paucity of documents actually describing the curriculum of medieval schools, historians know a good deal about the teaching of Latin grammar, far more than they know about the various elementary levels of learning. Mention of grammar schools and grammarmasters is relatively frequent, and a sufficient number of studies has been done on medieval grammatical texts to enable the historian to reconstruct, on a broad basis, the grammar curriculum. In contrast, elementary instruction, whether in school or elsewhere, has often been ignored or, at most, treated cursorily. Little is known about the elementary curriculum and even less about the number of such schools. Yet, at the point when children (*pueri*)[1] were beginning to learn their Latin grammar, most if not all would already have learned to read. They may also have been surpliced song scholars, trained to sing in the choir and therefore to read (or perhaps merely to memorize) portions of the liturgy. It was also possible for grammar scholars to have received prior training in writing.

Pre-Reformation historians know less about the elementary forms of education in part because of the difficulties they have differentiating grammar from elementary schooling. To some degree this is due to the fact that medieval people themselves did not always distinguish clearly between one level of instruction and another, but to a larger degree it is due to the lack of evidence concerning curriculum. When school statutes are extant or when information is available as to the books used in a particular school, the historian can be fairly sure of the level of instruction. Most of the documents from which one gleans the little we know about medieval education, however, provide scant insight into the curriculum. When no evidence for the usage of texts is available, other criteria must be developed by which one can judge the level of instruction and the type of school

---

[1] *Pueri*, as defined in fifteenth-century Latin-English and English-Latin dictionaries, referred to children and could include girls. While girls might, in theory, follow the full elementary and secondary curriculum described in this chapter, in practice the degree of their participation is problematic. For a discussion of the evidence for schooling of girls, see chap. 3.

involved. The age of the scholars who attended, where they went after leaving school, the number and gender of scholars, the location of the school, and the educational background of the schoolmaster all provide clues as to the level of education being pursued in any one instance. Other features that help distinguish a grammar from an elementary school are its formal foundation, an endowment, the existence of a separate school-house or boarding school, or proof of continuity over several centuries, i.e., evidences for a greater degree of institutionalization. These various distinguishing features of pre-Reformation English schools, apart from any evidence of curriculum, will be analyzed in Chapter three, while the curricular materials, especially the textbooks, are the focus of this chapter. Some of the evidence is drawn from other areas of England and some of it reaches back to Carolingian times. Together with the York diocesan documents, the sources make clear just how complex the educational curriculum of late medieval and early Tudor England could be.

As far back as 796, when Alcuin was schoolmaster at Tours, he wrote to Eanbald II, archbishop of York, to recommend that "Your grace . . . provide teachers for the boys. There should be classes for reading, singing, and writing separate from the clergy, and separate teachers for each class. . . ."[2] We do not know whether Eanbald incorporated this plan of study at York, but such clear differentiations in the curriculum as suggested by Alcuin were by no means absent elsewhere. A few years later, when Leidrad, archbishop of Lyon, established his schools, he was influenced by Alcuin in setting up two distinct schools—the *scola cantorum* for pre-paring teachers of the chant and the *scola lectorum* for preparing teachers in the study of scripture. At St. Gall, Ekkehard II taught writing, design, and painting techniques to children who had no aptitude for books. Indeed, it is clear from Pierre Riché's survey of European schools in the sixth through the eleventh centuries that distinctions between grammar and reading, and between reading, writing, and song schools were normal.[3]

---

[2] Phillip Jaffé, *Monumenta Alcuiniana*, Bibliotheca rerum germanicarum, no. 6 (Berlin, 1873), no. 72, 335. "Praevideat sancta sollertia tua magistros pueris, clero. Segregentur separatim orae illorum, qui libros legant; qui cantilene inserviant; qui scribendi studio deputentur. Habeas et singulis his ordinibus magistros suos, . . ." Translation from Stephen Allot, ed., *Alcuin of York—His Life and Letters* (York, 1974), 9.

[3] Rolph B. Page, *The Letters of Alcuin* (New York, 1909), 99; Leidrad, Epistola 30, *Monumenta Germaniae Historica, Epistolae*, Vol. 4 (Berlin, 1895), 543. "Nam habeo scolas cantorum, ex quibus plerique ita sunt eruditi, ut etiam alios erudire possint. Praeter haec vero habeo scolas lectorum, non solum qui officiorum lectionibus exerceantur, sed etiam qui in divinorum librorum meditatione spiritalis intelligentiae fructus consequantur." Pierre Riché, *Les Ecoles et l'enseignement dans l'Occident chrétien de la fin du V siècle au milieu du XI siècle* (Paris, 1979), 222, 236.

"L'enseignement élémentaire consiste, comme partout, et à toutes les époques, à apprendre à lire, écrire, chanter et compter, mais ces différentes techniques ne sont pas enseignées simul-

According to Riché, reading (equated with reading the psalter) was sometimes supplemented by writing and arithmetic. Often reading and song were complementary and taught by the same individual, although in the larger centers of learning, the responsibilities of the *cantor* and the *magister* were divided and even competitive. The psalter scholars (the majority) and the grammar scholars (fewer in number) were even more clearly distinct.[4]

Despite Alcuin's advice and Riché's conclusions, the evidence for differing levels of education in England does not emerge until after 1300. Prior to this, the term grammar probably indicated the principal subject of study in most schools, although reading, writing, and song may well have been included in the curriculum. Nicholas Orme has argued that the evidence does not allow historians to speak of physically separate elementary and grammar schools until the fourteenth and fifteenth centuries. Even by Tudor times the elementary and grammar levels were by no means completely distinct.[5] This has made the task of the historian of medieval English education difficult, but it is not an insurmountable problem. Medieval records are often specific enough, and they sometimes provide quite full information on the grammar schools. The problems develop in trying to decide whether elementary instruction is also being offered within the confines of a grammar school and in trying to document and detail elementary educational opportunities outside the grammar schools. With such problems, it is not surprising that very little research has been done on medieval elementary education,[6] and some of what has been written is confused.

Although A. F. Leach did not devote much time to investigating the

---

tanément ni à tous les élèves . . . nous distinguons deux groupes d'élèves, d'une part une grande majorité sachant lire, peut-être écrire, mais ayant mal bénéficié de l'enseignement du grammairien, d'autre part une minorité plus douée et capable d'aborder les auteurs et de se lancer dans l'étude des arts libéraux. . . . Mais auparavant, ne pouvons-nous pas faire une place à une troisième catégorie d'élèves? Alcuin, dans une lettre, fait allusion à trois groupes d'élèves: 'Ceux qui lisent, ceux qui chantent et ceux qui apprennent à écrire. . . .' Ainsi, les écoliers qui se font remarquer surtout par leur belle voix et leur capacité à écrire sont engagés vers un enseignement que l'on qualifierait de nos jours de technique, mais qu'il vaut mieux appeler 'spécialisé'. Ils forment la *schola lectorum*, la *schola cantorum* [et] la *schola scriptorum*."

[4] Riché, *Les Ecoles*, 221-52.

[5] Nicholas Orme, *Education in the West of England 1066-1548* (Exeter, 1976), 3.

[6] There are few places one can look for enlightenment on elementary instruction. See Kathleen Edwards, *The English Secular Cathedrals in the Middle Ages*, 2nd ed. (Manchester, 1967), 166-68; A. H. Thompson, "Song Schools in the Middle Ages," *Church-Music Society Occasional Papers*, no. 14 (1942); Frank Ll. Harrison, *Music in Medieval Britain* (London, 1958), chap. 1; Orme, *ESMA*, 60-70; William J. Frank Davies, *Teaching Reading in Early England* (London, 1973); and T. W. Baldwin, *William Shakspere's Petty School* (Urbana, Ill., 1943).

elementary curriculum, he assumed that reading and song were combined under the category of song school. He was followed in this assumption by J. W. Adamson, who argued that "in the light of contemporary events, it is reasonable to describe them [song schools] as schools which taught boys to read, if not to write."[7] This identification of song with reading has carried over into the work of Nicholas Orme.[8] In fact, it is clear from numerous documents that song and reading could be taught together. This is suggested by the late thirteenth-century lament in *Floriz and Blaunche-flur*, that "Ne can y in no scole syng ne rede without Blancheflour." In the plan of study proposed in Pierre Dubois's *De recuperatione terre sancte* and written between 1305-1307, the day began with the reading of the psalter, to be followed by instruction in song and in Donatus, "in accidentibus, declinationibus, et successive in aliis gramaticalibus," while a gloss in the *Corpus Juris Canonici* on "to keep school" defines it as "teaching the psalter and singing." Back in England, the music master at Warwick taught elementary reading, and this was probably true at most collegiate churches and cathedrals. In the sixteenth century the elementary schoolmaster attached to Exeter Cathedral directed "a free song school, the schoolmaster to have yearly from the said pastor and preachers xx marks for wages and his house free, to teach xi children freely to read, write, sing, and play upon the instruments of music and to teach [them] their A B C in Greek and Hebrew."[9] Nonetheless, as this chapter will argue, song schools did not always teach reading. More often reading schools did not teach song. In the cases where it is clear that both were taught by the same schoolmaster, the demands of each curriculum were different

---

[7] See, for example, A. F. Leach, *History of Warwick School* (London, 1906), 70-71; John William Adamson, *A Short History of Education* (Cambridge, 1919), 74; Clara P. McMahon, *Education in Fifteenth-Century England* (Baltimore, 1947), passim; and G. R. Potter, "Education in the Fourteenth and Fifteenth Centuries," *The Cambridge Medieval History*, Vol. 8, ed. C. W. Previté-Orton and Z. N. Brooke (Cambridge, 1936), 689. Although Adamson refers only to boys, girls also sometimes had access to a song and reading education. See chap. 3 below, pp. 69-70.

[8] Nicholas Orme, "Education and Learning at a Medieval English Cathedral: Exeter 1380-1548," *J. Eccl. Hist.* 32 (1981):268; *ESMA*, 63.

[9] *King Horn, Floriz and Blauncheflur, the Assumption of our Lady*, ed. J. Lumby, EETS, orig. ser., no. 14 (London, 1866), 71; Pierre Dubois, *De recuperatione Terre Sancte* (Florence, 1977), 160; *Corpus Juris Canonici*, ed. E. Friedberg, 2 vols. (Leipzig, 1879-1881), 2:col. 449, liber decretalium Gregorii IX, III, tit. i, cap. iii; the gloss, by Joli, Chanter of Paris, is cited in Hastings Rashdall, *The Universities of Europe in the Middle Ages*, 3 vols., rev. ed. (Oxford, 1936), 3:350, n 1; Leach, *History of Warwick School*, 65-71; R. Whiston, *Cathedral Trusts and Their Fulfillment*, 2nd ed. (London, 1849), 10-12. For the Exeter Cathedral song school, see also Nicholas Orme, "The Early Musicians of Exeter Cathedral," *Music and Letters* 59 (1978):395-410 and "Education and Learning at a Medieval English Cathedral," 268.

and often perceived as different by contemporaries. One cannot auto-matically assume that the same pupils were learning both. Thus, despite the evidence that song, reading, and sometimes grammar could be taught by the same schoolmaster, it is important to try to differentiate where warranted and no longer simply to assume that song schools taught reading and vice versa, or that medieval education, below university level, is adequately described in terms of its grammar schools.

LATIN GRAMMAR EDUCATION

Medieval grammar schools were expected to train their scholars to compose prose and poetry, both written and oral, in decent ecclesiastical Latin. As the scribbler on a flyleaf of a fifteenth-century Oxford register put it: "What is grammar? It is the art of writing and speaking correctly, containing the exposition of the poets."[10]

The most famous English grammarmasters, those whose writings be-came influential beyond their own schools, were John of Cornwall, school-master at Merton College, Oxford; possibly John Drury, schoolmaster of Beccles, Suffolk; and Richard of Hambury and John Leland, grammar-masters at Oxford; three of whom, John of Cornwall, Richard of Ham-bury, and John Leland, have been identified with an Oxford school of grammar which dominated English grammatical practices. R. W. Hunt, surveying the treatises of these three grammarians, points to the high level of grammatical theory in the writings of Richard of Hambury (d. circa 1294), who may have been a grammarian in the Arts faculty. In contrast, the extant writings of John Leland (d. 1428) are more elementary, con-sisting of his individual Latin lectures and a number of introductory English grammatical tracts. While Hunt judges that Leland's work shows a decline in the standard of grammar teaching by the end of the fourteenth century, David Thomson has more recently argued that Leland's work enabled grammarmasters to offer "more appropriate and practical material for the classroom than the learned *summae* of the earlier masters."[11] Toward

---

[10] *The Register of Congregation, 1448-1463*, ed. W. A. Pantin and W. T. Mitchell, Oxford Historical Society, new ser., 22 (Oxford, 1972), 408, quoted by Damian Leader, "Grammar in Late-Medieval Oxford and Cambridge," *History of Education* 12 (1983):9. "Grammatica quid est: ars recte scribendi recteque loquendi, poetarum enaracionem continens."

[11] J. N. Miner (Br. Bonaventure), "The Teaching of Latin in Later Mediaeval England," *Mediaeval Studies* 23 (1961):14-15; R. W. Hunt, "Oxford Grammar Masters in the Middle Ages," in *Oxford Studies Presented to Daniel Callus*, ed. R. W. Southern, Oxford Historical Society, new ser., 16 (Oxford, 1964), 16; Sanford B. Meech, "John Drury and His English Writings," *Speculum* 9 (1934):70-83; David Thomson, "The Oxford Grammar Master Revis-ited," *Mediaeval Studies* 45 (1983):299. See also Miner, "The Teaching of Grammar in England in the Later Middle Ages" (Ph.D. diss., University of London, 1959).

the end of the fifteenth century, with the foundation of Magdalen College in 1479, the grammar treatises from Oxford begin to exhibit a blend of traditional material with the newer Italian humanist grammars. Knowledge of the texts produced by Oxford grammarians was available within York diocese at Worksop Priory (Notts.) at the beginning of the fifteenth century when William Forster, himself an Oxford grammarmaster and a recently admitted canon at Worksop, bequeathed four grammars of John Leland and two of Richard of Hambury to the priory.[12] Later some of the grammar texts produced by Magdalen College grammarians circulated in the north.

Despite the Oxonian influence, it is questionable that there was ever any standard text for medieval grammarmasters to follow. There exist a good many medieval grammatical manuscripts which can be used to reconstruct a typical course of study, and nearly all of them are composite documents. Of twenty-five such manuscripts which have been examined and described by J. N. Miner, one characteristic stands out. Each manuscript is individualistic—a compilation of excerpts taken from a variety of Latin authors ranging chronologically from Aelius Donatus's *Ars Minor* (4th century A.D.) to the thirteenth-century *Catholicon* by Friar John Balbi of Genoa, but for the most part taken from thirteenth-century French and Italian grammatical masters. Many of the grammarmasters then added commentaries or tracts of their own devising, thereby adapting grammar texts to their particular needs.[13] Among the grammar texts bequeathed to Worksop Priory by William Forster, for example, was "De pronominibus sillabicatis auctore W. Foster."

Among the standard texts used by grammar teachers, the most popular were the *Ars Minor* of Donatus, of which over a thousand manuscript

[12] Emden, *BRUO*, 2:710-11; Susan Cavanaugh, "A Study of Books Privately Owned in England: 1300-1450," 2 vols. (Ph.D. diss., University of Pennsylvania, 1980), 1:353; Hunt, "Oxford Grammar Masters," 169, 186.

[13] Miner, "The Teaching of Latin," 1-20. One of the texts listed by Miner has been published, in part, by Sanford B. Meech, "An Early Treatise in English Concerning Latin Grammar," *University of Michigan Publications in Language and Literature* 13 (Ann Arbor, Mich., 1935), 81-125. The anonymous Latin and English grammar from Cambridge University, Trinity MS O.5.4, for example, uses the *Ars Minor* of Donatus, the *Doctrinale* of Alexander de Villa Dei, the *Catholicon* of John Balbi of Genoa, the writings of John of Garland, and the *Theodoli Ecloga*, among others. For a detailed description of this manuscript and twenty-three other Middle English grammatical tracts, see David Thomson, *A Descriptive Catalogue of Middle English Grammatical Texts* (New York, 1979), passim. Thomson stresses the individualistic, diversified and unstructured nature of these "texts." See Thomson, *A Descriptive Catalogue*, 21-25 where he concludes that "The manuscripts suggest that in most schools the instruction was made up of an individual and local amalgam of the old and the new, guided more by practical necessity and the availability of material than by a consistent idea of the curriculum."

copies and more than a hundred different manuscript versions survive from the eleventh through the fifteenth centuries along with some 360 incunabula editions, and the twelfth-century *Doctrinale* of Alexander de Villa Dei, of which there were some 280 incunabula editions. Other elementary grammars include Donatus's *Barbarismus*, which instructed in correct usage, and his *Ars Maior*, from which the *Barbarismus* was taken. Many additional grammar texts were elementary commentaries on Donatus's works or near word-for-word copies. Judging from surviving manuscripts, other popular grammar texts were the *Graecismus* of Eberhardus Bethuniensis, John of Garland's grammars, the *Catholicon* of John of Genoa, and the *Liber derivationum* of Hugutio of Pisa. Selections from these works were supplemented with short tracts on specific grammatical points; tracts (often in English) of the *Comparacio* (which treated comparison and its degrees), the *Informacio* and *Formula* (both of which treated Latin construction); *vulgari* or *latinitates* (translation sentences); and Latin verse compositions. These last were reading texts, often in abbreviated form, the most popular of which was the *Distichs of Cato*, a collection of Latin moral maxims which was printed at least 135 times before 1500. The *Ecloga* of Theodolus, a poetic dialogue between an Athenian shepherd and a young Jewess, with each extolling the history (or mythology) of his or her people, has survived in more than 120 manuscripts with at least 24 incunabula editions. At the end of the twelfth century, Alexander of Neckham recommended that schoolchildren, after learning their alphabet, other elementary matters, their Donatus, and Cato, turn to Theodolus. This sentiment was seconded by others, including Pierre Dubois. Theodolus's book can be documented in York diocese in the monastic library catalogues of Meaux, Austin Friars', York, and Whitby, but no surviving will mentions it.[14] Although it is extremely hazardous to make any judg-

---

[14] G. L. Bursill-Hall, "Teaching Grammars of the Middle Ages: Notes on the Manuscript Tradition," *Historiographia Linguistica* 4 (1977):1-29; "Medieval Donatus Commentaries," *Historiographia Linguistica* 8 (1981):69-97; H. R. Mead, "Fifteenth-Century Schoolbooks," *Huntington Library Quarterly* 3 (1939):37-42. Thomson, *A Descriptive Catalogue*, 23-28. For the Donatus, see Wayland J. Chase, ed. and trans., *The Ars Minor of Donatus*, University of Wisconsin Studies in the Social Sciences and History, no. 11 (Madison, 1926). An early printed *Doctrinale* (Camb. Univ. Lib. GW 935) has been published in facsimile by Stephen Gaselee for the Roxburghe Club (Cambridge, 1938). For the *Distichs* see Wayland J. Chase, ed. and trans., *The Distichs of Cato*, University of Wisconsin Studies in the Social Sciences and History, no. 7 (Madison, 1922) and Joseph Neve, *Catonis Disticha; Facsimiles, notes, liste des éditions du XVᵉ siècle* (Liège, 1926). On the *Ecloga* of Theodolus, see George L. Hamilton, "Theodolus: A Medieval Textbook," *Modern Philology* 7 (1909):1-17. For a list of other popular Latin verse readers, see Miner, "The Teaching of Latin," 7-10 and Miner, "The Teaching of Grammar," 99.

ments from bequests of grammar books in the surviving wills, the evidence from York diocese shows a marked preference for the *Cato* and the *Catholicon*, a combined Latin grammar and dictionary. It is peculiar that Donatus's *Ars Minor* (the *Donat* or *Accedence* as it was commonly called) was not mentioned more frequently in the wills as it was by far the most widespread as well as the most elementary of the Latin textbooks.[15] Since it was a rather brief text it was probably incorporated into other books or included among bequests of "all my grammar books."

Teaching the *Donat* sometimes began at the elementary rather than the secondary level of education, and reference to it as a textbook or to the existence of scholars called Donatists cannot be construed as proving the existence of a grammar school. The intermediate position of the Donatist scholar is clear from the thirteenth- or early fourteenth-century statutes of Warwick collegiate church.

> That all material for strife and disagreement, which we learn has hitherto arisen between the Master and Music Schoolmaster (*magistrum scolarum musice*) over the Donatists and little ones learning their first letters and the psalter (*Donatistas et primas litteras et psalterium addiscentes*) may be put a stop to for ever, after due inquiry in the matter and with the advice of our brethren, and so that the Masters and each of them may receive their due, and that undue encroachment of scholars on one side and the other may cease for the future; we decree and direct to be inviolably observed that the present Grammar Master (*magister grammatice*) and his successors shall have the Donatists, and thenceforward have, keep, and teach scholars in grammar or the art of dialectic, if he shall be expert in that art, while the Music Master shall keep and teach those learning their first letters, the psalter, music, and song.[16]

About 1400 it was required that the new grammar scholars who were elected into the Winchester College grammar school be taken from the elementary boys and choristers of the chapel who were already competently instructed in reading, song, and the *Old Donatus*. Similar requirements were specified for Eton College in 1443. Among household schools of the nobility the *Donat* was likewise taught to the younger children. In 1397

---

[15] There are at least ten references to the *Catholicon* and five to *Cato*. Donatus is mentioned twice. YML, D. & C., L 2/4, ff. 233, 235v, 255; BI, Prob. Reg. 2, ff. 413, 540; 3, ff. 358v, 359v, 424; 5, f. 486; 6, ff. 113, 133v; 7, f. 63; Reg. 16 (Scrope), f. 138; Reg. 20 (W. Booth), ff. 258, 273; Reg. 26 (Bainbridge), f. 138.

[16] Leach, *History of Warwick School*, 65-66.

John, the younger brother of Henry, Earl of Derby, was given his *Donat* at the age of seven and a half.[17]

By the end of the fifteenth century a new generation of grammarians emerged who had taught or studied at Magdalen College, Oxford, and one of the first tasks they turned to was a revision of the *Ars Minor*. Stimulated by several Italian revisions and by John Anwykyll's *Compendium totius grammatice*, John Stanbridge produced a number of elementary textbooks, which, although not substantially different from the medieval grammars, paid greater attention to classical materials.[18] With the help of the printing press, Stanbridge's works came into widespread use and retained their popularity well into the seventeenth century. Other elementary grammar texts, more clearly influenced by humanism, were Robert Whittinton's grammars, John Holt's *Lac Puerorum*, John Colet's *Aeditio*, and William Lily's *Rudimenta Grammatices*. By 1542 an authorized elementary Latin grammar, based largely on Lily's work, was in circulation.[19] Looking north, however, evidence in a 1512 lawsuit over the stock of a York bookseller suggests that Yorkshiremen were still turning to the older grammars, in particular the *Doctrinale* of Alexander de Villa Dei; although they were also likely to have used John Stanbridge's *Accidence* or Robert Whittinton's *Grammar*, both of which were published by York printers. A 1538 bookseller's inventory from York provides a mixed list of older grammatical works by John of Garland and Alexander de Villa Dei, as well as an *Expositio Donati*, along with newer works: a Greek alphabet, a grammatical text by Johann Reuchlin, Cicero's (?) *Copia Ver-*

---

[17] Thomas F. Kirby, *Annals of Winchester, from Its Foundation in the Year 1382* (London, 1892), 457; A. F. Leach, *Educational Charters and Documents, 589-1909* (Cambridge, 1911), 364-65; *VCH, Bucks.*, 2:159; K. B. McFarlane, *The Nobility of Later Medieval England* (Oxford, 1973), 43, 243 ff.

[18] John Stanbridge, *Accidence* (STC 2319.5-23155.2), *Vocabula* (STC 23177.5-23193.9), *Vulgaria* (STC 23194-23199), *Sum, es, fui (Gradus comparationum)* (STC 23155.4-23163.5), and *Parvula* (STC 23164.2-23175.5). The various editions of these last three works are listed by Eloise Pafort, "A Group of Early Tudor School Books," *The Library*, 4th ser., 26 (1946):227-61. For the Italian grammatical works by Nicolaus Perottus and Johannes Sulpitius, see STC 19767.3-19767.7 and STC 23425-23434.5. For John Anwykyll's *Compendium*, see STC 695-696. See also E. Gordon Duff, *Fifteenth-Century English Books* (Oxford, 1917), nos. 28-31, 346.

[19] H. S. Bennett, "A Check-List of Robert Whittinton's grammars," *The Library*, 5th ser., 7 (1952):1-14; John Holt, *Lac puerorum* (STC 13604-13606); John Colet, *Aeditio* (STC 5542-5543b). C. G. Allen, "The Sources of 'Lily's Latin Grammar,'" *The Library*, 5th ser., 9 (1954):85-100; Vincent J. Flynn, "The Grammatical Writings of William Lily, ?1468-?1523," *Papers of the Bibliographical Society of America* 37 (1943):85-113. The 1542 authorized grammar has been reprinted by Vincent J. Flynn, as *A Shorte Introduction of Grammar by William Lily* (New York, 1945).

borum and Johannes Despauterius's *Ars versificatoria*.[20] By 1546-1548, however, the first grammar schools in England to require proficiency in both Greek and Hebrew for their masters were Archbishop Holgate's foundations in the north at York, Hemsworth, and Malton.[21]

After the children finished with their grammatical rules, they turned to "making Latins," that is, making up or translating Latin sentences which were then parsed. This became the rudimentary exercise for late medieval grammar scholars and preceded the reading of Latin verse.[22] The books that contained these exercises, called *vulgaria* or *latinitates*, drew their material from mundane, secular matters and were limited only by the imagination and learning of the schoolmaster. They were sometimes racy and usually of contemporary interest—an obvious attempt on the part of the schoolmaster to provoke his scholars to learn. Some arresting examples from grammarmaster John Drury's *Parve Latinitates*, written in 1434, include:

J saw a nakyd man gaderin stoonys in hys barm.
Ego vidi nudus hominem colligere lapides in gremium suum.
Haddistu nouth to day a good stourid ars?
Habuisti ne hodie anum verberatum bene?
J haue drunkyn to-day many dyuers alis.
Ego bibi hodie multam seruiciam diuersam.[23]

With the coming of humanism, *vulgaria* were printed that incorporated the language of classical authors and, perhaps because they were meant for a wider audience, they were less adventurous in their subject matter.[24]

[20] Elizabeth Brunskill, "Missals, Portifers and Pyes," *The Ben Jonson Papers* 2 (1974):8; E. Gordon Duff, *The English Provincial Printers, Stationers and Bookbinders to 1557* (Cambridge, 1912), 53, 57; D. M. Palliser and D. G. Selwyn, "The Stock of a York Stationer, 1538," *The Library*, 5th ser., 27 (1972):207-19.

[21] York City Archives, Foundation Deed of Archbishop Holgate's School; *VCH, Yorks.*, 1:474-75; BI, Reg. 23 (Rotherham), f. 264v. One must question the extent to which this requirement was carried out, since the first master of Holgate's York school was Thomas Swanne, a Yorkshireman from Kirkby Overblow, who is not known to have graduated from either Oxford or Cambridge.

[22] The first grammar work to introduce "Latins" as exercises is that of John of Cornwall, written in the 1340s, although Cornwall was following a tradition reaching back to the thirteenth century. Hunt, "Oxford Grammar Masters," 175.

[23] Meech, "John Drury," 82-83. The first example may be a deliberately poor translation intended to illustrate the problem of following word order too closely. For other fifteenth-century *vulgaria* see W. Nelson, ed., *A Fifteenth-Century School Book* (Oxford, 1956); Nicholas Orme, "An Early-Tudor Oxford Schoolbook," *Renaissance Quarterly* 34 (1981):11-39; "A Grammatical Miscellany of 1427-1465 from Bristol and Wiltshire," *Traditio* 38 (1982):301-26; and Miner, "The Teaching of Grammar," 121-31.

[24] William Horman, *Vulgaria*, ed. M. R. James (Oxford, 1926); *The Vulgaria of John Stanbridge and the Vulgaria of Robert Whittinton*, ed. Beatrice White, EETS, orig. ser., 187 (London, 1932).

These *vulgaria* came under attack in turn by Roger Ascham, who proposed, in 1570, to replace them with examples taken directly from classical authors.[25]

However widespread the practice of making Latins may have been in Ascham's day, it was not always *de rigueur* in the earlier period. As William Langland complained, in *Piers Plowman*:

Grammer, the grounde of al,
  bigileth [foxes] now children,
For is noon of thise newe clerkes
  [schoolboys], whoso nymeth hede,
That can versifie faire ne
  formaliche enditen [write a letter],
Ne nauȝt oon among an hundred
  that an Auctour kan construwe,
Ne rede a lettre in any langage
  but in latyn or englissh.[26]

In 1357 Bishop Grandisson of Exeter circulated a letter in which he complained that too many students were passing on to reading poetry and meter without having grounded themselves sufficiently in Latin grammar.

We ourselves have learned . . . that among masters or teachers of boys and illiterate folk in our diocese, who instruct them in Grammar, there prevails a preposterous and unprofitable method and order of teaching . . . for these masters,—after their scholars have learned to read or repeat, even imperfectly, the Lord's Prayer, the Ave Maria, the Creed, and the Mattins and Hours of the Blessed Virgin, and other such things pertaining to faith and their soul's health, without knowing or understanding how to construe anything of the aforesaid, or decline the words or parse them—then, I say, these masters make them pass on prematurely to learn other advanced [*magistrales*] books of poetry or metre. Whence it cometh to pass that, grown to man's estate, they understand not the things which they daily read or say . . . moreover . . . they discern not the Catholic Faith.[27]

Bishop Grandisson closed his letter by enjoining the grammarmasters within each archdeaconry to "make them [the grammar pupils] construe

---

[25] Roger Ascham, *The Schoolmaster* (1570), ed. L. V. Ryan (Ithaca, N.Y., 1967), 13-14.

[26] *Piers Plowman: The B Version*, ed. George Kane and E. Talbot Donaldson (London, 1975), xv, 365 ff. (pp. 556-57).

[27] *The Register of John de Grandisson, Bishop of Exeter, A.D. 1327-1369*, ed. Francis C. Hingeston-Randolph, 3 vols. (London, 1894-1899), 2:1192-93; trans. G. G. Coulton, *Life in the Middle Ages*, 4 vols. (Cambridge, 1928), 2:113-14.

and understand the Lord's Prayer, the Ave Maria, the Creed, the Mattins and Hours of the Blessed Virgin, and decline and parse the words therein, before permitting them to pass on to other books. . . ."

To what extent matters of faith may have been construed in grammar schools outside Exeter diocese is impossible to assess. The practice was probably widespread, however, as evidenced by Archbishop Arundel's anxiety that English grammar schools might succumb to Lollard influence. In 1408 he decreed that "masters and such as teach children or any other, in sciences or in grammar instructing them in the first principles, shall in no wise meddle to instruct them in the Catholic Faith, in the Sacrament of the Altar or other Sacraments of the Church or any theological matters, neither shall interpret nor declare Holy Scripture in expounding the text, but as it hath been of old time accustomed."[28] John Lyndwood, in his gloss on this passage, makes it clear that teaching from scripture in a grammatical sense was customary, but that teaching scripture in a mystical or moral sense did not pertain to the faculty of the grammarmaster.[29] Despite Lyndwood's interpretation, Arundel's legislation, which appears to have failed in its effort to abolish schools for heretics,[30] may have effectively discouraged the use of scripture or the discussion of Catholic faith by orthodox grammarmasters. Many of the surviving texts used in grammar schools of the fifteenth century are markedly secular in tone.[31]

By the time of the Reformation, however, matters of faith and scriptural

[28] David Wilkins, ed., *Concilia Magnae Britanniae et Hiberniae*, Vol. 3 (London, 1737), 317. "Similiter, quia id quod capit nova testa inveterata sapit, statuimus et ordinamus, quod magistri sive quicunque docentes in artibus, aut grammatica, pueros, seu alios quoscunque in primitivis scientiis instruentes, de fide catholica, sacramento altaris, seu aliis sacramentis ecclesiae, aut materia aliqua theologica, contra determinata per ecclesiam, se nullatenus intromittant instruendo eosdem; nec de expositione sacrae scripturae, nisi in exponendo textum, prout antiquitus fieri consuevit; nec permittant scholares suos sive discipulos de fide catholica, seu sacramentis ecclesiae publice disputare etiam vel occulte: contrarium autem faciens, ut fautor errorum, et schismatum, per loci ordinarium graviter puniatur."

[29] William Lyndwood, *Provinciale* (Oxford, 1679), Book V, tit. 4, gl. ad consuevit: "Scil. Grammaticaliter, et sic secundum sensus Mysticos vel Morales non debent eam exponere, quia hoc non pertinet ad ipsorum facultatem sive doctrinam: et Culpa est se immiscere Rei ad se non pertinenti."

[30] Norman P. Tanner, *Heresy Trials in the Diocese of Norwich, 1428-31*, Camden Society, 4th ser., 20 (London, 1977), 29-30.

[31] The *Speculum Parvulorum*, written by William Chartham, a monk of Christ Church, Canterbury, in the first half of the fifteenth century, is a significant exception. See J. N. Miner, "The Use of the Disputation in England's Medieval Grammar Schools" (Paper presented at the International Congress on Medieval Studies, Kalamazoo, Mich., 1982). For a discussion of (and emphasis on) the religious content in late medieval grammar texts, see Miner, "The Teaching of Grammar," passim.

materials were once again taught in the grammar schools. This was probably the case at Doncaster in 1528 when Simon Robinson, the vicar, left
"to Peter Mydleton the hoole bible, if he will continue the scole and do
well, or els not." Thomas Magnus's grammar school foundation at Newark
in 1530 specified that the masters not only compel the scholars to learn
grammar and rhetoric but also "teach and inform their scholars in knowledge of the ten commandments, the articles of the faith, the understanding
of the holy psalms and hymns."[32] Thomas More's comment in 1532 was
that, "After the psalter chyldren were wont to go to theyr Donat & theyr
Accydence / but now they go strayte to scrypture."[33] Such was probably
the case at Dalton, Lancashire late in 1536, where William Rede was
teaching from Erasmus's *Paraphrases* and attacking papal authority, a
circumstance that raised suspicions of heresy. In 1546 the grammar school
goods inventoried at Brough under Stainmore (Westmorland) by the chantry commissioners included "vi bookes of the Byble called *Glosa Ordinaria*,
thole Byble in Latten, ix other bookes, as *Ortus Vocabulorum* and *Catholicon*."[34] With the exception of William Rede's school, these examples
reflect a Catholic, rather than a Protestant, teaching tradition.

The availability of books, evident in Bishop Grandisson's circular, in
the school library at Brough, and even in the Lollard schools, is interesting,
since some historians, describing the practice of medieval grammar schools,
speak of rote learning in which schoolchildren had no books except perhaps
wax tablets or small notebooks in which they jotted the lessons of the day.[35]
In such cases students had to rely on their memories, which grammarmasters sharpened by the use of inquisitorial techniques. The following
example illustrates a dialogue that might be employed in such a classroom.

---

[32] BI, Reg. 27 (Wolsey), ff. 163-163v; Cornelius Brown, *A History of Newark-upon-Trent*,
2 vols. (Newark, 1904-1907), 2:190.

[33] *The Complete Works of St. Thomas More*, Vol. 8, ed. Louis A. Schuster, Richard C. Marius,
James P. Lusardi, and Richard J. Schoeck (New Haven, 1973), 11.

[34] Christopher Haigh, *The Last Days of the Lancashire Monasteries and the Pilgrimage of Grace*,
Chetham Society, 3rd ser., 17 (Manchester, 1969), 52; R. L. Storey, "The Chantries of
Cumberland and Westmorland, part 2," *Transactions of the Cumberland and Westmorland Anti-
quarian and Archaeological Society*, new ser., 62 (1962):147.

[35] J. J. Bagley, *Life in Medieval England* (London, 1960), 92. "A good memory served the
medieval schoolboy well, for he had no reference or textbooks . . . handwritten books were too
scarce for general possession, and dictionaries did not exist." Philip W. Rogers, *A History of
Ripon Grammar School* (Ripon, 1954), 38. "The absence of textbooks for the boys seems strange
. . . the lessons we see are all verbal." Joan Simon, *Education and Society in Tudor England*
(Cambridge, 1966), 50. "[Latin rules] were expounded orally and learned by heart . . . books
at this time were essentially a luxury product, costing more than the average teacher could well
afford."

Es tu scholaris? Sum.

Quod legis? Non lego sed audio.

Quid audis? Tabulam, vel Donatum vel Alexandrum vel logicam vel musicam.[36]

In rural areas of the north the children were still being taught their grammar by rote as late as the first decade of the sixteenth century. Roger Ascham, the best known of sixteenth-century schoolmasters, who was raised in Kirby Wiske in the North Riding, recalled

> . . . when I was young, in the North, they went to the grammar school little children; they came from thence great lubbers, always learning and little profiting: learning without book everything, understanding within the book little or nothing. Their whole knowledge, by learning without the book, was tied only to their tongue and lips, and never ascended up to the brain and head, and therefore was soon spit out of the mouth again.[37]

There is, however, evidence from York diocese that points to the increasingly general use of books by grammar scholars at the end of the Middle Ages. About 1380, John Waldby, an Augustinian friar of York, noted in a sermon in the city that ". . . if the master is away, boys in school fail to apply themselves to their books. But as soon as they hear his stern voice, their eyes are on the page." Wills provide considerable evidence for the practice of leaving grammar books to young boys for their use in school, and a few wills from schoolboys include bequests of texts.[38] One example of the former occurred in 1465 when John Elwyn of Hedon left all his grammar books to the boys of the grammar school at Hedon. Among the Middleton manuscripts at Nottingham University there is a thirteenth-century grammar treatise which, from the evidence of various scribblings, came into the hands of schoolboys from the north of England in the fifteenth century; other, similar fifteenth-century man-

---

[36] A. E. Shaw, "The Earliest Latin Grammars in English," *Transactions of the Bibliographical Society* 5 (1898-1900):44-45.

[37] Ascham, *The Schoolmaster*, 79.

[38] MS Caius College, Cambridge 334, ff. 177 *et seq.*, cited in G. R. Owst, *Preaching in Medieval England* (Cambridge, 1926), 64-65. For a detailed analysis of the grammar books bequeathed to young scholars in York diocese, see chap. 7 below. In addition, John del Man, son of John Man, citizen and tapiter of York, left all his grammar books to Thomas Garland in 1438 (BI, Prob. Reg. 3, ff. 544v-545). Robert Hunter, scholar in York, left all his books to Thomas, son of Robert Elleryngton, in 1446 (BI, Prob. Reg. 2, f. 159). In 1457 Adam Tyldesley, son of Thomas Tyldesley of Hilton, a grammar scholar at Southwell, left his portable breviary to the parish church of Dene (BI, Reg. 20 [William Booth], f. 272).

uscripts are Bodleian 638 and PRO C 47/34/13 Miscellanea.[39] Nor is mention of the use of books by scholars limited to the grammar level. As we shall see, elementary students sometimes had their own primer, psalter, or *Donat*. Or, lacking that, they used the books in church, as the vicar of Hornby (North Riding) feared when he left a large portifor (breviary) to his church in 1439.[40] Outside York diocese, in the city of Lincoln, the grammarmaster in the early fifteenth century had a particularly large library of 112 volumes containing 674 separate items. Many of his grammar books, which included Donatus's *Ars Minor*, the *Catholicon* of John Balbi, a *Catholicon* of his own composing, Cato, Aesop, Theodolus, Priscian's *In Majore* and the *Elementarium* of Papias, must have at times been in the hands of his pupils.[41]

The availability of texts to schoolchildren increased throughout the fifteenth century, and once the printing press reached England, it became possible to buy school texts for a few pennies. In the 1512 lawsuit at York referred to above, 300 missals, portifors, primers, and other little paper books in Latin and English were estimated to be worth approximately £10. Among the books sold at Oxford in 1520 were sixteen notebooks of Whittinton and Stanbridge and one new grammar book, all for 1s. Further down the list are two primers and two A B C's sold for 10d., twenty-four A B C's in paper sold for 10d. and twelve A B C's in parchment sold for 1s. 2d. The inventoried stock of a York bookseller in 1538 suggests even cheaper schooltexts. The *exposicio hymnarum*, a song schooltext, was valued at 1d., an imperfect grammar of John of Garland at 1d., a "bounshe of doctourinalez" (probably the *Doctrinale* of Alexander de Villa Dei) at 2d., and an *exposicio super donatum* at 2d.[42] The availability

---

[39] BI, Prob. Reg. 4, f. 66; *Test. Ebor.*, 2:270. Nicholas Orme describes the Middleton MS Mi LM 2: "Here we find their names inscribed: 'Johannis Wapplode', 'Johannes Cole de Wodyl' and, ungrammatically, 'iste liber constat Radulfe Savage'. Master Savage, who describes himself as 'bonus puer', was apparently the author of various scribbles throughout the book, including the observation "Willelmus Cayso est pravus puer'." Orme, *ESMA*, 127. See also Historical Manuscripts Commission, *Report on the Manuscripts of Lord Middleton Preserved in Wollaton Hall* (London, 1911), 212-13. For a description of the Bodleian MS, see Ethel Seaton, *Sir Richard Roos c. 1410-1482: Lancastrian Poet* (London, 1961), 105-106. For the volume in the PRO, see N. R. Ker, *Medieval Manuscripts in British Libraries*, Vol. 1 (Oxford, 1969), 180.

[40] YML, D. & C., L 2/4, f. 251: ". . . quod idem portiforum taliter servetur quod per pueros vel clericos in ecclesia predicta addiscentes et erudientes non violetur nec ullo modo sordidetur . . ." See also E. G. Cuthbert F. Atchley, "The Halleway Chauntry," *Bristol and Gloucestershire Archaeological Society* 24 (1901):111.

[41] Charles Garton, "A Fifteenth Century Headmaster's Library," *Lincolnshire History and Archaeology*, 15 (1980):33.

[42] Brunskill, "Missals, Portifers and Pyes," 13, 25; Falconer Madan, ed., "The Daily Ledger

of cheaper books made it possible for Lord Darcy, when he began to found his free grammar school at Whitkirk (West Riding) in 1520, to supply books "safely to be kept by the said master to the use of the . . . school," while Archbishop Holgate stipulated that the scholars in his new grammar schools were to read psalms and scripture during church service every Sunday and holiday privately to themselves, although they had to share books to do it. In 1542 Wilfrid Borrowe, probably the rector or vicar at Kirkby Lonsdale, left to the grammar school "the rest of my bowkes not before geven to the Scowle at Kirkby."[43]

Even with greater accessibility of books, however, memorization, often enhanced by the use of interrogatories, remained fundamental to late medieval and early Renaissance learning. Erasmus makes this point several times in his *Colloquies*. In "Off to School," one of his schoolboys remarks that he has yet to memorize the previous day's fairly long lesson. He fears that he cannot do it, and his schoolmate sympathizes. "I hardly know the lesson well enough myself," Sylvius responds, and they soon agree to take turns repeating the lesson, one reciting and the other looking at the book. Later Erasmus remarks that whoever is too giddy-minded to fix in memory what he has learned is unfit for learning.[44] Unlike the parish scholars of Ascham's childhood village, however, Erasmus's schoolboys were learning from their own texts. There must have been, as the foregoing pages suggest, enormous differences in available resources and teaching effectiveness from one grammar school to the next.

In the better grammar schools students were expected not only to read Latin but also to speak it. In 1459 the choristers at Wells were told that, if "at dinner or supper time, they shall want something on the table they shall ask for it in Latin not in English. . . ." While, during a visitation of Southwell Minster's grammar school in 1484, it was noted with disapproval that "they do not speak Latin in school but English." The unknown Magdalen College author of a late fifteenth-century collection of schoolboy dialogues noted that, "If I had not used my English tongue so greatly, for which the master hath rebuked me oft times, I should have been far more cunning in grammar. Wise men say that nothing may be more profitable to them that learn grammar than to speak Latin." Another

of John Dorne, 1520," *Collectanea*, 1st ser., part 3, 74-177; 2nd ser., appendix, Oxford Historical Society, nos. 5, 16 (Oxford, 1885, 1890); Palliser and Selwyn, "The Stock of a York Stationer," 213-19.

[43] PRO, SP 1/21, 128v; *L & P, Henry VIII*, 3 (1519-1521), i, 394; York City Archives, Foundation Deed of Archbishop Holgate's School, f. 4v; Preston Record Office, Lonsdale, Archdeaconry of Richmond, Original Wills, Box 300 B 1543-1610.

[44] *The Colloquies of Erasmus*, trans. C. R. Thompson (Chicago, 1965), 43-45; 461.

vulgaria from the early sixteenth century makes a similar point: "If thu cannyst not exprese the conseytes of thi mind in latyn, this is the cause and noon eles, that thu art wont more to thi mother tong than to latyn, wich thyng hurtes gretly not only the but also thi scole felowis."[45]

As the above evidence suggests, any very high standard of Latinity in casual or even classroom conversation was little adhered to. As early as the 1340s in the south of England, grammar scholars began to learn their lessons by composing and versifying English to Latin and back rather than, as had been the custom, from French into Latin and back.[46] A number of Latin grammar treatises in English survive from the fifteenth century, suggesting that it may have been difficult for schoolchildren to learn their grammar from books wholly in Latin.[47] John Bracebridge, the early fifteenth-century grammarmaster at Lincoln, owned a Cato, glossed in English for the benefit of his scholars, and John of Cornwall's *Speculum grammaticale*, based on Donatus and probably including English.[48] Latin-English dictionaries also became popular, especially the *Medulla Grammatice*, which was probably compiled in the first third of the fifteenth century and is regularly bequeathed in northern wills thereafter.[49] Although the Latin to English dictionaries suggest Latin scholars versed in English, the fifteenth century also saw the production of English-Latin dictionaries, the *Promptorium Parvulorum* and the *Catholicon Anglicum*, which suggest English scholars being taught Latin in English. The *Promptorium Parvulorum*, in particular, was written specifically for children, and was printed at least six times between 1499 and 1528. It was not until the early sixteenth century that grammar school statutes begin to specifically

---

[45] *Dean Cosyn and Wells Cathedral Miscellanea*, ed. A. Watkin, Somerset Record Society, no. 56 (London, 1941), 106; A. F. Leach, ed., *Visitations and Memorials of Southwell Minster*, Camden Society, new ser., no. 48 (London, 1891), 49. ". . . non locuntur latinum in scola sed anglicum." Nelson, *A Fifteenth-Century School Book*, 22; Orme, "An Early-Tudor Oxford Schoolbook," 24. The discussion of the use of English speech in the grammar curriculum follows Orme, ESMA, 96-101.

[46] *Polychronicon Ranulphi Higden*, Vol. 2, trans. and commentary by John Trevisa, ed. C. Babington, Rolls Series, no. 41 (London, 1896), 157-61. See also W. H. Stevenson, "The Introduction of English as the Vehicle of Instruction in English Schools," in *An English Miscellany Presented to Dr. Furnivall* (Oxford, 1901), 421-29.

[47] Thomson, *A Descriptive Catalogue*; Meech, "John Drury"; Shaw, "The Earliest Latin Grammars in English"; Sanford B. Meech, "Early Application of Latin Grammar to English," PMLA 50 (1935):1012-32; Meech, "An Early Treatise in English concerning Latin Grammar," 81-125.

[48] Garton, "Fifteenth Century Headmaster's Library," 35-36.

[49] YML, D. & C., L 2/4, f. 349; L 2/5a, f. 100; BI, Reg. 26 (Bainbridge), f. 141; BI, Prob. Reg. 2, ff. 17, 312; 3, f. 318; 4, ff. 18, 67.

require their scholars to speak Latin and not English,[50] but by the 1560s, Roger Ascham's estimation of the Latin spoken "now commonly, in the best schools in England," was such that "confusion is brought in, barbarousness is bred up so in young wits as afterward they be not only marred for speaking but also corrupted in judgment," and he recommended the use of English in teaching Latin grammar.[51]

Regardless of how much English was included in the curriculum, most medieval grammar scholars eventually learned to speak Latin, and once they were capable of doing so they were ready to engage in disputations. At the grammar-school level these exercises traditionally concerned themselves with logic and grammar, although they must also have included debates on faith and the sacraments, both of which topics Archbishop Arundel forbade to grammar scholars in 1408.[52] Disputations were held at Merton grammar school in the 1340s where John of Cornwall, famous for first introducing English as a vehicle of instruction, was grammar-master. They also took place at St. Albans, Eton, Winchester, and Crediton in the fourteenth and fifteenth centuries, and John Stow's recollections provide evidence that disputations were still practiced in the grammar schools of early Tudor London when he was a schoolboy. Although they were no longer concerned with questions of logic, he notes that "the arguing of the Schoole boyes aboute the principles of Grammar hath beene continued even till our time; for I myselfe in my youth have yearelie seen on the Eve of S. Bartlemew the Apostle, the schollers of divers Grammar schooles repaire unto the Churchyard of S. Bartlemew, the Priorie in Smithfielde, where upon a bank boorded aboute under a Tree, some one Scholler hath stepped up, and there hath apposed and answered, till he were by some better Scholler overcome." As a child Stow could also have heard the disputations "bothe in privat houses and in the commen scholes" on the question "whether the pope might dispence with the brother to mary his brother's wyfe after carnall knouledge."[53] According to John

---

[50] *Promptorium Parvulorum sive clericorum, lexicon Anglo-Latinum princeps*, ed. A. Way, 3 vols., Camden Society, nos. 25, 54, 89 (London, 1843-1865); *The Promptorium Parvulorum: The First English-Latin Dictionary*, ed. A. L. Mayhew, EETS, ex. ser., no. 102 (London, 1908); *Catholicon Anglicum, an English-Latin Wordbook dated 1483*, ed. S.J.H. Herrtage, EETS, orig. ser., no. 75 (London, 1881). *VCH, Lancs.*, 2:581-85; 601.

[51] Ascham, *The Schoolmaster*, 17.

[52] Wilkins, *Concilia*, 3:317. For the text see note 28 above. For this reference and additional evidence that disputations were commonly employed in grammar schools, see Miner, "The Use of the Disputation in England's Medieval Grammar Schools," 11-13.

[53] A. F. Leach, ed., *Educational Charters and Documents, 589 to 1909* (Cambridge, 1911), 300-301; *VCH Bucks.*, 2:161-62; Registrum J. Whethamstede, in *Chronica Monasterii S. Albani*, ed. H. T. Riley, Rolls Series, no. 28, part 6, vol. 2 (London, 1873), app. C, 312; *Registrum*

Rous, who was writing in the 1480s, disputations took place up to his time in the cathedral churches and in certain well-known colleges (of which York diocese boasted four) and in the friaries.[54] These disputation exercises helped prepare boys to go on to the university, and consequently writers of grammars, such as one Master John Versor in the fifteenth century, advertised the dialectical virtues of their various texts. "[Here is] the exceedingly useful production of Master John Versor dealing with the lesser Donatus in an extraordinarily charming fashion and with superlatively good arguments through the knowledge of which young scholars may arrive very easily at the very best possible manner of arguing and debating."[55]

Insofar as it is possible to generalize about late medieval grammar schools, we can say that they were concerned primarily with the very practical objective of teaching Latin in both speech and written composition. Teaching Latin reading was not the primary task of the grammar schools. After beginning with the *Donat* and the basic grammatical rules, the grammar scholar proceeded to "making Latins" with the aid of various *vulgaria*, dictionaries, and more complex grammars, from there turning to the reading and writing of Latin verse and to disputations. The result should have been to produce scholars who could read and speak a fluent "bastard" Latin which, although highly anglicized in syntax and vocabulary, was sufficient for both ecclesiastical and secular administrative purposes; and who could probably write the same administrative Latin in a very practical, legible cursive hand. The subject matter of these late medieval grammatical texts and exercises was concerned with the events of everyday life, although occasionally it contributed (perhaps through biblical quotations) to a scholar's religious training.

READING EDUCATION

In contrast with the comparative variety of grammar texts and the relative latitude grammarmasters exercised with regard to curriculum, the

---

T. Brantyngham, ed. F. C. Hingeston-Randolph (London, 1901), part 1, 378-79; John Gough Nichols, ed., *Narratives of the Days of the Reformation*, Camden Society, orig. ser., no. 77 (London, 1859), 220.

[54] John Rous, *Historia Regum Angliae*, ed. T. Hearne (Oxford, 1716), 73-74. ". . . sic in hodiernum diem in ecclesiis cathedralibus, & quibusdam nobilibus collegiis, & locis religiosis fratrum iiii ordinum mendicantium servantur lecturae & disputationes fructuosae. . . ."

[55] Charles Thurot, "Notices et extraits de divers manuscrits latins pour servir à l'histoire des doctrines grammaticales au moyen âge," *Notices et extraits des manuscrits de la Bibliothèque impériale* (Paris, 1868) 22:iii, 487.

elementary school texts were uniform, allowing for little pedagogical initiative. Church service books formed the basis for the standard reading curriculum. They acquainted the beginning scholar with the rituals of the liturgy and with selected prayers or biblical passages, particularly from the psalter.

The youngest pupils in the elementary reading schools were called "petty" scholars, deriving from "petites," the Anglo-Norman word that characterized the youngest children at a school. Petty scholars began by learning their A B C's followed by numbers, the Hail Mary or the Lord's Prayer in Latin and English. These first lessons were sometimes written upon a parchment pasted to a wooden tablet. Such a wooden "booklet" was described in a late fourteenth-century alphabetic poem on the Passion:

A place, as man may se
Quan a chyld to scole xal set be,
 A bok hym is browt,
Naylyd on a brede of tre,
That men callyt an abece,
 Pratylych i-wrout.
Wrout is on the bok withoute
.v. paraffys grete and stoute,
 Rolyd in rose-red;
That is set withoutyn doute
 In tokenyng of Cristes ded.
Red letter in parchemyn
Makyth a chyld good and fyn
 Lettrys to loke and se.[56]

Earlier, circa 1340, the Dominican friar, Robert Holcot, commented that "Boys when they are first instructed are not able to learn anything subtle, but only simple things. So they were first taught with a 'book' of large letters affixed to a piece of wood, and progress afterwards to learning letters from a more advanced book."[57] By the end of the fifteenth century a hornbook, a piece of board about 9 inches by 5 inches with a handle and a transparent sheet of horn covering it, was commonly used. A B C's in paper and parchment were also readily available, as is evident from

[56] MS Harleian 3954, f. 87, printed in T. Wright and J. O. Halliwell, eds., *Reliquiae Antiquae*, 2 vols. (London, 1845), 1:63. See also MS Sloane 2593; MS Bodleian 2643, f. 152, and MS Advocates 18.7.21, f. 122v. These last two are listed in Carleton F. Brown, *A Register of Middle English Religious and Didactic Verse*, 2 vols. (Oxford, 1916-1920), 2:nos. 899, 925.

[57] Beryl Smalley, *English Friars and Antiquity in the Early Fourteenth Century* (Oxford, 1960), 332.

the 1520 bookseller's list of John Dorne at Oxford.[58] Some of these, selling for only a penny, were probably single leaves, although the A B C's in parchment selling for three pennies may have been small books, perhaps not unlike the fourteenth-century English A B C of six leaves at the Hunterian Museum, Glasgow, or the little book of eight leaves printed at Venice in 1494 and described as an *Alphabetum et preces pro pueris*.[59] It was probably one of these booklets, and not a wooden tablet or hornbook, that is described in the late fourteenth-century poem *God Speed Me*:

Croys was maad al of reed
In þe bigynnynge of my book
That is clepid God me spede
In þe firste lessoun þat I took
Thanne I lerned a and be
And oþir lettres by here names.
But alwey God spede me
That is me nedeful in alle games
If I pleyde in felde oþir in medes.[60]

The petty child, just beginning his letters, may have encountered less Latin than English by the fifteenth century. At Hull in 1454, the petties learned their alphabet, table graces, and the elements of English spelling and reading. At Lincoln about 1410 the grammarmaster owned two English tracts on the Ten Commandments and one on the seven deadly sins, which he probably used for instructing the younger children.[61] One of the early extant printed A B C's, probably published about 1538, contains, in English, the alphabet, some table graces, the seven works of mercy, Ten Commandments, and seven deadly sins. The Pater Noster, Hail Mary, and the Creed were given in both Latin and English, and the book ends with two untranslated pages of Latin from the Antiphoner "to helpe

[58] Andrew W. Tuer, *The History of the Hornbook*, 2 vols. (London, 1897); Falconer Madan, ed., "Day-Book of John Dorne, Bookseller in Oxford, A.D. 1520," *Collectanea*, 1st. ser., Oxford Historical Society, no. 5 (Oxford, 1885), 71-177 passim, but see especially the index on p. 145.

[59] "Day-Book of John Dorne," 128, 145. W. H. Allnutt, *An Early Sixteenth-Century A B C in Latin after the Use of Sarum* (Oxford, 1891), 8-9. Allnutt includes, in facsimile, a four leaf vellum copy of a Latin A B C, printed about 1538 and, as of 1891, deposited in the library at Lanhydrock.

[60] M. C. Seymour, ed., *On the Properties of Things: John Trevisa's Translation of Bartholomeus Anglicus De Proprietatibus Rerum*, 2 vols. (Oxford, 1975), 1:40.

[61] Hull Corporation Archives, Bench Book IIIa, f. 38; Garton, "Fifteenth Century Headmaster's Library," 36.

a prest to syng," which the children were undoubtedly expected to memorize without necessarily understanding.[62]

While the petty school curriculum appears relatively straightforward, the scarcity of evidence for petty schools and scholars as well as the elusive, sometimes confusing quality of the evidence we have, assures us that our generalizations must remain tentative. Sometimes contemporaries did not recognize a clear distinction between these beginners and other elementary scholars who were readers. For example, in a dispute at the collegiate church of Warwick in 1316, mention was made of the petties who were learning to read their letters and the (Latin) psalter. Alternatively, petty learning might be subsumed under the general grammar curriculum, as at the Hungerford Almshouse where the warden was to teach boys and others "from the beginning of learning unto such season as they have sufficient or competent [knowledge] of grammar." On the other hand, two examples from the fifteenth century illustrate instances when the petty scholar was clearly differentiated from the more advanced student. In the constitution for the almshouse at Ewelme in 1437 it was directed that, if the schoolmaster had no more than four "childer that actually lernes gramer, besides petettes and reders," he should assist at matins and evensong. In 1477 the statutes for the Ipswich schools defined petties as those scholars learning their A B C's and song; they were distinguished from the primer and psalter scholars who were learning to read.[63] Here, however, the petty and song scholars are grouped together, which reminds us once more how difficult it is to differentiate one scholar or one school from another and how variable the medieval school curriculum could be. While the exercise is not entirely quixotic, since it is clear that contemporaries similarly sought to differentiate one curriculum from another, the results can never be more than approximate.

The A B C "books" served as an introduction to the elementary primer, so-called, Bishop Hilsey of Rochester explained in 1539, "because I suppose that is the first book in which tender youth was instructed in." It was the *primus liber* of the aspiring reader,[64] notwithstanding the earlier A B C's. There are few extant examples of a simple English primer from

[62] Evelyn S. Shuckburgh, ed., *The ABC Both in Latyn and Englysche* (London, 1889).

[63] A. F. Leach, "Some Results of Research in the History of Education in England," *Proceedings of the British Academy* 6 (1913-1914), 451-52; Orme, *Education in the West of England*, 144; Historical Manuscripts Commission, *Ninth Report* (London, 1883), 216-22; Leach, *Educational Charters and Documents*, 422-23.

[64] *The Manual of Prayers, or the Prymer in Englyshe and Latyn* (STC 16009-16010), intro.; Edwyn Birchenough, "The Prymer in English," *The Library*, 4th ser., 18 (1937-1938), 177-78.

before the sixteenth century. One, written at the end of the fourteenth century, incorporates the A B C's and is followed by the exorcism, the Lord's Prayer, Hail Mary, the Creed, the Ten Commandments, the seven deadly sins, the seven principal virtues, seven works of mercy bodily, seven works of mercy ghostly, five bodily wits, four cardinal virtues, seven gifts of the Holy Ghost, Corinthians 13, and the Beatitudes and Sayings of St. Augustine. Another, a small vellum manuscript of the fifteenth century, begins with the alphabet followed by the Lord's Prayer, Ave, Creed, an explanation of the Ten Commandments, "the sevin dedeli sinnes, the vii vertuis, the five bodeli wittis, the v gosteli wittis, the vii yiftis of þᵉ holigost, the vii werkis of merci bodeli, the vii werkis of merci (gosteli), the foure cardinal vertuis, the xvi condicions of charite, the foure tokenysse of saluacion, A deuoute meditacion of Richarde Hampole, and [a treatise on] the name of Ihū."[65] The most common surviving English primer is the lengthier Book of Hours. One example (from 1420-1430), which has been published by the Early English Text Society, consists of the Office of the Holy Virgin, the Offices of the Dead, the Penitential and Gradual Psalms, the Litany and Commendations.[66]

Prior to 1349 French was the only vernacular language permitted in schools, and, although it was from then on being gradually displaced by English, Oxford University statutes circa 1380 ordered grammarmasters to use both English and French in teaching. For the elementary instruction of French, French primers were available. One early fifteenth-century French primer includes, in French, an explanation of the Creed, the seven sacraments, the Ten Commandments (in prose and verse), excerpts from various sermons, the Veni Creator, seven deadly sins and seven cardinal virtues, the Pater Noster, Hail Mary, and other prayers, a poem about the path to paradise, a chapter from the Gospel of St. John, and, in Latin, some hymns and prayers and a chapter from St. Luke.[67]

---

[65] George A. Plimpton, *The Education of Chaucer* (Oxford, 1935), 18-34; Allnutt, *An Early Sixteenth-Century A B C*, 8; Bodleian Library, Rawl. MS c. 209.

[66] Henry Littlehales, ed., *The Prymer or Lay Folks Prayer Book*, 2 vols., EETS, orig. ser., nos. 105, 109 (London, 1895-1897), ed. from Cambridge University MS Dd. 11. 82 ab. Two other English primers (both written c. 1400) have been edited by Henry Littlehales, *Pages in Facsimile from a Layman's Prayer Book in English c. 1400 A.D.* (London, 1890), ed. from British Library MS 27, 592 and *The Prymer, or Prayer-Book of the Lay People in the Middle Ages*, 2 vols. (London, 1891-1892), ed. from MS G. 24 in St. John's College, Cambridge. Another primer (B.M. Add. 17010) has been edited by William Maskell, *Monumenta Ritualia Ecclesiae Anglicanae*, Vol. 3, 2nd ed. (Oxford, 1882).

[67] Orme, *ESMA*, 71-75; Helen Suggett, "The Use of French in England in the Middle Ages," *TRHS*, 4th ser., 28 (1946):61-83; Plimpton, *Education of Chaucer*, 40-79.

Primers were usually in Latin,[68] but as these examples show, vernacular primers were not unknown. The simpler versions, whether in Latin or the vernacular, were certainly used in elementary education. The more complex Books of Hours were commonly used by the laity as a devotional manual during the church service, but they could also be used as school-texts, as Bishop Grandisson's 1357 circular, which instructed teachers to parse the Matins and Hours, illustrates.[69]

Why there now exist so few manuscript copies of the simplest elementary English primer remains something of a mystery. One possibility is that both French and English were more often learned colloquially by hearing and then improved by vocabulary-building treatises such as that of the thirteenth-century *Treaté sur la langue française* by Walter of Bibbesworth.[70] One further reason may be the ephemeral nature of such slight texts, and another might be anti-Lollard sentiment, which tended to be suspicious of all religious materials in the vernacular. In 1408 Archbishop Arundel required episcopal licenses for all vernacular versions of or extracts from the Bible,[71] and although it is not clear that this applied to primers, Margaret Deanesly notes arraignments for possession of English primers in 1429 and in the 1510s.[72] By 1511, however, John Colet was requiring the children at St. Paul's school to learn the catechism in English and providing them with a short English treatise on the articles of the faith, the seven sacraments, a discourse on charity, and various precepts of living. This primer was then printed as an introduction to Colet's *Aeditio.*[73] The next printed English primer may have been published on the Continent in 1529, although it is no longer extant. In 1534 the first

---

[68] For Latin primers, see Edgar Hoskins, *Horae Beatae Mariae Virginis or Sarum and York Primers with Kindred Books and Primers of the Reformed and Roman Use* (London, 1901); *Horae Eboracenses: The Prymer or Hours of the Blessed Virgin Mary according to the Use of York*, ed. C. Wordsworth, Surtees Society, no. 132 (Durham, 1920).

[69] Karis Crawford, "Prymers in England: An Untapped Source for Fifteenth-Century Studies" (Paper presented at the International Congress on Medieval Studies, Kalamazoo, Mich., 1977); *Register Grandisson*, 1192-93. A sentence of John Drury's *Parue Latinitates* also shows the book of hours in the hands of schoolchildren: "Primarium meum iacet in gremio meo qui scio matutinas sancte marie." Meech, "John Drury," 82. One of the Latin Books of Hours, printed at Paris for F. Byrckman of London in 1514, was specifically intended "pro pueris." (STC 15916).

[70] M. T. Clanchy, *From Memory to Written Record: England, 1066-1307* (Cambridge, Mass., 1979), 151-54. See also W. Rothwell, "The Role of French in Thirteenth-Century England," *Bulletin of the John Rylands University Library* 58 (1976):458-64.

[71] Wilkins, *Concilia*, 3:317.

[72] Margaret Deanesly, *The Lollard Bible and Other Medieval Biblical Versions* (Cambridge, 1920), 357, 368.

[73] J. H. Lupton, *A Life of John Colet*, 2nd ed. (London, 1909), 279, 285-90. The earliest surviving copy of Colet's *Aeditio* is, however, 1527 (STC 5542).

licensed English primer appeared in London, to be followed by over forty other printed versions by 1550, all of which reflect the influence of the Reformation.[74] It was not until 1550, however, that a Statute at Large ordered the destruction of all pre-Reformation service books, including primers in Latin or English other than those authorized by the King.[75] This Edwardian statute not only helps explain the lack of extant pre-Reformation elementary primers, whether in Latin or English, it testifies to the existence of such primers even as late as 1550.

In 1545 Henry VIII issued an authorized English primer. Henry (or his counselors) hoped to discourage the "adversity of primer books that are now abroad, whereof are almost innumerable sorts" by requiring that the royal primer

> be frequented and used in and throughout all places of our said realms and dominions, as well of the elder people, as also of the youth, for their common and ordinary prayers, willing, commanding, and straightly charging, that for the better bringing up of youth in the knowledge of their duty towards God, their prince, and all other in their degree, every schoolmaster and bringerup of young beginners in learning, next after their A, B, C, now by us also set forth, do teach this Primer, or book of ordinary prayers unto them in English; and that the youth customably and ordinarily use the same until they be of competent understanding and knowledge to perceive it in Latin. At what time they may at their liberty either use this Primer in English, or that which is by our authority likewise made in the Latin tongue, in all points correspondent unto this in English.[76]

Earlier than this, evidence for the use of English primers in the schools is not very satisfactory. Of the printed versions only Bishop Hilsey of Rochester's 1539 abridged English primer is specifically entitled "for the

---

[74] Charles C. Butterworth, *The English Primers (1529-1545)* (Philadelphia, 1953), 11-17. An ecclesiastical commission in 1530 condemned such an English primer, and the evidence from subsequent heresy trials confirms its existence. Ibid., passim, esp. 305-309; STC 15986-16052.

[75] *Statutes of the Realm* (London, 1819), 4:110; C. H. Williams, ed., *English Historical Documents*, Vol. 5 (London, 1967), 853. John Hennig, "Primer Versions of Liturgical Prayers," *Modern Language Review* 39 (1944):331. See also the 1547 injunctions given by Edward VI as well as the royal articles of inquiry and Archbishop Cranmer's articles of inquiry of the same year, printed in Edward Cardwell, ed., *Documentary Annals of the Reformed Church of England*, Vol. 1 (Oxford, 1844), 20, 30-31, 57-58.

[76] This copy of the royal injunction was included in the preface to King Henry's Primer printed by Richard Grafton 1545-1546. For it and other primers, see Edward Burton, ed., *Three Primers Put Forth in the Reign of Henry VIII* (Oxford, 1834); Butterworth, *The English Primers*, passim.

educacyon of chyldren."[77] Most surviving English manuscript primers are expensive illuminated texts probably commissioned, and possibly licensed, by a wealthy family or monastery.[78] At York, however, we know of one bookseller whose stock of 300 volumes included large numbers of primers in both English and Latin. Although they were not specifically described as schooltext primers, the fact that they were being sold along with *Doctrinales* and alphabet books strongly suggests that they were. The fifteenth-century scholars at Hull learning to read in English probably used an English primer, and in 1519 when Bishop Fitz James of London forbade the teaching of reading in English at his newly founded grammar school at Bruton, English primers must surely have been available.[79] The practice of chaining a *Medulla Grammatice* in the parish church suggests the ability of parish clergy (and their scholars) to handle both Latin and English.[80] Even were primers and other service books in Latin, they could be annotated in English for the use of schoolchildren, as may have been the case in 1394 when John de Pykering, rector of St. Mary's Castlegate in York, left "two books marked for the assistance of the children, one for matins and vespers, and the other for mass."[81] Finally, evidence for the use of English in grammar education argues strongly but indirectly for the availability of English primers.

After learning the elementary primer, a reading scholar would move on to learn the psalm *De profundis*, perhaps the *Dirige* and *Placebo* (the funeral masses), parts of the daily mass, particularly the Matins and Hours of the Virgin, and finally, the entire psalter.[82] The teaching of the psalter required the student to recognize and pronounce (i.e. read) the Latin, although not necessarily to understand it grammatically. As Pierre Riché notes, "Up to the end of the Middle Ages, to be a psalter scholar means

[77] STC 16011. It consists of, among other things, an almanac, the alphabet, the Ten Commandments, the Creed, various prayers, the Matins, Compline, and the Pater Noster. The only copy is at the British Library b.35 b.13.

[78] Crawford, "Prymers in England," 6-7, 14 n 20.

[79] Brunskill, "Missals, Portifers and Pyes," 25, 27, 29-30, 33; Hull Corporation Archives, Bench Book IIIa, f. 28; F. W. Weaver, "Foundation Deed of Bruton School," *Somerset and Dorset Notes and Queries* 3 (1892-1893):245.

[80] BI, Prob. Reg. 2, f. 17; 3, f. 318; 4, f. 18.

[81] *Test. Ebor.*, 1:194-95. ". . . duos libros notatos pro ministerio puerorum, unum pro matutinis et vesperis, et alterum pro missa. . . ."

[82] Thomas More described the elementary curriculum in 1532 in his *Confutation of Tyndale's Answer*. "Then haue we ferther yet besyde Barns boke, the a b c for chyldren. And bycause there is no grace therin / lest we shold lakke prayours, we haue the prymer, and the ploughmans prayour, and a boke of other small deuocyons, and then the hole psalter to." *The Complete Works of St. Thomas More*, vol. 8, part i, ed. Louis A. Shuster, Richard C. Marius, James P. Lusardi, and Richard J. Schoeck (New Haven, 1973), 11.

to know how to read."[83] Throughout late medieval York diocese various testators made it clear that the scholars of the parish were expected to know their entire (Latin) psalter.[84]

Translating the psalter or other parts of the service into English in the schools was not unheard of. Margaret Deanesly mentions one writer who, in the middle of the Wycliffite controversy, refers to a practice of translating the epistles and gospels in the schools, as well as the psalms, while the author of the late fourteenth-century *The Chastising of God's Children* forbade the saying of the daily office in English (thereby testifying to the practice).[85] In addition, there were several English translations of the psalter available, the most famous of which was Richard Rolle's, although it is doubtful that these would have been used, except in conjunction with a Latin text, in the elementary schools where one of the purposes was to train scholars who could minister in the church services. They were, however, occasionally bequeathed by York testators.[86] Ideally the training of the reading scholar who had passed beyond his primer was entirely in the Latin of the church services.

These elementary lessons were sometimes specified in the statutes of a school. At Ipswich grammar and reading school the statutes in 1477 divided the pupils into the petties who learned their A B C's and song, the primer scholars, the psalter scholars, and the grammar scholars. In 1519 Bishop Fitz James, founder of Bruton grammar school, excluded the petty and reading scholars in his statutes, declaring that the schoolmaster "shall not teche his scolers song nor other petite lernyng, as the crosse rewe, redyng of the mateyns or of the psalter or such other small thyngs, nother redying of Englisshe, but such as shall concern lernynge of grammar." In 1526, when William Pettiplace made provision for a chantry school at Childrey, Berkshire, he specified that the children should be taught the alphabet, three basic prayers, everything necessary to help the priest at mass, the collects, psalms, prayers for the dead, and table graces. These all required a reading knowledge of Latin. However, the reading of English was not neglected as the students had to learn in English the articles of the faith, the Ten Commandments, the seven deadly sins, the seven sacraments, the manner of confession, and various precepts about

---

[83] Riché, *Les Ecoles et l'enseignement*, 223. "Jusqu'à la fin du Moyen Age, être *psalteratus* signifie savoir lire."

[84] BI, Reg. 14 (Arundel), ff. 29v-30; Reg. 18 (Bowet), f. 356; Prob. Reg. 2, f. 577; 4, f. 1; Reg. 28 (Lee), ff. 168-69.

[85] Deanesly, *Lollard Bible*, 190; *The Chastising of God's Children*, ed. Joyce Bazire and Eric Colledge (Oxford, 1957), 71, 221.

[86] YML, D. & C., L 2/4, ff. 112v, 261, 331v; BI, Prob. Reg. 2, f. 63v.

good manners. The regulations for the Clerk's school in Skipton-in-Craven (Yorks.), although written for the foundation of the school in 1555, probably reflect earlier practices at the parish school. The clerk was directed "to teach the children to spell and to read the A B C, called the A B Cs, the Primer and Psalter in Latin and not in English."[87]

The use that scholars made of the service books sometimes became a matter of concern. In 1439 the vicar of Hornby in the North Riding worried that the children who were learning in the church would injure or soil the large breviary that he was bequeathing to remain in the choir. In 1481 the parish clerk in St. Nicholas parish church, Bristol, was ordered not to take any book out of the choir for the children's use without license of the procurator. The children still posed a problem at Bristol in 1524 when William Brigemen, the clerk of All Saints, left an inventory including thirty books bequeathed to the church "under the condicion that no children shuld be tawte apon the seid bookes. . . ."[88]

Thus the education of the reading scholar prepared him (or her) to read English (or possibly French) and Latin books of a limited ecclesiastical nature. There was none of the diversity of texts and individuality of treatment that marked the grammar curriculum. What texts there were, other than the very elementary A B C and primer books, were the service books which would be readily available in any parish church or chapel. Such an education provided the reading scholar with enough Latin to read the psalter and a thorough knowledge of the fixed parts of the daily service. It was a useful education for those planning to go into the Church, while it provided the building blocks for further self-education for others. If one did well, there was the possibility of moving to a grammar school where training in the composition and speaking of Latin was acquired. Thus, when William Langland, in *Piers Plowman*, tells how his father and friends "fonde me to scole" till he could understand the Latin of the Bible, he could conceivably be referring to a reading school education, although it is clear elsewhere that he was quite familiar with fourteenth-century grammar and grammar schools. His description of the tools from which he derived his living, his "*pater-noster* and my prymer, *placebo* and

[87] Leach, *Educational Charters and Documents*, 422-23; *VCH, Suffolk*, 2:326; Weaver, "Foundation Deed of Bruton School;" PRO, PCC, Prob. 11/23 6 Jankyn, quoted in *VCH, Berks.*, 2:275-76; A. M. Gibbon, *A History of the Ancient Free Grammar School of Skipton-in-Craven* (Liverpool, 1947), app. C.

[88] YML, D. & C., L 2/4, f. 251; J. R. Bramble, "Ancient Bristol Documents, Nos. II and III," *Proceedings of the Clifton Antiquarian Club 1884-8*, 1, pt. 2 (1888):148; Atchley, "The Halleway Chauntry," 111-14.

dirige, and my sauter som tyme and my sevene psalmes," can also serve to describe a reading school curriculum.[89]

WRITING EDUCATION

While there is abundant evidence of teaching reading in the elementary school curriculum, the actual number of instances we can document of elementary schoolmasters teaching writing is small. They may not have taught it as a matter of course, perhaps because schoolmasters were not always trained writers. Writing was a difficult art, compared, by Meister Eckhart, to the art of learning an inner solitude. "To acquire this art, one must practice much, however disagreeable or difficult it may be, however impossible it may seem,"[90] although the more relaxed cursive hand of the fourteenth and fifteenth centuries may have been easier to acquire than the bookhand of an earlier period.[91] Failure to teach writing could just as easily have been the result of the high price of paper (still at 4d. a quire in the sixteenth century) or, as was the case in the city of York, the antagonism of the scriveners' gild.[92] In the absence of paper, nearly every medieval scholar had a wax writing tablet, but this afforded little practice except perhaps in forming letters.

Writing at an elementary-school level in York diocese was available in

[89] *Piers Plowman, Selections from the C Text*, ed. Elizabeth Salter and Derek Pearsall (Evanston, Ill., 1967), C Text, 6:35-37, 45-47 (pp. 78-79). For Langland's schooling, see John E. Wells, *A Manual of the Writings in Middle English, 1050-1400* (New Haven, 1916), 252; Nicholas Orme, "Langland and Education," *History of Education* 11 (1982):251-66; and Janet Coleman, *Piers Plowman and the "Moderni"* (Rome, 1981).

[90] Meister Eckhart, *The Talks of Instruction*, trans. R. B. Blakney (New York, 1941), 9-10.

[91] The cursive hand first emerged in the twelfth century as the demand for documents and the need to write quickly developed. By the thirteenth century cursive was also being used for books. According to M. T. Clanchy, the average standards of writing were improving, "presumably because more clerks were getting an appropriate education," although "to explain how such elegance and consistency were achieved in the majority of local documents remains an outstanding and probably insoluble problem." Clanchy, *From Memory to Written Record*, 102-103.

The forms found in the York ecclesiastical archives include the Anglicana formata and, increasingly after the 1380s, the Secretary hand, or a mixture of the two. Although some of the materials, especially the legal documents, are hurried, idiosyncratic, and not calligraphic, generally the documents display a hand described by John Lawson as "meticulous stylized . . . systematically abbreviated but clear and grammatical . . . the result of long and careful schooling, . . ." John Lawson, *A Town Grammar School Through Six Centuries* (London, 1963), 15; see also T.A.M. Bishop, *Scriptores Regis* (Oxford, 1961), 6-7, 13; M. B. Parkes, *English Cursive Book Hands 1250-1500* (Oxford, 1969), intro.

[92] Joyce W. Percy, ed., *York Memorandum Book*, Vol. 3, Surtees Society, no. 186 (Gateshead, 1973), 194-97, 206-11.

1402 at Rudby parish when Sir John Depeden, knight, proposed to send John Fitz Richard either to the parson of Rudby or to the treasurer's household at York, to learn to read and write. In 1487 William Dowson of Hornsebek was bequeathed enough goods to support him in school until he learned to read and write. Later, in 1526, Hugo Starkey of Olton (Chester), knight, granted "Richard Gratewod 40s., 20s. thereof to bestow on hym to lerne to wryte and redd w^t John Lech. . . ."[93] Writing and doing accounts were specifically mentioned as part of the elementary curriculum at Acaster Selby, Yorks. (circa 1470), Rotherham, Yorks. (1483), Brough under Stainmore, Westm. (1509), and Rolleston, Staffs. (1524); while writing was envisioned alongside the grammar curriculum of a projected school at Leadenhall, London, in 1459. In 1500 William Pygg, chantry priest, left the schoolmaster of Newark a writing desk (*cathedram pro scriptore*).[94] By 1547 a royal injunction ordered chantry priests to "exercise themselves in teaching youths to read and write," and the chantry certificates from 1546 to 1548 give several examples of such priests teaching writing in addition to reading or grammar.[95]

Despite the fact that writing schools were sometimes founded alongside grammar schools, they seem to have been considered part of a more elementary curriculum. Archbishop Rotherham included instruction in writing at Rotherham so that the many youths of the area who were able but did not wish to enter the priesthood could be trained in the mechanical arts and for other concerns. The lowliness of the salary there (£5 6s. 8d.) in relation to the salaries for teaching song and grammar, as Nicholas Orme points out, also points to the relative lowliness of the subject.[96] Bishop Sherborne of Chichester echoed this assessment in his foundation at Rolleston by relegating those boys to writing who were too dull or lazy for the grammar school curriculum.[97] In the best of all possible worlds, as we know from Erasmus's *Colloquies*, petty scholars at the beginning of the sixteenth century were expected to have paper, pen, and ink with them when they arrived in school. John Colet, when he refounded St. Paul's school, expected his entering grammar scholars to know already how to read and write both English and Latin. Similarly, Archbishop Holgate's foundation of a grammar school within York in 1546 was for scholars

[93] BI, Prob. Reg. 3, ff. 88v-89, printed in *Test. Ebor.*, 1:296; BI, Prob. Reg. 5, f. 319; G. J. Piccope, ed., *Lancashire and Cheshire Wills and Inventories from the Ecclesiastical Court, Chester*, Vol. 1, Chetham Soc., old ser., no. 33 (Manchester, 1857), 12.

[94] Appendix B below; Orme, *ESMA*, 78, 297, 309; *VCH, Notts.*, 2:202.

[95] Cardwell, ed., *Documentary Annals*, 1:20; Leach, *ESR*, ii, 66, 98, 251-52, 300, 307, 312.

[96] *EYS*, 2:104-85; Orme, *ESMA*, 78.

[97] Chichester Diocesan Record Office, Cap 1/14/5, f. 28; Orme, *ESMA*, 78.

who were expected "to use and exercise wrytinge of their Lattyns and lessons [in] their owne handes."[98] In light of these examples, Bishop Stillington's foundation at Acaster Selby circa 1470, which included separate writing, song, and grammar facilities, with separate masters for each, reflects an elevated conception of the scrivener's art, due perhaps to the influence of Stillington's father, a scrivener at York.[99]

Since writing, if it was taught at all, was usually taught as part of the elementary curriculum, it is not surprising to find evidence among scriveners that their apprentices lacked sufficient Latin grammar. In 1497 the London scriveners' gild pointed to this lack, "wherethrough oftentimes they err, and their acts and feats been incongruous, and not perfectly done to the great reproach and slander of the said fellowship." The remedy was to insist upon examination of apprentices before the wardens. If a boy was found wanting, he was to be sent "to grammar school unto such time as he have or by reasonable capacity may have positive grammar."[100]

By the turn of the sixteenth century York diocese had peripatetic scriveners who wandered from school to school teaching elementary pupils for a few weeks in the year, after which the writing in the school would be neglected. At Giggleswick, in 1507, the master set aside three weeks for the children to practice writing under a scrivener.[101] It was far easier to learn to write in the towns where the scriveners kept private writing schools, teaching not only the everyday cursive hand of the time but also business methods, forms of correspondence, and accounts.[102] A school bill from Nottingham, dated 1532, shows that John Burton paid 4d. to 6d. a week first to the scrivener of the Long Rowe, then to William Cost, and finally to Master Holyhed for twenty-five weeks' worth of writing lessons for William Meryman.[103] Writing schools undoubtedly were common in London by the late fourteenth century, but the evidence we have for this is indirect, based, for the fifteenth century, on evidence from gilds that their members could write. Colet's assumption that his scholars at St. Paul's could write argues for the availability of writing masters in six-

---

[98] *The Colloquies of Erasmus*, 45; Lupton, *A Life of John Colet*, 2nd ed. (London, 1909), app. B, 285-86; York City Archives, Foundation Deed of Archbishop Holgate's School, f. 7v.

[99] Appendix B below; *Register of the Freemen of the City of York, 1272-1558*, Vol. 1, ed. F. Collins, Surtees Society, no. 96 (Durham, 1897), 59, 81.

[100] *The Case of the Free Scriveners of London (1749)*, 25-26, cited in Joan Simon, *Education and Society in Tudor England* (Cambridge, 1966), 15.

[101] Edward A. Bell, *A History of Giggleswick School from Its Foundation: 1499-1912* (Leeds, 1912), chap. 3.

[102] John Lawson and Harold Silver, eds., *A Social History of Education in England* (London, 1973), 70, 114.

[103] *VCH, Notts.*, 2:222.

teenth-century London. Juan Luis Vives, whose *Linguae Latinae Exercitatio* or *School-Boy Dialogues* (1529) most probably reflects a London environment, directs his two reading scholars to a separate writing master.[104]

In York the number of scriveners who are recorded as freemen increases by about 50 percent between 1350 and 1500. By the mid-fifteenth century the gild, responding perhaps to the needs of its increased membership, made it illegal for any priest with an annual salary above seven marks to teach writing to any apprentice, hired-man, or servant, or to write texts for profit. Apparently some of the priests, probably the poorer ones, continued to teach writing, for a controversy later arose between the scriveners' gild and Sir William Inceclyff, chantry priest in the chapel of Foss Bridge, who was teaching children to write and selling the books produced.[105] The main concern of the scriveners was that the clergy not engage in competitive trade by selling their books; it was not illegal for them to teach writing or produce books gratis. Eventually, however, the power of the scriveners' gilds declined with the growing popularity of printing. As William Horman noted in his 1519 *Vulgaria*, "Pryntynge hathe almooste undone scryveners crafte."[106] And writing, as suggested by the 1547 royal injunction and the mention of writing instruction in chantry certificates, was now the province of parish clergy, even in the more remote areas.

An individual whose education included all or a substantial portion of the elementary education described above was considered lettered and sometimes labeled literate (especially after 1300), although he would not be literate in the more technically correct sense of the word, that is, learned in Latin grammar and writing.[107] A late fifteenth- or early sixteenth-

---

[104] *Tudor School-Boy Life: The Dialogues of Juan Luis Vives*, trans. Foster Watson (London, 1970), chap. 10.

[105] The numbers of scriveners, based on the freemen's register, are 19 (1350-1399), 18 (1400-1449), and 27 (1450-1509); *VCH, Yorkshire: City of York*, 116; Percy, *York Memorandum Book*, 3:194-97, 207-11.

[106] William Horman, *Vulgaria* (1519), 125. See also p. 135.

[107] Herein literacy is defined as the ability to read a printed or written text in either Latin or the vernacular. Ability to write more than one's signature is taken as a priori evidence of literacy. Signatures alone, since they are infrequent due to the use of seals or the sign of the cross, do not provide an adequate index. The term *literatus*, which was used throughout the Middle Ages, generally describes an individual with a facility in Latin. According to John of Salisbury, "[Latin] grammar alone has the unique privilege of making one 'lettered' . . . anyone who spurns grammar, is not only not a 'teacher of letters,' but does not even deserve to be called 'lettered.' " John of Salisbury, *The Metalogicon*, trans. D. D. McGarry (Berkeley, 1962), 71. By the fourteenth century, however, an individual with only minimal Latin reading skills might also

century brass in Spofforth parish church (W. Riding) spells out the distinction that the ordinary rural parishioner understood between those who were lettered and those who were unlearned.

With humble prayer I beseech thee
That this scripture shall here or see,
To say *De Profundis*, if you lettered be,
For the soules of Jone my wife and me.
Thomas Middleton, sometyme man of law,
Under this stone am laid full lawe;
If thou be unlearned, and cannot reed,
For our soules and All Christen soules med,
Say a Pater Noster, an Ave, and Creed.[108]

The lettered were equated with those who could say their *De Profundis*. This is interesting in view of the fact that children being educated in the parishes and performing during the funeral services are described in the wills of the end of the fourteenth through the sixteenth centuries not only as little clerks or literate children, or toward the latter half of the fifteenth century as parish scholars, but also as children saying (or singing) *De Profundis*. If in fact, as the earlier discussion of the reading school curriculum suggests, children learned their *De Profundis* after mastering their primer, it is probable that children who knew their 129th Psalm were literate. However, Psalm 129 is short; it was popular; and it is likely that all song scholars were acquainted with it. It could easily have been learned by rote,[109] despite Thomas Middleton's assumption, and one needs to be cautious in assigning literacy to those children.

SONG EDUCATION

Song schools were primarily places in which choristers were taught the singing required in church services. The training included plainsong and, increasingly throughout the later Middle Ages, polyphony. Song scholars were expected to recite the psalter and hymnal, parts of which they might

---

be characterized as *literatus*. The more traditional *homo literatus*, as defined by John of Salisbury, is herein referred to as latinate or learned in Latin. For a further discussion of these issues, see J. Hoeppner Moran, "Literacy and Education in Northern England, 1350-1550: A Methodological Inquiry," *Northern History* 17 (1981):1-23.

[108] *Test. Ebor.*, 3:209.

[109] In 1531 Sir William Bulmer the elder, knight, attached to his will an Order for the Master, brother priests and beadmen at St. Elen chapel, Wilton. He expected every beadman, if he did not already know them, to memorize the psalms *De Profundis* and *Miserere*. BI, Prob. Reg. 10, f. 105; printed in *Test. Ebor.*, 5:314.

learn by heart. As a result, the degree of literacy attained in many song schools, especially those at the parish level, must remain questionable despite clear evidence that some song scholars were not only trained in reading but also in Latin grammar. John Merbecke, organist of St. George's Chapel, Windsor, in the 1540s, makes an illuminating comment about his song school education. He "in a maner never tasted the swetnes of learned Letters, but [was] altogether brought up in your highnes College at Wyndesore, in the study of Musike and plaiying Organs, wherin I consumed vainly the greatest part of my life." John Stevens, who cites Merbecke, sees this as "unmistakable testimony to the vocational bias even of a royal song-school." Erasmus also had a low opinion of the level of learning among choristers as well as a negative reaction to English church music. "The choristers themselves do not understand what they are singing, . . . Words nowadays mean nothing. . . . Money must be raised to buy organs and train boys to squeal and to learn no other thing that is good for them. . . . Boys are kept in the English Benedictine Colleges solely and simply to sing morning hymns to the Virgin."[110]

Song schools existed at all ecclesiastical levels—in the cathedrals, monasteries, hospitals, collegiate churches, occasionally chantry chapels, and parish churches—and in the aristocratic and royal households. Throughout York diocese, in York Cathedral and the ancient collegiate churches of Beverley, Ripon, and Southwell, choristers attended grammar schools attached to the church but separate from the song school.[111] At York, for example, the Dean and Chapter Acts of 1421, and again in 1432, make it clear that not only the choristers, but also the deacons and acolytes, were to attend the grammar school on pain of expulsion.[112] At Ripon collegiate church, during a visitation by Archbishop Kemp in 1439, it was noted that deacons, subdeacons, choristers, and clerks of the church attended the grammar school.[113]

But elsewhere this was not always the practice. In Lincoln, Lichfield, and Wells Cathedrals the choristers did not learn their grammar from any grammarmaster but rather from the songmaster. Similarly at St. David's in Wales, the precentor was to instruct two (later seven) choristers in both grammar and song. At Exeter the master of the choristers taught

---

[110] Orme, "Education and Learning at a Medieval English Cathedral," 268-69; *Tudor Church Music* 10 (1929):159. John Stevens, *Music and Poetry in the Early Tudor Court* (London, 1961), 304; J. A. Froude, *Life and Letters of Erasmus* (New York, 1895), 122-23.

[111] Edwards, *English Secular Cathedrals*, 166; *EYS*, 1:94-95, 151; Leach, *Visitations and Memorials of Southwell Minster*, lxv, 57.

[112] YML, D. & C., Acts H2/1a, f. 36a; H2/3a, f. 21a.

[113] *EYS*, 1:151.

them reading and song; whether they learned Latin grammar remains unclear.[114]

It is possible that the choristers in some cathedral or collegiate churches would also have attended independent reading schools. In 1499 one of the vicars choral of Southwell, Master Lawrence Pypys, was teaching boys in his chantry. This was not the grammar school, of which John Barre was the grammarmaster and John Babthorp his assistant. It was not the Minster song school either. It was most likely a petty or reading school, and the choristers may have been welcome. At Ripon Minster, from 1391 to 1394 the sexton taught a school, which may well have been a reading school for choristers and others.[115]

Among other collegiate establishments and in the monasteries there was sometimes a less than clear-cut distinction between the masters of the various schools. At Warwick collegiate church in 1316 and at Howden collegiate church in 1394 the songmaster also taught the elementary reading pupils. At Leicester Abbey in 1440 Bishop Alnwick of Lincoln enjoined the abbot to provide a serviceable teacher to instruct the younger canons and almonry boys in elementary knowledge and grammar. And in 1447 he enjoined the master of the novices in Nutley Abbey to instruct the novices in both reading and song. At Gloucester Abbey in 1515 and Cirencester Abbey in 1538, the master of the children taught both song and Latin grammar, although the young brethren and thirteen boys of the clerks' chamber who were taught grammar at Gloucester were not all taught song. Plainsong and descant (counterpoint) were taught to only five or six boys. Other monasteries divided teaching duties between more than one master.[116] Nonetheless, even when the same master handled several teaching assignments, the differences in curriculum remained clear in the minds of contemporaries, and students being taught in grammar

---

[114] A. F. Leach, "Lincoln Grammar School, 1090-1906," *The Journal of Education* (Aug. 1906):524-25; Henry Bradshaw and Christopher Wordsworth, *Lincoln Cathedral Statutes*, 3 vols. (Cambridge, 1892-1897), 2:95. At Lincoln, however, by 1307, the precentor was employing a separate grammar tutor for the choristers. Edward Yardley, *Menevia Sacra*, ed. F. Green, Cambrian Archaeological Association, supplementary vol. (London, 1927), 372; *Dean Cosyn and Wells Cathedral Miscellanea*, 98-109; Orme, *Education in the West of England*, 80-82; Orme, "Education and Learning at a Medieval English Cathedral," 268-69.

[115] Leach, *Visitations and Memorials of Southwell Minster*, 67; J. T. Fowler, ed., *Memorials of the Church of SS Peter and Wilfred, Ripon*, Vol. 3, Surtees Society, no. 81 (Durham, 1888), 105, 113, 118.

[116] Leach, *Educational Charters and Documents*, 274-75; *EYS*, 2:85; A. H. Thompson, ed., *Visitations of Religious Houses in the Diocese of Lincoln, 1420-1449*, 3 vols., Lincoln Record Society, nos. 7, 14, 21 (Horncastle, 1914-1929), 2:214; 3:260. See also Thornton Abbey, ibid., 3:379; Orme, *Education in the West of England*, 203-204, 207.

or reading were not always the same students being taught song. This is the case not only in cathedral, collegiate, and monastic establishments, but also at the parish level where reading and song schools were becoming increasingly evident throughout our period. At Sibthorpe (Notts.) collegiate parish church, founded in 1342, the song schoolmaster also taught reading to the choristers and other parish children who wanted to learn their letters. In 1438 John Bee of Bishopburton (E. Riding) bequeathed 6d. to each child in the parish church who was either singing or reading. At a later date (1548) and further afield, the schoolmaster at Montgomery parish church in northern Wales, who was hired to teach grammar, "taught but yonge begynners onelye to write and syng, and to reade soo farre as the accidens Rules, and noo grammer, sythens the feast of Sainte Michell the archangell last past."[117]

Despite the confusion of teaching duties, which is not unusual throughout this period, one can argue that separate levels of education and even separate schools were understood to exist. A good example of this comes from Howden collegiate church. In 1393 the prior of Durham appointed a master of the song school for a five-year period. The songmaster held office only a year, at which time another chaplain was collated to both the reading and song schools, as customary. In 1401 a new master was appointed to the same school of reading and song, while John Lowyke, a layman, was given permission to hold an additional reading school if he desired. Then, from 1409 until 1412 and again in 1456 the reading and grammar schools were taught by the same individual, while the song school was separate.[118] Similar flexibility was exhibited at Northallerton (N. Riding) where, in 1322, only a master of the grammar school is mentioned. By 1377, and again in 1385, the master of the grammar school was also appointed to teach song. In 1426 there was a separate appointment to the reading and song school, and in 1440 John Levesham, chaplain, was collated to the position of master of all three schools.[119]

Flexibility with regard to teaching duties allowed an institution to adjust to the availability of masters and the fluctuations in the school-attending population. Despite the shifting responsibilities of the schoolmasters, the curriculum was unlikely to have changed, and the fees probably made clear the level of education being offered to any one scholar. A good example of this comes from Ipswich, where the bishop of Norwich fixed "quarterage" payments to the schoolmaster in 1477 at 10d. for gram-

[117] Thompson, "Song Schools in the Middle Ages," 17; BI, Prob. Reg. 3, f. 562v; Leach, ESR, ii:312.

[118] EYS, 2:xvii-xxi, 85-87.

[119] Ibid., 60-62; VCH, Yorks., 1:445-46.

marians, 8d. for psalter scholars, and 6d. for primerians, excluding the petty scholars called Apesyes and Songe. Similarly at Newland (Gloucs.) in 1446 the students who learned the alphabet, matins book, and psalter were to pay not more than 4d. a term, while those who studied grammar were to pay not more than 8d. At Hull in 1454 the grammarmaster was allowed to charge 8d. per quarter for grammar and 6d. for reading. A later example, slightly beyond our time frame but still relevant, concerns Francis Willoughby at Walden School in 1555. Family account books give the cost of his schooling for one quarter ending September 15 at 3s. 4d., with an extra 5s. to learn singing and an additional 12d. to learn writing.[120]

No general conclusions can be made as to how many song scholars were likely to have received a reading and/or grammar education or vice versa. Circumstances varied at every level and in each locale. At York Cathedral the endowed choristers, who were restricted to twelve in number, were privileged scholars at the grammar school, receiving their education free of charge. The remainder of the cathedral grammar scholars, who were at least sixty in number, paid for any song school education they may have had, either at the cathedral school or perhaps at a parish song school.[121] In 1367 Master Adam of York, the precentor, complained that

> Whereas by immemorial custom the keeping school in the city of York, for teaching boys singing, ought to be held in a certain place belonging to the cathedral church, the appointment and removal of the rector or master of which was appurtenant to the precentorship; yet divers chaplains, holy water carriers, and many others actually keep song school for the instruction of boys in singing, in parish churches, houses and other places in York, to the no small prejudice and grievance of the Precentor and his precentorship, and in manifold breach of the liberties of the cathedral church.[122]

Archbishop Thoresby of York reacted by censoring the practice, but apparently it continued. In 1411 the visitation of inferior ministers within the cathedral noted that song schools were being conducted without license by the personnel of the cathedral itself, and throughout the rest of our period no more recorded efforts were made to abolish the song schools.[123]

---

[120] VCH, Suffolk, 2:326; Orme, Education in the West of England, 159-61; Lawson, A Town Grammar School, 17; University of Nottingham Library, Mi LM 26, f. 53; Historical Manuscripts Commission, MSS of Lord Middleton, 411.

[121] Test. Ebor., 1:86, 262-63; Valor Ecclesiasticus (1825), V, 6.

[122] BI, Reg. 11 (Thoresby), f. 142v.

[123] YML, Visitation and Chapter Act Book E L2/3a, f. 34.

A similar situation occurred in Lincoln. According to Bishop Alnwick, most of the forty-six parish churches within Lincoln were holding song schools, a practice that had formerly been forbidden but by 1439 was generally accepted as long as the song scholars were not from outside the parish in which they were being taught.[124]

Despite the abundance of song schools, not every grammar or reading scholar would have received a song school education. Evidence from Beverley Minster suggests this. In 1312 Roger of Sutton, the school-master, argued that only seven choristers should be admitted free to the grammar school. However, the senior clergy decided that no limit needed to be set as to the number of choristers admitted free, provided that none of the grammar scholars who were not choristers attempted to defraud the schoolmaster by wearing a habit in choir.[125] At the parish level, York diocesan wills frequently mention scholars in the parish churches who did not wear surplices and therefore were not singing in the choir.[126] Much earlier, in the Winchester diocesan statutes (1262 x 1265), Church officials were concerned about scholars not learning to sing. The clergy were directed to induce parents "to let their boys learn singing after they know how to read the psalter, so that after they have learnt higher subjects they may not be obliged to go back to this, or not having learnt it be less fit for divine service." By 1545 Roger Ascham lamented that the teaching of plainsong and pricksong (or descant), which was considered an important part of eloquence training by many humanists, was being neglected to the point where, for every student then entering the university who had learned to sing, there were six who had received no musical education whatsoever.[127]

---

[124] "The precentor shall . . . appoint and prefer the song master in the city and those in the county of Lincoln, excepting only schools on prebendal estates and those which certain curates hold for their own parishioners in their own parishes, or which are held by the parish clerks of the same, for we will not that such persons be hindered by the precentor from educating and instructing the small boys of their parishes in song." Thompson, "Song Schools," 17.

[125] EYS, 1:94-95; Leach, *Memorials of Beverley Minster: The Chapter Act Book*, Vol. 1, Surtees Society, no. 98 (Durham, 1898):293. ". . . habentes considerationem ad antiquas consuetudines ecclesiae et scolarum praedictarum, decrevit numerum puerorum coristarum in praedictis scolis non esse artandum, sed omnes, quotquot fuerint, in ecclesia coristae in scola quieti sint et liberi quoad ipsum Magistrum; et quod ipse Magister, vel aliquis successorum suorum, nomine salarii nihil exigat ab eisdem: verumtamen injunxit Succentori quod in fraudem Magistri scolarum ad portandum habitum in choro pueros non admittat."

[126] Appendix B, passim.

[127] F. M. Powicke and C. R. Cheney, ed., *Councils and Synods*, Vol. 2 (Oxford, 1964), i:713-14; "Inducantur insuper parentes puerorum quod ipsos pueros postquam psalterium legere sciverint cantum addiscant, ne postquam forte maiora didicerint ad hoc discendum redire co-

Nor was a reading or grammar education for choristers always possible, especially at the parish level, if only because many of the song schools existed without accompanying reading or grammar instruction. This may have been the case within the city of York's parishes. While we already know that song schools were common in the city parishes by the 1360s, the only evidence for fourteenth-century reading schools comes from St. Mary's Castlegate and perhaps from St. Leonard's Hospital. Middleham, a collegiate parish church founded in the West Riding in 1478, contained only a song school, as did a large number of other parish churches. At Newark, the priest who was to teach "plain song, prick song, descant, and to play at the organs" was to freely teach all persons and children that wanted to attend. There was no stipulation that any of the singers be scholars, either of a reading or a grammar school. A similar situation could occur in the monasteries, where Nicholas Orme suggests that some of the song scholars specialized in music, not receiving any other education.[128]

The financial incentives were such that it made sense to become a chorister. In 1428 Robert Holme, merchant and former mayor of York, made a quadripartite agreement between himself, the commonalty of York, a chaplain who was to sing masses for the benefit of his soul, and the Dean and Chapter of York, who were to supply four boys attending and wearing surplices at the annual obit for his father and later for Holme himself. The four boys, who were probably from the cathedral song school, were each given 2d., while 11s. were paid annually to the vicars choral of the cathedral.[129] The 1502 will of Thomas Herdsong of York left funds to find a mass at St. Michael's Spurriergate every Saturday, to be sung with note by men and children. The churchwarden's accounts for this same parish show annual expenses to the children for obits.[130] Further afield, in Wotton-under-Edge (Gloucs.) at the time of the Reformation, one John More remembered singing the morrow mass, especially the *Confiteor* and *Oremus pro Animabus*, as he knelt in his surplice beside the chantry priest. For a penny the priest would include the names of any other persons in

gantur, vel tanquam huiusmodi inscii ad divinum obsequium sint suo perpetuo minus apti." Roger Ascham, *Toxophilus*, in *English Works of Roger Ascham*, ed. W. A. Wright (Cambridge, 1904), 14-16; Leach, *History of Warwick School*, 65.

[128] J. Hoeppner Moran, *Education and Learning in the City of York, 1300-1560* (York, 1979), 18-19; James Raine, ed., "The Statutes Ordained by Richard Duke of Gloucester, for the College of Middleham," *Archaeological Journal* 14 (1857):163; Brown, *History of Newark-upon-Trent*, 2:206; Orme, *ESMA*, 247.

[129] Leach, *York Memorandum Book*, 3:149-51.

[130] BI, Prob. Reg. 5, f. 5; PR Y/MS/3 Churchwardens' Draft Account Book, St. Michael's Spurriergate, 1537-1548.

his intercessions, and the boys were given the odd penny.[131] The wills of the period, from the end of the fourteenth century until the time of the Reformation, are replete with references to the penny or pennies given to children who sang at funerals.

Insofar as it was possible for song scholars to learn to sing by rote, they did not need either a reading or grammar school education, despite evidence that many of them were readers or grammar scholars. They may have been interested only in becoming "singing-men" such as the singing-man at Walsingham Priory, a yeoman peasant who came to Cromwell's attention in connection with the Walsingham conspiracy in 1537.[132] Scores of such singing-men, about whom we know almost nothing, but whose educational level could not have been high, were being employed by the English monasteries on the eve of the dissolution.

Thus, while we have evidence that the cathedral choristers usually received training in Latin grammar, this was not necessarily the case for parish choristers or for those boys singing in the monastic Lady Chapels. We cannot be sure that these song scholars received even a reading education, although many of them surely did. In addition, training in grammar and reading was not necessarily, perhaps not usually, accompanied by training in song. These patterns, the chorister without a reading or grammar education and the scholar without song school training, are illustrated best in the following, much-cited passage from Chaucer's Prioress's Tale:

A litel scole of Cristen folk ther stood
Doun at the ferther ende, in which ther were
Children an heep, ycomen of Cristen blood,
That lerned in that scole yeer by yere
Swich maner doctrine as men used there,
That is to seyn, to syngen and to rede,
As smale children doon in hire childhede.

Among thise children was a wydwes sone,
A litel clergeon, seven yeer of age,
That day by day to scole was his wone,
And eek also, where as he saugh th'ymage
Of Cristes mooder, hadde he in usage,
Of hym was taught, to knele adoun and seye
His *Ave Marie*, as he goth by the weye. . . .

[131] Orme, *Education in the West of England*, 198.
[132] G. R. Elton, *Policy and Police* (Cambridge, 1972), 146.

This litel child, his litel book lernynge,
As he sat in the scole at his prymer,
He *Alma redemptoris* herde synge,
As children lerned hire antiphoner;
And as he dorste, he drough hym ner and ner,
And herkned ay the wordes and the noote,
Til he the firste vers koude al by rote.

Noght wiste he what this Latyn was to seye,
For he so yong and tendre was of age.
But on a day his felawe gan he preye
T'expounden hym this song in his langage,
Or telle hym why this song was in usage;
This preyde he hym to construe and declare
Ful ofte tyme upon his knowes bare.

His felawe, which that elder was than he,
Answerde hym thus: "This song I have herd seye,
Was maked of our blisful Lady free,
Hire to salue, and eek hire for to preye
To been oure help and socour whan we deye.
I kan namoore expounde in this mateere;
I lerne song, I kan but smal grammeere."[133]

The elementary schools of late medieval England offered various kinds of education. For Chaucer's "litel clergeon" it provided a reading education which depended upon the primer and other service books for texts. Although some of this material, particularly at the beginner's level, was in English or possibly French, most of it would have been in Latin, for one of the goals of a reading education was to educate boys who could help minister in the church and perhaps eventually go into the priesthood. Writing and doing accounts were not completely neglected; writing, in particular, became more widespread toward the end of our period. A song school education, although distinct from that of the reading school, might include reading skills and probably acquainted most students with a written text. For that unknown proportion of song scholars who mainly memorized their hymns and psalms, it is debatable whether, outside the choir, they could be considered literate. Although Nicholas Orme suggests that someone "who could pronounce Latin words must be presumed to be able to

---

[133] Chaucer, "The Prioress's Tale," *The Complete Works of Geoffrey Chaucer*, ed. F. N. Robinson, 2nd ed. (Boston, 1933), 161-62.

read and understand English,"[134] we need to know more about the methods used in teaching song before we can be sure.

Training in reading, whether in song schools or, more obviously, in a reading school, was of great use, not only to the young boy looking to a career in the Church but also to the child with no interest in becoming a cleric. Depending upon the skill of the schoolmaster, a student's own capabilities, and the length of time spent learning, the reading scholar would leave with a limited reading knowledge of the vernacular and a more extensive knowledge of the Latin of the Church. He (less likely she) might also, but not necessarily, acquire some writing skills. Such an individual should be able to read a posted bill in English, the Book of Hours in Latin or English, a deed of release, a will or a manor court entry in Latin, to procure a scrivener to write a needed document and, possibly, to make copies of any of these texts. For the purposes of late medieval society, a person with these skills would be literate but, being unacquainted with Latin grammar, not latinate.

In conclusion, although the late medieval pre-university educational milieu is characterized by variety and flexibility, four distinct if sometimes overlapping levels of education do emerge from the evidence. The division into reading, writing, song, and grammar schools is not unique to York diocese. Examples from other parts of England suggest similar patterns. Nor are the divisions recent. Despite a lack of evidence from England prior to 1300, they appear to have their roots in Carolingian times. The task of the next two chapters is to evaluate the surviving evidence for schools in light of the different levels of learning and, in compiling a list of York diocesan schools, to more clearly distinguish grammar from reading, and song from both reading and grammar.

[134] Orme, "Education and Learning at a Medieval English Cathedral," 268.

CHAPTER 3

Scholars, Schoolmasters, and Schools

It is one thing to explain the overall differences between elementary and grammar education and another to discover the level of instruction available in specific instances. The identification of individual pre-Reformation schools as grammar, reading, writing, and/or song has been difficult for historians because so few of the surviving documents describe or even hint at the curriculum. A. F. Leach, in his book *The Schools of Medieval England*, refers to "the darkness of our ignorance of the curriculum in our ancient [i.e., medieval] schools."[1] The only concrete information he provides comes from Cardinal Wolsey's 1528 statutes, ordered for his short-lived schools at Ipswich; an Eton timetable available for 1528; and the curricula at Eton and Winchester partially preserved in statutes for a school at Saffron Walden in 1530. The various forms (or levels) at these schools were concerned primarily with Latin learning. Latin grammar teaching was based on Stanbridge's *Accidence*, Lily's grammar, and the late fifteenth-century grammatical works of Giovanni Sulpicius of Veroli, while the writing of Latin prose and verse was learned from, among others, Cicero's *Letters*, Valla's *Elegantiae*, and Lucian's *Dialogues* (in translation). All these works are typical of a humanist education and offer little insight into the medieval curriculum. With the exception of Stanbridge's *Accidence*, which we know was available in the north of England, the books used in these prestigious southern English schools are meaningless for understanding the curricula in York diocesan schools which, even as late as 1548, betray almost no humanist influence.[2]

Part of the difficulty in investigating the curriculum of particular schools is, as Nicholas Orme has pointed out, that medieval writers often defined schools according to their constitution rather than their curriculum.[3] In his effort to reconstruct the medieval curriculum Orme turned to the surviving schoolbooks, as has also been done in Chapter two above, but schooltexts cannot help the historian who hopes to differentiate one school from another along curricular lines. Unless a grammarmaster is specified

[1] Leach, *SME*, 300.
[2] See Chapter seven below.
[3] Orme, *ESMA*, 59.

or a school specifically labeled, the historian of medieval education has traditionally had limited success in discovering the level of education being offered in particular cases. For example, one can point to the versifying William Paston was doing at Eton in 1479 to tell us something about the curriculum there, but this kind of evidence is rare.[4] Partial library catalogs, which also tell us something about the curriculum, survive from St. Paul's, Winchester, Eton, Brough under Stainmore (Westm.), and Rotherham schools, but there is no way to reconstruct the libraries of most schools, if indeed they existed.[5] Finally, foundation statutes, although they become more numerous toward the end of our period, include surprisingly little information on curriculum. Consequently we must develop other criteria for deciding whether a given school or schoolmaster offered one type of education or another. In the absence of direct evidence there are a variety of other, more indirect indicators that help the historian make an informed, or at least defensible, judgment. Fortunately, the sources for York diocese are especially full with regard to schools and present a superb opportunity in this chapter for developing such indices. As before, however, the evidence from York has occasionally been supplemented by information for education from outside the diocese.

SCHOLARS

One obvious approach to deciding what level of education was being offered in a particular school might be the age of its scholars. In fact, the age of late medieval and early Tudor scholars is no more than a clue to the curriculum being taught and cannot be considered a definitive guide unless taken in conjunction with other information. Children attending the reading schools were usually youngsters between the ages of seven to ten or twelve, although from time to time one finds references to petty scholars as young as four or five years of age or evidence that suggests that youths could stay in the reading schools up to the age of fifteen or more.[6]

---

[4] Norman Davis, ed., *Paston Letters and Papers of the Fifteenth Century*, 2 vols. (Oxford, 1971-1976), 1:650-51.

[5] Edith Rickert, "Chaucer at School," *Modern Philology* 29 (1932):257-74; W. H. Gunner, "Catalogue of Books Belonging to the College of St. Mary, Winchester, in the Reign of Henry VI," *Archaeological Journal* 15 (1858):59-74; M. R. James, "Chapel Inventories," *Etoniana* 27 (1921):444; R. L. Storey, "The Chantries of Cumberland and Westmorland, part 2," *Transactions of the Cumberland and Westmorland Antiquarian and Archaeological Society*, new ser., 62 (1962):147; M. R. James, *A Descriptive Catalogue of the Manuscripts in the Library of Sidney Sussex College, Cambridge* (Cambridge, 1895), 5-8.

[6] In 1531 Sir Thomas Elyot recommended instruction in Greek or Latin earlier than age

Students in the grammar schools might be anywhere from eight to eighteen or nineteen years of age, although the more common grammar school age was from ten to fifteen or sixteen. New grammar scholars elected into Winchester College were to be taken from the elementary boys and choristers of the chapel who were from eight to twelve years. They could stay until the age of eighteen. Similar requirements were instituted at Eton, although in 1479 William Paston was still there at the age of twenty. In the statutes for Wotten-under-Edge in 1384, it was declared with regard to the grammar scholars that "age on their first admission shall not exceed ten years (though we do not intend absolutely to forbid such admission before that age, supposing the persons admitted are of sufficient ability)." They were then to remain at the school for six years. The Statutes of St. Alban's almonry boys in 1339 state, "let them [the poor scholars] be admitted to live there for a term of five years at the most, to whom this period suffices for becoming proficient in grammar." Any grammar scholar in a less structured school might, however, attend it on and off for more than five or six years.[7] Archbishop Rotherham, in making provisions for six poor children, choristers, to be instructed in grammar, song, and writing at Rotherham school, did not specify a starting age but only a school-leaving age of eighteen.[8]

It was not so uncommon for adults to be scholars in the grammar

---

seven, while William Forest, in a plea for universal schooling in 1548, recommended that all children begin school at four. David Cressy, ed., *Education in Tudor and Stuart England* (New York, 1976), 70, 95. For other opinions and some specific examples of young scholars aged four or five, see William J. Frank Davies, *Teaching Reading in Early England* (London, 1973), 61-64. In 1551 Sir John Savile was sent to learn under the curate of Elland at the age of five. J. W. Clay and John Lister, eds., "Autobiography of Sir John Savile, of Methley, Knight, Baron of the Exchequer, 1546-1607," *YAJ* 15 (1900):421-22. Sixteenth-century admissions to Merchant Taylor's school in London, which offered reading instruction, included boys as young as five years of age. Richard De Molen, "Ages of Admission to Educational Institutions in Tudor and Stuart England," *History of Education* 5 (1976):211, 213. That there were older youths in the reading schools is suggested by the ages of admission to grammar at Winchester College. In the fifteenth and sixteenth centuries boys were admitted as late as ages fourteen to sixteen. Quite possibly they came directly from a reading education. Ibid., 212. In the early sixteenth century a husbandman entered school at Tickhill at age four and left at age fifteen, while a yeoman attended the same school from age eight to fifteen. It is conceivable that this was a reading school. J. S. Purvis, *Select XVIth Century Causes in Tithe*, YAS rec. ser., no. 114 (Leeds, 1949), 107, 108. In 1283 a scholar at Clitheroe (Lancs.) left school [scolas reliquit] when he was nineteen or twenty because he was beaten so badly. W. Brown, ed., *Yorkshire Inquisitions*, Vol. 4, YAS rec. ser., no. 37 (Leeds, 1906), 92. This may have been an elementary school since there is no subsequent record of its existence or any suggestion that it was a grammar school.

[7] *VCH, Hamps.*, 2:261ff; VCH, *Bucks.*, 2:159; Davis, ed., *Paston Letters*, 1:650-51; A. F. Leach, *Educational Charters and Documents, 589 to 1909* (Cambridge, 1911), 296-97, 338-39.

[8] Leach, *ESR*, ii, 293.

schools. Bishop Grandisson, in his 1357 mandate *Pro pueris informandis*, implied that *pueri* were not the only ones taught in the grammar schools of Exeter diocese when he addressed himself to the "Master or teachers of children and of the unlearned of our diocese." At Winchester, although in general the grammar students were not allowed to stay beyond the age of eighteen, founder's kin could be admitted up to the age of twenty-five. Examples from further north abound. In 1473 William Cowper of Wollaton (Notts.) taught men as well as boys in grammar, while an indenture from the newly endowed grammar school of Manchester (Lancs.) in 1515 specified "that such a fit person . . . shall freely, and without anything being given therefore or taken by him, teach and instruct others, as well youths as grownup persons, in his learning and wisdom." In 1530 Thomas Magnus's statutes for the grammar school at Newark provided the income for two secular priests, "whereof . . . one should have sufficient cunning and learning to teach grammar . . . freely teaching and instructing all persons and children that would at Newark come to school with [him]."[9]

An accepted age for entering the universities was fifteen or sixteen, perhaps even fourteen, but many scholars matriculated later. Twenty was not an unusual age for entering university, as evidenced by the early fifteenth-century "Mirror of the Periods of Man's Life." "Quod resoun, 'in age of xx. ʒeer, Goo to oxenford, or lerne lawe.' "[10] Nicholas Orme cites the case of John Boryngton, who, after teaching grammar at the city school of Exeter for nine years, received a rectory and thereby university support in 1437 when he was in his late twenties or older. Such delayed learning must have been common in late medieval York diocese, as the large number of licenses for university study combined with letters dimissory to proceed to the priesthood suggests.[11] One wonders just what

[9] *The Register of John de Grandisson, Bishop of Exeter, A.D. 1327-1369*, ed. F. C. Hingeston-Randolph, 3 vols. (London, 1894-1899), 2:1192-93; *VCH, Hamps.*, 2:261 ff.; A. F. Leach, ed., *Visitations and Memorials of Southwell Minster*, Camden Society, new ser., no. 48 (London, 1891), 13; *VCH, Lancs.*, 2:581; Cornelius Brown, *History of Newark-upon-Trent*, 2 vols. (Newark, 1904-1907), 2:206.

[10] "The Mirror of the Periods of Man's Life," in *Hymns to the Virgin*, ed. F. J. Furnivall, EETS, orig. ser., no. 24 (1867), 61. For a discussion of the wide range of ages of entering university students in the sixteenth century, see De Molen, "Ages of Admission," 215-18, subsequent comments by Kenneth Charlton and Lawrence Stone in *History of Education* 5 (1976):221-27, and Lawrence Stone, "The Size and Composition of the Oxford Student Body 1580-1909," in *The University in Society*, 2 vols. (Princeton, 1974), 1:32. For testamentary evidence from northern England showing how common it was to enter either Oxford or Cambridge at age fifteen, see PRO, PCC, Prob 11/24 Thower 16 (will of Rauf Hedworth) and BI, Prob. Reg. 9, f. 462; *Test. Ebor.*, 5:279.

[11] Nicholas Orme, "Education and Learning at a Medieval English Cathedral: Exeter 1380-1548," *J. Eccl. Hist.* 32 (1981):270-71; BI, Reg. 9-23, passim.

might be considered the upper age for schooling to which Thomas More was referring in 1527 when he commented on the relatively high rate of illiteracy among the English "and many now to olde to begynne to go to scole . . . ."[12] Obviously, English schooling in the late Middle Ages exhibited flexibility with regard to age, which makes it difficult for the historian to judge a school's curriculum on the basis of its scholars' ages.

Song schools seem to have been for any child above early childhood who had a decent and as yet unbroken voice, although older individuals (vicars choral, chaplains, monks, clerks, and laity) sang with them and often outnumbered the children in the choir. Occasionally adults were to be found in the song school, as at Newark in 1530, where the statutes of the song school specified free instruction to all "persons and children that wanted to attend," although the choristers actually singing at the church were limited to six.[13] Most children remained in these song schools until their voices broke, and then either continued in reading or grammar or went into an occupation. Some of the song scholars stayed on, however. They may have remained as parish clerks singing in the local church, or, if they were sufficiently trained, become vicars choral in a collegiate or cathedral church or singing-men there or in a monastery or private chapel. The York statutes of about 1317 observed that a boy who was musical and had a good voice could in the course of time become a censerbearer (thurifer), a subdeacon, deacon, and, if he were worthy, a vicar choral.[14] Thus, while the age of a scholar is not always useful in determining the kind of education involved, information on a scholar's subsequent career, as in the case of a vicar choral or singing-man, can help greatly.

Some of the pupils learning reading must have left their education at the age of ten, twelve, or perhaps even fifteen or sixteen, to enter a craft, or to work as husbandmen or yeomen. Unfortunately, the lack of school registers as well as the dearth of records reflecting the lives of artisans and yeomen means that we cannot know what proportion might have done so. We can, however, illustrate the point. One of the best examples comes from the will of Sir John Depeden, knight and Lord of Healaugh, dated 1402. In it he gave £20 to John, the son of John FitzRichard, in order that he might be placed either in the custody of Master John de Neuton, treasurer of York, or of Sir Robert Wyclif, parson of Rudby (N. Riding),

[12] *The Complete Works of Sir Thomas More*, Vol. 9, ed. J. B. Trapp (New Haven, 1979), 13.

[13] Brown, *History of Newark*, 2:186.

[14] *York Cathedral Statutes* (Leeds, 1900), 12. For attendance at the song school and the subsequent careers of choristers at Exeter, see Orme, "The Early Musicians of Exeter Cathedral," *Music and Letters* 59 (1978):398-99.

until he learned "aliqualiter intelligere et scribere." After this he was to be sent to London to learn the art of fishmonger, grocer, or mercer. In an earlier will of 1391, provision was made for John Ysaak, son of Robert att Hall, chaplain, to go to school until he learned to say his psalter and then to be put into a craft.[15] One might reasonably conclude that a school at Harwood (W. Riding) that was attended circa 1505 by Richard Robynson, yeoman, when he was about ten years old, was offering a reading education. Both his age and Robynson's subsequent occupation argue for this assessment. But how should one judge the early sixteenth-century school at Tickhill (W. Riding) that a yeoman and a husbandman attended for seven and eleven years respectively, until they were fifteen or more?[16] Quite possibly they were learning reading despite their somewhat advanced ages. The long years of education suggest Latin grammar, but the occupations of the two men make this seem unlikely. One needs to be careful, however, and not automatically assume that occupational level is a sure guide to a person's educational training. Despite the solid statistical data published over ten years by David Cressy, which shows a close correlation between levels of literacy and occupational status in Tudor England,[17] the results are not always predictable in any particular case. For example, after the dissolution of the monasteries, individuals who had been trained in grammar at the monastic schools and had become lay officials within the monasteries could turn to husbandry. We have evidence for this at Monk Bretton within York diocese when John Foxe, husbandman, who had been chamberlain of the priory before 1536, testified at York in 1574.[18] Peter Heath notes the case of a maltman from Braughing (Herts.) who first learned his letters and then his grammar from a vicar's chaplain in the 1460s. In 1531 Sir Thomas Elyot deplored the irrational behavior of parents who took away from schoolmasters ". . . theyr aptist and moste propre scholers, after they be well instructed in speakyng latine . . . and either be brought to the courte, and made lackayes or pages, or els are bounden prentises."[19]

---

[15] *Test. Ebor.*, 1:296; BI, Prob. Reg. 1, f. 50v.

[16] Purvis, *Select XVIth Century Causes*, 68, 107, 108.

[17] David Cressy, "Occupations, Migration and Literacy in East London, 1580-1640," *Local Population Studies*, no. 5 (1970):53-60; "Literacy in Pre-Industrial England," *Societas* 4 (1974):229-40; "Educational Opportunity in Tudor and Stuart England," *History of Education Quarterly* 16 (1976):301-20; "Levels of Illiteracy in England, 1530-1730," *Historical Journal* 20 (1977):1-23; "Social Status and Literacy in North-East England, 1560-1630," *Local Population Studies*, no. 21 (1978):19-23; *Literacy and the Social Order: Reading and Writing in Tudor and Stuart England* (Cambridge, 1980).

[18] J. S. Purvis, "New Light on the Chartularies of Monk Bretton Priory," *YAJ* 37 (1948):68.

[19] Peter Heath, *The English Parish Clergy on the Eve of the Reformation* (London, 1969),

One can assume, however, that professionals and university students, as well as higher clergy and lay administrators, would have once been grammar students, and it was not unusual for a merchant to have been trained in grammar. In the will of Sir Richard Bassett of Fledborough (Notts.), knight, dated June 15, 1522, the testator requested that his two sons be kept at the grammar school. Subsequently, he noted, one was to go into law and the other was to become a merchant. Earlier, at the end of the fourteenth century, a London mercer sent his son to Oxford for more than a decade. When the young man came back to London, he was apprenticed to his father's company. Although Sylvia Thrupp notes that this case was probably unusual, she does argue that most London merchants of the fourteenth and fifteenth centuries had some training in Latin.[20] In general, although the subsequent career of a scholar rather than his age as a student is a surer indicator of the kind of school attended, life is never totally predictable. Grammar-educated maltmen do occur, and it is best to be cautious. Knowledge of the subsequent occupation of a scholar, while helpful, is not sufficient for judging the nature of his education.

The presence of women or girls in a school argues for the teaching of elementary learning rather than Latin grammar. Unfortunately, however, information on women scholars arises infrequently, in part because the Latin texts so often refer to *pueri*, which can cover girls as well as boys, and possibly in part because girls were seldom in the schools. By the late Middle Ages the girls in English nunneries were being taught to read the vernacular (French and, after the fourteenth century, English) rather than Latin. Girls could also be taught in a household where they might learn to read both French and English and perhaps the Latin primer or psalter. In 1463 Brian Roucliffe, speaking of his daughter-in-law and the granddaughter of Sir William Plumpton, reported that she "speaketh prattely and french and hath near hand learned her sawter." Young girls might also be taught by anchorites or their servants. *The Ancren Riwle*, from the thirteenth century, states quite firmly that, "An anchoress must not become a schoolmistress, nor turn her anchoress-house into a school for children. Her maiden may, however, teach any little girl concerning whom it might be doubtful whether she should learn among boys."[21]

---

appendix 2(b); Sir Thomas Elyot, *The Boke Named the Governour*, ed. H. S. Croft, 2 vols. (New York, 1967), 1:163.

[20] BI, Prob. Reg. 9, f. 311; *Test. Ebor*, 5:147-49; Sylvia Thrupp, *The Merchant Class of Medieval London 1300-1500* (Ann Arbor, Mich., 1948), 161.

[21] Power, *Med. Eng. Nunneries*, 260-84; *Plumpton Correspondence*, ed. Thomas Stapleton, Camden Society, no. 4 (London, 1839), 7-8; *The Nun's Rule; Being the Ancren Riwle Modernized*, ed. James Morton (London, 1924), 319.

It was not unusual for girls to learn alongside boys. It occasionally occurred that the convents admitted young boys as well as girls, and other schools besides those mentioned above taught children of both sexes. The "parish town clerk" in one of Skelton's late fifteenth-century poems kept a song school "for lordes and ladyes. . . . He techyth hem so wysely to solf and to fayne That neither they singe wel prike song nor plain." The 1472 will of William Ecopp, rector of Heslerton (Yorks.) requested thirteen children, including five boys, certain children of William Gibson, and others, poor children, boys as well as girls, to be present, in togas and tunics all of one color, in the choir at the time of his funeral masses on the day of his burial and eight days after. It is entirely possible, as Dorothy Gardiner suggests, that the girls were part of the song school. It is difficult to see why they should be so arrayed in the choir at funeral masses for any other reason.[22] We know of another girl, Elizabeth Garrard, age eight, at school in London toward the end of the fifteenth century. Her teacher, a priest, was accused in the Court of Chancery of having "ravysshed" her within three weeks of her arrival. The priest, William Barboure, reported that he had promised in good faith to "instructe and teache . . . Elizabeth . . . the *Pater Noster, Ave*, and *Credo* with ferther lernyng as at that tyme he taught other yong chyldren to the nowmber of xxx[ti]."[23]

Girls might also have been taught by schoolmistresses such as Elyn Skolemastre of Taunton in 1494 or Matilda Maresflete, "magistra scolarum" in Boston in 1404. And certainly women were both teaching and attending Lollard schools from the end of the fourteenth century on. None of these examples suggest Latin learning, although there may have been an occasional exception such as Johanna Fitzhonor, a nun at Dartford in 1481 who was allowed a preceptor "in grammatica et lingua Latina," or Agnes Smyth, the concubine of a vicar choral at York Cathedral who was reported in 1462 to be "bene literata." Such instances are, however, occasional, and one can cautiously conclude that the presence of girls in a school is evidence for its elementary nature.[24]

[22] "Volo quod Willelmus Ecopp, Johannes frater ejus, Johannes Snowball, Johannes Danby, Johannes Scarlett, et quidam de pueris Willelmi Gybson, et caeteri innocentes de maxime egenis villae, tam de masculis quam de puellis, ad numerum xiii . . . (videlicet pueri masculi habeant togas, et puellae tunicas vocatas kirtyls de uno colore), sint praesentes in choro tempore exequiarum mearum, et missarum, tam diebus sepulturae meae quam octavo." BI, Prob. Reg. 4, f. 178; *Test. Ebor.*, 3:200; Dorothy Gardiner, *English Girlhood at School* (Oxford, 1929), 77-78; *The Complete Poems of John Skelton*, ed. Philip Henderson (London, 1931), 121.

[23] C. T. Martin, "Clerical Life in the Fifteenth Century," *Archaeologia* 60, pt.2 (1907):359-60.

[24] *Somerset Medieval Wills (1383-1500)*, ed. F. W. Weaver, Somerset Record Society, no. 16 (London, 1901), 323; *VCH, Lincs.*, 2:451; Margaret Aston, "Lollard Women Priests?" *J.*

SCHOOLMASTERS

Another factor to be weighed, although also full of ambiguities, is the status and training of the schoolmaster. Grammarmasters were not necessarily university graduates, and, from the very earliest notices, were often married laymen or clerks. In his educational study of the six counties in the west of England, Nicholas Orme has located the names of 150 schoolmasters alive between 1200 to 1548 and teaching within these counties. Only 31 can be clearly proven to be graduates of either university. Another 88 are equally clearly non-graduates, and the remainder cannot be categorized. Out of the total of about 150, a majority were priests (83). Of the other 67, 15 were in minor orders and the remaining 52 were probably clerks or laymen. Some unknown proportion of these non-priestly schoolmasters would have been married.[25] Among the twelve known grammarmasters at York Cathedral teaching between 1266 to 1535, four (perhaps five) are known to have taken university degrees. At least three were clergy, and another three were married laymen.[26] The better grammar schools tried to hire grammarmasters with an M.A., but with the scarcity of trained teachers after the plague these schools were forced to accept masters with only B.A.'s. In 1368 Symon de Beckyngham, the chancellor of York Cathedral, appointed John de York, B.A., to the mastership of the grammar school, waiving the rule that the master should be an M.A. and be appointed for only three or five years. Similar conditions prevailed at Lincoln, where the cathedral chapter appointed John Muscham to the grammar school in 1351 on the condition "that if a master of arts should come and ask for the school he should be admitted, since by custom the teaching of the school belongs to an M.A." Even Oxford schoolmasters were no longer required to have an M.A. at the end of the fourteenth century, and among the eight grammarmasters known to have taught at York Cathedral between 1400 and 1548, none are known to have had an M.A., and only one appears to have had a B.A.[27] With a dearth of M.A.'s to teach grammar, the universities may have established a new *magister in grammatica* degree toward the end of the fourteenth century, but the numbers who received the M. Gram. were never large— David Thomson counts twenty-one and sixty-three at Oxford in the four-

---

Eccl. Hist. 31 (1980):441-61; British Library, Additional MS 32446, f. 11v, quoted by A. G. Little, "Educational Organization of the Mendicant Friars in England," *TRHS*, new ser., 8 (1894):51; J. S. Purvis, *A Medieval Act Book* (York, 1943), 49.

[25] Nicholas Orme, *Education in the West of England 1066-1548* (Exeter, 1976), 18-19.

[26] J. Hoeppner Moran, *Education and Learning in the City of York, 1300-1560* (York, 1979), appendix.

[27] *VCH, Lincs.*, 2:423; Orme, *ESMA*, 151; Moran, *Education and Learning*, appendix.

teenth and fifteenth centuries respectively. Among the York Cathedral grammarmasters two are known to have received it.[28]

Grammarmasters might hold an M.A., B.A., M. Gram., B. Gram., or a license for teaching from either Oxford or Cambridge, but there was no rule enforced or even enforceable that made them prerequisites, and Nicholas Orme stresses that qualified grammarians whose graduate status was doubtful could nonetheless prove to be excellent schoolmasters.[29] In fact, by the early sixteenth century both the B. Gram. and M. Gram. degree were being granted not just for university study, but also for teaching experience. Thus Thomas Hartwell, who received his M. Gram. from Cambridge in 1520, had no university training but did have nine years' grammar teaching to recommend him; while, in 1513, a Thomas More supplicated for the B. Gram. at Oxford with fourteen years' teaching experience but no years of study.[30] On the other hand, reference to a master with a B.A., M.A., M. Gram., B. Gram., or possibly a license to teach assures us that a grammar school was being conducted, despite the fact that neither the M. Gram. nor the B. Gram. necessarily meant that the teacher was university trained. In York diocese most of the grammarmasters were probably qualified more by experience than university education. Among the more than fifty B. Gram.'s from Oxford between 1501 and 1540 only two can unquestionably be associated with York (William Beaumont at Halifax in 1516-1517 and Christopher Holdsworth at York in 1531).[31] Yet there are notices for nearly seventy grammar schools in the diocese between 1500 and 1548.[32] As a result, information with regard to the university education of a teacher is only helpful in determining the status of a school in a small number of instances.

Although late medieval grammarmasters were, in general, modest in

[28] Moran, *Education and Learning*; R. W. Hunt, "Oxford Grammar Masters in the Middle Ages," in *Oxford Studies Presented to Daniel Callus*, ed. R. W. Southern, Oxford Historical Society, new ser., no. 16 (Oxford, 1964), 163-93. David Thomson argues, however, that the M. Gram. at Oxford was not new in the fourteenth century but already in existence before c. 1310. David Thomson, "The Oxford Grammar Masters Revisited," *Mediaeval Studies* 45 (1983):298-310. For the numbers of M. Gram.'s at Oxford, see Thomson, "Oxford Grammar Masters," 301. For a description of the requirements for the M. Gram., see Damian Leader, "Grammar in Late-Medieval Oxford and Cambridge," *History of Education* 12 (1983):9-14.

[29] Orme, *Education in the West of England*, 19; for a fuller description of the training of medieval grammarmasters, see Orme, *ESMA*, 151-56.

[30] *Grace Book Γ, 1501-1542*, ed. W. G. Searle (Cambridge, 1908), 176, cited in Leader, "Grammar," 12; Emden, *BRUO, 1501-1540*, 399.

[31] Emden, *BRUO, 1501-1540*, passim. Of the five M. Gram.'s listed in Emden, four incepted at Cambridge.

[32] Chapter four and Appendix B below.

their achievements and reputations,[33] the masters of the larger or more prestigious schools were better respected, better known, and consequently better documented than the teachers of smaller, rural grammar schools or than teachers of reading and song schools. In particular, grammarmasters in the northern towns, whether they were graduates or non-graduates, lay or in orders, were often held in high esteem by the rest of the community. At Scarborough, grammar schoolmaster Hugh Rasyn was bailiff in 1421-1422 and elected to the parliamentary common in 1422. In 1366/7 the "magister scolarum" of Beverley's grammar school was the second-highest ranked individual assessed for a tax to cobble the streets; while William Hardynges, the grammarmaster from 1436 to 1456, was a steward of the great gild of St. John, thrice borough governor, and one of those named to greet Henry VI on his visit to Beverley.[34] Sometime after 1327 the grammarmaster of Preston, Master Ralph, was considered of sufficient reputation to be recommended as penitencer for the archdeaconry of Richmond. In 1415 Richard Marshall, the schoolmaster at Preston, was enrolled in the Merchant gild, having paid a substantial admission fee of three shillings. And between 1400 and 1550 three different grammarmasters of Preston had fathers, uncles, or brothers who were mayors of the town.[35] Various grammarmasters of York Cathedral were freemen of the city, members of the great Corpus Christi gild, or related to the leading citizens of the city; while one, John Hamundson, was the brother-in-law of the mayor of Hull. The grammarmaster at Richmond in the 1480s was so highly considered that the prior of Durham went to great lengths to convince him (against the wishes of the burgesses and gentlemen of the town) to leave Richmond and come to teach at Durham.[36] The prestige (and probably the pay) of being grammarmaster in the larger towns was such that the rector of Bilborough was willing to leave his position to become the master of Nottingham in 1512.[37]

The town grammarmasters seem to have been in a strong competitive

[33] Nicholas Orme, "Schoolmasters, 1307-1509," in *Profession, Vocation and Culture in Later Medieval England*, ed. C. H. Clough (Liverpool, 1982), 218-41.

[34] Arthur Rowntree, ed., *The History of Scarborough* (London, 1931), 139 n 112; BI, Prob. Reg. 2, f. 356; *Test. Ebor.*, 2:209; *EYS*, 1:101; John Lawson, "Beverley Minster Grammar School in the Middle Ages," *University of Hull Studies in Education* 2 (May 1954):161.

[35] Rosalind M. T. Hill, ed., *The Register of William Melton: Archbishop of York, 1317-1340*, Canterbury and York Society, no. 70 (Torquay, 1977), 34; Hill, *The Labourer in the Vineyard: The Visitations of Archbishop Melton in the Archdeaconry of Richmond* (York, 1968), 8; W. A. Abram, *Memorials of the Preston Guilds* (Preston, 1882), 14; *VCH, Lancs.*, 2:570-71.

[36] Moran, *Education and Learning*, appendix; L. P. Wenham, "Two Notes on the History of Richmond School, Yorkshire," *YAJ* 37 (1950):369-72.

[37] *VCH, Notts.*, 2:218.

position, which was probably helped by the dearth of grammarmasters after the black death in 1349 and throughout the fifteenth century. They often moved about from place to place, presumably to better their positions. Thus John de York, master of York Minster's grammar school, brought an action for departure in 1374, citing the statute of laborers against William de Wirsall, clerk and teacher in the grammar school. William, according to John, had left his employ before his one-year term of service was completed.[38] Stephen Moys, grammarmaster at Richmond from 1392/3 until 1397, is to be found at Newark from 1405 to 1435; while Thomas Ridley, grammarmaster at Nottingham from 1429 until 1432, had moved to a position as grammarmaster at St. Leonard's Hospital, York, by the time of his death in 1448.[39] John Hamundson, master at York Minster from 1465 until his death in 1472, had earlier (1456) been appointed headmaster at Howden after receiving his B.A. from Oxford. And in 1444 the mayor of Hull tried to entice the grammarmaster of Scarborough to Hull to fill a vacancy. He may have succeeded, for nothing more is known of a grammar school at Scarborough.[40]

The esteem in which grammarmasters were generally held did not prevent them from occasionally running afoul of the law. In 1348 Richard, the chamberlain and formerly master of the schoolhouse at Ripon, was ordered to be arrested together with 139 others, presumably for causing a riot. The grammarmaster of Preston, an individual of some local importance as we have already seen, was indicted along with others in 1358 for rioting in connection with a pardon of a murderer. And Master William Hardynges, whose credentials have already been cited, was expelled from the freedom of Beverley for pasturing his cows on the commons a few years before he became one of the governors of the city.[41] The fourteenth- and fifteenth-century grammarmasters of Nottingham, who in other respects seem to have been well-considered by their townspeople, have, with the exception of a successful plea for school fees owed in 1395, a continuous and frustrating history of pleas for unpaid debts or pleas brought against them for unpaid rent. With puzzling consistency the juries found against the schoolmasters. The historian, tracing the legal

---

[38] PRO, CP 40/499 (De Banco), 449 Hill., f. 377v.

[39] Wenham, "History of Richmond School," 371; Brown, *History of Newark-upon-Trent*, 2:155, 160, 163, 177; *VCH, Notts.*, 2:217; YML, M 2/6e, Register of Wills, from the Peculiar of St. Leonard's Hospital, f. 43.

[40] BI, Prob. Reg. 4, f. 85; *Test. Ebor.*, 3:198-99; Emden, *BRUO*, 2:865; John Lawson, *A Town Grammar School Through Six Centuries* (Oxford, 1963), 16. For additional evidence of mobility, see Orme, "Schoolmasters, 1307-1509," 221-22.

[41] *VCH, Yorks.*, 1:426, 431; *VCH, Lancs.*, 2:570.

complaints by and against the Nottingham masters, finally sympathizes with Thomas Ridley in 1431-1432 when he reacts by burning down the walls, closes, and enclosures of his rented property. This may, of course, explain Ridley's decision to move from Nottingham to St. Leonard's, York. A later Nottingham grammarmaster, George Somer, invokes less sympathy, as we find him presented and successfully indicted for willful murder in 1532.[42] One final example concerns William Burton, grammarmaster of St. Leonard's, York at the end of the fifteenth century. In 1491 the following complaint was heard before the mayor and council:

> . . . one John Paynter was brought before York council to answer for having said to William Burton, schoolmaster of St. Leonard's Hospital, that the Earl of Northumberland was a traitor and betrayed King Richard. In defence Paynter said that he heard Burton say that King Richard was a hypocrite, a crouchback, and was buried in a dyke like a dog; and he answered and said that he lied, for the King had buried him like a noble gentleman. Two priests who were present at the time testified that the schoolmaster had called King Richard a caitiff, and said he was buried like a dog, but that Paynter in rebuking him had said nothing about the Earl; and the Prior of Bolton Abbey, also present, wrote that the schoolmaster had said concerning King Richard that he never loved him, and that he was buried in a dyke; but that all who were present in the house and heard him supposed that he was distempered either with ale or wine.[43]

Although the schoolmaster's political sentiments proved distressing, his opinions were nonetheless of some importance. These notices of illegal or unpopular activities, rather than documenting the low status of medieval grammarmasters, as most educational historians have asserted, may indicate the extent to which the grammarmasters of these towns influenced public opinion, or, from the point of view of the courts, could serve as examples to the public. In general, the grammarmasters in the northern towns seem to have associated as equals with and sometimes as leaders of the more prominent citizens. Consequently any evidence that a schoolmaster is esteemed locally is an indicator that, whatever else he might teach, he probably teaches grammar.

We know less about the status of grammarmasters in monastic and

[42] *Records of the Borough of Nottingham*, 4 vols. (London, 1882-1889), 1:246-49, 262-63, 2:12-15, 122-23, 128-29; 3:140-41, 372, 396, 453-58; 4:26-31. In 1425 and 1517, the usher and the guardians respectively of the grammar school also lost pleas at court. 2:406; 3:48-51.

[43] C. B. Knight, *A History of the City of York* (York, 1944), 308; the full account is in *York Civic Rec.*, 2:71-73.

country schools. Monastic schools were generally taught by one of the older and more learned monks or by a recent graduate, perhaps more normally a secular than a regular, from one of the universities.[44] Many monasteries were lucky to get grammarmasters at all. This would seem to have been true in the Lincoln diocesan monasteries during the first half of the fifteenth century, when the episcopal visitors recorded numerous instances of insufficient grammarmasters.[45] A lack of monastic grammar-masters has also been noticed for the west of England, at Bruton (1452), Keynsham (1526), Tewkesbury (1378), and Tywardreath (1513).[46] The evidence from York diocese with regard to grammarmasters in the monasteries is extremely scanty and it was not unusual for the monks or friars to get their grammar education outside the cloister. One example of a teacher within the cloister walls in the diocese is at Tickhill friary in the beginning of the sixteenth century. But it is not clear what the status of the school was; the school seems to have attracted neighborhood boys who did not become friars, and the master does not fit the usual pattern as he was chaplain to an aristocratic corrodiary (or pensioner) who resided within the friary.[47]

Grammar teachers in rural parishes are also shadowy figures whose tenure might be brief. In 1345 Richard de Bury, the bishop of Durham, thought well of the "masters of country schools and instructors of rude boys" as sources for his book collecting,[48] but rural parishes often had problems retaining the services of an instructor in grammar. The parson of Bilborough, in 1505, was taking in boarding pupils in grammar for fees of 9s. per twelve weeks or 9d. per week, but he did not remain long at Bilborough. In 1513 he was offered the position of grammarmaster at Nottingham, which he accepted. Pocklington, although fully endowed with a grammar school in 1514, nevertheless seems not to have had a schoolmaster there by 1548. Master Clegborowe, who had been school-master at Kneesall (Notts.) for sixteen years in the early sixteenth century, finally left to go north to a better preferment. His successor, Master Baxter, actually taught at Newark and only kept school at Kneesall when

---

[44] Orme, *ESMA*, 240. See also the examples of those teaching monastic grammar listed in his *Education in the West of England*, chap. 4.

[45] A. Hamilton Thompson, ed., *Visitations of Religious Houses in the Diocese of Lincoln, 1420-1449*, 3 vols., Lincoln Record Society, nos. 7, 14, 21 (Horncastle, 1914-1929). The following monasteries lacked sufficient grammar teachers at one time or another: Dunstaple, Newnham, Peterborough, Thornton, Canons Ashby, Elsham, Kyme, Leicester, and Wellow.

[46] Orme, *Education in the West of England*, chap. 4.

[47] Purvis, *Select XVIth Century Causes*, 107-108.

[48] Richard de Bury, *Philobiblon: The Text and Translation of E. C. Thomas*, ed. M. Maclagan (Oxford, 1960), 94-95.

the plague was at Newark.[49] The uncertain availability of parish teachers is nicely illustrated by Archbishop Rotherham, who, looking back to his early days (c. 1430), described the gratitude he felt for the opportune but unexpected arrival of a grammarmaster in the little village of Rotherham: "We stood there in that time, without letters; we should have stood there untaught, illiterate, and rough for many years, had it not been that by God's grace a man learned in grammar arrived, from whom, as from a primal font we were, by God's will, instructed, and, under God's leadership, came to the state in which we are now, and others arrived at great positions."[50] In 1480, when Rotherham began to consider endowing a collegiate church and school at Rotherham, there was no grammar education then available.

The grammar schools which did survive or spring up in the rural areas of the north were sometimes taught by the rector, vicar, or curate, as at Bilborough, South Dalton (E. Riding), Kirkby Kendal (Westm.), South Duffield (E. Riding), Cottingham (E. Riding), Wilforth (Notts.), and perhaps Kinoulton (Notts.). This may also have been the case, in the early and mid-fifteenth century, at the parish churches of Bainton and Beeford (both in the E. Riding).[51] Thomas Gascoigne, in his *Liber Veritatum*, praises an unnamed rector, identified by Angelo Raine with the rector of Bainton, who supported twenty students at school and at the university.[52] Gascoigne also cites the rectory of Ormyshede (Ormside, Westm.?) where,

[49] *VCH, Notts.*, 2:218-21; A. F. Leach, "The Foundation and Refoundation of Pocklington Grammar School," *Transactions of the East Riding Antiquarian Society* 5 (1897):63-114; C. J. Kitching, "The Chantries of the East Riding of Yorkshire at the Dissolution of 1548," *YAJ* 44 (1972):182; PRO, Chantry certificates: E 301/119; Brown, *History of Newark-upon-Trent*, 178.

[50] *EYS*, 2:110.

[51] R. L. Storey, ed., "The Chantries of Cumberland and Westmorland, part 2," 169-70 (Kirkby Kendal); James Raine, ed., *Wills and Inventories from the Registry of the Archdeaconry of Richmond*, Surtees Society, no. 26 (Durham, 1853), 33-34 (Kirkby Kendal); W. D. Macray, *Register of Magdalen College, Oxford*, new ser., 1 (London, 1894), 84; A. F. Leach, ed., *Memorials of Beverley Minster: The Chapter Act Book*, Vol. 1, Surtees Society, no. 98 (Durham, 1898), 42-43, 114, 169 (South Dalton); W. Brown, ed., *The Registers of John le Romeyn, Lord Archbishop of York, 1286-1296 and of Henry of Newark, Lord Archbishop of York 1296-1299*, 2 vols., Surtees Society, nos. 123, 128 (Durham, 1913-1916), 1:285-86 (Kinoulton), 2:324 (South Dalton); W. Brown and A. H. Thompson, eds., *The Register of William Greenfield, Lord Archbishop of York, 1306-1315*, Vol. 3, Surtees Society, no. 151 (Durham, 1936), 1 (Cottingham). See also 176-77, 208; BI, Prob. Reg. 4, f. 66 (Wilforth); BI, Reg. 29 (Holgate/Heath), f. 74 (South Duffield); Mill Stephenson, "Monumental Brasses in the East Riding," *YAJ* 12 (1893):198; 14 (1898):507 (Bainton); *Yorkshire Church Notes 1619-1631 by Roger Dodsworth*, YAS rec. ser., no. 34 (Leeds, 1904), 217 (Beeford).

[52] Angelo Raine, *History of St. Peter's School, York, A.D. 627 to the Present Day* (London, 1926?), 58; Thomas Gascoigne, *Loci e Libro Veritatum*, ed. J. Thorold Rogers (Oxford, 1881), 112. "Novi enim unum rectorem, qui, ex bonis unius ecclesiae, quam unicam habuit, exhibuit ad scolam et ad studium viginti juvenes, et fecit ipsos sacerdotes."

once it was appropriated by York monks, education, the promotion of students, and the maintenance of scholars perished.[53] One has to be cautious about the location of some of these rectory schools, however. It occasionally happened that a rector was nonresident, conducting a school in one of the larger towns rather than in his rural parish. A pertinent example, although not from northern England, occurred in 1463 when Robert Fabell, master in grammar and rector of Beckington, was licensed to absent himself and keep a grammar school elsewhere for four years in order to raise money to meet creditors and execute repairs. William Burton, the tutor to two nephews of Archbishop Melton, who accompanied the boys to school at Newark in 1333, was also the rector of Kirkbymoorside. Two centuries later, in 1542/3 the rector of Thirbergh was charged with pluralism for also teaching at Rotherham College. In 1458 Richard Wetwang, rector of Stokesley, was probably keeping a school within the city of York as was Nicholas de Ferriby, vicar of Weston, in 1375. And the last grammarmaster at Durham Priory was Robert Hartburne, the rector of Kimblesworth.[54] By 1548 an increasing number of parish grammar schools were being conducted by chantry or stipendiary chaplains rather than by rectors or vicars.[55]

It was not usual for the rector or vicar to run the parish reading or song school. These were conducted by a parish chaplain, chantry chaplain, parish clerk, or, as at Hull, the town clerk. As early as 1234 a canon embodied in Gregory IX's decretals ordered that every parish clerk should have enough learning to enable him to sing with the priest, read the epistle and lesson, and conduct a school. In an effort to regulate such clerk's schools, the abbot of Bury St. Edmunds in 1268 prohibited the clerks in Bury from teaching the psalter or singing without a license. And in order to insure that the clerks were sufficiently literate, and also to aid impoverished scholars, a synod at Exeter in 1287 decreed that when there was a school in a town or castle within ten miles of any parish, some scholar

---

[53] Gascoigne, *Loci e Libro Veritatum*, 5. "Et consimiliter habent monachi Eborum ecclesiam de Ormyshede . . . appropriatam; et studium et promocio studencium et exhibicio ad studium pereunt." Gascoigne's diatribes against appropriated rectories include numerous repetitive descriptions of the educational support provided by resident rectors for their parishioners in unappropriated benefices. See pp. 3-4, 70, 74, 106-107, 113-14, 135, 148-49, 198.

[54] *The Register of Thomas Bekynton, Bishop of Bath and Wells 1443-65*, eds. H. C. Maxwell-Lyte and M.C.B. Dawes, 2 vols., Somerset Record Society, nos. 49, 50 (London, 1934-1935), 1:317, 400-401; BI, Reg. 9B (Melton), ff. 44v, 59v, 61v, 533, cited by L. H. Butler, "Archbishop Melton, His Neighbors and His Kinsmen, 1317-1340," *J. Eccl. Hist.* 2 (1951):66; J. S. Purvis, *Educational Records* (York, 1959), 24-25; Moran, *Education and Learning*, 11; J. T. Fowler, ed., *Rites of Durham*, Surtees Society, no. 107 (Durham, 1903), 91-92, 274.

[55] Approximately 200 different grammar schools are listed in the 1546/8 chantry certifications, most of which were being taught by chantry or stipendiary chaplains. Leach, *ESR*, ii:passim.

should be chosen as parish clerk or holy water carrier.[56] This scholar, in turn, might hold school for those even younger, as is apparent from an anecdote of Matthew Paris. "It happened that an agent of the Pope met a petty clerk carrying water in a little vessel, with a sprinkler and some bits of bread given him for having sprinkled some holy water, and to him the deceitful Roman thus addressed himself: 'How much does the profits yielded to you by this church amount to in a year?' To which the clerk, ignorant of the Roman's cunning, replied: 'To twenty shillings, I think.' Whereupon the agent demanded the percentage the Pope had just demanded on all ecclesiastical benefices. . . . And to pay that sum this poor man was compelled to hold school for many days, and by selling his books in the precincts, to drag on a half-starved life."[57] What little evidence there is suggests that it may not have been uncommon to find parish clerks teaching elementary schools in the thirteenth century.

In contrast, the instructions for parish clerks which are extant from 1450 to 1530 make no mention of teaching as one of the duties expected.[58] The role that the parish clerk may have played as schoolteacher in the thirteenth century perhaps gave way in the face of increasing numbers of chantry and stipendiary chaplains who had no cure of souls, and who made their living by singing masses for the dead and sometimes teaching schools. In addition, as the number of individuals in minor orders declined rapidly in the fourteenth and fifteenth centuries, while large numbers of priests were being ordained, it is likely that the parish clerk declined in importance.[59]

[56] *Corpus Juris Canonici*, ed. E. Friedberg, 2 vols. (Leipzig, 1879-1881), 2:part 2, col. 449, liber decretalium Gregorii IX, III, tit. i, cap. iii, 448: "Ut quisque presbyter, qui plebem regit, clericum habeat, qui secum cantet, et epistolam et lectionem legat, et qui possit scholas tenere, et admonere suos parochianos, ut filios suos ad fidem discendam mittant ad ecclesiam, quos ipse cum omni castitate erudiat."; *VCH, Suffolk*, 2:311; F. M. Powicke and C. R. Cheney, eds., *Councils and Synods*, Vol. 2 (Oxford, 1964), ii:1026-27. "A nostris maioribus sepe audivimus recitari beneficia aque benedicte intuitu caritatis fuisse ab initio instituta ut ex eorum proventibus pauperes clerici exhiberentur in scolis et ibidem taliter proficerent ut aptiores et magis ydonei fierent ad maiora. Ne igitur quod tam salubriter extitit institutum per temporis lapsum redeat in abusum, statuimus quod in ecclesiis, que a scolis civitatis vel castrorum nostre diocesis ultra decem non distant miliaria, aque benedicte beneficia solis scolaribus assignentur."

[57] Quoted in P. H. Ditchfield, *The Parish Clerk* (London, 1907), 44, from Matthew Paris, *Chronicon Maiora*, ed. H. R. Luard, 7 vols., Rolls Series (London, 1872-1883), 5:172.

[58] J. Wickham Legg, ed., *The Clerk's Book of 1549*, Henry Bradshaw Society, no. 25 (London, 1903). Legg has printed the constitutions of the parish clerks of Trinity Church, Coventry (1462), at All Saints, Bristol (1455-1469), at St. Nicholas, Bristol (1481), and St. Michael's, Cornhill (before 1538). See also: *The First Churchwardens' Book of Louth, 1500-1524*, ed. R. C. Dudding (Oxford, 1941), 13-14; "Records and History of St. Stephen, Coleman Street," *Archaeologia* 50 (1887):49-50.

[59] J. Hoeppner Moran, "Clerical Recruitment in the Diocese of York, 1340-1530: Data and Commentary," *J. Eccl. Hist.* 34 (1983):19-54.

The parish clerk did not altogether lose his role or income as teacher, however. The few pieces of evidence we have suggest that he sometimes taught song and, more rarely, reading. The accounts of St. Giles, Reading state that 12s. were "pay'd to Whitborne the clerk towards his wages and he to be bound to teach ii children for the choir." At Faversham, in 1506, it was ordered that "the clerks or one of them, as much as in them is, shall endeavour themselves to teach children to read and sing in the choir, and to do service in the church as of old time hath been accustomed, they taking for their teaching as belongeth thereto." And in Bristol, as has already been noted in Chapter two, the parish clerk was ordered not to take any choir books for the children to learn from without permission.[60]

There are only a few examples from York diocese that show parish clerks involved in teaching. In 1521 Henry Smyth, formerly parish clerk of St. Sampson's (where he may have conducted a school), was granted the office of clerk in St. William's Chapel on Ouse Bridge, provided that he "should sing divine service in the choir of the chapel, play the organ, or teach boys." It is also reported from Nottinghamshire that, in the fifteenth century, one John Waterall gave a house to the clerk of the parish of Edenstowe rent-free to teach children in. It is not obvious what kind of school was being conducted, nor is the original documentation cited in this instance.[61] With the disappearance of the chantries and the chaplains who occupied them in 1548, the role of the parish clerk in teaching reemerged, and in 1571 Archbishop Grindal of York could enjoin the parish clerk to "be able to read the first lesson, the Epistle, and the Psalms, with answers to the suffrages as is used, and also that he endeavour himself to teach young children to read, if he be able so to do."[62]

Prior to 1548, however, and throughout the fourteenth and fifteenth centuries, it would appear that most of the teaching in reading and grammar at the parish level had fallen into the hands of the chaplains, of whom there were a great number.[63] Evidence from the chantry surveys, wills, and other documents suggest that most parish schools, whether reading or grammar, were taught by parish or chantry chaplains. Two chaplains who taught schools, for example, were an unnamed chantry priest amortized in 1512 by Harold Staunton of Newark to be a teacher of grammar,

---

[60] Ditchfield, *The Parish Clerk*, 45; J. R. Bramble, "Ancient Bristol Documents, Nos. II and III," *Proceedings of the Clifton Antiquarian Club 1884-8*, 1, pt. 2 (1888):148; F. F. Giraud, "On the Parish Clerks and Sextons of Faversham, 1506-1593," *Archaeologia Cantiana* 20 (1893):205.

[61] Joyce W. Percy, ed., *York Memorandum Book*, Vol. 3, Surtees Society, no. 186 (Gateshead, 1973), 239; BI, Prob. Reg. 8, f. 3; Brown, *History of Newark-upon-Trent*, 2:178.

[62] Ditchfield, *The Parish Clerk*, 54.

[63] See below, Chapter five.

and William Kingston, appointed in 1539 by the former abbot of Top-holme "[to] synge at hongsynger in Yorkshyre & teache & bringe up children in vertue & lernyng."[64] Appendix B provides numerous similar instances.

Townspeople and parishioners could feel quite strongly about the education provided by these chaplains. In 1526 the mayor of Preston in Lancashire, with other burgesses, stormed into the chantry of Sir Roger Lewyns armed with "bylles, swords, and bucklers" where they broke a coffer, carried off chalices, vestments, books, and "juelles" belonging to the chantry and put Lewyns "in great perell of his lyfe" because he had neglected his duty of keeping a school.[65] Earlier, about the year 1503 in the town of Walsall (Staffs.), the "best of the commyns" assembled and sealed the following letter to Sir Henry Vernon, patron of a chantry there:

> We have a chaplain and true bedeman of yours amongst us, whose name is Sir John Staple. We hear that you intend to take him away from us. He has always been ready to maintain the service of God. He has caused charity amongst the people, where else there would have been much discord and debate. He has kept a school, and taught the poor children of the town of his charity, taking nothing for his labour. He has done many more good deeds, specially to the poor people. That he should thus depart were the greatest loss to the poor town of Walsall that it has ever had by the departure of any priest.[66]

Neither Lewyns nor Staple are listed in Emden's biographical registers of Oxford and Cambridge, and in the absence of other information it is not possible to know whether they taught (or would have taught) grammar, a more elementary curriculum, or a combination of both. What is clear is that, whatever the level of learning, it was highly valued but could be quite transient.

In sum, it is reasonable to suppose that a schoolmaster who had some local stature, who had his M.A., B.A., M. Gram., B. Gram., or a university license for teaching grammar (and who would be likely to be called "Master"), or who was a rector or vicar would probably be teaching a grammar school. This, of course, does not preclude the possibility that he might also have taught reading pupils, although in the larger grammar schools an usher, assistant scholar, or parish chaplain would perform that function. Toward the end of our time period, however, it becomes in-

---

[64] PRO, PCC Prob. 11/17 9 Fetiplace; Prob. 11/26 19 Crumwell.

[65] *VCH, Lancs.*, 2:570.

[66] Historical Manuscripts Commission, *The MSS of the Duke of Rutland Preserved at Belvoir Castle*, Vol. 1 (London, 1888), 17.

creasingly common to find chantry or stipendiary chaplains (without university degrees or perhaps any university experience) teaching grammar. The emergence of this kind of grammar school coincides with the decline in those taking degrees in grammar at the universities, as grammar teaching became increasingly a local (and not a university) responsibility during the latter part of the fifteenth century.[67] Parish chaplains were also likely to be found teaching reading schools. After the turn of the fourteenth century parish clerks are only occasionally to be found teaching song and sometimes reading.

SCHOOLS

The clearest evidence for the type of a school being conducted usually comes from records of a formal foundation and/or endowment. In many cases these documents have survived, and they become increasingly common just prior to the Reformation when endowing schools was in vogue. There are several types of foundations that were characteristic of the late medieval period.[68] Roughly classified, they are: 1) those of the cathedral and ancient collegiate churches, e.g., York, Beverley, Ripon, Southwell, and probably Howden in York diocese; 2) those of chantry colleges, for example, Newark, Pontefract, Middleham, Rotherham, Acaster Selby, Sibthorpe, and possibly Hemingbrough;[69] 3) those of monastic origin, e.g., Guisborough, Furness, Monk Bretton, Newburgh et al.;[70] 4) a few

[67] Kenneth Bartlett, "The Decline and Abolition of the Master of Grammar: An Early Victory of Humanism at the University of Cambridge," *History of Education* 6 (1977):6.

[68] This list is based on the classification presented in W. E. Tate, "Some Sources for the History of English Grammar Schools, part 1," *BJES* 1 (1952-1953):173.

[69] A. H. Thompson has distinguished two classes of collegiate churches: 1) those of the more ancient cathedral model, in which category he includes (for York diocese) York, Beverley, Ripon, Southwell, and Howden; and 2) the later colleges of chantry priests. Among the latter he includes Hemingbrough, Sibthorpe, Lowthorpe, Rotherham, Pontefract, Acaster Selby, and Middleham. The fifteen chantry priests of Newark had customs which resembled that of a chantry college, although they were not formally incorporated. The primary difference Thompson finds is that the older, cathedral models included a prebendary system and nonresident canons. A. H. Thompson, "Notes on Colleges of Secular Canons in England," *The Archaeological Journal* 74 (1917):139-98. Although Thompson defines Hemingbrough as a chantry college, it did have three prebendaries and might best be seen as a transition foundation between the two types, but closely modeled on Howden.

[70] There are important distinctions which must be made among the variety of schools which could be maintained in monasteries. Most of the monastic schools were held only for novices and were not open to any larger public. Some monasteries had almonry schools, which were usually small reading and grammar schools. The children who attended them were often poor children from nearby parishes, relatives of the monks, or, as at Furness, children of the mon-

hospital and almshouse schools, e.g., St. Leonard's in York or Ewelme (Oxon.); 5) occasional schools held in the friaries, e.g., Tickhill and York; 6) a number of gild schools, such as Pocklington, Pickering, Middleton, Topcliffe, and York; 7) many schools attached to chantries or stipendiary services supported either by a perpetual or short-term chantry foundation or by stocks contributed by the parishioners, e.g., Bedale, Bolton-upon-Dearne, Boroughbridge et al.; and 8) a few independent town schools not closely associated with ecclesiastical foundations, e.g., Richmond, Lancaster, and Nottingham.

A further category of school, which was not likely to be endowed, was the independent private or household education available, in York diocese, at Leckenfield, Wollaton, Halsham, perhaps Hinderskelfe, Wressle, Nostell, and at several households in the city of York. Private education could be provided in the homes of the aristocracy, in an abbot's household, or in the household of high-ranking ecclesiastical officials. There is no valid way to distinguish, institutionally, between the household education offered in the household of, say, the Percies or the archbishop of York, from the education provided by a rector or a cathedral parson in his household.[71] The differences are primarily ones of social status. Generally, following Nicholas Orme's practice, one may apply the term "private" to these schools in comparison with the more "public" nature of the other schools listed above. Within such a household, the children would have received, besides a grammar education, an education in manners and an entrée into the higher reaches of society. Other schools that also usually offered a grammar education were the monastic schools, the schools attached to cathedral and ancient collegiate foundations, and the town schools, although some reading was often available for beginning pupils. However, when schools are found supported by chantries, gilds, hospitals, almshouses, or from the funds of parishioners, the school could just as easily have been a reading rather than a grammar school. Song schools, on the other hand, could be found within any one of the above institutions or households.

Increasingly during the period under consideration, schools were being

---

astery's tenants. Occasionally fee-paying scholars attended these schools as appears to have happened at Guisborough Priory in the thirteenth century and at many of the nunneries throughout this period. Other monasteries had schools for choristers which might include an education in grammar as well as song. Such was the case at Bridlington, at Durham, and probably at other large monasteries, particularly Benedictine monasteries, about which we have no information. For a discussion of almonry schools, see J. N. Miner, "The Teaching of Grammar in England in the Later Middle Ages" (Ph.D. diss., University of London, 1959), 202-12.

[71] Moran, *Education and Learning*, 10-11.

endowed. Early on, in the twelfth and thirteenth centuries, it was usual for chantry colleges, almshouses, hospitals, monasteries, and individual chantries to be endowed without schools, the schools being added later as a secondary function. By the second half of the fifteenth century and the early sixteenth century, however, it became common for benefactors to stipulate that their gifts were for educational as well as religious purposes. Schools that were thus specifically endowed or founded were almost exclusively grammar schools, although they might admit some elementary pupils. Examples of such foundations include Nottingham, Preston, Hull, East Retford, Lancaster, Pocklington, and Giggleswick. Very few of these newly endowed schools included elementary teaching as part of their statutory requirements, although there were efforts in that direction. Both Archbishop Rotherham and Bishop Stillington, founders, respectively, of Rotherham and Acaster Selby collegiate churches in the second half of the fifteenth century, attempted to endow elementary education, but these foundations did not find many imitators. In the north, the only other endowed schools that explicitly incorporated an elementary education in the curriculum were an endowed writing, grammar, and song school at Brough under Stainmore (Westm.) in 1506, and the grammar and reading schools established and endowed in York, Malton, and Hemsworth by Archbishop Holgate from 1546 to 1548. In this latter case the reading was supplementary, to be carried out by one of the grammar scholars. Although there is no foundation deed extant for Giggleswick, elementary education may have been endowed there, if not in 1507 then in 1545.[72]

The attitude among some of the founders of grammar schools was distinctly unfavorable to elementary pupils. In the 1528 statutes for Sedbergh, the grammarmaster and his advanced students were specifically denied the task of teaching elementary pupils free; they could teach more humble subjects but they must charge a fee; the endowment of the school was not to cover this function. The 1526 foundation of Faversham, in Kent, allowed entrance only to the pupil who could already "say and read his mattins, evensong, seven Psalms, Latin dirge and commendations." While at Rolleston (Staffs.) Bishop Sherburne of Chichester, in his 1524 foundation statutes, allowed elementary teaching only for pupils who were too lazy or stupid to benefit from the grammar curriculum.[73]

Throughout England there are few examples of an elementary school

---

[72] See Appendix B below.

[73] *EYS*, 2:305; A. F. Munden, *Eight Centuries of Education in Faversham*, Faversham Papers, no. 9 (Kent, 1972), 5; Leach, "Some Results of Research in the History of Education in England," *Proceedings of the British Academy* 6 (1913-1914):453; Orme, *ESMA*, 78.

endowed separately from a grammar foundation. Within York diocese there is only one clear instance of an endowed elementary school: the 1342 reading and song school at Sibthorpe College.[74] Another possible example comes from York in 1528 when Thomas Drawswerde, an alderman and carver, left

> iii tenements lyeng in Sancte Martyne parishe . . . for the sustentacion and fynddyng of the chantre preist, to praye for my sall, my wiffes' salles and all Cristen salles, for to syng every nyght *Sancte Deus, Sancte Fortis*, frome the Trinitie Sondaye to Michaelmes, after the discretion of the curate; and for to teche vii childer of the parishe, and to take nothyng of them; and every weike ons to saye *Placebo* and *Dirige*, with *Commendacion* and *Messe* of *Requyem* for all Cristen salles.[75]

Drawswerde did not dwell on the level of education to be offered, but the very fact of endowment, in the absence of any other information, suggests that these scholars may have been learning Latin grammar; and this conclusion is supported by the knowledge of Latin displayed by some of St. Martin's parishioners in the 1550s.[76]

Twelve choristers at York Cathedral and Beverley Minster held endowed positions, and song schools were regularly endowed along with grammar schools, as for example at Rotherham, Acaster Selby, Newark, Brough under Stainmore, and Fotheringhay (Northampts.). A song school was endowed at Middleham in 1478 as part of the larger college chantry foundation.[77] Only at Blackburn (Lancs.) was the possibility of an endowed song school entirely on its own ever raised, and this was to be established only if a grammarmaster could not be found.[78] Thus, evidence for endowment of a school is a strong indicator of a grammar school, although some endowed institutions supported more than one kind of school.

Other arguments for the existence of a grammar school might be proof that the school had its own schoolhouse, was a boarding school, had a large number of students, and/or existed continuously over several centuries. Separate schoolhouses or boarding schools rarely existed for just a reading or song school. Usually a porch, chantry, spare aisle, or transept

[74] See Appendix B below.

[75] BI, Prob. Reg. 9, f. 448; *Test. Ebor.*, 5:267-69.

[76] Claire Cross, "Lay Literacy and Clerical Misconduct in a York Parish during the Reign of Mary Tudor," *York Historian* 3 (1980):10-15.

[77] See Appendix B below.

[78] *VCH, Lancs.*, 2:590.

within the church served for its use. At Durham, a song school for six children was held

> . . . in ye Centorie garth in vnder ye south end of ye church . . . betwixt two pillers adioyning to ye ix alter Dour . . . wch said schoole . . . was verie fynely bourded wth in Rownd about a mannes hight about ye waules and a long deske [did reach] frome one end of ye scoole to thother to laie there bookes vpon, and all the floure Bourded in vnder foote for warmnes, and long formes sett fast in ye ground for ye Children to sitt on. And ye place where ye m^r did sitt & teach was all close bordede both behinde and of either syde for warmnes.[79]

In 1496 Roger Bell, age thirty-eight, recalled attending school in the conventual church at Kirkham Priory within five feet of the font. At Southwell one of the vicars choral was holding a reading or, possibly, a song school in his chantry, thereby disturbing the minster services.[80] The chantry certificates, which sometimes give information as to the existence of a schoolhouse, provide no example of a reading school with a separate building. Nevertheless, some reading and song schools, especially within the larger towns, may have had their own buildings. In 1367 Master Adam, precentor of York, complained of the numerous song schools held in parish churches, houses, and other places in York. And in 1487 Sir William Akers, a priest of York and brother in St. John's gild, bequeathed "a prynted cloth at the oder hows where my childer lernis." Leach suggests that a 1512 reference in Nottingham to "the tofalle [i.e., lean-to] that the chyldern lerne inne" is a reference to an elementary school building.[81]

The need for separate schoolhouses for reading and song schools, however, was not a pressing one, for they usually had smaller numbers of students than did the grammar schools. Most song schools educated between six and sixteen boy choristers, the largest schools being found in the new collegiate foundations of the fifteenth century.[82] There were twelve choristers at York, and this was the usual number for English cathedrals.

---

[79] Fowler, *The Rites of Durham*, 62.

[80] Purvis, *Educational Records*, 11; Leach, *Visitations and Memorials of Southwell Minster*, 67.

[81] BI, Reg. 11 (Thoresby), f. 142v; Prob. Reg. 5, f. 371; *VCH, Notts.*, 2:218.

[82] There were, for example, sixteen choristers at Eton and Winchester, at King's College and at New College. Frank Ll. Harrison, *Music in Medieval Britain* (London, 1958), 32-34. These choirs were often more than twice as large, but the other singers would have been adults. The choir at St. Leonard's, York, in the thirteenth and fourteenth centuries, appears to have had thirty choristers. It is not clear how many of these were children, although fourteen boys with habits were in the grammar school in 1280. Rotha Mary Clay, *The Medieval Hospitals of England* (London, 1909), 26; William Dugdale, *Monasticon Anglicanum*, Vol. 6, pt. 2, new ed. (London, 1830), 607; A. Raine, *History of St. Peter's School, York*, 42.

There were twelve choristers at St. Leonard's Hospital in 1535, ten children singing at Guisborough parish church in 1452 and at Stillington parish in 1505, twenty-four scholars singing at Thirsk in 1521, nine children with surplices at Rudby in 1474, thirteen children singing at Lund in 1520, and six children singing at Topcliffe parish church in 1548.[83] Notices of numbers of reading scholars from York diocese range from a possible thirty at Guisborough in 1452, to eighteen at Howden in 1401, thirteen plus scholars at Wetwang in 1530, nine scholars at Knaresborough in 1522, seven scholars at St. Martin's Coney Street in 1528, and six scholars in 1539 taught by the priest of the Lady gild in Topcliffe.[84] Eileen Power found a similar range in the numbers of girls being educated in the nunneries throughout England, including thirty or forty or more at Polesworth in 1537, twenty-six at St. Mary's Winchester in 1536, about eighteen at Stixwould in 1440, nine at Swaffham Bulbeck in 1483, and only two at Littlemore (1445) and Sopwell (1536).[85] In most of these instances it is not clear whether these are totals or only a proportion of the students. Thirty scholars in the reading schools may not have been unusual. William Barboure, the priest cited earlier for molesting Elizabeth Garrard, taught "the *Pater Noster*, *Ave* and *Credo* with ferther lernyng" to thirty children, while John Lawson estimates the average size for an elementary seventeenth-century village school in the north at twenty or so.[86]

Numbers in the grammar schools were substantially higher—over sixty (and probably over a hundred) at York Cathedral, at least thirty-three at Beverley, seventy both at Winchester and Eton, sixty to eighty at Campden (Gloucs.), fifty at Ipswich, and, by 1548, 100 at Lancaster and 120 at Skipton in Yorkshire.[87] In the 1550s we have notices of seven score scholars

[83] BI, Reg. 16 (Scrope), f. 139; *Test. Ebor.*, 1:262-63 (York); *Valor Ecclesiasticus*, Vol. 5 (London, 1825), 17-18 (St. Leonard's); BI, Prob. Reg. 2, f. 258 (Guisborough); 4, f. 121 (Rudby); 9, f. 124 (Lund), f. 174 (Thirsk); YML, D. & C., L 2/5a, f. 71 (Stillington); Leach, *ESR*, ii:284 (Topcliffe).

[84] BI, Prob. Reg. 2, f. 269v (Guisborough); British Library, MS Cotton Faustina A VI, f. 100v; *EYS*, 2:85 (Howden); YML, D. & C., L 2/5a, f. 155 (Wetwang); *Wills and Administrations from the Knaresborough Court Rolls*, Vol.1, ed. F. Collins, Surtees Society, no. 104 (Durham, 1902), 14-15 (Knaresborough); BI, Prob. Reg. 9, f. 448; *Test. Ebor.*, 5:267-69 (St. Martin's); Leeds Central Library, Archives Department, Richmond Archdeaconry, Will Register 1, 2, 3 & A, ff. 175, 187 (Topcliffe).

[85] Power, *Med. Eng. Nunneries*, 265.

[86] Martin, "Clerical Life in the Fifteenth Century," 359-60; John Lawson, *Primary Education in East Yorkshire, 1560-1902*, East Yorkshire Local History Society, no. 10 (York, 1959), 6.

[87] *Test. Ebor.*, 1:86 (York); BI, Prob. Reg. 2, f. 353v (Beverley); Leach, *Educational Charters and Documents*, 324-25, 412-13 (Winchester and Eton); *VCH, Gloucs.*, 2:28 (Campden); PRO, DL 1/37 c. 16 (Lancaster); Leach, *ESR*, ii:301 (Skipton).

at Blackburn (Lancs.) and Pocklington (East Riding).[88] An average of sixty-six scholars attended the thirteen grammar schools for which enrollment information is given in the chantry certificates.[89] These chantry schools would tend, however, to be smaller than cathedral or town schools. Finding over one hundred students in a grammar school is a common occurrence. The specific figures Nicholas Orme has discovered from the west of England range from 20 to 30 to 120 to 140.[90] In 1473 the grammarmaster at Wollaton was restricted to twenty-six grammar students after complaints from the schoolmaster of Nottingham, while the chantry certificates mention only thirteen children supported freely (others may have paid to attend) at Royston grammar school.[91] Although there are instances of grammar schools with less than twenty students, these were not common. Generally, in an unendowed school a schoolmaster charged an average fee of 8d. per pupil per term or 2s. 8d. a year, calculating four terms in a year per pupil. At this rate a grammarmaster who had no extra income or independent benefice would need at least fifty scholars to provide himself with a modest (£6-7) annual income. The wide range of grammar student attendance a master could expect is well-illustrated in a fifteenth-century Latin grammar manuscript which contains the following dialogue: "Of noumbre, as how many scolers be in the scole? Quot scolares sunt in scola? XX, XL, C et cetera."[92]

While evidence for a large number of pupils is a strong indication of the existence of a grammar school, continuity of a school over several centuries is an equally strong argument. The larger student body, probable need for a separate schoolhouse and boarding facilities, and the reputation of an established school with successful graduates would all contribute to greater continuity for grammar schools than for elementary schools. A quick glance at the documentation on York diocesan schools in Appendix B will substantiate this statement. There is scarcely a school that can be shown to have existed for more than a century that cannot also be shown to have been a grammar school. And in those few instances, e.g., Malton, where a longstanding school cannot be proven absolutely to have been a grammar school, the suspicion is nevertheless that a grammar school was involved and that further findings will bear this out.

[88] PRO, DL 5, f. 271; Leach, "The Foundation and Refoundation of Pocklington Grammar School," 89.

[89] Leach, *ESR*, ii:63, 68, 74, 75, 81, 86, 97, 190, 268, 269, 292, 301. Brisworth, with thirty scholars (p. 152), is omitted since it is not described as a grammar school.

[90] Orme, *ESMA*, 122; Orme, *Education in the West of England*, 21.

[91] Leach, *Visitations and Memorials of Southwell Minster*, 13; Leach, *ESR*, ii:292, 308-309.

[92] Sanford B. Meech, "An Early Treatise in English Concerning Latin Grammar," *University of Michigan Publications in Language and Literature* 13 (Ann Arbor, Mich., 1935), 110.

Among the numerous schools documented for York diocese, there are several that previous historians have found difficult, if not impossible, to classify. One of these is the school at Wakefield. It is an excellent case for testing the various criteria developed in this chapter. The earliest records for the school at Wakefield occur in the manor court rolls from before 1275 to 1338, during which time two different rectors of the school are mentioned. Prior to 1275 and probably later, the rector of the school of Wakefield was one Robert, who has been identified with Robert, son of Roger de Wyrinthorp. If so, he was a substantial landowner and a layman with a family. The schoolmaster [rector of the schools] from 1296 until 1338 was Master John de Wakefield, a chaplain and a man of some wealth and prominence in Wakefield.[93] The school may have continued throughout the fourteenth century. It is claimed that Henry of Wakefield, bishop of Ely in 1373, and Richard Flemyng, bishop of Lincoln in 1420, were educated at Wakefield,[94] although Flemyng, who was born in Crofton near Wakefield, might just as easily have received his grammar education at the school in Crofton.[95] Other prominent individuals who may have received their education at Wakefield include Master Thomas of Wakefield, chancellor of York in 1290; John Forman, vicar of Royston (1450-1502); Thomas Knolles, vicar of Wakefield (1502-1547) and president of Magdalen College (1527-1535); Richard Lyster, chief justice of the King's Bench, 1546; Robert Wakefield, linguist, d. 1537; and Thomas Robertson, vicar of Wakefield (1546-1557) and master of Magdalen College (1526-1534).[96] About 1360 a Wakefield man sent his son away to school at Thornhill (a village about five miles west of Wakefield),[97] an action that is suggestive and could point to a lack of educational facilities in Wakefield at the time. Evidence from wills shows the presence of boy clerks and scholars in Wakefield from 1427 to 1546; one of the wills refers to those who do service in the church and can say their Latin.[98] Although John Walker argues that a school was endowed as part of a chantry both in 1322 and 1480, the records of the chantry foundations

---

[93] John W. Walker, *Wakefield, Its History and People*, 2 vols., 2nd ed. (Wakefield, 1939), 2:363-64.

[94] Ibid., 366.

[95] A grammar school is mentioned at Crofton in 1372. See Appendix B below.

[96] Walker, *Wakefield*, 2:366-67.

[97] *Calendar of Inquisitions Post Mortem*, Vol. 14 (London, 1952), 182.

[98] BI, Prob. Reg. 2, ff. 317, 529; 3, f. 494; 6, ff. 61, 91v, 92, 96; 8, ff. 86-87; 9, ff. 6, 38, 260, 299v, 404; 10, f. 47. The will which mentions the service in Latin (9, f. 38) is printed in *Test. Ebor.*, 5:74. For Thomas Knolles's will in 1546, which also mentions scholars, see Macray, *Register of Magdalen College*, 1:130.

do not prove it.[99] In 1548 the chantry commissioners reported that in the Thurstone chantry one Edward Wood, fifty-two years of age and well-learned, taught youths at Wakefield. Nothing is mentioned regarding his teaching of any Latin grammar although the reference to being well-learned usually implied that capability. In none of the documents is there any mention of a schoolhouse, and it has been suggested that the school met in the north aisle of the parish church.[100]

Neither Leach nor Orme has posited a grammar school at Wakefield. Nevertheless, the evidence is relatively full and sufficiently suggestive to warrant reexamination. The boy clerks knew Latin, although not necessarily Latin grammar. The continuity of the school and the number of possible distinguished graduates argue for its being a grammar school, but the lack of a schoolhouse and failure to mention grammar in the chantry certificates suggest a reading school. The identification of Robert, the first-known schoolmaster, is too tentative to be helpful, but the rector of the school between 1296 and 1338, Master John de Wakefield, was, from his title, possibly, although not necessarily, a university graduate. He was sufficiently wealthy to endow a chantry in 1322. Edward Wood, the master in 1548, was well-learned. He was probably university-trained, as the chantry surveyors were chary in their use of this term, and he may be the same Edward Wood who received his B.A. from Oxford in 1522.[101] It is significant that they record him teaching youths rather than children. The lack of any evidence for a school at Wakefield between 1338 and 1427, as well as the existence of two late fourteenth-century grammar schools (Crofton and Thornhill), each within five miles of Wakefield, argues against Wakefield's school having had an uninterrupted history. However, this same circumstance strongly suggests that the Wakefield school was a grammar school whose absence may have stimulated the emergence of the new foundations. Finally, the most convincing proof of a grammar school at Wakefield is the unthinkable incongruity of having Thomas Knolles and Thomas Robertson, both vicars of Wakefield between 1502 and 1557 and respectively also president and master of Magdalen College, Oxford with its well-known association with grammar teaching, as the resident vicars of a parish without a grammar school.[102] Considering the temper of the times, one would expect that, if Wakefield had been

[99] Walker, *Wakefield*, 2:364-65.

[100] Leach, *ESR*, ii:304; Walker, *Wakefield*, 2:365-66.

[101] Emden, *BRUO, 1501-1540*, 636.

[102] Walker, *Wakefield*, 2:365-67; Robertson was also the author of a collection of four grammatical tracts, printed in Basel in 1532, and one of the commissioners who produced Lily's Latin grammar, 1545. Emden, *BRUO, 1501-1540*, 487-88.

without a grammar school by the beginning of the sixteenth century, either Knolles or Robertson would have founded one.

In this fashion, using the criteria developed in this chapter and following the scanty documentary leads for York diocese, one is able to assemble the data for late medieval education on a more rigorous and disciplined basis. The result, detailed below, is an educational scenario in late medieval York diocese of far greater variety and more remarkable vitality than previously suspected.

CHAPTER 4

The Schools of York Diocese

The methodological considerations of the last two chapters, which help us to distinguish among the variety of schools in late medieval England, are applied throughout this chapter in compiling and analyzing the educational data from York diocese. The resulting chronology of educational growth as well as the combined totals of schools differ substantially from earlier estimates of pre-university education in late medieval England and strongly suggest that the two hundred years prior to the Reformation were a far more important period, educationally, than historians have supposed.

In the course of the last eighty years several lists of medieval schools have been compiled. The first of these, by A. F. Leach, recorded ninety-two schools in York diocese prior to the dissolution of the chantries in 1548. Sixty-three of these were considered by Leach to have been grammar schools, and the remaining twenty-four were a mixture of reading, writing, and song schools.[1] Unless an institution was specifically described as a reading or song school, Leach tended to find a grammar school there. The mere mention of scholars was sufficient evidence for Leach to posit a grammar institution, and only occasionally did he reserve judgment.[2] In addition, Leach assumed that many of the grammar schools were long-lived institutions, evidence for whose foundations was either lost (but very early and usually associated with a collegiate or cathedral church) or, for the fifteenth and sixteenth centuries, traceable to a gild or chantry foundation. Thus, in the case of Doncaster, which had a grammarmaster in 1351 and, so Leach thought, a school again in 1528, Leach was willing

---

[1] For a listing, see J. Hoeppner Moran, "Educational Development and Social Change in York Diocese from the Fourteenth Century to 1548" (Ph.D. diss., Brandeis University, 1975), app. B. There was an earlier attempt by Nicholas Carlisle to enumerate endowed grammar schools in *A Concise Description of the Endowed Grammar Schools in England and Wales*, 2 vols. (London, 1818). Carlisle's list was completely superseded by Leach's work.

[2] Although Leach assumed that it was "only in places where there was a grammar school that scholars are mentioned" (*VCH, Yorks.*, 1:457), he did not consider the scholars at Topcliffe in 1519 grammarians, perhaps because the chantry certificate mentioned only a song school. (*VCH, Yorks.*, 1:478; Leach, *ESR*, ii:284). Nor was he convinced that Wakefield, despite the mention of scholars in 1546, was a grammar school. Again, the chantry certificate did not specify a grammar school at Wakefield. *VCH, Yorks.*, 1:440-41; Leach, *ESR*, ii:304.

to assume that the school had a continuous history, the facts of its foundation being obscured in the pre-1351 mists of Yorkshire history.[3] Despite these problems, Leach uncovered abundant and invaluable material bearing on education in the diocese. His most important contribution was a two-volume collection of documents on Yorkshire schools, which can be supplemented by his articles on schools in the *Victoria History of the Counties of England* for Yorkshire, Lancashire, and Nottinghamshire.

Half a century later, in 1956, P. J. Wallis and W. E. Tate published a register of old Yorkshire grammar schools in which they identified sixty-five pre-Reformation grammar institutions.[4] This was fifteen more than Leach had counted within the county. Unfortunately the documentation of these schools was not always complete, and one is left to wonder where to find information on a schoolmaster at Settrington in 1525 or an educational endowment in 1455 at Cawthorne. A far more accurate, although conservative listing of schools is the more recent one by Nicholas Orme in his *English Schools in the Middle Ages* (1973). Orme finds seventy-three schools in York diocese prior to 1530. Of these, however, only thirty-six are labeled grammar. Orme is cautious and unwilling to posit a grammar school unless the documentation specifically mentions one. Thus, at Kinoulton, Wakefield, Kelk, South Dalton, Guisborough Priory, Pontefract, and Thornhill, where it appears highly likely that grammar schools existed, Orme has resisted applying a label. He is also scrupulous about dates, calling a school continuous only when notice of its existence occurs every twenty-five years. This is a practice that he relaxes in his later book on education in the west of England, but it produces, for the unrevised York lists, some significant underestimates.[5]

Despite problems, these lists provide a superb starting point for the study of grammar education within York diocese. They do not, however, offer much help in evaluating the availability of elementary education. Leach noticed reading, writing, and song schools only inadvertently. Wallis and Tate excluded them from consideration, and Orme, while noting a number of undefined schools, made specific mention of only fifteen elementary schools in York diocese.

Documenting primary schools has been one of the most perplexing

[3] *EYS*, 1:22; *VCH, Yorks.*, 1:446.

[4] P. J. Wallis and W. E. Tate, "A Register of Old Yorkshire Grammar Schools," *The University of Leeds Institute of Education, Researches and Studies*, no. 13 (1956):64-104.

[5] Beverley, for example, which surely had a grammar school continuously throughout the Middle Ages, is listed as providing a grammar education for less than 160 years between 1100 and 1548. Orme, *ESMA*, 296; John Lawson, "Beverley Minster Grammar School in the Middle Ages," *University of Hull Studies in Education* 2 (May 1954):151-67.

problems in medieval (as well as early modern) educational history. The scarcity of references is due to the ephemeral nature of such schools, the lower assessment society usually accords elementary teaching, and the lack of institutionalization that results. Since few teachers of elementary subjects required a separate building or enjoyed an endowment, there is seldom any mention of them in land and tenement grants. The reading teacher, exercising less authority than a grammarmaster, did not often appear in witness lists. Prominent individuals, thinking back on their educational experiences, rarely recalled their early educational years. And if they did, as in the cases of Thomas Cranmer and Roger Ascham, their recollections were sometimes negative. This scarcity of evidence has been responsible for the almost complete neglect that some historians of education have accorded medieval elementary schools.[6]

In fact, historians have known from a variety of scattered documents that elementary schools were not so unusual. Mention of them occurs sporadically in bishops' registers, legal records, chronicles, town archives, and chantry certificates. The already strong evidence for large numbers of grammar schools argues for the availability of a reading education, and the growing number of literate merchants, tradesmen, and yeomen throughout the fifteenth century likewise implies the existence of developing and accessible elementary schooling.[7] Until now, however, the most comprehensive information on medieval elementary education in England has been drawn from the chantry surveys of 1546 and 1548 which cover only schools still in existence at these dates. Nor do they mention primary education with any degree of consistency. The commissioners were mainly interested in continuing the grammar schools, and primary schools, even when noticed, were not recommended for further support.

The best source for medieval elementary schools, many of which were parish schools, are the wills of the period, which, from time to time, also yield new information on the grammar schools. The evidence they provide is cryptic. The will, for example, of John Bowmer in 1492 left a penny "to every child that canne syng" at his funeral. Since he specified that his burial was to take place in Holy Trinity church, Acaster Malbis (W. Riding), I have assumed that a song education was available and have accordingly posited a song school within the parish. In 1480 Henry Huse

---

[6] James Bowen, *A History of Western Education*, Vol. 2 (London, 1975), 163, 322. For Cranmer's and Ascham's reactions, see J. G. Nichols, ed., *Narratives of the Days of the Reformation*, Camden Society, orig. ser., no. 77 (London, 1859), 218, 238-39 and Roger Ascham, *The Schoolmaster* (1570), ed. L. V. Ryan (Ithaca, N.Y., 1967), 79.

[7] J. Hoeppner Moran, "Literacy and Education in Northern England, 1350-1550: A Methodological Inquiry," *Northern History* 17 (1981):1-23.

of Flintham, requesting burial at Flintham, left 2d. to every child reading the lesson and 1d. to every literate child. Clearly a reading education was available at Flintham. Reading schools are suggested when testators mention the scholars of the parish or, prior to 1450, boy clerks.[8] Generally the references to schools, scholars, literate children, children that sing, boy clerks, or schoolmasters are, like the above examples, brief and non-descriptive, but they occur more frequently over an extended period of time than in any other single source.

While, ideally, it would be nice to have fuller references to scholars and schools in order to be sure that our designations of reading and song, in particular, are well-founded, in practice this is not possible. Therefore, in making a determination of the kind of learning involved, I have taken the wills at face value. Mention of scholars, without specific reference to grammar, suggests a reading school. Evidence for children singing suggests a song school. The presence of children or scholars saying *De Profundis* offers evidence for petty learning. It must be emphasized that these are tentative descriptions awaiting further research and greater clarification.

Nor can the wills provide us with a definitive survey of late medieval parish education. The testators whose wills are extant were a very small proportion of the population,[9] and there are some parishes that are unrepresented by a single surviving late medieval will. In addition, the wills survive unevenly throughout the period of this study. Whereas prior to 1390 less than two hundred wills are extant per decade, by 1520 the surviving wills number in the thousands per decade. To a certain degree, therefore, the growing references to elementary parish scholars that are analyzed in this chapter are a reflection of the increase in testamentary sources. But for a variety of reasons, which are detailed in Appendix A, the evidence for expanding elementary education cannot be explained away entirely on the basis of the vagaries of documentation. In the final analysis, by utilizing the prior researches of Leach and Orme in particular and adding the information gathered primarily, but not exclusively from wills, it has been possible to compile a list of schools, documented in Appendix B, that shows a substantial growth in education before 1548. It is a list that may be fairly comprehensive, if only by reason of the high numbers and predictable distribution of these schools throughout York diocese.

The number of grammar schools that can be identified with a degree of certainty as existing in York diocese prior to 1548 is eighty-five. The

---

[8] See Appendix B below.
[9] See Appendix A below.

TABLE 1

First Documented Date for Grammar Schools
in York Diocese, pre-1300 to 1548

Dates	Confirmed or Probable	Possible
11th c.-1300	13	
1301-1350	7	
1351-1400	7	1
1401-1450	5	
1451-1500	8	1
1501-1548	45	4
Total	85	6

SOURCE: Appendix B.

TABLE 2

Number of Grammar Schools in York Diocese
during Each Fifty-Year Period, pre-1300 to 1548

Dates	Confirmed or Probable	Possible
11th c.-1300	13	
1301-1350	15	
1351-1400	19	1
1401-1450	20	
1451-1500	25	1
1501-1548	68	4

SOURCE: Appendix B.

chronological distribution of first references to these schools is displayed
in Table 1 and the totals existing during each fifty-year period are indicated
in Table 2. There may also have been sixteenth-century grammar schools
at Bingley, Boroughbridge, Kippax, and Worsborough as well as a private
grammar school (taught by Nicholas de Ferriby) in the city of York in
1375 and a second grammar school at Ripon in the late fifteenth century.
The evidence for these, however, is thus far inconclusive, and for purposes
of tabulation they have been labeled as possible grammar schools.

We know of only thirteen grammar schools within the diocese before
1300, five of which (the four minster schools and the school at St. Leonard's Hospital, York) appear to have survived continuously throughout
this period. Fifteen grammar schools appear on the record for the first

half of the fourteenth century (seven of them documented for the first time), and this moderate climb in numbers of known grammar schools continues in the second half of the fourteenth century, when another seven new schools come to our attention. Relative to the fourteenth century and in marked comparison with the first half of the sixteenth century, there are few grammar schools whose first mention occurs between 1401 and 1450. Those which do appear for the first time are: 1) Scarborough (1407), 2) Belvoir Castle (1412/13), 3) Rotherham (grammarmaster there c. 1430, not founded until 1483), 4) Sherburn in Elmet (1435), and 5) Hornby (1439). Of these, Scarborough's grammarmaster may have been teaching prior to 1400. By the time he surfaces in the records he was a respected leader in the community, and he died in the 1420s.[10] It is also highly likely that the household grammar school at Belvoir Castle had been in existence some years before. The school at Sherburn, whose grammar status is somewhat tentatively ascribed, may have had its origins as early as 1321. This leaves Rotherham and Hornby (N. Riding), and it is noteworthy that Archbishop Rotherham, in referring to the grammarmaster at Rotherham, emphasized his unexpected arrival.[11] One concludes that the first half of the fifteenth century was not a likely time for grammar school foundations. This situation changes by the second half of the fifteenth century, when first references to schools return to fourteenth-century levels. Eight schools come to our notice for the first time between 1451 and 1500, and at least two sixteenth-century grammar schools (Giggleswick and the school associated with St. John's gild, York) may have been functioning by the late fifteenth century.[12]

New foundations were needed as older grammar schools disappeared. The schools at Kinoulton, Kelk, and South Dalton ran into trouble (in 1289, 1304/5 and 1304-1306 respectively) with ecclesiastical officials who were bent on maintaining a monopoly on grammar teaching within their particular jurisdiction.[13] The boarding school at Guisborough Priory was subjected to criticism by Archbishop Wickwane in 1280 for being a

[10] Arthur Rowntree, ed., *The History of Scarborough* (London, 1931), 139, n 112; BI, Prob. Reg. 2, f. 516.

[11] *EYS*, 2:110. ". . . sine literis stetimus, stetissemusque sic indocti, illiterati, et rudes ad annos plurimos, nisi quod, gracia Dei, vir in gramatica doctus supervenerit, . . ."

[12] *VCH, Yorks.*, 1:460; Edward A. Bell, *A History of Giggleswick School from Its Foundation: 1499-1912* (Leeds, 1912); J. H. Moran, *Education and Learning in the City of York: 1300-1560* (York, 1979), 13.

[13] A. F. Leach, ed., *Memorials of Beverley Minster: The Chapter Act Book*, Vol. 1, Surtees Society, no. 98 (Durham, 1898), 42-43, 48, 114, 169; W. Brown, ed., *The Register of John le Romeyn, Lord Archbishop of York, 1286-1296*, Vol. 1, Surtees Society, no. 123 (Durham, 1913), 285-86.

financial burden on the house. It is likely that this archiepiscopal concern, plus a fire that destroyed much of the priory in 1289, put an end to the school.[14] We do not know why the grammar schools at Dunham (pre-1351), Old Malton (1245, 1391), the Augustinian Friary at York (second half of the fourteenth century), and Hemingbrough (1394) disappear from view. The grammar schools at Crofton (1372) and Thornhill (c. 1361) may have succumbed to competition from the Wakefield school, which itself seems to have experienced a hiatus for nearly eighty years after the plague. We might add to this list the grammar school at East Retford (1318, 1393) which apparently did not continue into the fifteenth century, although it was reestablished in 1518, and the longstanding schools of Pontefract and Nottingham for which there are no references between 1267 and 1437 for Pontefract and none between 1289 and 1382 for Nottingham. These were followed, in the fifteenth century, by the disappearance of two schools along the Yorkshire coast—Scarborough after 1444 and Hedon after 1465—and by the long silence of the Northallerton schools, from 1440 until 1548. There are a sufficient, although not necessarily alarming, number of "lost" grammar schools to give some substance to William Byngham's petition to Henry IV for the training of grammarmasters at Cambridge. Byngham, the rector of St. John Zachary in London, after travelling from Hampton to Coventry and then to Ripon (unfortunately for our purposes transversing only a corner of York diocese) reported that, ". . . your seyd poure besecher hath founde . . . lxx Scoles voide or mo that weren occupied all at ones within l yeres passed, bicause that ther is so grete scarstee of maistres of Gramer, whereof as now ben almost none."[15]

Despite these setbacks York diocese experienced a very slight rise in grammar schools between the late fourteenth century and the first half of the fifteenth century, followed by a modest increase (to twenty-five) by 1500. At the turn of the sixteenth century an explosion in grammar education seems to have taken place, resulting in a dramatic five- to six-fold increase in the evidence for new grammar schools. This striking

[14] W. Brown and A. H. Thompson, eds., *Cartularium Prioratus de Gyseburne*, Vol. 2, Surtees Society, no. 89 (Durham, 1894), 360-62; *Chronicon Domini Walteri de Hemingburgh*, ed. H. C. Hamilton (London, 1849), 2:18-19.

[15] A. F. Leach, *Educational Charters and Documents 598 to 1909* (Cambridge, 1911), 402-403; *CPR*, Henry VI, 3:295. The sentiments behind Bingham's petition were supported in 1447 by four London rectors who asked Parliament "to considre, the grete nombre of gramer Scoles, that somtyme were in divers parties of this Realme, beside tho that were in London, and howe fewe ben in thise dayes, . . ." and to allow the establishment of grammar schools in their parishes. *Rot. Parl.*, 5:137.

expansion of grammar teaching, occurring evenly throughout the fifty-year period, provides substantial support for the thesis, propounded by Lawrence Stone, of an educational revolution in the sixteenth century, although it begins earlier than Stone envisioned, being pre- as well as post-Reformation.[16] Efforts at explanations for such a significant rise in grammar education might include the growth in population of York diocese, which may have begun by the end of the fifteenth century or perhaps a bit earlier. Whether this rise was partially responsible or not, it cannot begin to explain an increase in available grammar institutions of the magnitude of 300 percent. More important was the growing interest and involvement of the laity, especially the gentry and wealthier townspeople. Toward the end of the fifteenth century, they began to found, govern, and send their children to these schools in far greater numbers than previously. They supplemented but did not displace the educational involvement of the Church, which was also on the rise in the fifteenth and sixteenth centuries, as will be argued below in Chapter six. A further factor was the introduction of the printing press and the increased production of grammar texts that resulted. The popularity of works by the new grammarians, especially Stanbridge and Whittinton, and the remarkably large number of editions produced, not only by London presses but also by the presses of York, must have provided a substantial impetus to the founding of new schools, the training of grammarmasters, and the availability of books to students.

Beyond these developments, which will be discussed in greater detail in Chapters six and seven, another, hitherto unnoticed change was taking place. Parish reading and song schools begin to surface in the historical records of the fourteenth century, at least within York diocese. They emerge in increasing numbers in the fifteenth century, numbers that cannot be explained away simply in terms of increased availability of sources.[17] The evidence argues strongly for an educational trend in fifteenth-century York diocese that prepared more and more individuals to the point where they could benefit from and would perhaps demand grammar instruction. Discovery of such a development should not be surprising. It is common sense to suppose that a growth in grammar schools would necessitate the earlier expansion of elementary education, but the magnitude of that growth is remarkable.

The major documentary source for reading schools and parish scholars,

[16] Lawrence Stone, "The Educational Revolution in England, 1560-1640," *Past and Present*, no. 28 (1964):42-47.

[17] See Appendix A below.

the wills of the period, are relatively less abundant for the fourteenth century than for the later period and nonexistent for the thirteenth century. Present findings for the years before 1400 should therefore be viewed as inconclusive (see the discussion in Appendix A). The existence of schools at Yarm (1139-1140), Lancaster (early thirteenth century), Cockermouth (second half of the thirteenth century), Helmesley (thirteenth century), Sheffield (c. 1297), Sherburn in Elmet (1321), Hovingham (c. 1310), Leeds (1341-1400), Fairburn (1348), Barnsley (1370), and possibly Bainton (1375) are known because of the chance mention of a scholar or schoolmaster. Often it is impossible to guess as to whether reading, grammar, or both were taught in these schools. A fourteenth-century school at Sibthorpe is unique in that we know the circumstances of its foundation and endowment as a song and parish reading school.[18] Only occasionally in the fourteenth century does one chance upon a will such as that of John Frankys of Hedon in 1391 who left bequests to the scholars saying their psalters in four separate parishes, or that of the rector of St. Mary's Castlegate in York who left annotated service books to his parish scholars in 1394.[19] Since wills, although not numbering in the thousands, are still numerous at least as early as 1340, the lack of reference to parish scholars before the 1390s is possibly indicative of a relative dearth of parish schools for this earlier period.

Another group of pre-1400 reading schools about which we have fuller information are those held in nunneries, of which there are notices for twelve within York diocese.[20] The presence of young children being brought up in the nunneries comes to our attention through archiepiscopal injunctions against the practice. Despite these injunctions it is likely that convent schools continued to exist, as they brought in needed revenues to these notoriously poor institutions. However, we only have the evidence (such as it is) from Swine and Nun Appleton in the fifteenth century and Esholt in the sixteenth century to support this assumption.[21]

Even without further evidence of the numbers and continuity of convent schools, the known reading schools increase substantially after the turn of

---

[18] A. Hamilton Thompson, "The Chantry Certificate Rolls for the County of Nottingham," *Transactions of the Thoroton Society* 16 (1912):108-19; "Song Schools in the Middle Ages," *Church-Music Society Occasional Papers*, no. 14 (1942):22-23.

[19] BI, Reg. 14 (Arundel), ff. 29v-30; Prob. Reg. 1, f. 81; *Test. Ebor.*, 1:195.

[20] Marrick (1252), Arden (1306), Arthington (1315-1318), Esholt (1315, 1318), Hampole (1313-1314), Keldholme (1318), Moxby (1314), Nunburnholme (1318), Nunkeeling (1314), Sinningthwaite (1315), Rosedale (1315), St. Clement's, York (1310, c. 1312, 1317). See Appendix B below.

[21] Power, *Eng. Med. Nunneries*, 579-80.

TABLE 3

FIRST DOCUMENTED DATE FOR READING SCHOOLS
IN YORK DIOCESE, PRE-1300 TO 1548

Dates	Confirmed or Probable	Possible
11th c.-1300	7	2
1301-1325	13	
1326-1350	2	
1351-1375	2	
1376-1400	9	
1401-1425	8	
1426-1450	19	2
1451-1475	12	1
1476-1500	16	
1501-1525	37	5
1526-1548	36	3
Total	161	13

SOURCE: Appendix B.

NOTE: Includes all schools that have been labeled as "either reading or grammar." Six petty schools (Blyth, 1481; Bolton Percy, 1505; Sutton-on-Derwent, 1505; Flawforth, 1515; Rylstone, 1524; and Kirkby Lonsdale, 1529) have also been included.

the fourteenth century, and especially after 1425. By far the greater proportion of reading schools discovered thus far date from 1401 to 1548. Adding these to the pre-1400 schools just described, we have a total of 161 confirmed or probable and 13 possible reading schools.[22] Tables 3 and 4 provide a distribution of the reading schools, documenting the years in which they first come to our attention (Table 3) and the numbers known within each twenty-five-year period (Table 4).

The first documented date for a reading school comes from the twelfth century when a school at Yarm is mentioned, although it is possible that Bridlington Priory was also providing some elementary instruction in the 1130s. Six known reading schools date from the thirteenth century and twenty-six from the fourteenth. If we disregard the eleven fourteenth-century convent schools, which come to our notice before 1320 and were

[22] The schools which cannot be definitely assigned as either reading or grammar have been included.

TABLE 4

NUMBER OF READING SCHOOLS IN YORK DIOCESE
DURING EACH TWENTY-FIVE-YEAR PERIOD,
PRE-1300 TO 1548

Dates	Confirmed or Probable	Possible
11th c.-1300	7	2
1301-1325	14	2
1326-1350	4	
1351-1375	5	
1376-1400	13	2
1401-1425	12	2
1426-1450	26	4
1451-1475	23	4
1476-1500	24	2
1501-1525	54	8
1526-1548	55	9

SOURCE: Appendix B.

NOTE: Includes all schools which have been labeled as "either reading or grammar." Six petty schools (Blyth, 1481; Bolton Percy, 1505; Sutton-on-Derwent, 1505; Flawforth, 1515; Rylstone, 1524; and Kirkby Lonsdale, 1529) have also been included.

probably functioning earlier, we are left with fifteen new reading schools in the fourteenth century. This is in marked contrast to the notices for fifty-five new reading schools within the fifteenth-century. It is particularly interesting to note that during the first half of the fifteenth century, when grammar education was in the doldrums, reading schools are coming to our attention in greater numbers, increasing from thirteen between 1376 and 1400 to twenty-six between 1426 and 1450. It is, of course, possible that the climb in numbers is artificially produced due to better documentation in the fifteenth century. Nonetheless, the will evidence is plentiful in the 1390s and substantial in the 1340s. Thus, the pattern of schools discovered may represent a real increase in the availability of elementary education.

In the last quarter of the fifteenth century sixteen new references to reading schools surface. Since several of the late fifteenth-century reading schools had appeared earlier, the number of existing schools climbs from twelve between 1401 and 1425 to twenty-three from 1476 to 1500. In all, we know of forty-one different reading schools throughout the diocese in the second half of the fifteenth century in comparison with thirty in the first half of the century, an increase of 37 percent. This result is far less likely to be due to documentary distortion since the number of extant wills rises at a much slower rate throughout the fifteenth century.[23] One can conclude, then, that the total number of reading schools functioning in York diocese increased throughout the fifteenth century, with the biggest jump, a jump of 125 percent, occurring in the second quarter of the century. By 1500 there were, roughly, double the numbers known to have existed at the end of the fourteenth century.

By 1548 those numbers had doubled again. As Tables 3 and 4 illustrate, between 1501 and 1548 the number of first references to reading schools rises to seventy-three. The total number of schools functioning is ninety-four, fifty-four in the first quarter of the sixteenth century and fifty-five in the second quarter, with evidence for continuity in fifteen instances. On the basis of these statistics, it is understandable how Matthew Wytham of Brettanby, who died somewhere in York diocese in 1545, might have thought he could bequeath pennies to scholars at his funeral regardless of where he was buried.[24] Wytham may have been overly optimistic, however, for even with the impressive growth in schools documented here, less than 25 percent of the approximately seven hundred parishes in York diocese would have had reading schools at one time or another in the late Middle Ages, while at his death, as far as we now know, only one-third of those would have then had scholars in the parish.

In addition to the grammar and reading schools, references have been noted to a total of eighty-four song schools prior to 1548. Except for the schools attached to the collegiate or cathedral foundations of York, Beverley, Ripon, Southwell, Howden, and Sibthorpe as well as the song schools in St. Leonard's Hospital, the peculiar of Northallerton and Pontefract Castle, all other references to song schools are post-1400. This lack of evidence for song schools in parish churches prior to 1400 (or even 1425) agrees well with the history of the use of polyphony in the Ordinary of the mass and of choral and antiphonal performances.[25] Table

[23] See Appendix A.

[24] James Raine, ed., *Wills and Inventories from the Registry of the Archdeaconry of Richmond*, Surtees Society, no. 26 (Durham, 1853), 55-57.

[25] Frank Ll. Harrison, *Music in Medieval England* (London, 1958), chap. 4, esp. p. 197. Harrison's evidence is primarily post-1450, but John Wyclif's earlier condemnation of "deschaunt, countre note, and orgon" in church argues for the increased popularity of liturgical polyphony by the end of the fourteenth century. John Wyclif, "Of Feigned Contemplative Life" in *Fourteenth Century Verse and Prose*, ed. K. Sisam (Oxford, 1921), 123-25. Evidence from the Old Hall manuscript shows that polyphonic choral settings for the mass were being composed

TABLE 5

SONG SCHOOLS IN YORK DIOCESE, PRE-1300 TO 1548

Dates	First Notice of a Song School	Existing Song Schools
11th c.-1300	5	5
1301-1350	2	7
1351-1400	2	9
1401-1450	8	16
1451-1500	30	50
1501-1548	37	47
Total	84	

SOURCE: Appendix B.

5 shows the extent to which it became more common, in the fifteenth century, for the average parish church to have a choir, however small, and a song school. Churches with either reading or grammar schools often also had a song school, although many parishes appear to have had song schools independent of any accompanying elementary or grammar education.[26] The implication of Thomas Middleton's will of 1492, which requested burial wherever God disposed but assumed that there would be children in surplices there, is that song schools were commonplace in the parish churches of his time.[27]

The extent to which historians have underestimated the number and growth of schools, particularly elementary schools, in the century and a

---

for the royal chapel, perhaps between 1370 and 1420. Richard H. Hoppin, *Medieval Music* (New York, 1978), 509. The evidence for song scholars in some parishes in the first half of the fifteenth century suggests that polyphonic music may have been sung at mass, with boys, in the parish churches before the second half of the fifteenth century. Table 5 and Appendix B below. At their simplest, these parish choirs may have sung plainsong while a clerk or two sang faburden. For more on the parish choirs, see Nicholas Temperley, *The Music of the English Parish Church*, 2 vols. (Cambridge, 1979), 1:7-10, 2:3, 21-25.

[26] See Appendix B below, passim. For confirmation of the growing number and significance of parish song schools by the second half of the fifteenth century, see Roger Bowers, "Choral Institutions within the English Church—Their Constitution and Development 1340-1500" (Ph.D. diss., University of East Anglia, 1975), 1006-1007.

For example, the churchwarden's accounts of St. Michael's Spurriergate in York (1518-1528, 1537-1548) show continuing expenses for a songmaster, song books, surplices ("yᵉ chyldren geyre or albys"), and choristers. There is no evidence whatsoever for other additional activities. YML MS Add 220/2; BI, PR Y/MS/3.

[27] BI, Prob. Reg. 5, f. 422.

half before the Reformation is especially apparent when one looks at the city of York. York is also a good case study because it illustrates the severe limits of the educational monopolies that some of the higher clergy tried to exercise.[28]

Previous historians have identified, at various times in medieval and early Tudor York, a theological, grammar, and song school at the cathedral; a song and grammar school at St. Leonard's Hospital; a reading and grammar school founded by Archbishop Holgate in 1546; a school at St. Mary's Abbey (perhaps thirteenth century in origin); a thirteenth-century synagogue (*schola*) for the Jewish community which surely housed a Hebrew school; parish schools at St. Michael-le-Belfrey, St. Martin's, Coney Street, and Holy Trinity, King's Court; a 1546 school in the Merchants' Hall; schools of philosophy and/or theology at the Franciscan, Dominican, and Augustinian friaries; and a school for girls at St. Clement's nunnery.[29] There are, in addition, scattered references in the published literature to a late fourteenth-century school at Holy Trinity Hospital, Fossgate, which did not exist.[30] This seemingly full catalog of educational facilities for the city actually reflects perhaps one-half of the available resources.

[28] The following discussion of education in the city of York is based, to a large extent, upon Moran, *Education and Learning*, 5-14, 18-19, 26-27.

[29] For the schools at the cathedral and for Archbishop Holgate's foundations, see *VCH, Yorks.*, 1:416-23, 474-75; *EYS*, 1:1-80b; Angelo Raine, *History of St. Peter's School, York, A.D. 627 to the Present Day* (London, 1926?); E. N. Jewels, *A History of Archbishop Holgate's Grammar School, York 1546-1946* (York, 1963); G. E. Aylmer and Reginald Cant, eds., *A History of York Minster* (Oxford, 1977), 67-73, 200-203. The evidence for a school at St. Mary's Abbey is in Raine, *History of St. Peter's School*, 36-37. For the schools at St. Leonard's Hospital, see *VCH, Yorks.*, 3:339-43; Raine, *History of St. Peter's School*, 42; *Valor Ecclesiasticus temp. Henr. VIII*, Vol. 5 (London, 1825), 17-18. The synagogue school is noted by R. Barrie Dobson, *The Jews of Medieval York and the Massacre of March 1190* (York, 1974), 45. For the parish schools and the school at Merchants' Hall, see D. M. Palliser, *Tudor York* (Oxford, 1979), 174-75. Power, *Med. Eng. Nunneries*, 580, argues convincingly that St. Clement's had a school for girls, but that possibility is carried to extremes by W. E. Tate, *A. F. Leach as a Historian of Yorkshire Education* (York, 1963), 38. For information on the friary schools, see, *inter alia*, Francis Roth, *The English Austin Friars*, 2 vols. (New York, 1966), passim; William J. Courtenay, *Adam Wodeham: An Introduction to His Life and Writings* (Leiden, 1978), 45-49; A. G. Little, "Educational Organization of the Mendicant Friars in England," *TRHS*, new ser., 8 (1894):49-70; L. M. Goldthorp, "The Franciscans and Dominicans in Yorkshire," *YAJ* 32 (1935-1936), 264-320, 365-428; Bede Jarrett, *The English Dominicans* (London, 1921), esp. 49-64; Maura O'Carroll, "The Educational Organization of the Dominicans in England and Wales 1221-1348: A Multidisciplinary Approach," *Archivum Fratrum Praedicatorum* 50 (1980):23-62; and William Hinnebusch, *The History of the Dominican Order*, Vol. 2 (New York, 1973), chaps. 1-3.

[30] *VCH, Yorks.*, 3:350; Maud Sellers, ed., *York Memorandum Book*, 2 vols., Surtees Society, nos. 120, 125 (Durham, 1912-1915), 2:lxv. The original statutes read, "Item volumus et ordinamus, quod in dicto Hospitali sint tresdecim pauperes et debiles personae continuè et

St. Peter's school at the minster, York's best-known grammar school, catering, probably, to over a hundred of the better students from the north of England, has a history from the twelfth century to 1548 that is relatively well-documented and adequately summarized elsewhere.[31] But St. Peter's was not the only grammar school in the city. There was a longstanding grammar school of royal foundation at the hospital of St. Leonard's, the statutes of which provided for a master, thirteen chaplain-brethren, up to four secular priests, eight sisters, thirty choristers, two schoolmasters (in grammar and song), an unknown number of lay *conversi*, and 206 sick poor folk. Beneath the infirmary, in a building called the "Barnhous," space was also provided for nursing abandoned infants and for bringing up orphans and other indigent children. The grammar school educated the choristers, but the school was also open to other children, some of whom were recruited from the orphanage on the hospital grounds and some of whom may have come from the hospital's extensive manors in the north. Sometime prior to 1341 the chancellor of York Cathedral made an effort to suppress the school. In that year the dean and chapter received an order from Edward III not to impede William de Marton in the management of St. Leonard's grammar school which, it was stated, "has been in existence time out of mind."[32] The school continues to emerge intermittently from the records in 1393, 1448, 1491, and 1535, surviving until the dissolution of the hospital in 1539. Although we learn very little about the school itself from these references, we do discover details about the schoolmasters, one of whom, Nicholas de Ferriby in 1393, had been a fellow at Cambridge and was a member of a family prominent among the ranks of late fourteenth-century diocesan and cathedral clergy.[33] Twenty years earlier, in 1375, the same Nicholas de Ferriby was teaching grammar

---

personaliter commorantes, et duo pauperes clerici, scolas exercentes, . . ." William Dugdale, *Monasticon Anglicanum*, Vol. 6, pt. 2, new ed. (London, 1830), 737; BI, Reg. 11 (Thoresby), f. 169. See also Joyce W. Percy, ed., *York Memorandum Book*, Vol. 3, Surtees Society, no. 186 (Gateshead, 1973), 145 and Leach, *ESR*, ii:283.

[31] Moran, *Education and Learning*, 5-8. See also Raine, *History of St. Peter's School*.

[32] *VCH, Yorks.*, 3:336-44; Dugdale, *Monasticon Anglicanum*, Vol. 6, pt. 2, 607; Rotha Mary Clay, *The Medieval Hospitals of England* (London, 1909), 26, 156; *Valor Ecclesiasticus*, 5:17-18; Raine, *St. Peter's School*, 42.

[33] This is probably the same Nicholas de Ferriby who became canon of York in 1379 and died in 1404. The dates argue for the identification. For information on him and other Ferribys, see Emden, *BRUC*, 225; Emden, *BRUO*, 2:678-79 where Emden appears to have conflated two William de Ferribys, one of whom was the Master of St. Leonard's for a brief period in the 1390s. YML, D. & C., L 2/4, ff. 67-68, 135v-36; *Test. Ebor.*, 1:103-105; R. Barrie Dobson, "The Later Middle Ages, 1215-1500," in *A History of York Minster*, ed. Aylmer and Cant, 60; YML, D. & C., H 1/3a, ff. 70 seq.

within the capitular jurisdiction in the city, at which time the chapter threatened to have him excommunicated if he did not relinquish his school. It was argued that Master Ferriby was furnishing a pernicious example, causing scandal to many and disturbing and gravely prejudicing the chancellor and grammarmaster of the cathedral.[34] One suspects that he must have been competing most effectively with St. Peter's school. It has been assumed, because of Ferriby's later connection with St. Leonard's, that this was a further effort to suppress the hospital school, but there is no strong evidence behind this assumption. Ferriby may well have been conducting his own private grammar school elsewhere in the city, perhaps even under the protection of his brother, John de Ferriby, prebendary, master of the fabric, and later subtreasurer of the cathedral.

For all its vigilance the cathedral chapter did not police its own ranks very effectively. By 1300 it had long been customary for the residentiary canons and other dignitaries to provide education within their households, among which the household "school" of the treasurer was especially prominent.[35] According to R. B. Dobson, "Northern knights and even bishops were prepared to pay considerable sums to secure the admission of the sons of their relatives and friends to the *familia* of a residentiary canon; and it was in this way that many Yorkshire boys began their own clerical careers."[36] This was undoubtedly the intent of Archbishop Melton when, in 1335, he handed his young nephews, Thomas and John, over to the care of William Yafford, a canon of York.[37] In 1411 a visitation of the cathedral by the dean and chapter reported that grammar and song schools were also being carried on by the inferior ministers, most probably the

---

[34] YML, D. & C., H 1/3a, f. 122; *EYS*, 1:24-25.

[35] In 1402 John Depeden, knight and Lord of Healaugh, left £20 to John, the son of John FitzRichard and requested that he be placed in the custody of John de Newton, treasurer of York, until he learned "aliqualiter intelligere et scribere." BI, Prob. Reg. 3, f. 88v; *Test. Ebor.*, 1:296. The 1432 will of Robert Wolveden, treasurer of York, left goods to all the gentlemen's sons committed to him for education. YML, D. & C., L 2/4, f. 235; *Test. Ebor.*, 3:92. Another treasurer, William Poteman, mentions, in 1492, the sons of gentlemen who had been with him from less than four to as many as eight years. BI, Reg. 23 (Rotherham), f. 352; *Test. Ebor.*, 4:82. About 1488 the rector of Leconfield, Master John Smerte, requested that his nephew be tutored and governed by William Sheffield, official of the court of York. This is probably the same William Sheffield who was soon to become treasurer and later dean. BI, Prob. Reg. 5, f. 372; Emden, *BRUC*, 521-22.

[36] Dobson, "The Later Middle Ages, 1215-1500," 104.

[37] BI, Reg. 9B (Melton), f. 541v; cited in L. H. Butler, "Archbishop Melton, His Neighbors and His Kinsmen," *J. Eccl. Hist.* 2 (1951):66. The importance of the household of the canons is emphasized in the 1290 statutes of the cathedral where it is stated that their households are extraparochial and come under the direct control of the canon or his deputy. *The Statutes of the Cathedral Church of York*, 2nd ed. (Leeds, 1900), 20-21.

parsons and vicars choral, without license from the chancellor or precentor.[38] This is also suggested in the will of William Staneley (proved in 1396) who left 2d. to every boy "moranti in orto magistri mei," his master being Thomas de Garton, one of the cathedral parsons.[39] These sorts of educational arrangements appear to have continued in the fifteenth century.[40]

Occasionally a nonresident rural rector living within the city or a city cleric is noted as having maintained a household of boys, and private chaplains, either on their own or within the household of the wealthier merchant and gentle families, acted as tutors. William Burgh, chaplain, in his will of 1458 left 13s. 4d. to Robert his cousin, who was staying "ad magistrum" Richard Wetwang, clerk. Wetwang was the rector of Stokesley, but probably maintained a household in the city of York.[41] In 1480 William Akers, priest, left "to Malde Bowmer a prynted cloth at the oder hows where my childer lernis." In 1525 William Smyth, notary of York, requested that "Sir John Conyers prest haye the guyding of my thre sones . . . and he to bring theym up in lernyng to they may come to yere of discrescion," while the 1535 will of Richard Oliver, rector of All Saints, North Street, makes it clear that he kept several boys in his household.[42] The extent to which Latin grammar was imparted in any of these cases must have fluctuated greatly depending upon the ability and expectations of the pupils as well as the teachers, but one ought not to underestimate the potential of even the most informal household education. A case in point, which has already been mentioned in Chapter three, is that of William Holbek, a vicar choral within the cathedral whose situation was brought to the attention of the capitular court in 1462. Holbek had been living for seven years with Agnes Smyth, a former servant, during which time he had taught her letters so that Agnes was described as "bene literata." What interested the court was not the fact that he was teaching her Latin, however, but rather that he had had several children by her.[43]

[38] YML, D. & C., L 2/3a, ff. 36-37.

[39] YML, D. & C., L 2/4, f. 112.

[40] Later cathedral parsons sometimes left service books to their boys. In 1452 Robert Buktrout, a parson in York Minster, left his best portable breviary to William Robynson, his boy; and in 1475 Richard Clynt, another Minster parson, left his parchment portifor to his boy George. YML, D. & C., L 2/4, ff. 270, 331v.

[41] BI, Prob. Reg. 2, ff. 365, 484; Test. Ebor., 2:248-49. This may have been the situation with Nicholas de Ferriby, vicar of Weston, who was teaching grammar in York in 1375. See note 33 above.

[42] BI, Prob. Reg. 5, f. 371; YML, D. & C., L 2/5a, f. 142; Test. Ebor., 5:207-208; BI, Reg. 28 (Lee), ff. 168-69; Claire Cross, "York Clerical Piety and St. Peter's School on the Eve of the Reformation," The York Historian 2 (1978):5.

[43] J. S. Purvis, A Medieval Act Book (York, 1943), 49.

In 1528 another threat to the cathedral chapter's asserted monopoly over grammar education came from a newly endowed school at St. Martin's Coney Street. The school seems to have already been in existence, on an informal, fee-paying basis for over a century, for in 1408 John Wardell, citizen of York, left 1d. to each of the seven boys reciting psalms in St. Martin's. In 1432 bequests were left to the small clerks of St. Martin's, and in 1452 Robert Belton, an apothecary of York, left 26s. 8d. to be distributed, among others, to the poor scholars at St. Martin's.[44] Such a school could not have escaped the notice of the dean and chapter since the parish was under capitular jurisdiction and subject to visitations throughout the fifteenth century.[45] There are two plausible explanations for the failure of the dean and chapter to complain. First, it is possible that no Latin grammar was taught in the school, although it seems unlikely that an endowed parish school would not have provided at least the rudiments of Latin grammar. Subsequent testimony by several parishioners of St. Martin's who were, they deposed, more familiar with the Latin of the services than was the vicar himself, suggests that Latin grammar was taught in the school.[46] It is more probable that the dean and chapter did not feel they could interfere in a parish school that explicitly catered only to its own parishioners. An earlier case which suggests the importance of this distinction occurred in 1289 when the schoolmaster of Nottingham appealed to Archbishop John le Romeyn because a grammar school at Kinoulton was drawing students from beyond its parish boundaries, thereby infringing the right of Nottingham's school.[47] It would have ill-behooved the chapter to quarrel with parochial grammar schools since, as early as

---

[44] In 1528, Thomas Drawswerde, alderman and carver of York, left 4d. to the scholars of St. Martin's parish and endowed a chantry priest "to teche vii childer of the parishe, and to take nothyng of them." BI, Prob. Reg. 9, f. 448; *Test. Ebor.*, 5:267-69. For earlier references to the scholars at St. Martin's, see BI, Prob. Reg. 2, f. 577v; BI, Prob. Reg. 3, f. 334; YML, D. & C., L 2/4, f. 254; BI, Prob. Reg. 2, f. 315.

[45] For the visitations of St. Martin's see YML, D. & C., L 2/3a, ff. 11v-12, 20, 40.

[46] Claire Cross, "Lay Literacy and Clerical Misconduct in a York Parish during the Reign of Mary Tudor," *The York Historian* 3 (1980):10-15.

[47] Brown, *Register of John le Romeyn*, 1:285-86. It is also possible that the common law was beginning to impinge on the educational monopolies of the Church. Carlo Cipolla cites the 1441 case of a schoolmaster at Gloucester (appointed by Llanthony Abbey) who sought damages against a rival teacher. The common lawyers rejected the suit, remarking that teaching "is a virtuous and charitable thing to do, helpful to the people, for which he cannot be punished by our law." Carlo Cipolla, *Literacy and Development in the West* (Harmondsworth, 1969), 44. For a full text of the case and an extended discussion of the lessening of ecclesiastical control over education, see J.E.G. de Montmorency, *State Intervention in English Education* (Cambridge, 1902), chaps. 1, 2, and appendix. There is no modern treatment of the relationship between common law, the Church, and educational monopolies.

the tenth century, an English ecclesiastical council had decreed that priests should "always have in their houses (or churches) a school such as school-masters have and, if any devout person wishes to entrust his little ones to them for instruction, the priest ought to receive them with the greatest pleasure and teach them kindly."[48] The *Novum Registrum* (1440) of Lincoln Cathedral makes it clear that parish schools in that diocese were exempted from the chancellor's (and the chapter's) monopoly.[49]

In the sixteenth century the grammarmaster of St. Peter's felt much less compunction with regard to a grammar school maintained by St. John's gild. The school, which may have functioned from the 1480s and probably attracted scholars from more than one parish, drew a complaint from Master Christopher Holdsworth in 1531 that grammar was being taught there, but there is no evidence that the chapter took action. The fact that Robert Morres (or Morris), the priest named by Holdsworth, was subsequently elected by city officials in 1555 to conduct a school on Ousebridge suggests that he continued to teach within the city after 1531.[50] Finally, in 1546, at a time when St. Peter's school may have been experiencing difficulties, if in fact it was functioning at all, Archbishop Holgate established a new grammar school, headed by a master who was to be trained to teach Hebrew and Greek as well as Latin. The school was set up as a corporate body "in dede and in name," explicitly independent of any capitular control and capable of engaging in legal actions on its own.[51] Such an institutionally independent school was new to the city of York but recalls the earlier grammar foundations at Winchester and Eton and, in York diocese, the schools at Acaster and Rotherham.

[48] Leach, *Educational Charters and Documents*, 36. "Presbiteri semper debent in domibus suis ludimagistrorum scholas habere, et si quis devotus [homo] parvulos suos eis ad instructionem concedere velit, illos quam libentissime suscipere et benigne docere debent." David Wilkins, ed., *Concilia Magnae Britanniae et Hiberniae*, 4 vols. (London, 1737), 1:270.

[49] "Idem etiam Cancellarius scholas omnes grammaticae in civitate et comitatu Lincolniensi pro suo libero conferat arbitrio; scholis cantus, et illis quae sunt in praebendis, ac aliis quas tenent ecclesiarum rectores, vel caeteri curati, aut eorum parochiales clerici, in suis parochiis pro suis parochianis in fide et literatura erudiendis, duntaxat exceptis." Christopher Wordsworth, ed., *Statuta Ecclesiae Cathedralis Lincolniensis* (London, 1873), 24.

[50] J. S. Purvis quotes from the "Office Book" of 1531. "Mr. Chris. Holdsworth ludi literarii Magister Ebor. contra do. Robt. Morres capellanum gilde S. Johannis Baptiste eiusdem civitatis vocatum Talyer Prest . . . quare non debet eidem silencium impori ne doceat grammaticam." Purvis, *Educational Records* (York, 1959), 4, n 1. The school which William Akers was teaching in 1480 may have been associated with the same gild, since Akers includes the brethren of St. John's among his legatees. BI, Prob. Reg. 5, f. 371; see above, p. 86. For the school on Ousebridge, see York City Archives, York Corporation Records House Book, XXI, ff. 20v, 108v; *VCH, Yorkshire: City of York*, 124, 516; *York Civic Records*, 5:97-98.

[51] Deed of Foundation of the Free School of Robert Holgate, York (Archbishop Holgate Society Rec. Soc., no. 1, n.d. [1948?]). One of the originals is in the York City Archives.

In addition to the various grammar facilities available within York, there were a number of hitherto unnoticed song and reading schools. Ten scholars are mentioned at St. Michael le Belfrey parish at the turn of the sixteenth century. St. Mary's Castlegate would appear to have had a parish school from the late fourteenth century up to at least the mid-fifteenth century; while the parish of St. Sampson and St. William's chapel on Ousebridge each had sixteenth-century schools. The chantry school at St. Martin, Coney Street, already mentioned as a probable grammar school, undoubtedly also provided a reading and possibly a song education.[52] There was a sixteenth-century song school at St. Michael, Spurriergate and possibly also at St. John del Pyke parish church. Song and/or reading schools were held throughout the fifteenth century at Holy Trinity in King's Court; St. Olave; St. Martin, Micklegate; St. Michael, Ousegate; and possibly also at All Saints, North Street.[53]

[52] In 1496 Isabella Saxton, widow of Master John Saxton, left 12d. to be divided among the "clericulis" of St. Michael's, while John Petty, mayor of York, mentioned ten scholars there in 1508. YML, L 2/4, f. 323; L 2/5a, ff. 76v-77. John de Pykering, rector of St. Mary's Castlegate (d. 1394), left "duos libros notatos pro ministerio puerorum, unum pro matutinis et vesperis, et alterum pro missa in choro ecclesiae predictae." BI, Prob. Reg. 1, f. 81; *Test. Ebor.*, 1:195. The 1447 will of Frater Nicholas Wartre, rector of St. Mary's, left 4d. to each boy in a surplice who ministered in the parish services. BI, Prob. Reg. 2, f. 268v; see also f. 272. In 1508 William Chimney, alderman and draper of York, left 1d. to each scholar at St. Sampson's. BI, Prob. Reg. 8, f. 3. The teacher of these scholars may have been Henry Smyth, who, in 1521, was granted the clerkship of St. William's Chapel on Ousebridge with the proviso that he teach boys. He was described as formerly clerk of the parish of St. Sampson's. *York Memorandum Book*, 3:239. Henry Smyth was still the clerk of St. William's in 1541 when he promised to "maik a showe of syngyng and other mellody after the best facon as he could devyse on the leyds of the said chappell." *York Civic Records*, 4:60. He probably taught song as well as reading. For the school at St. Martin's, Coney Street, see above, pp. 85, 109.

[53] The 1503 will of Thomas Herdsong of York left funds to find a mass every Saturday to be sung with note by men, children and organs, and to pay the parish clerk 8d. and the chantry priest 6s. 4d. for this service. BI, Prob. Reg. 9, f. 5. Early churchwarden's accounts for St. Michael's show annual expenses to the children for obits and for their surplices. They also include expenses for "ye verse boke," for "wryttyng of a sequence," for writing a mass, for mass books, coucher books, a legend of saints, a Bible, a processional, a hymnal, and other books as well as for the organist and organ repairs. YML MS Add 220/2; BI, PR Y/MS/3 (Churchwarden's Accounts, St. Michael's Spurriergate, 1518-1528, 1537-1548). In the 1430s both John Cartwright and his widow left pennies to the little clerks ministering daily in Holy Trinity, King's court. BI, Prob. Reg. 3, ff. 387v, 480. For 1463, see the wills of William Touthorp and his widow who both left pennies to the small boys with surplices at Holy Trinity. BI, Prob. Reg. 2, ff. 485, 599. For St. Olave's, see BI, Prob. Reg. 2, ff. 365, 395v-96, 597; 4, f. 26. In 1435 Thomas Pynchebek, chaplain, left 2d. to each "clericulo" who continued to sing in St. Martin's, Micklegate. BI, Prob. Reg. 3, f. 445. See also ibid., f. 307 and 2, f. 439v. The 1488 will of Nicholas Vicars, grocer of York, left 5s. to all the small clerks in St. Michael's, Ousebridge. BI, Prob. Reg. 5, f. 355v. For information on All Saints, North Street, see p. 108 above. St. John del Pyke is discussed in footnote 54 below.

Elementary education was not confined to the parishes. Twelve small clerks are mentioned at Holy Trinity Priory in 1439. The nunnery of St. Clement, just south of the city walls, may have conducted a school for young girls throughout our period and until its dissolution, although clear evidence for young girls at the convent comes only from the first half of the fourteenth century. There may have been a reading school at the Merchants' Hall in 1546. Both St. Leonard's Hospital and the school founded by Archbishop Holgate in 1546 made provision for reading, while St. Leonard's included a song school, and some of the Holgate scholars were also trained to sing in the choir.[54] In addition to the song schools already mentioned, in 1367 Master Adam, the cathedral precentor, cited (and Archbishop Thoresby threatened to censure) the numerous chaplains, holy water carriers, and others who were keeping song schools in the city and ignoring the cathedral monopoly on teaching boys singing. But by 1411 song schools were being conducted without license even by the personnel of the cathedral itself.[55]

The city of York was not bereft of centers for higher education either. The minster theological lectures continued at least throughout the fourteenth century, and there is evidence that the friaries continued to maintain high educational standards within their cloistral schools. Although I have found no evidence for the educational activities of the Carmelites, the Dominican priory may have had a school of theology and most probably a school of philosophy which rotated periodically to other convents.[56] It certainly had thirty-four cells, each with a study, all of which were burned in 1456.[57] York was one of seven custodial schools for English Franciscans

---

[54] For Holy Trinity Priory, see BI, Prob. Reg. 3, f. 590; 2, f. 168. For St. Clement's nunnery, see Power, *Med. Eng. Nunneries*, note B: School Children in Nunneries, esp. p. 580; *VCH, Yorks.*, 3:129; W. Brown and A. H. Thompson, eds., *The Register of William Greenfield, Lord Archbishop of York, 1306-1315*, Vol. 2, Surtees Society, no. 149 (Durham, 1934), 80-81, 126-27. For a school at Merchants' Hall, see Palliser, *Tudor York*, 174-75. St. Leonard's Hospital, which provided a grammar education for the children in its orphanage, would have had to provide reading training. It also had a song school, a songmaster being mentioned in 1280, thirty choristers in 1376 and twelve choristers in 1535. Raine, *St. Peter's School*, 42; *VCH, Yorks.*, 3:340; *Valor Ecclesiasticus*, 5:17-18. Archbishop Holgate's foundation freed both the grammarmaster and his usher from teaching reading, turning that task over to one of the other scholars. Foundation Deed, f. 8v. Some of Holgate's schoolboys sang in the choir at St. John del Pyke and may have attended a song school there. Ibid., f. 4v.

[55] BI, Reg. 11 (Thoresby), f. 142v; *EYS*, 1:22-23; YML, D. & C., L 2/3a, ff. 36-37.

[56] Hinnebusch, *The History of the Dominican Order*, 2:chap. 2.

[57] Moran, *Education and Learning*, 25-26. In 1456 Archbishop William Booth granted forty days of indulgence to all who helped the York Dominicans, whose "cloister and building have been destroyed by fire" together with "books, chalices, vestments and other goods, the jewels deposited in the buildings and thirty-four cells and *studia*." BI, Reg. 20 (W. Booth), f. 187;

and, because of overcrowding at the university convents by the second quarter of the fourteenth century, the custodial schools probably grew in importance.[58] That the Franciscan school continued into the fifteenth century is attested by reference to a master of the school of the Grey Friars in the will of George Darell of Sessay, esquire, who left him a chair and two benches for his chamber in 1433. Fifty years later, Brother Robert Bewchampe, the master of the students of the Friars Minor in York, was authorized as a preacher within the diocese. According to A. G. Little, the Franciscan custodial school would have been theological, one of seven designated for study before candidates progressed to the *studium generale* of the universities. Little has argued that seculars were admitted to these schools, but there is no proof of such a practice at York.[59]

Fuller information survives for the Augustininan friary, which was founded around 1271, quite possibly by Giles of Rome, a leading philosopher and theologian of the order. There was a close connection between Giles, the Maulay family of Yorkshire, and the Austin friars of York, as Giles of Rome dedicated two of his philosophical works to Sir Stephen Maulay, while Lady Margaret Maulay was buried in the York Austin Friary.[60] The friary was designated as a *studium concursorium*, an ambiguous term that seems to indicate it had a school of both philosophy and theology. In the second half of the fourteenth century it had two masters, which would suggest a *studium* of the highest level.[61] Song, grammar (more remedial than beginning), and logic were also taught within the friary to the novices and younger students: the latter may have entered the convent at an age as early as ten, but were expected to have already acquired the rudiments of reading, writing, and liturgical singing and to have mastered their primer and psalter.[62] In addition, no one was allowed

James Raine, ed., *The Fabric Rolls of York Minster*, Surtees Society, no. 35 (Durham, 1859), 240. The friary had further problems in 1474 when the master general ordered the prior to expel certain brethren, "fratres malae vitae de dicto conventu, quos judicaverit scandalosos." British Library, Add MS 32, 466, f. 9v. For circumstantial evidence that the York Dominicans had a school of theology, see O'Carroll, "The Educational Organization of the Dominicans," 23-62.

[58] Courtenay, *Adam Wodeham*, 46-47.

[59] BI, Prob. Reg. 3, f. 355v; *Test. Ebor.*, 2:28; BI, Reg. 23 (Rotherham), f. 43v; Little, "Educational Organization of the Mendicant Friars in England," 66-69; A. G. Little, *Studies in English Franciscan History* (Manchester, 1917), 168-71. Courtenay stresses that the custodial schools taught more philosophy than theology. Courtenay, *Adam Wodeham*, 46-47.

[60] Roth, *The English Austin Friars*, 1:24; 2:29.

[61] Ibid., 1:146-47. The only convents which had been allowed two masters in the past were Paris, Oxford, Cambridge, and Lyon.

[62] Ibid., 1:136-41. The General Chapters of the Order, from 1351 to 1362, allowed the

to progress to university without knowing how to preach to the laity and without having done so at least ten times in the vernacular.

In contrast with the fairly full and rather impressive documentation for education and learning within the York friaries, the evidence for a monastic role in education throughout the rest of the diocese is slight. The earliest definite notice relates to Guisborough Priory, an Augustinian monastery which maintained a boarding school for laity in the north Yorkshire moor country of the thirteenth century. In 1266 Archbishop Wickwane, writing to the prior, gave his consent to the request of John Blaby, a local land-owner, to send his two boys to be educated at the priory "et subesse discipline et regimini illius doctoris qui pueros pauperes quos in domo vestra sustentatis pio caritatis intuitu instruit et informat."[63] Several years later this school, which was now attracting both powerful and poor, was in danger of being a burden to the priory, and Wickwane allowed its continuance only if the chancellor of York was convinced that the school remained useful and fruitful to the monastery. The lack of any further reference to the school, in addition to evidence of Guisborough's more precarious financial condition later, suggests that the school was discontinued.[64]

In only nine other monasteries and one friary do we have definite evidence of educational activities. In 1450 the recent (perhaps 1447) privileges and exemptions that Henry VI had granted to Bridlington Priory, an Augustinian priory on the eastern seacoast, were affirmed with the condition that they continue to keep twelve choristers with a master to teach them grammar and song. In 1472 Ralph Snaith of Pontefract put his two sons into the Augustinian priory of Nostell for their board and learning. This was probably a grammar school in the prior's household.[65] The remaining monastic schools, at Newburgh, Whitby, Furness, Kirkham Priory, Monk Bretton Priory, Holy Trinity Priory in York,

---

order to receive into the priesthood even those with no Latin. This was a temporary expedient due to the plague. In 1402 the English Parliament passed a law forbidding the mendicant orders to accept boys before the age of fourteen. *Rot. Parl.*, 3 (Sept. 30, 1402).

[63] C. R. Cheney, "Letters of William Wickwane, Chancellor of York, 1266-1268," *EHR* 47 (1932):633; Brown and Thompson, *Cartularium Prioratus de Gyseburne*, 2:19-20.

[64] Brown and Thompson, *Cartularium Prioratus de Gyseburne*, 2:360-62; the *Chronicon Domini Walteri de Hemingburgh*, Vol. 2, ed. H. C. Hamilton (London, 1849), 18-19 mentions a fire in 1289 which consumed many of its books. See also Brown and Thompson, *Cartularium Prioratus de Gyseburne*, 2:353-57. In the 1330s the priory received a license to sell a corrody and some of its books because of financial distress. D. Robinson, ed., *The Register of William Melton, Archbishop of York, 1317-1340*, Vol. 2, Canterbury and York Society, no. 71 (Torquay, 1978), 158.

[65] *Rot. Parl.*, 5:188; BI, Prob. Reg. 4, ff. 185-86; *Test. Ebor.*, 3:204.

and possibly the Gilbertine monastery at Old Malton, seem to have been almonry schools, open to local children who might also receive board and/or lodging there.[66] Such almonry scholars would normally have received a grammar education. Even A. F. Leach, whose bias against the monasteries was manifest, concluded that "most of them learnt to read and sing and some got a more or less good grammatical . . . education there."[67] Some of the boys would eventually become monks, more perhaps became secular clergy, others returned to the lay world, and some stayed on at the monasteries as lay officials, as was the case with the chamberlain at Monk Bretton Priory, who had been an almonry scholar there in his youth.[68] Finally, the school at Tickhill friary must have been unusual for a friary. It was open to laity and provided an education, whether in grammar or reading we do not know, for a yeoman and a husbandman from the neighborhood. The schoolmaster was chaplain to one of the lay residents and perhaps not directly attached to the friary.[69] In the aggregate, the evidence for monastic schooling in York diocese is slim. Only eleven houses are known to have held schools for outsiders out of a total of approximately seventy-five religious houses within the diocese.

We have better evidence for the educational role of the nunneries in York diocese. Eileen Power tentatively estimated, on the basis of the early fourteenth-century York diocesan visitations of Archbishops Greenfield and Melton and of Bishop Alnwick of Lincoln's visitations (1440-1445), that two-thirds of all nunneries in the two dioceses boarded and taught small children. Her references, with the addition of one to Keldholme nunnery which she missed, point to fourteen such nunneries within Yorkshire. They represent a little over half the known Cistercian and Benedictine nunneries for the county. Sometimes only one or two children are mentioned (mostly girls, although five Yorkshire nunneries seem to have also admitted boys), and it is common to find only a single reference between the thirteenth century and 1537, the exception being Esholt (W. Riding) where mention is made of children living there in 1315, 1318, and 1537. Eileen Power's conclusion that these children at the nunneries

---

[66] See Appendix B below. These almonry schools came into being due to the abolition of child oblation. The monks may have hoped that the education invested in local boys would result in novices for the monastery. The multiplication of private masses throughout the fourteenth and fifteenth centuries as well as the popular new liturgical polyphony, which required more serving boys and choristers, meant that often the monks made good use of almonry boys even if they did not become novices.

[67] Leach, *SME*, 230.

[68] J. S. Purvis, "New Light on the Chartularies of Monk Bretton Priory," *YAJ* 37 (1948):68.

[69] J. S. Purvis, *Select XVIth Century Causes in Tithe*, YAS rec. ser., no. 114 (Leeds, 1949), 107, 108.

were receiving an education is convincing although the evidence is indirect. Whatever education they did receive was not extensive, probably more petty learning and vernacular instruction than Latin reading, and the number of children involved was small, perhaps two to ten per convent, although there is one example of thirty to forty children in a convent.[70] Despite these limitations, the nuns' schools must have been a significant aspect of medieval education in the thirteenth and fourteenth centuries when other reading facilities were less available, and they provided almost the only alternative to a household education for girls. Unfortunately, the documentation for these schools in York diocese is minimal from the late fourteenth century until the dissolution, and it is possible (although the financial exigencies of the nunneries argue against it) that their educational role declined.

Similarly small in numbers and equally difficult to document are the household schools. The survival of household records from the Percy, Roos, Lancaster, and Willoughby estates allows us brief glimpses of expenses in aristocratic households. Some of these had their own chapels with choristers and song masters, such as those at Pontefract Castle, Leconfield Manor, and Wollaton Hall.[71] A grammarmaster was also often available to teach children of the family, gentlemen and yeomen boys of the household, neighborhood children, perhaps the sons and maybe the daughters of stewards and other household officials. The Roos family manuscripts, preserved at Belvoir Castle, show household expenses for gentlemen wards and scholars, for varieties of books (including Bartholomaeus Anglicus's *De Proprietatibus Rerum*), for poor scholars, for a schoolmaster in 1539, and for *three* schoolmasters in 1540, although their teaching duties are not specified. A 1544 inventory mentions the schoolhouse. The Willoughby material from Lord Middleton's manuscripts provides a similar picture.[72] One gains the impression of a very active educational milieu and one wonders to what extent this may have been common in aristocratic households by the sixteenth century. Hints of additional aristocratic household schools come from Pontefract in the eleventh century,

[70] Power, *Med. Eng. Nunneries*, 260-84, 579-81.

[71] *John of Gaunt's Register, 1379-83*, ed. E. C. Lodge and R. Somerville, 2 vols., Camden Society, 3rd ser., 56, 57 (London, 1937), 1:41, 90, 177; 2:278; Thomas Percy, ed., *The Regulations and Establishment of the Household of Henry Algernon Percy, the Fifth Earl of Northumberland at His Castles of Wressle and Leckonfield in Yorkshire, 1512*, new ed. (London, 1905), 311-13, 318; Historical Manuscripts Commission, *Report on the Manuscripts of Lord Middleton Preserved at Wollaton Hall* (London, 1911), 382-86.

[72] Historical Manuscripts Commission, *The MSS of the Duke of Rutland Preserved at Belvoir Castle*, Vol. 4 (London, 1905), 260-345; *MSS of Lord Middleton*, 101-465.

from Sheffield in the thirteenth, Halsham in 1472, and Hinderskelfe in 1525. The sixteenth-century school at Topcliffe, which was under the tuition of the Earl of Northumberland's steward, might also have been a household school.[73]

In contrast with the paucity of materials on education in religious houses and aristocratic households, there is an abundance of references to grammar, reading, and song schools at the parochial, public level. Approximately 90 percent of the schools listed in Appendix B are either parish reading and song schools or public grammar schools perhaps associated with a chantry, gild, or parish church. The importance of the numbers of these public schools needs to be stressed, despite the fact that the totals mask an uncertain educational milieu which is not very stable at the elementary level, of untested competence, and, despite rapid growth, still not widely available. The numbers mark a significant increase over the numbers of public schools previously known in pre-Reformation York diocese. If we take the best previous list, that of Nicholas Orme, one can see the difference. Orme documents twenty-five such schools for York diocese between 1500 and 1530, excluding schools in the religious houses and private household schools.[74] Appendix B below documents a total of approximately one hundred schools between 1500 and 1530, excluding the private schools in religious houses and aristocratic households.

Orme's overall statistics for York (twenty-one from 1350 to 1399, nineteen from 1400 to 1449, twenty-four from 1450 to 1499, and twenty-five from 1500 to 1530) support a thesis that late medieval and early Tudor England experienced a continuously slow rise in available educational facilities. The documentation in Appendix B reveals, instead, rapid and dramatic growth in song and reading education after 1400 and in grammar education after 1500. Perhaps the most startling new evidence is the tremendous rise in elementary education in the fifteenth and sixteenth centuries. When all the reading schools, song schools (counted for these purposes as elementary, although some choristers may have been trained in grammar), and combined reading and song schools are counted (Chart 1), one sees an impressive climb. Beginning in the fifteenth century the number of elementary institutions of all kinds rose so quickly as to more than triple in one hundred years. By 1500 the elementary schools were nearly three times as numerous as the grammar schools, and even with the rapid development of grammar education from 1500 to 1548, the elementary schools continued to outpace the number of grammar schools by 124 to 68.

[73] See Appendix B below.
[74] Orme, *ESMA*, app.

Chart 1

THE GROWTH IN ELEMENTARY AND SECONDARY (GRAMMAR) EDUCATION IN YORK DIOCESE, PRE–1300 TO 1548

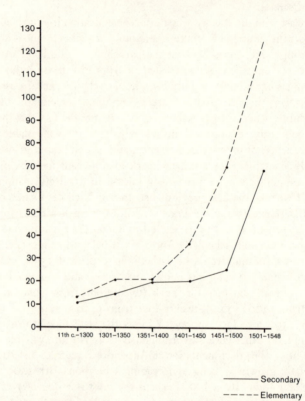

NOTE: Although it has been argued in chapter two above that combined song and reading schools probably taught reading skills which were to some extent distinct from training in song, for the purposes of this chart, a combined song and reading school has been counted as one learning center.

The number of known schools must, of course, always represent some unknown proportion of the actual numbers. For a variety of reasons it is clear that our list is incomplete. Except in a few instances, for example at Giggleswick, Ripon, and Howden, the documentation for diocesan grammar schools does not mention any accompanying reading education. Prior to 1300, however, before the pre-university curriculum evolved into more clearly defined stages, reading had been closely integrated with grammar. This practice continued, as the sixteenth-century foundations that restricted grammar schools to teaching grammar clearly indicate, and the researcher will never know exactly how many grammar schools also offered elementary education. The amount of information available on education within the religious houses is also inadequate and surely underrepresents their contribution. If Eileen Power is correct in estimating that two-thirds of all nunneries had schools, then the Yorkshire numbers are an underenumeration. In addition, the larger Benedictine monasteries at any rate must have had song schools associated with their Lady Chapel choirs.[75] Schools for novices certainly existed in more than the one friary for which we have information. Nor can all the parish schools have been accounted for. The missing wills from the fourteenth century as well as some from the 1410s and 1420s surely contained references to schools and scholars which are now lost from view. The several thousand wills that survive from 1530 to 1548, which have yet to be read systematically, undoubtedly contain additional references to scholars at funerals, despite the growing disillusionment with masses and prayers for the dead. And finally, there are several schools whose existences first come to light in the 1550s but whose beginnings may date from the period of this study. One example will illustrate this. In his autobiography Sir John Savile, who raised himself up from a minor gentry family near Halifax, described his early educational history in some detail. At the age of five he learned his alphabet and English catechism under Richard and Hugh Gledhill, clerk and curate of Elland. A year later (toward the end of the reign of Edward VI) he started to learn his Latin accidence at Rastrick under Robert Ramsden. In 1553 he read through some of Aesop's Fables under Richard Gledhill at Elland. The following two years he studied part of the *Sacred Dialogues* of Castalion under Robert Hutton at Halifax and then read the *Disticha Moralia* of Cato at Huddersfield and partly at Okes Farm, near Almondbury, under Ramsden. During 1557-1558 he worked at Newhall, the mansion of John Nicholl in Elland, under John Henshowe (earlier the schoolmaster at Hawkshead?), reading Virgil and learning grammar. Then at Rastrick he studied with Ramsden again, this time reading Terence, and from 1558-1561 he spent his time at Halifax under Richard Best reading Ovid, Horace, Virgil, Cicero, and Eutropius.[76]

---

[75] Roger Bowers, "Obligation, Agency, and *Laissez-faire*: The Promotion of Polyphonic Composition for the Church in Fifteenth-Century England," in *Music in Medieval and Early Modern Europe*, ed. Iain Fenlon (Cambridge, 1981), 7. See also Bowers, "Choral Institutions within the English Church—Their Constitution and Development 1340-1500" and *Church and Cathedral Choirs in Late Medieval England* (forthcoming).

[76] J. W. Clay and John Lister, eds., "Autobiography of Sir John Savile, of Methley, Knight, Baron of the Exchequer, 1546-1607," *YAJ* 15 (1900):421-22; see also M. W. Garside, "Halifax Schools prior to 1700 A.D.," in *Papers, Reports, etc. Read before the Halifax Antiquarian Society* (Halifax, 1924), 185-86.

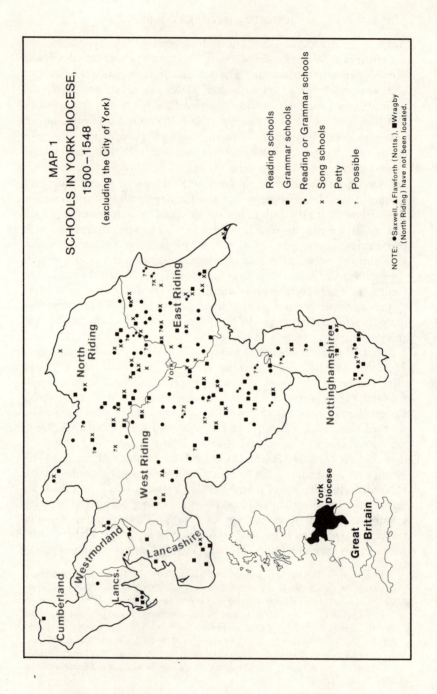

MAP 1

SCHOOLS IN YORK DIOCESE, 1500–1548

(excluding the City of York)

• Reading schools
■ Grammar schools
•̷ Reading or Grammar schools
× Song schools
▲ Petty
? Possible

Cumberland

Westmorland

Lancs.

North Riding

West Riding

York

East Riding

Lancashire

Nottinghamshire

York Diocese

Great Britain

NOTE: ● Saxwell ▲Flawforth (Notts.), ■Wragby (North Riding) have not been located.

Only one of these places, Halifax, is known to have had a pre-1548 school, although the inhabitants of Rastrick in 1605 testified that there had from "time immemorial been an ancient chapel within the township of Rastrick, called St. Matthew's chapel, within which divine service had been celebrated and also a school [held] for the education of youth."[77] Nor are any of the schoolmasters, with the possible exception of Henshowe, who may have taught at Hawkshead (Lancs.) in the 1530s, previously known.

Although the list of schools compiled here is incomplete, it probably pinpoints a high rather than a low proportion of the existing educational facilities. When the geographical distribution of these schools is taken into account, it would appear that we have at least a representative sample of schools which cover the diocese in a way that one might expect and that lends confidence to our findings.

One heavy (and early) concentration of schools is between Doncaster and York, extending into Nottinghamshire roughly along the old Roman road and primary line of communication between northern and southern England. By 1548 an impressive number of schools existed in the dales region northeast of York toward Richmond, and another group of largely elementary schools can be found in the northwest East Riding and southeast North Riding. The West Riding was graced with numbers of schools scattered mainly throughout the southern two-thirds. A high percentage are grammar schools, most of which were founded in the early sixteenth century—a reflection of economic growth and population pressures. There are several notable educational blank spots in the diocese. The north Yorkshire moors, the western area of Nottinghamshire toward the Derbyshire border, and the northwest section of the North Riding seem to have had virtually no educational resources. But these were also the regions with the lowest population densities.

Very few schools are documented in Richmond archdeaconry until quite late in the period under consideration here. This is in part because fewer documents, especially the wills, have survived for this area, but it is also because the archdeaconry was a region with few population centers and it remained somewhat culturally isolated from the rest of the diocese. To some extent, however, the dearth of schools in the Lancashire section of Richmond was compensated for by a proliferation of schools just across the border in the diocese of Lichfield.[78]

---

[77] John Lister, "The Old Free Chapels in the Parish of Halifax," in *Papers, Reports, etc. Read before the Halifax Antiquarian Society* (Halifax, 1909), 36.

[78] For example, Clitheroe in 1283, Blackburn (endowed in 1524), Winwick (1546-1548), and Whalley in 1548. In addition, there were schools at Manchester, Leyland, Middleton, Bolton, Burnley, Standish, and Pendleton. Helen M. Jewell, " 'The Bringing Up of Children

The educational map of York diocese on the eve of the Reformation presents a picture substantially different from the analysis offered twenty years ago by W. K. Jordan in his volume on the rural charities of England from 1480 to 1660. Jordan's limited pre-Reformation sources provided evidence for only eight schools in Yorkshire by 1480. His conclusion, that Reformation Yorkshiremen had inherited meager educational resources from the Middle Ages and had had to build on "most limited [educational] foundations left from the ruin of the medieval world,"[79] is no longer acceptable. The wills upon which Jordan based his study, when examined in greater number and supplemented with a wider range of primary and secondary sources, suggest the opposite conclusion. The educational resources of late medieval York diocese were substantial and expanding. They provided a solid foundation on which late Tudor and Stuart Englishmen could build. As a factor in understanding the Reformation, the spread of education should now be seen not merely as a consequence but also as a precursor to the religious upheavals of the sixteenth century.

Thus far this study has delineated the kind of education available in York diocese from 1340 to 1548. It has also charted the references to schools, schoolmasters, and scholars in the primary sources. The remaining chapters suggest some of the causes and consequences of these educational changes. It is not my purpose to try to provide all the answers. This could, for example, involve us in questions as to the impact of plague and of benefit of clergy, the decline of feudalism, the relative distribution of wealth, the rise of the gentry, changing attitudes toward the clergy, and a host of other questions which are at present unanswered and perhaps unanswerable. It is, however, my purpose to link the educational materials with other late medieval currents of change—changes in clerical recruitment, lay literacy, lay literary interests, and the laicization of society. By focusing on these issues some understanding of the reasons for educational growth as well as some appreciation of the results of that growth will emerge.

---

in Good Learning and Manners': A Survey of Secular Educational Provision in the North of England, c. 1350-1550," *Northern History* 18 (1982): app. For Pendleton and Standish, see Christopher Haigh, *Reformation and Resistance in Tudor Lancashire* (Cambridge, 1975), 43.

[79] W. K. Jordan, *The Charities of Rural England, 1480-1660* (London, 1961), 299, 301.

CHAPTER 5

The Church and Educational Change

For the causes and consequences of the educational developments described in the previous chapters, the first and most obvious place to look is among the ranks of the clergy, since they functioned as the educational elite of late medieval English society. In particular, the elementary curriculum, based as it was on the liturgy, was essential training for any aspiring mass or parish priest. It is common sense to suppose that one of the first results of an increase in the availability of elementary education, and especially of a reading education, would be an increase in clergy, particularly at the parish level. The results of an investigation of the ordination records between 1345 and 1525 are displayed in Charts 2-6, smoothed out by the use of a five-year moving average.[1] The charts show that, for York diocese, the correlation does indeed exist, and that the increase in clerical recruitment in the second half of the fifteenth century was a dramatic one. This chapter evaluates alternative explanations for the increase in ordinations after 1460 and argues that a growing demand for clerical services and the increased availability of elementary and grammar education are relevant, and perhaps essential, for understanding the climb in clerical recruitment. In order to better understand the late fifteenth-century developments, however, it is helpful first to look briefly at the ordination trends of the fourteenth and early fifteenth centuries.

York diocese lost a great number of clergy during the plague years of the fourteenth century. In 1348-1349, the year the plague first appeared, the death rate for beneficed clergy has been estimated as 36.54 percent in Nottingham archdeaconry and 35.36 percent in Cleveland. It was even higher elsewhere—44.91 percent in the archdeaconry of York and 48.11 percent in the East Riding. Although we have no comparable figures for

---

[1] The ups and downs of clerical recruitment throughout this period were dramatic; the specific annual totals along with a detailed explanation for the various shifts, have been published in J. Hoeppner Moran, "Clerical Recruitment in the Diocese of York, 1340-1530: Data and Commentary," *J. Eccl. Hist.* 34 (1983):19-54. The article also documents the sources for the ordination data, details the methodology of using ordination lists, and charts the ordinations of regular priests. Their numbers remain remarkably stable throughout the entire period.

Chart 2

CLERICAL ORDINATIONS YORK DIOCESE
1345–1380

(5 year moving average)

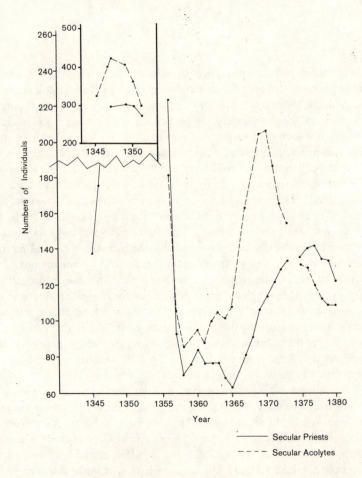

unbeneficed clergy; their death rate was unlikely to have been much less. The later plagues, in 1361-1362 and 1369, had a less severe impact on the beneficed clergy; approximately 6 percent died in 1361-1362 and 13 percent in 1369.[2] The losses in all three instances were rapidly made good.

[2] A. Hamilton Thompson, "The Pestilences of the Fourteenth Century in the Diocese of York," *The Archaeological Journal* 71 (1914):111-13, 115-16.

Between 1349 and 1350 the number of priests ordained rose from 185 in 1348 to 724 in 1350, while the five-year moving average reaches 300 in 1349. Recovery was less dramatic in the 1360s, although a glance at Chart 2 shows a noticeable upswing subsequent to 1365. By the time the 1377 poll tax was being assessed, York diocese had an estimated population of 2,290 secular clergy, over 800 of whom were beneficed and approximately 1,500 of whom were not.[3] J. C. Russell, the chronicler of Britain's medieval population, was sufficiently impressed and puzzled by the number of unbeneficed clergy in 1377 to suggest that, "in view of the large surplus of clerks in 1377 it is doubtful if the number of secular clerks increased at all in the period (1377 to 1550)."[4] By looking at the ordination data of the fifteenth and early sixteenth century, one can readily see that Russell's suggestion is borne out, with regard to York diocese, only up to 1460. After this date he could not have been more wrong.

After a gap in the records from 1380 until 1392, the ordinations show a substantial decline among secular priests, whose numbers average 111 per annum from 1392 to 1400 and 86 from 1401 to 1410. Clerical recruitment at York in the fifteenth century reached its nadir in 1405.[5] Thereafter decline was arrested, and the averages of secular ordinations to the priesthood remain remarkably stable throughout the first half of the fifteenth century. At the acolyte level, the 1450s saw a significant downturn. And the average recruitment level of secular priests, which had been growing slowly in the first four decades of the fifteenth century, fell back in the 1450s. There are no immediately obvious reasons for this mid-century downward trend, although it is possible that the plagues of the 1430s (which seem to have been particularly severe among children) may help account for it.[6]

By the 1460s, however, the ordination figures began to move upward, increasing steadily throughout the rest of the fifteenth and early sixteenth century, climbing from a low of 75 in 1453 to a peak of 363 in 1508.

[3] John Topham, "Subsidy Roll of 51 Edward III," *Archaeologia* 7 (1785):345. The poll tax for 1377 lists 1,790 beneficed and 1,481 unbeneficed clergy in York diocese, i.e., a total of 3,271. J. C. Russell calculates the proportion of regular to secular clergy throughout England as 10,600:24,900 (30 percent regular, 70 percent secular), which would leave York diocese with an estimated population of 2,290 secular clergy in 1377. J. C. Russell, "The Clerical Population of Medieval England," *Traditio* 2 (1944):179. Since the regular clergy were nearly all beneficed, their numbers (981) deducted from the 1,790 beneficed clergy results in 809 beneficed secular clergy. A. Hamilton Thompson gives a figure of 750 benefices in York diocese. *VCH, Yorks.*, 3:80-88.

[4] Russell, "The Clerical Population of Medieval England," 179.

[5] An exceptionally low number of acolytes recorded in 1478 seems to be the result of scribal neglect.

[6] See Moran, "Clerical Recruitment," for a fuller analysis of this decline.

Chart 3

CLERICAL ORDINATIONS YORK DIOCESE
1380–1420

(5 year moving average)

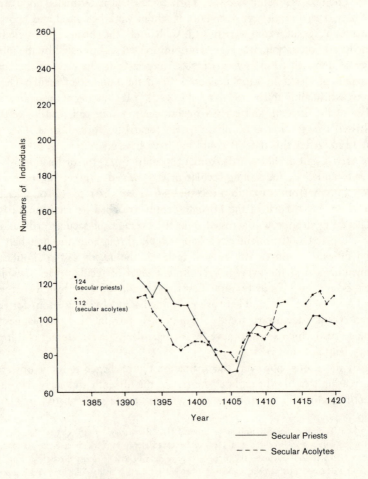

The five-year moving average reaches its peak at 239 in 1509. Assuming an average life expectancy after ordination of between twenty-five and thirty years for those men ordained in the latter half of the fifteenth century,[7] there would have been a total of between 4,111 and 4,736 secular

[7] Margaret Deanesly, *The Lollard Bible and Other Medieval Biblical Versions* (Cambridge,

clergy in York diocese in 1500.[8] This would exceed the 1377 poll tax numbers for York by 1,821 to 2,446 priests. Even were there an underestimate of 10 percent (rather than the 5 percent suggested by Russell) in the poll tax numbers, it can still be argued that the ordination records for York show an increase of as much as 63-88 percent in the population of the secular clergy between 1377 and 1500.[9]

An underlying condition of this increase may have been a rise in the general population. However, the population recovery for England from 1440 to 1500 has been estimated as only around 30 percent (from 1.17 million to just over 1.50 million), and recent scholarship suggests that this may be too high.[10] Even were there a population increase of this magnitude, it need not translate itself into greater numbers of clergy.

Nor does an explanation for this increase rest with any sudden influx of ordinands into York diocese from elsewhere. From 1427 to 1500 there is an estimated growth of from one or two individuals to perhaps twenty individuals coming *into* York diocese each year with letters dimissory, i.e., diocesan letters that permit an ordinand from one diocese to be

---

1920), 159; J.R.H. Moorman, *Church Life in England in the Thirteenth Century* (Cambridge, 1945), 53; J. C. Russell, *British Medieval Population* (Albuquerque, N.M., 1948), 185, table 8.10.

[8] These totals are calculated by using model life tables for males from Western Europe. Ansley J. Coale and Paul Demeny, *Regional Model Life Tables and Stable Populations* (Princeton, 1966), ii:3, 7 (levels 2 and 6). The tables used are those which show life expectancies at age twenty-five of approximately twenty-five and thirty years. The population at age twenty-five has been converted to a base of 1,000, and the declining number of survivors calculated accordingly. Since the tables are presented in five-year intervals, the results have been graphed and the numbers for intermediate years taken from the graph line. The number of ordinations was then multiplied by the proportion surviving from the year of ordination to 1500. All the secular priests ordained between 1445 and 1500 and living in the year 1500 were then added up to give the total number of survivors. For reservations on applying the Coale-Demeny tables to late medieval England, see Robert S. Gottfried, *Bury St. Edmunds and the Urban Crisis 1290-1539* (Princeton, 1982), 48-50. The major difficulty appears to be with the birth rates and with infant mortality rather than with the death rates.

[9] See note 3 above for the total of 2,290 secular clergy in the diocese in 1377. Adding 10 percent for underevaluation results in a figure of 2,519 as an outside estimate. Russell, "Clerical Population of Medieval England," 179; Russell, *British Medieval Population*, 131-39, 143-46, esp. tables 6.5 and 6.7. Taking an average life expectancy of twenty-five years after ordination, the number of secular clergy in 1500 would be 4,111 (or 63 percent more). Assuming an average life expectancy of thirty years after ordination, the numbers are 4,736 in 1500, an 88 percent increase over the inflated poll tax figures of 2,519.

[10] T. H. Hollingsworth, *Historical Demography* (Ithaca, N.Y., 1969), app. 3, esp. fig. 10. For more pessimistic assessments, see John Hatcher, *Plague, Population and the English Economy, 1348-1530* (London, 1977); Robert Gottfried, *Epidemic Disease in Fifteenth-Century England* (New Brunswick, N.J., 1978); R. Barrie Dobson, "Urban Decline in Late Medieval England," *TRHS*, 5th ser., 27 (1977):1-22.

Chart 4

CLERICAL ORDINATIONS YORK DIOCESE
1420–1460
(5 year moving average)

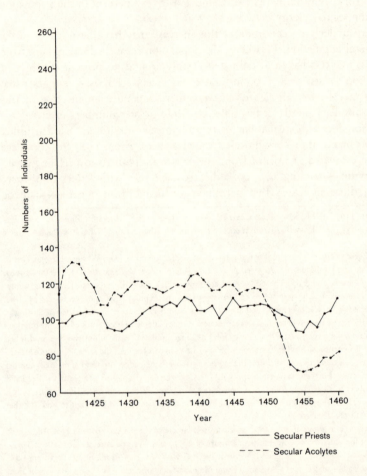

ordained by the bishop of another. However, there is a far greater growth in those *from* York being granted letters dimissory for ordination outside the diocese. Under Archbishop Kemp (1425-1452) the number of letters dimissory recorded average only three per year, while under Archbishop William Booth (1452-1464) they average twenty-four, and under Archbishop Rotherham (1480-1500), forty-four.[11] In the final analysis, the

[11] BI, Regs. 19, 20, 23. See also Peter Heath, *English Parish Clergy on the Eve of the*

Chart 5

CLERICAL ORDINATIONS YORK DIOCESE
1460–1500

(5 year moving average)

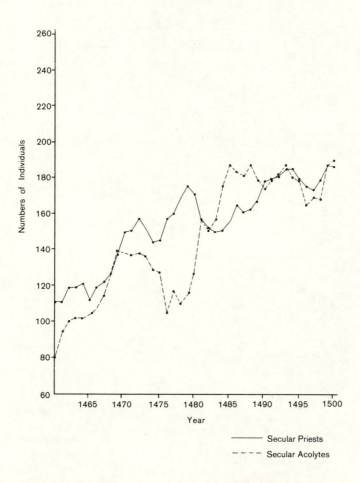

growing number of letters dimissory from York only leave us with a greater increase to explain.

To what extent is it possible to argue that stepped-up clerical recruitment was being facilitated by a relaxation of standards? For example, the greater

---

Reformation (London, 1969), app. 3. For some comments on the difficulty of drawing conclusions from the records of letters dimissory, see Moran, "Clerical Recruitment," n 99.

Chart 6

CLERICAL ORDINATIONS YORK DIOCESE
1500–1525

(5 year moving average)

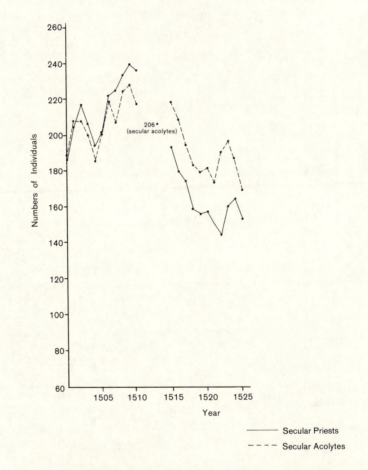

Year

———— Secular Priests

– – – – Secular Acolytes

freedom of choice in terms of place of ordination, which is suggested by the number of letters dimissory, argues for a Church hierarchy in the second half of the fifteenth century that did not place many difficulties in the path of aspiring priests. In general, however, there is little to suggest that recruitment procedures were more lax in the later fifteenth century than they had been earlier.[12] Although additional ordinations (beyond the

[12] For an extended discussion on this point, see Moran, "Clerical Recruitment," 26-31.

canonical six per year) were occasionally allowed in the fourteenth century, there is no evidence for them in the fifteenth century. Rapid promotions up the ordination ladder (usually within twelve months and often less) were common throughout the period 1340-1530. Although evidence with regard to examinations of prospective ordinands is not plentiful at any time in the medieval period, references do occur sporadically throughout this period, suggesting that examination procedures continued, however effective or ineffective they may have been.[13]

The fact that a larger proportion of acolytes were going on to the priesthood could suggest a lowering of educational standards for higher orders. Prior to 1348 G. G. Coulton has estimated that only 36.2 percent of the beneficed clergy from four dioceses (Exeter, Bath and Wells, Winchester, and Worcester) were priests, a figure he finds compatible with A. H. Thompson's results for preplague Lincoln and York dioceses.[14] Subsequent to 1380, in the diocese of York, the proportion of acolytes to priests equalized, with the result that the individual who remained in minor orders must have been a rarity in the century and a half before the Reformation. If this development does reflect a lowering of standards, then the question it raises is why, for the next eighty years, there should have been relatively so few clergy recruited. It is far more likely that the Church's reforming goal of a priest in every benefice was responsible for this change. The abuse of beneficed clergy without priestly orders having cure of souls had been attacked energetically prior to 1348. But reform along these lines may have become more pressing in the face of recurrent plague and the attendant spiritual needs of the people. Quite possibly the fact that benefit of clergy was no longer based on the tonsure but rather on reading ability also made minor orders less attractive.[15] Whatever the reason, the nearly universal tendency for acolytes to move into higher orders occurred too early to contribute to the spurt in clerical recruitment of the second half of the fifteenth century.

There were two other changes that facilitated ordination procedures during the period 1340-1530, although neither helps explain the rise in recruitment in the 1460s. First, it was customary for titles to be presented by a prospective ordinand. These offered proof that he had a living whereby he could support himself, and if a title proved insufficient, the ordaining bishop was, according to ecclesiastical law, held responsible. Thus, in the twelfth and thirteenth centuries titles were examined carefully,

[13] Ibid. See also pp. 144-47 below.

[14] G. G. Coulton, *The Black Death* (London, 1929), 39-43.

[15] C. B. Firth, "Benefit of Clergy in the Time of Edward IV," *EHR* 32 (1917):182-84; Leona Gabel, *Benefit of Clergy in England in the Later Middle Ages* (Northampton, Mass., 1929), passim.

and ordinands presented a variety of titles to prove financial independence. At York between 1342 and 1347 many ordinands were offering five marks or a piece of land (often one messuage) from a patron. Other titles were from one's own patrimony or benefice, from a university, from a monastery, or from a hospital. In 1346 and 1347 approximately 27 and 21 percent respectively of the titles came from religious houses, many of them titles from houses outside the diocese by letters dimissory. It was a confusing array of titles, which was undoubtedly difficult to deal with administratively. But by 1348 monastic titles had risen to approximately 36 percent of the total and by 1349 they represented 68 percent. Beginning in December 1348, possibly as the result of a diocesan decision, a majority of all titles were from religious houses and in the subsequent years, up until the Reformation, this became an almost universal practice.[16] Such *pro forma* titles, which clearly made for administrative ease, may have opened up major orders (which were the only ones requiring a title) to individuals who had access to neither patrimony nor patron. While this procedural change probably facilitated recruitment during the initial plague years, by the 1460s it was no longer a novelty, and we have no information that would suggest that titles became cheaper or monasteries more willing to sell them as time went by.

A second development that made ordinations easier to administer was the increased frequency with which they were held exclusively in the city of York, or sometimes at Cawood. In the fourteenth century (and up through the archbishopric of Henry Bowet), ordinations were regularly held in many parts of the diocese.[17] By 1420 this was no longer the case. The prospective ordinand, even if he were simply seeking the minor order of acolyte, now usually had to travel to York. While this may have regularized the process to some degree (and perhaps helps account for the nearly complete ordination lists of this period), the costs of travelling to and lodging in York were an added financial burden in an already fairly expensive process.

There is no doubt that entering clerical orders required an investment. In addition to the costs of travel and lodging (which have to be considered at each step up the ordination ladder), there was the cost of buying or renting a title, ordination fees (which might run about 6s. 8d.), a few pennies for the tonsure, and the cost of equipment. A surplice, for example, might cost about 12s. and service books another few shillings.[18] All of

[16] Moran, "Clerical Recruitment," 30-31.

[17] For example, Howden, Beverley, Newark, Thirsk, Warter, Ripon, and Doncaster.

[18] Margaret Bowker, *The Secular Clergy in the Diocese of Lincoln, 1495-1520* (Cambridge, 1968), 40; J. F. Williams, "Ordination in the Norwich Diocese during the Fifteenth Century," *Norfolk Archaeology* 31 (1956):353-54.

these expenses came on top of the major cost of education, resulting in considerable expense for the less wealthy aspirant. Some of these concerns manifest themselves in the wills of the period. Particularly apt is the 1538 will of Thomas Atkinson of Clint (West Riding), a yeoman, who specifies that "Robert Atkynson, my son, shall have hys fyndyng of my sayd wyffe, either at Yorke or elles where it shalbe thought beste, so that he may folowe the scole unto suche tyme yt he may gette orders and be preiste, and that he shall have his tytle and singynge geyr boughte at the coste of my sayd wyffe."[19]

Despite these financial disincentives, more and more men, in the second half of the fifteenth century, were seeking and gaining entry into higher orders. A look at the opportunities open to the newly ordained clergy can help us comprehend the motives that prompted such an influx of ordinands.

One of the most often mentioned consequences of the Black Death was the desertion of poor cures for the sometimes more lucrative but usually less demanding office of mass or chantry priest.[20] Throughout the fourteenth and early fifteenth centuries, the demand for chantry priests, mass priests, gild chaplains, and household chaplains continued strong, and the most recent research suggests a growth in foundations of chantries and payments to stipendiary chaplains, especially in the north in the second half of the fifteenth century and even into the sixteenth century despite discouraging legal and financial restraints imposed under the Tudors.[21] In terms of perpetual chantries, the 1535 *Valor Ecclesiasticus* notes a total of at least 424 chantries in the county of Yorkshire alone, the largest proportion of which were founded from 1450 to 1500.[22] In county Lancashire, much of which was within York diocese, the movement for founding chantries only begins to be well documented after 1450 and was

---

[19] *Wills and Administrations from the Knaresborough Court Rolls*, Vol. 1, ed. F. Collins, Surtees Society, no. 104 (Durham, 1902), 26.

[20] Archbishop John Thoresby (1352-1373), in an effort to stem an influx of clergy away from *cura animarum* and into stipendiary positions, ordered no chaplain to receive more than six marks (£4) as an annual salary. Some chantry positions could bring as much as £10 per annum. Thoresby, in the introduction to his constitution, speaks of the "difficult attitude and grasping demands which stipendiary chaplains have so far in these days shown and made . . . owing to the lack and scarcity of such chaplains." R. M. Woolley, *The York Provinciale* (n.p., 1930), bk. 3, tit. 13.3.

[21] Alan Kreider, *English Chantries: The Road to Dissolution* (Cambridge, Mass., 1979), chap. 3, esp. fig. 2.

[22] *Valor Ecclesiasticus temp. Henr. VIII*, Vol. 5 (London, 1825), passim. See also William Page, ed., *The Certificates of the Commissioners Appointed to Survey the Chantries, Guilds, Hospitals, etc. in the county of York*, Vol. 1, Surtees Society, no. 91 (Durham, 1894), vii; Joel Rosenthal, "The Yorkshire Chantry Certificates of 1546: An Analysis," *Northern History* 9 (1974):30-31.

in full swing on the eve of the dissolution. Within the walls of the city of York alone, references have been discovered to a total of approximately 140 different perpetual chantries. In order to cope with the large number of chantry priests, chantry colleges were formed throughout the diocese at Hemingborough, Sutton-in-Holderness, and Lowthorp in the East Riding, at Acaster Selby, Rotherham, Pontefract, and Middleham in the West Riding, and at Newark and Sibthorp in Nottinghamshire. Most of them were fifteenth-century creations. The number of chaplains serving both the minster and parish chantries of York was sufficient to warrant the formation of a college for the city chaplains (at Peaseholme Green) in the fifteenth century and St. William's College for the minster priests in 1461. In addition, Richard III had begun founding a college for one hundred chaplains who would serve just one chantry chapel at the cathedral. Although he died before the scheme reached fruition, his vision is a reminder of the tremendous capacity of the chantry system to absorb or attract large numbers of clergy.[23]

Whereas we have sufficient documentation from the late Middle Ages to be fairly sure of the numbers and locations of the perpetual chantries, it is nearly impossible to establish meaningful statistics on the number of stipendiary grants to chaplains chanting masses for the dead for more modest time periods. By the end of the fourteenth century, it was becoming common for a testator to bequeath sums of money to a mass priest. By the beginning of the sixteenth century this practice was the norm within the diocese. The result was, that by 1526-1527 the secular clergy assessed for taxes in the North and East Ridings included 99 rectors, 139 vicars, 101 chantry priests (presumably serving perpetual chantries), and 510 stipendiary chaplains, i.e., chaplains employed for saying masses for limited time periods.[24] In terms of percentages there were two and a half times more clergy engaged in saying masses for the dead than those engaged in cure of souls and five times more stipendiary than chantry priests.

No similarly comprehensive data is available for other parts of the diocese, a deficiency that has been remedied somewhat for the West Riding by R. B. Smith in his book on *Land and Politics in the England of Henry*

[23] Kreider, *English Chantries*, 90-91; R. Barrie Dobson, "The Foundation of Perpetual Chantries by the Citizens of Medieval York," in *Studies in Church History*, Vol. 4, ed. G. J. Cuming (Leiden, 1967), 24; A. Hamilton Thompson, "English Colleges of Chantry Priests," *Transactions of the Ecclesiological Society*, new ser. 1, no. 2 (1943):92-108; James Raine, ed., *The Fabric Rolls of York Minster*, Surtees Society, no. 35 (Durham, 1859), 87.

[24] "The Fallow Papers," *YAJ* 21 (1911):243-52 and "The East Riding Clergy in 1525-6," 24 (1916):62-80. This excludes eighteen prebendaries, sixteen vicars choral, and seventeen pensioners from the East Riding.

VIII (1970). By using the *Valor Ecclesiasticus* and supplementing it with the *Liber Valorum* of the same year and information from the clerical subsidy of 1523, Smith has calculated the early sixteenth-century clerical population of the West Riding as follows: 62 rectors, 108 vicars, and 269 chantry priests. Stipendiary chaplains are not mentioned, although judging from the North and East Riding statistics, their number would more than double the totals.[25]

Even in places without a large collegiate establishment the number of clergy attached to one establishment could be considerable. At the beginning of the sixteenth century there were as many as five chaplains in the small rural parish of Bubwith, twenty-five in what is now the modern parish of Hull, seven at Bridlington, six priests in one chantry at Northallerton, and fifteen in one parish church at Newark. One gets an idea of the numbers involved by examining wills, for testators sometimes enumerated the crowd of chaplains they expected to be present at their funeral services or to pray subsequently for their souls. In 1470 Elizabeth Medelay planned for seven chaplains and six clerks at her funeral in the village of Clementhorp. About the same time, thirteen chaplains were expected at a funeral in Holy Trinity, Hull, and, in 1503, William Wright provided for twelve chaplains at his burial in New Malton. Earlier, in 1390, John Yhole, a citizen of York, left monies to twenty-eight chaplains celebrating at St. Wilfrid's in York, 3s. 4d. to the parish chaplain and 2s. to each of the rest of the chaplains continuing to celebrate there. Isolda de Acaster, wife of John, a citizen and merchant of York, followed a few years later (in 1395) with a bequest of £100 to twenty chaplains for one year's worth of prayers and 12s. for each remaining chaplain within the city of York. This was topped, a year later, with the will of Robert Holm, merchant of York, who left £500 for twenty-five chaplains to pray for his soul the space of four years at St. Trinity, Goodramgate in York. If the twenty-five priests could not be found, ten were to be employed until the money was used up. In addition to this, Holm left 2s. to every chaplain within York who continued to say services and had not yet been promoted to a benefice. In 1436 Thomas Bracebridge left 4d. to every rector and chaplain within the parish churches of York and its suburbs. He estimated the total cost at 100s., suggesting that there were then some 260 parish clergy in or near the city. In the 1469 will of John Coupland, citizen of York, there was a bequest of 8d. to every parish chaplain of All Saints, North Street who would attend his funeral, but in his further bequest of 4d. to other chaplains the testator felt it necessary to specify that only the first

[25] R. B. Smith, *Land and Politics in the England of Henry VIII* (Oxford, 1970), 93.

twenty extraparochial chaplains would qualify. In 1466, Sir Robert Lound, himself a chaplain from York, felt that although he did not know exactly where he would die and be buried, he could count upon the fact that there would be at least twelve chaplains there. Later, in 1521, Nicholas Bosvile of Denaby (West Riding) left 40s. for six score priests to sing masses for his soul.[26]

These large numbers of parochial clergy were supplemented by chaplains in domestic chapels of the nobility, gentry, higher clergy, and well-to-do merchants. The register of Archbishop Waldby, covering only ten months between March 1397 and January 1398, records twenty-six licenses for oratories in private houses. The register of the archdeaconry of Richmond for 1442-1477, covering the most remote area within the diocese, also lists numerous licenses for private oratories, and subsequent archiepiscopal registers continued to issue them in large numbers, often allowing masses to be said privately on behalf of one individual in a variety of places within the diocese over a period of several years or during the pleasure of the petitioner. In 1410 Master Thomas Walkington, archdeacon of Cleveland, left his three personal chaplains £48 for three years of prayers. Thomas Nelson, citizen of York, had three chaplains in his household in 1463, and in 1466 Henry Hertlington, esquire, left £12 for three years to his domestic chaplain. The household book of Henry, fifth Earl of Northumberland (1474-1527) gives full details as to the organization of his chapel staff, including references to eleven chaplains.[27] It is no wonder that, in 1528, Sir Thomas More complained "that we sholde not haue suche a rabell that euery meane man must haue a preste in his house to wayte vppon his wyfe whiche no man almost lacketh nowe . . ."[28] Clearly, the opportunities for newly ordained priests were there.

[26] BI, Prob. Reg. 1, ff. 43, 81, 100-103; Prob. Reg. 3, f. 488; Prob. Reg. 4, ff. 97, 135, 160, 265; Prob. Reg. 6, f. 82v; Prob. Reg. 9, f. 263; *Test. Ebor.*, 6:5; PRO, PCC, Prob. 11/14 Holgrave 28, will of Jane Hastynges. See also "The East Riding Clergy in 1525-6," 62; *Yorkshire Chantry Surveys* 92 (1895), 222; A. Hamilton Thompson, *The English Clergy and Their Organization in the Later Middle Ages* (Oxford, 1947), 134; Dobson, "The Foundation of Perpetual Chantries," 37-38.

[27] David M. Smith, ed., *A Calendar of the Register of Robert Waldby, Archbishop of York, 1397* (York, 1974); A. Hamilton Thompson, ed., "The Register of the Archdeacons of Richmond, 1442-1477, part i," *YAJ* 30 (1930):38-39; James Raine, ed., *Wills and Inventories . . . of the Northern Counties of England*, Surtees Society, no. 2 (London, 1835), 50 (Walkington); Dobson, "The Foundation of Perpetual Chantries," 37 n 1 (Nelson); BI, Prob. Reg. 4, f. 236 (Hertlington); Thomas Percy, ed., *The Regulations and Establishment of the Household of Henry Algernon Percy*, new ed. (London, 1905), 311-13, 316-17.

[28] *A Dialogue Concerning Heresies*, ed. M. C. Lawler, Germain Marc'hadour, and Richard C. Marius, *The Complete Works of St. Thomas More*, Vol. 6, pt. 1 (New Haven, 1981), 301.

Still, it is one thing for a society to increase its demand for religious services and another for the Church to supply that demand. Considering the low levels of clerical recruitment between 1390 and 1460 in light of a continuing and indeed increasing demand for priests, it is possible that the Church was experiencing a manpower crisis in the first half of the fifteenth century.[29] One of the ways the Church may have responded to this problem was to promote the availability of education in the expectation that it would produce a larger pool of aspiring and educated clergy.

With regard to raising the educational level of the higher clergy, a concerted effort had been made in the twelfth and thirteenth centuries to strengthen education in the cathedral churches. The Third Lateran Council (1179) ordained that a grammarmaster should be appointed in every cathedral, and Fourth Lateran (1215) extended this educational reform by decreeing that metropolitan churches should also appoint a theologian to instruct clergy in scripture and prepare them for pastoral work. In 1219 Pope Honorius III responded to the possible scarcity of such teachers by allowing the church hierarchy to send promising clerics to the university for the study of theology for five years, during which time they were to enjoy the fruits of their benefices.[30] The culmination of this effort was achieved with the promulgation of the constitution *Cum ex eo* by Boniface VIII in 1298. *Cum ex eo* provided an educational opportunity at the university for any clergyman who was not yet ordained to the priesthood or even to the subdiaconate, and who had only one living with cure of souls. It was an educational subsidy which was meant, as Leonard Boyle explains it, for the "young and uncommitted." "Boniface's constitution was not designed to provide teachers of theology, or to cater to canons or other beneficed clergy; its purpose was to promote a literate parochial clergy directly, and its application was strictly confined to clerics who were destined for an ordinary and unencumbered *cura animarum*."[31]

That a great many English clergy took advantage of this opportunity is testified to by the Dominican preacher John Bromyard, who complained (c. 1348) that too many of the clergy were frittering away their time at the university, and by Leonard Boyle, who documents a remarkably large number of licenses granted in England in the fifty years after the promulgation of *Cum ex eo*, including 105 licenses in Winchester diocese between 1305 and 1316 and 400 licenses in Exeter between 1307 and

---

[29] R. L. Storey, Review of *A Calendar of the Register of Henry Wakefield* in *EHR* 89 (1974):379.

[30] Leonard E. Boyle, "The Constitution 'Cum ex eo' of Boniface VIII," *Mediaeval Studies* 24 (1962):264.

[31] Ibid., 274.

1326.[32] In York diocese, during the archiepiscopacy of William Melton (1317-1340), forty-three licenses for study were issued within the archdeaconry of Cleveland alone.[33] By the 1340s, however, these licenses to study declined significantly and never regained popularity. This may have occurred because *Cum ex eo* was specifically designed for the beneficed cleric in minor orders, an increasingly rare category of clergy. In addition, *Cum ex eo* was irrelevant to the needs of the growing numbers of unbeneficed chaplains. To the extent that the fifteenth century saw an increase in university-educated clergy, the credit must go to the university colleges which made substantial and growing provisions for clerical education and promotion, rather than to *Cum ex eo*.[34]

By the fifteenth century the increased proportion of graduate clergy was considerable in some dioceses. Out of 671 institutions to benefices in Bath and Wells between 1443 and 1465, one-fifth went to university graduates. At Lincoln the proportion of beneficed clergy with M.A.'s (clearly the cream of the crop) rose from 3 1/2 percent to 11 1/2 percent between 1421-1431 and 1495-1520. The proportion of graduate clergy presented to parish livings in Norwich diocese between 1503 and 1528 was one-sixth the total, while fully one-third of all those admitted to and vacating parochial livings in London under Bishop Tunstall (1522-1530) were graduates.[35] These figures are in somewhat marked contrast to York diocese where, in the archdeaconry of Richmond in 1525-1526, there was not one graduate and, in the letters dimissory registered in the diocese between 1452 and 1530, only 2.7 percent were for university graduates.[36]

Thus, despite ecclesiastical efforts extending over several centuries, the clergy of York diocese scarcely benefited from efforts to raise clerical standards to the university level. How pessimistic this conclusion seems depends in large part on the extent to which one judges that a university education was appropriate for a parish priest, beneficed or not. One might ask, as Roy Haines does, how suitable, in contemporary opinion, was it for a man intending to exercise *cura animarum* in a parish to pursue a university curriculum. Haines notes that "the basic outline of priestly knowledge and expertise as expounded by Grosseteste, Pecham (in *Igno-*

[32] Ibid., 283, 297.

[33] D. Robinson, ed., *The Register of William Melton, Archbishop of York, 1317-1340*, Vol. 2, Canterbury and York Society, no. 71 (Torquay, 1978), passim.

[34] Roy M. Haines, "The Education of the English Clergy during the Later Middle Ages: Some Observations on the Operation of Pope Boniface VIII's Constitution *Cum ex eo* (1298)," *Canadian Journal of History* 4 (1969):18-19.

[35] Orme, *ESMA*, 19; Bowker, *Secular Clergy*, 44-45; Heath, *English Parish Clergy*, 81.

[36] PRO E 35/61; Heath, *English Parish Clergy*, 82, app. 3.

rantia sacerdotum), Quivil or Thoresby, had no connection with the Arts course at a university." Pecham's syllabus, for example, included fourteen articles of faith, the Ten Commandments, two precepts of the Evangelist, seven works of mercy, the seven "capital" sins, the seven principal virtues, and the seven sacraments.[37] This prescription for the *ignorantia sacerdotum* was reissued in York diocese by Archbishop Neville (1465-1476) and in 1518 by Cardinal Wolsey.[38] Earlier synodal statutes, issued first at Wells (1258?) and then at York (1259) likewise specified that parish rectors and vicars know (and teach their parishioners) such basic knowledge as the Ten Commandments and the seven sacraments.[39] The similarity between these catechetical expectations and the elementary curriculum described above is readily apparent.

Going somewhat beyond these minimal expectations, William de Melton, chancellor of York, in his (1510?) sermon delivered to York candidates for ordination, sketched the depth of knowledge hoped for. "No one should receive holy orders who has not gained at least a moderate knowledge of good letters, meaning Latin. He should be able to read a Latin book, especially the scriptures, readily and accurately. A priest ought to know enough grammar to be able to study from books and improve himself without the aid of teachers."[40] Melton's criteria were echoed in Convocation in 1531 when regulations for ordination were issued. No one was to receive the subdiaconate unless "so versed in the Epistles and Gospels, at least those contained in the Missal, as to be able to explain their grammatical meaning to the examiner."[41] Such expectations are significant, not only because they required only a minimal training in Latin grammar, no more than what one might expect from an elementary education with a few years at a grammar school or a few years of tutoring by a competent clerk or priest, but also because of the underlying assumption that the ordinands might not be likely to receive further schooling.

From York diocese there are several examples of parish clergy with

[37] Haines, "Education of the English Clergy," 15-16; Roy M. Haines, "Education in English Ecclesiastical Legislation of the Later Middle Ages," in *Studies in Church History*, Vol. 7, ed. G. J. Cuming and D. Baker (Cambridge, 1971), 170.

[38] David Wilkins, ed., *Concilia Magnae Britanniae et Hiberniae*, 4 vols. (London, 1737), 3:599-605, 662-65; Woolley, *York Provinciale*, 1-3.

[39] *Councils and Synods II, 1205-1313*, ed. F. M. Powicke and C. R. Cheney (Oxford, 1964), i:609-10.

[40] William de Melton, *Sermo Exhortatorius cancellarii Eboracensis hiis qui ad sacros ordines petunt promoveri* (STC 17806), 5-6. The sermon is discussed in Heath, *English Parish Clergy*, 70-73.

[41] Philip Hughes, *The Reformation in England*, 3 vols. (London, 1950-1954), 1:84-85.

only an elementary or some grammar school education to recommend them. Although there is no evidence for any grammar school at Rothwell parish, in 1440 a testator left 2d. to every scholar in the parish who had not yet been ordained priest. These parish scholars may well have been going directly from an elementary curriculum into the priesthood. Robert Scalinge, the vicar of Langtoft in 1556, was born and educated for the priesthood in Bulmer parish where he could remember how, in 1503, "he did use sometymes to say mattyns with Parson Jakson then Parson of Bulmer . . ." As far as we know, there was no grammar school in Bulmer. If Scalinge picked up any grammar education, it would probably have been after he was ordained priest (in 1521) and had left his native parish (in 1522). Reading and writing were considered sufficient training for the priesthood by Elizabeth Symson of Bellerby who, in 1535, stipulated that her son "Christofer be founde at scole to he canne write and rede and if he will be prest." Thomas Atkinson may have had either an elementary or grammar education in mind for his son in 1538 when he requested, as noted above, that he be supported "of my sayd wyffe, either at Yorke or elles where it shalbe thought beste, so that he may folowe the scole unto suche tyme yt he may gette orders and be preiste. . . ."[42]

The hypothesis that these instances exemplify a relatively widespread phenomenon is substantiated by the ordination registers. In the fifteenth and early sixteenth centuries the candidates for acolyte were generally identified in terms of their home parishes. And the title received by acolytes when they were ordained into major orders came increasingly from monasteries or convents near their home parishes. One cannot escape the conclusion that these prospective priests were travelling to York with the backing and education provided by local individuals, whether from the parish priests, the local religious house, or a combination of the two. It is doubtful that they were all able to take advantage of the grammar schools in their area, and in many cases there were none nearby. What grammar education many of these ordinands must have received would have had to come from close association with the rector, vicar, or chaplains in their parish.

Taking Archbishop Rotherham's register (1480-1500), in which the ordinands from the archdeaconry of Richmond were recorded separately, it is notable that Richmond, which we know as the most remote and sparsely populated of the five archdeaconries, was supplying almost exactly

[42] BI, Prob. Reg. 2, f. 38; J. S. Purvis, ed., *Select XVIth Century Causes in Tithe*, YAS rec. ser., no. 114 (York, 1949), 93; Leeds Central Library, Archives Department, Richmond Archdeaconry, Will Register 1, 2, 3, & A, f. 139; *Wills and Administrations from the Knaresborough Court Rolls*, 1:26.

one-fifth of the clergy ordained during these years.[43] Richmond was, moreover, without the educational resources of the rest of York diocese and certainly, before 1500, not well-supplied with grammar facilities. Nor would the Richmond parish clergy have been capable of providing any very sophisticated grammar education for their parish scholars, for, as was noted above, not a single university graduate was to be found among their ranks in 1525-1526. It is therefore quite likely that many Richmond ordinands had only a reading education to recommend them.

Although the level of learning attained by most parish and mass priests was not high, some learning was requisite, and its availability was on the increase. According to the statistics presented in Table 4 (Chapter four), the first large climb in numbers of reading schools occurred in the second quarter of the fifteenth century, ten to thirty-five years before clerical recruitment began to grow. From then until about 1510 clerical recruitment kept pace with the growth of reading institutions and the new spurt in grammar school foundations. The sequence of events would strongly suggest that the increased availability of a reading education contributed significantly to soaring clerical recruitment, although it is quite possible that the grammar schools, despite their numerical stability, were opening their doors to larger numbers of scholars during the same period. The parallel between the growing number of elementary and secondary scholars and the rising rate of ordinations can most graphically be seen by examining the letters dimissory from York between 1452 and 1514.

Under William Booth (1452-1464) only 15.4 percent of letters dimissory went to scholars. By 1465 the proportion of scholars is far greater. Between 1465 and 1476, 39.4 percent of all ordinands seeking orders outside the diocese were scholars, and the proportion rises steadily until the archiepiscopacy of Christopher Bainbridge (1508-1514) when it reaches a height of 52 percent. Although the percentage of scholars declines under Wolsey, actual numbers per annum are higher than previously. The table of scholars granted letters dimissory not only parallels the rise and subsequent leveling off in ordinations, it also exhibits a leap in numbers (between Rotherham and Bainbridge) similar to the climb in both elementary and grammar education after 1500 (Tables 2 and 4 above).

If, as has been argued above, the rise in ordinations is related not only to heavy demand for clerical services, but also to the increased availability of elementary and grammar education, one would expect to find some awareness of this relationship or at least some concern for pre-university education among the Church hierarchy. The most obvious question is

---

[43] BI, Reg. 23 (Rotherham), ff. 372-468.

TABLE 6

SCHOLARS LISTED IN LETTERS DIMISSORY, 1452-1530

Archbishop	No. Scholars Listed in Letters Dimissory	Average No. Scholars Listed per annum	% Scholars of Total No. Letters Dimissory Registered
Wm. Booth (1452-1464)	45	3.5	15.4%
Neville (1465-1476)	58	4.8	39.4%
L. Booth[a] (1476-1480)	1	—	—
Rotherham (1480-1500)	341	16.2	38.7%
Savage (1501-1507)	106	15.1	45%
Bainbridge (1508-1514)	147	21	52%
Wolsey (1514-1530)	364	21.4	34%

SOURCE: Peter Heath, *English Parish Clergy on the Eve of the Reformation* (London, 1969), app. 3.

[a] Due apparently to scribal negligence, letters dimissory were rarely recorded under L. Booth.

whether the Church promoted parochial education and, if so, for what reasons?

Although Leonard Boyle has argued that thirteenth-century conciliar legislation on education was primarily focused on supplying graduates for cathedral chairs,[44] the English ecclesiastical hierarchy, at any rate, did concern itself with education at the parish level. As early as 994, the *Liber legum ecclesiasticarum* recommended that priests keep schools and teach young children for free.[45] The early eleventh-century so-called "Canons of Edgar," possibly issued by a northern synod, assert that "it is right

[44] Boyle, "The Constitution 'Cum ex eo,' " 266.

[45] Wilkins, *Concilia*, 1:270; A. F. Leach, *Educational Charters and Documents, 589-1909* (Cambridge, 1911), 36-37. "Ut presbiteri per villas scholas habeant, et gratis parvulos doceant."

that priests readily teach the young, and instruct them in crafts, that they may have help in church," an expectation closely echoed in one of Ælfric's pastoral letters of the same period.[46] Sometime between 1200 and 1215, in one of the earliest sets of diocesan statutes (perhaps from London), priests were advised to teach their parishioners in English the Lord's Prayer, the Creed, general confession, the articles of faith, and the value of the sacrament of confession.[47] The York synodal statutes (1241 x 1255), which were reiterated in Wolsey's *Provinciale* of 1518, required rectors and all those to whom *cura animarum* belonged to instruct and inform those committed to their care in right faith and good conduct. In addition, the clergy should give themselves over to good studies, devoting their time to prayer and reading.[48] Earlier statutes from Salisbury (1219 x 1228), reissued for Durham (1228 x 1236), provide a benefice for those schoolmasters who instruct poor scholars in grammar. Subsequently, the Winchester diocesan statutes of 1295 directed rectors and parish priests to teach boys in the parish their Lord's Prayer, Creed, Ave Maria, and how to read the psalter. Provision was also made for scholars to be assigned as holy water carriers, a position that carried with it certain financial rewards.[49] Two sermons of Master William de Rymyngton, chancellor of Oxford, which were preached at York in 1372 and 1373, criticized parish clergy for not instructing their parishioners sufficiently in sacred literature. In the fifteenth century Bishop Pecok, preaching at Paul's Cross, argued that bishops should leave elementary instruction to the parochial clergy, while Thomas Gascoigne, chancellor of Oxford circa 1450, expected the parish clergy to preach frequently and extend education.[50] By 1529 the Convocation of Canterbury explicitly directed "rectors, vicars and chantry priests that after divine service they shall employ themselves in study, prayer, lectures or other honest affairs or business, which becomes their profession: namely, by instructing boys in the alphabet, in reading, in singing or grammar." Finally, in 1537, Bishop Latimer of Worcester

---

[46] *Councils and Synods I, 871-1204*, ed. D. Whitelock, M. Brett, and C. Brooke (Oxford, 1981), i:314, 331. For Ælfric's letter, see p. 331 n 1: "Sed vos sacerdotes debetis docere pueros et adolescentes vel iuvenes et habere in eis adiutorium ad ecclesiastica officia implenda."

[47] Ibid., ii:1057-58, 1070-71.

[48] *Councils and Synods II*, i:485; Woolley, *York Provinciale*, 26.

[49] *Councils and Synods II*, i:94; *VCH, Hants.*, 2:253-54. "Item, precipimus quod aliquod competens beneficium magistro prebeatur qui gratis in gramatica facultate pauperes scolares instruat iuxta posse suum, . . ."

[50] Joseph McNulty, "William of Rymyngton, Prior of Salley Abbey, Chancellor of Oxford, 1372-3," *YAJ* 30 (1931):231-47; G. R. Owst, *Literature and Pulpit in Medieval England* (Cambridge, 1933), 273-75; Thomas Gascoigne, *Loci e Libro Veritatum*, ed. J. Thorold Rogers (Oxford, 1881), xli-xlii, lxi, 3-5.

enjoined that "everyone of you that be chantry priests do instruct and teach the children of your parish such as will come to you at the least to read English," an order that Bishop Bonner of London repeated in 1542 not only to chantry priests but also to parsons, vicars, and stipendiary priests.[51] Sporadically but consistently throughout this period, the ecclesiastical hierarchy evinced concern for and tried to promote the educational efforts of its parish clergy. The rationale appears to have been a mixed one of producing scholars and educating parishioners, both at a very basic level. Nor was this the end of the Church's concern with education. In addition to facilitating a university education for some clergy, issuing summaries of the knowledge required for cure of souls, and exhorting and requiring clergy to establish parish schools and educate parishioners, the ecclesiastical hierarchy tried to establish minimal standards of Latin literacy for those entering orders. It is unclear how successful they were.

Prior to the plague there was clearly some concern for the educational quality of the candidates. Both H. S. Bennett and Nicholas Orme cite examples of more than cursory examinations for literacy from the thirteenth- and fourteenth-century ordination records. Additional evidence for the seriousness with which examinations were taken in various parts of England prior to the plague years comes from J.R.H. Moorman's account of Church life in England in the thirteenth century as well as from the work that Roy Haines has done in the diocese of Worcester.[52] The evidence from York is scanty but does suggest that there was some effort to maintain educational standards. Archbishop Giffard's register records examinations for prospective acolytes and subdeacons held previous to the September ordinations in 1273 when the candidates from St. Leonard's Hospital, York, were "examinati leniter," while nearly two hundred others were more straitly examined. A similarly large group of prospective deacons and priests were listed as being examined the following year. Twenty-seven years later the register of Archbishop Corbridge refers to examinations to be held at St. John, Beverley, for candidates to all four orders. Archbishop Corbridge's concern for examination of learning manifested

[51] W. Frere and W. M. Kennedy, *Visitation Articles and Injunctions of the Period of the Reformation*, Vol. 2, Alcuin Club Collections, no. 15 (London, 1910), 17, 56, 63, 85. Wilkins, *Concilia*, 3:865. See also the 1538 injunctions of the bishop of Exeter. Ibid., 844-45.

[52] Orme, *ESMA*, 16-17; H. S. Bennett, "Medieval Ordination Lists in the English Episcopal Registers," in *Studies Presented to Sir Hilary Jenkinson*, ed. J. C. Davies (Oxford, 1957), 20-34; Moorman, *Church Life*, 198-201; Roy M. Haines, *The Administration of the Diocese of Worcester in the First Half of the Fourteenth Century* (London, 1965), 172. The discussion of ordination examinations in York follows material previously presented in Moran, "Clerical Recruitment," 27-29.

itself also in his statutes for the chapter at Southwell Minster where he ordered that no one be ordained or beneficed except after examination before the chapter. A similar procedure was followed at York Minster in 1344 when Robert Swetemouth, the subchanter, presented a list of candidates for orders to the chapter, by whom each was examined and approved. In fact, the regular presence of examiners is suggested by a 1334 commission to the bishop of Norwich to ordain, in any church of the city or diocese of York, persons presented by the dean of Christianity in York and his fellow examiners.[53]

References to examinations do not disappear between 1348 and the Reformation, but they are not plentiful. A 1397 commission to the bishop of Whithorn as suffragan specifies one of his duties as that of conferring minor orders on suitable candidates after due examination. In 1421 the York Chapter Acts record the examination of eleven young clerks of the cathedral by some of the canons. Three of them were pronounced competent in Latin, three quite unsatisfactory, and the rest more or less satisfactory in that they attended class regularly. Unfortunately, the documents do not tell us to what extent these examinations determined the ordination schedules of these boys. In 1474, on a small slip attached to one of the ordination folios, there is a list of what would seem to be candidates from Richmond archdeaconry. Several names are ticked off and appear on the official list of those ordained the following day. All the aspiring acolytes, one subdeacon, and five priests fail to appear in the official record.[54] This may indicate some effort to control the flow of candidates from Richmond archdeaconry, which was the most remote and least well educationally supplied area of York diocese. And forty years later, Richard Thornton testified in the bishop of Lincoln's Court of Audience that he had been examined before ordination at York: "M. doctor Tate examined hym and admytted hym to the order of prestehode in a lytle house beside thaff chapitre house of the mynster."[55]

Despite precautions, unworthy candidates managed to get ordained. In 1481 Archbishop Rotherham's register records a dispensation to John

---

[53] *The Register of Walter Giffard, Lord Archbishop of York, 1266-1279*, ed. W. Brown, Surtees Society, no. 109 (Durham, 1904), 194-98; William Brown, ed., *The Register of Thomas of Corbridge, Lord Archbishop of York, 1300-1304*, Vol. 1, Surtees Society, no. 138 (Durham, 1925), 2-3; A. F. Leach, ed., *Visitations and Memorials of Southwell Minster*, Camden Society, new ser., no. 48 (London, 1891), 201-16; YML, D. & C., H1/1a, f. 11; Rosalind M. T. Hill, ed., *The Register of William Melton: Archbishop of York, 1317-1340*, Vol. 1, Canterbury and York Society, no. 70 (Torquay, 1977), 108.

[54] Smith, *Calendar of the Register of Robert Waldby, Archbishop of York*, 3; YML, D. & C., H2/1a, f. 36; BI, Reg. 22 (G. Neville), ff. 228-29.

[55] Lincoln Record Office, Cj. 2, ff. 100ff.; cited in Bowker, *Secular Clergy*, 41.

Gedney of Beverley, who, "in the time of our predecessor Laurence [Archbishop Booth, 1476-1480] fraudulently caused himself to be ordained to the subdiaconate by William, Bishop of Dromore, by causing another to appear for him at the examination in literacy, from the consequences of this act so that he may proceed to higher orders."[56] The 1510? sermon by William de Melton, the chancellor of York Cathedral, noted that although examinations were being held at York, requirements were lax, and he listed a variety of frauds by which candidates achieved ordination, including pretending to have a university degree in order to be exempt from the examination.[57] One can conclude, therefore, that while there is no evidence that examinations were not performed, opportunities for fraud did exist. In addition, the large numbers presenting themselves for ordination in the aftermath of the fourteenth-century plagues or by the end of the fifteenth century must have involved logistical difficulties for their examiners, and it is unrealistic to suppose that all were examined scrupulously. The problem was "not that learning was unexamined . . . but that a very little learning was deemed adequate. Yet some compromise with reality was unavoidable if the Church were to recruit personnel in sufficient numbers . . ."[58]

Many authorities within the Church testified to the fact that examinations had become too perfunctory and superficial. Thomas Gascoigne complained that the promotion to the priesthood of unworthy candidates was one of the greatest scandals of his time. John Colet's sermon to the Convocation at St. Paul's in 1511/12 reiterated the theme:

> Let those lawes be rehersed, that do warne you fathers that ye put nat ouer soone your handes on euery man, or admitte vnto holy orders. For ther is the well of euils, that, the brode gate of holy orders opened, euery man that offereth hym selfe is all where admytted without pullynge backe. Therof spryngeth and cometh out the people that are in the church both of unlerned and euyll pristes.

Thomas Starkey was similarly critical. "For this admitting of frail youth without convenient proof of their virtue and learning is the ground and mother of all misorder in the Church and religion." Even among the higher officials of the Church, "commonley you shall find that they can no thing do but patter up their matins and mass, mumbling up a certain

[56] E. E. Barker, ed., *The Register of Thomas Rotherham, Archbishop, 1480-1500*, Vol. 1, Canterbury and York Society, no. 69 (Torquay, 1976), 192. For the original, which Barker paraphrases, see BI, Reg. 23 (Rotherham), f. 203v.

[57] Melton, *Sermo Exhortatorius*.

[58] Heath, *English Parish Clergy*, 18.

number of words no thing understood."[59] William de Melton, in his 1510? sermon for the ordinands, also referred to the ignorance of the clergy (*rudium et stolidorum clericorum*) as one of the scandals of the time, and William Allen, writing to Dom Maurice Chauncey in 1577, recalled the pre-Reformation clergy, "the common sort of curates had in old time, as you may better than I remember their want then in manner even of necessary knowledge."[60]

Thomas More's *Dialogue against Tyndale* (1528) is perhaps the most convincing evidence of widespread clerical ignorance precisely because he was refuting Tyndale's vehement attack on the English clergy. More discounted much of Tyndale's criticism as exaggerated, but even he could not pretend that all was well. His interlocutor in the *Dialogue*, after urging that the English clergy were vice-ridden and seldom willing to teach laity, received the following response from More:

> I wote well there be therein many very lewde and naught. And surely where so euer there is a multytude it is not without myracle well possyble to be other wyse. But nowe yf the bysshops wolde ones take vnto presthed better ley men and fewer . . . all the matter were more than halfe amended.[61]

One of the reasons for such relatively minimal educational standards for ordination must surely have been that a very large percentage of those entering the clergy after 1460 (and before) would never have expected to obtain a benefice or even to become a vicar or curate. To ask of them that they be good grammarians would have meant overeducating them for the tasks they would be expected to perform. Even beneficed clergy in York diocese (63 percent of whose benefices had been appropriated by the time of the Reformation) fared relatively poorly. In 1535 Archbishop Lee wrote that the livings in York diocese were so poor and unattractive that he was lucky to find incumbents who could understand what they read and administer the sacraments. No question of an understanding of grammar was even suggested, and Lee was sure that in everything else the clergy would need outside counsel.[62]

---

[59] Gascoigne, *Loci e Libro Veritatum*, 18-20; J. H. Lupton, *A Life of John Colet*, 2nd ed. (London, 1909), 300; Thomas Starkey, *A Dialogue between Reginald Pole and Thomas Lupset*, ed. K. M. Burton (London, 1948), 126, 181.

[60] Melton, *Sermo Exhortatorius*; Hughes, *The Reformation in England*, 1:84.

[61] *A Dialogue Concerning Heresies*, 295.

[62] Henry Ellis, ed., *Original Letters, Illustrative of English History*, 4 vols., 3rd ser. (London, 1846), 2:338; John Strype, *Ecclesiastical Memorials*, 7 vols. (London, 1816), 1:302. See also Heath, *English Parish Clergy*, 74.

TABLE 7

LEVEL OF LEARNING AMONG THE CHANTRY CHAPLAINS
IN THE COUNTY OF YORK, 1548

Categories	West Riding	City of York	North & East Ridings[a]	Total No.	%
Learning not described[b]	53	0	10	63	19
Not learned; unlearned; no learning	21	9	6	36	11
Meanly learned; indifferently learned; of little learning[c]	12	61	44	117	35
Somewhat learned; indifferently well-learned	23	5	7	35	10
Learned; good learning; well-learned	3	12	68[d]	83	25
Total	112	87	135	334	100

SOURCE: William Page, ed., *The Certificates of the Commissioners Appointed to Survey the Chantries, Guilds, Hospitals, etc. in the County of York*, Vol. 2, Surtees Society, no. 92 (Durham, 1895), 371 ff.

[a] The only complete surviving returns from the East Riding are from Hull and Beverley.

[b] Many of these are described as blind, sick, or, in four cases, just deceased.

[c] The terms "indifferently learned" and "meanly learned" appear to be interchangeable. In the returns for the city of York three chantry chaplains who held more than one chantry were described as meanly learned in one instance, indifferently learned in another.

[d] Thirty-nine of the sixty-eight chantry chaplains listed as having good learning were attached to the town of Beverley, most of them in chantries within the minster. The level of learning of the chantry chaplains in Beverley was significantly higher than those in York.

In the 1548 returns for the county of York, the chantry commissioners noted the level of learning of the chantry priests. The data are summarized in Table 7. With the single exception of the chantry chaplains in Beverley, the results were unimpressive. Forty-six percent of all the chantry priests were either unlearned or "meanly" learned, while only 35 percent were either somewhat learned or well learned. If the chantry priests exhibited such a low level of educational competence, then the stipendiary chaplains, who ranked lower in the ecclesiastical hierarchy and were more numerous, must have had an even more depressing record. With the dissolution of the chantries many of these lower clergy were thrown back into a lay world where the level of their education must not have distinguished them appreciably from the laity who, as we shall see in Chapter six, had also benefited from the developments in education.

If one cannot actually prove that the increasing demand for chantry priests in York diocese, buttressed by longstanding ecclesiastical concerns for education, stimulated schooling, or that the development of education then promoted an increase in the ranks of the clergy (we could only do the last with the help of school registers and ordination records), we have nonetheless argued and documented a highly plausible chain of events. There can be no doubt that after 1460 York diocese experienced an upsurge in the number of men seeking admittance to the order of priesthood, and the available evidence for the early sixteenth century suggests that, whereas the growth may have stopped after 1510, a continuing high rate of re-cruitment was maintained at least until Wolsey's demise in 1529. This development was likely due to the growing demand for parish and private chaplains and the expanding opportunities for elementary and grammar education. There were undoubtedly many individuals who hoped to take advantage of that demand to peform a function that offered a modest, somewhat secure, living and required only a moderate, sometimes even minimal, investment in education. It is clear that there were a number of these parish chaplains, chantry chaplains, and perhaps even some curates and vicars with no more than a reading school education behind them. While this may have met the immediate needs of the Church, it was ultimately to work to its disadvantage. As we shall see in Chapter six, the same schools that were educating the parish clergy were also helping to create a new class of literate laity with less of a vested interest in the continued vitality of the Church and with a sense of equality or even superiority toward the similarly or sometimes less well educated clergy. While the Church concerned itself with supplying the priests demanded for private oratories, for chantries, and for obits and trentals, the aspiring clerk became less convinced that entering the Church was a necessary step in his road to success. If the York diocesan situation was at all typical, by the time of the Reformation the Church was overburdened with chaplains who were trained, at most, for cure of souls and often capable of little more than chanting the services. It was a situation that did not augur well for the Church at a time when laity were becoming increasingly capable of considering religious questions for themselves.

CHAPTER 6

Literacy and the Laicization
of Education

References to reading and song scholars increase in number throughout the fifteenth and sixteenth centuries, while the availability of grammar schools expanded markedly between 1500 and 1548. In fact, the educational developments that were taking place within late medieval York diocese are sufficiently great to tempt one to speak of a pre-Reformation revolution in education. Whereas the previous chapter argued that a growth in clerical recruitment accompanies these changes and partially explains them, this chapter examines lay involvement in education and the extent of lay literacy. It suggests that the evolving laicization of society was a cause and also a consequence of educational expansion.

There is no doubt that most members of the English upper classes[1] by the fourteenth century were literate; that is, they could read and write in either French or English and oftentimes both.[2] And many members of the English upper classes were latinate; they could read Latin, knew some Latin grammar, and often boasted large libraries.[3] A few of the aristocratic laity were authors and scholars in their own right.[4] Among the north country wills in the Prerogative Court of Canterbury, many, although not the majority, of the noble wills provide some indication of literacy or

---

[1] In the late fourteenth century and first half of the fifteenth, there was not yet the sharp distinction between nobility and gentry common to the sixteenth century. Although the distinction became clearer after 1450, this analysis will include as members of the upper class both the aristocracy and gentry, including squires who became armigerous in the fourteenth century. See K. B. McFarlane, *The Nobility of Later Medieval England* (Oxford, 1973), app. a, chap. 1 and chap. 8; N. Denholm-Young, *The Country Gentry in the Fourteenth Century* (Oxford, 1969), chap. 1.

[2] McFarlane, *Nobility of Later Medieval England*, chap. 6.

[3] For the various degrees and definitions of literacy, see Chapter two, p. 18 above.

[4] McFarlane, *Nobility of Later Medieval England*, chap. 6. McFarlane mentions William de la Pole, Duke of Suffolk; John Montagu, Earl of Salisbury; and Henry, Duke of Lancaster. One might add, for the fifteenth century, Sir Richard Roos; Anthony Woodville, Earl Rivers; Stephen Scrope, esquire; and Sir Thomas Malory. Geoffrey Chaucer, described in 1372-1373 as *armiger*, should also be included as a member of the lower nobility. Denholm-Young, *The Country Gentry*, 23-24.

interest in education; this is equally true for the women as for the men. And, although many of the northern gentry whose wills were apt to be registered at York rather than Canterbury were more concerned with the disposition of their land and jewels than with books or the training of their children, evidence is not lacking of their literacy and concern with education.

Although approximately two dozen individuals scattered throughout the York diocesan wills are characterized as *literatus* (i.e., latinate), there is only one instance, early in our period, when the adjective is used to describe a member of the armigerous class. This occurred in 1349 when William de la Zouch, the archbishop of York, referred to his young kinsman Anketill Mallory as *armiger literatus*.[5] The failure to identify other nobility as *literati* is curious, as we know that Latin literacy among the aristocratic and knightly classes was not unusual from the twelfth century onwards.[6] It is possible that literate knights were becoming less remarkable and hence less remarked upon.

It is certainly common to find the nobility or gentry writing or signing their wills, although a signature alone is not always conclusive evidence of literacy.[7] In 1391 Sir William Moubray of Colton drew up his own last will and testament at York in French. In 1422 Sir Roger Salvyn, a Yorkshire knight dying at the Franciscan friary in York, wrote his will in English, as did Sir Hugh Willoughby, knight, of Nottinghamshire, in 1443. Sir John Markynfelde, knight, wrote an indenture (in English) separate from his will in 1448.[8] In 1457 Sir Thomas Rokes, a knight with lands in Halifax, wrote his own will in Latin, and in 1464 Peter Ardern, knight and Baron of the Exchequer with lands in Little Driffield, Howby, Easingwold, and Galtres Forest, Yorkshire, penned his will in a combination of English and Latin, as did Alexander Nevill in 1453 and Henry Percy, Earl of Northumberland, in 1485. By 1498 Sir Richard York, knight, heard his will read (in Latin), answered in Latin, wrote a

---

[5] *Test. Ebor.*, 1:56.

[6] Ralph V. Turner, "The *Miles Literatus* in Twelfth- and Thirteenth-Century England: How Rare a Phenomenon?" *American Historical Review* 83 (1978):928-45; M. T. Clanchy, *From Memory to Written Record: England, 1066-1307* (Cambridge, Mass., 1979), chap. 7; Denholm-Young, *The Country Gentry*, 2.

[7] J. Hoeppner Moran, "Literacy and Education in Northern England, 1350-1550: A Methodological Inquiry," *Northern History* 17 (1981):8; Clanchy, *From Memory to Written Record*, 183-84.

[8] BI, Prob. Reg. 1, f. 29v, printed in *Test. Ebor.*, 1:158-61; described by McFarlane, *Nobility of Later Medieval England*, 45; PRO, PCC, Prob. 11/2A and 2B (Reg. March, 49), printed in *NCW*, 31-32; BI, Prob. Reg. 2, ff. 180-82, 186-88, printed in *Test. Ebor.*, 2:130-34; BI, Prob. Reg. 2, f. 190.

note in Latin at the end, and signed his name to the codicil.[9] By the beginning of the sixteenth century the gentry and aristocracy of York diocese increasingly either wrote or signed their wills.[10]

Evidence of writing ability needs to be supplemented with evidence for reading ability gathered primarily from what we can discover about book ownership.[11] Since so few medieval inventories have survived, wills provide the best information we have, although they mention only an unknown, and perhaps relatively small, proportion of those books actually in the hands of testators. How ill-advised drawing conclusions about book ownership from wills can be is obvious when one compares, for example, the will of the thirteenth Earl of Oxford, dated 1509, which mentions three books, with the inventory of his library, which mentions sixty to sixty-five volumes.[12]

Among the 148 wills of Yorkshire gentry between 1376 and 1482, 24, or 16 percent, mention books. At the national level, and further up the social scale, the statistics are somewhat better. Among the extant wills of English peers and peeresses between 1350 and 1500, 28 percent mention books, mostly service and devotional books.[13] Women, in proportion to the number of extant wills, were more likely to bequeath books than were men.[14] York diocesan gentlewomen often left small personal libraries such as that of Elizabeth la Zouche in 1380, who mentions a "Tristrem" and

[9] PRO, PCC, Prob. 11/4 Stockton 12, extract printed in *NCW*, 256; PRO, PCC, Prob. 11/5 Godyn 19, extract printed in *Test. Ebor.*, 4:102-103n and *NCW*, 257; BI, Prob. Reg. 2, ff. 351-52; Reg. 23 (Rotherham), ff. 347-49, printed in *Test. Ebor.*, 3:304-10; PRO, PCC, Prob. 11/11 Horne 36, printed in *Test. Ebor.*, 4:134-37.

[10] The growing number of nobility either writing their wills or signing them can be readily seen by looking through the first five volumes of the *Test. Ebor.* While there is only one example from the earliest volume, the numbers gradually increase. See *Test. Ebor.*, 1:158-61; 2:110-14; 130-34, 207-208; 3:25-27, 178-81, 273-78, 304-10; 4:15-16, 117-18, 128-29, 134-37, 149-54; 5:32-34, 73-76, 110-12, 129-32, 144-46, 166-70, 306-19. The practice is more prevalent in the wills registered at the Prerogative Court of Canterbury.

[11] For a discussion of the limited usefulness of signatures for determining literacy in the Middle Ages, see Moran, "Literacy and Education."

[12] W. H. St. John Hope, "The Last Testament and Inventory of John de Veer, Thirteenth Earl of Oxford," *Archaeologia* 66, 2nd ser., 16 (1915):311-12, 317, 338, 341-42, referred to in Joel Rosenthal, "Aristocratic Cultural Patronage and Book Bequests, 1350-1550," *Bulletin of the John Rylands University Library* 64 (1982):546. Susan Cavanaugh makes this point in the introduction to "A Study of Books Privately Owned in England: 1300-1450," 2 vols. (Ph.D. diss., University of Pennsylvania, 1980).

[13] M.G.A. Vale, *Piety, Charity and Literacy among the Yorkshire Gentry, 1370-1480* (York, 1976), 5, 29-30; Rosenthal, "Aristocratic Cultural Patronage," 536.

[14] Rosenthal, "Aristocratic Cultural Patronage." Among the extant wills of peers and peeresses, 48 percent of all women's wills mention books, while only 18 percent of the male testators left books.

a "Lanchelot," a breviary, a psalter, and other books.[15] In 1448, Agnes Stapelton, wife of Sir Brian Stapelton, bequeathed a library which consisted of three French books, pseudo-Bonaventure's *Life of Christ* (in English), the *Prick of Conscience, Chastising of God's Children*, a tract entitled *Vice and Virtues*, a book with prayers, a primer, and a large psalter. Although devotional and moral treatises were the most common books bequeathed by women testators, romances were also popular. For example, in 1432 Joanna Hilton left "unum librum de Romanse cum Decem Preceptis Alembes" and "unum librum de Romanse de Septem Sages" to her sister and niece respectively. Earlier she had been bequeathed a French *Romance of the Rose*.[16] Such women must have read the vernacular (either English or French) with greater ease than they would a Latin text. The will of Dame Jane Huddelston illustrates this nicely. Her 1518 will describes the way her son cheated her out of dowry lands in Yorkshire by asking her to sign a Latin document she could not read and which he misrepresented to her. She attempted to right the situation in her will, which was written in English.[17]

Among the male testators, John Morton, knight, bequeathed a Latin *Policronicon*, "unum librum de Anglico, vocatum Gower" (which he left to Joan, Countess of Westmoreland) and *De Gestis Romanorum* in 1431. Earlier, Thomas Ughtred, knight, had left a library of service books, including two missals, two portifors, a gradual, and an ordinal, in addition to a *Brut*.[18] In 1458 Sir Thomas Chaworth of Nottinghamshire left two *policronicons* (one in English and one in Latin), a *Grace de Dieu* and an *Orilogium Sapienciae*, both in English, and "a newe boke of Inglisse, yᵉ which begynnyth with yᵉ lyffe of Seynt Albon and Amphiabell and other mony dyvers lyfez . . . ," including, probably, several of Chaucer's tales and various works by Lydgate. Chaworth also bequeathed a book of fines and eight service books. He owned, but did not bequeath, the English translations of Guido delle Colonne's *Historia Trojana* and Bartholomaeus Anglicus's *De Proprietatibus Rerum*.[19] Peter Ardern, mentioned above, left a library of twenty-eight volumes. These included several service

[15] A. Gibbons, ed., *Early Lincoln Wills*, Lincoln Record Series, no. 1 (Lincoln, 1888), 91-92.

[16] PRO, PCC, Prob. 11/3 Luffenam 35, printed in *NCW*, 48-49; BI, Prob. Reg. 3, f. 347, printed in *Test. Ebor.*, 2:23-25 and *NCW*, 35. The identity of the romance beginning "cum Decem Preceptis Alembes" is unclear.

[17] PRO, PCC, Prob. 11/9 Ayloffe 18, extract printed in *NCW*, 96-97.

[18] BI, Prob. Reg. 2, ff. 653v-54, printed in *Test. Ebor.*, 2:13-15; BI, Prob. Reg. 3, f. 68v, printed in *Test. Ebor.*, 1:241-45.

[19] BI, Reg. 20 (William Booth), ff. 275-76, printed in *Test. Ebor.*, 2:220-29; Cavanaugh, "A Study of Books Privately Owned," 181-83.

books; numerous law volumes; a variety of English books, including Boethius's *Consolation of Philosophy*, the *Legend of Saints*, a book on hunting, and pseudo-Bonaventure's *Life of Christ*; a grammar and a *Catholicon*; and two or three Latin texts.[20] The Thornton manuscript, compiled about 1440 by Robert Thornton, esquire, of East Newton, Yorkshire, shows a more diverse literary culture than is suggested by any of the wills. His commonplace book includes the *Morte Arthure*, a variety of other romances, tracts by William Nassington and Richard Rolle, as well as numerous religious prayers, hymns, and moral treatises.[21] The wills, unfortunately, are often most opaque when we would like them to be most expansive, and there are numerous examples among the upper-class testators of those who left, for example, "all my books concerning the law of the land," "all my books . . . of my chapel," or simply, "all my books."[22]

Although references to books are relatively frequent, almost no other of the York nobility whose wills are extant exhibit the well-rounded commitment to learning and literacy of Thomas Bowes, a Yorkshire gentleman who became keeper of the king's "exchaunges, money and cunage" and who, in 1479, not only left a library of several service books and a Bible, but also wrote his own will and set aside £30 for his son William to attend school.[23] Generally throughout the fourteenth and early fifteenth centuries the wills of Yorkshire gentry show little concern for the education of their own children or that of others.[24] Only toward the end of the fifteenth century do they begin to mention educational benefactions.[25]

[20] PRO, PCC, Prob. 11/5 Godyn 19, extract printed in *Test. Ebor.*, 4:102-103n.

[21] J. O. Halliwell, ed., *The Thornton Romances*, Camden Society, no. 30 (London, 1844), xxvi-xxxvi.

[22] See, for example, the wills of John Pigot (BI, Prob. Reg. 2, f. 544v); Sir John Scot (Prob. Reg. 3, f. 259); William Nevill of Rolston, knight (Reg. 26 (Bainbridge), f. 138v); and Margaret Plays, widow of William Plays, knight (Prob. Reg. 3, f. 44).

[23] PRO, PCC, Prob. 11/7 Logge 12, extract printed in *NCW*, 260.

[24] Vale, *Piety, Charity and Literacy*, 27. A similar picture emerges from an examination of aristocratic wills between 1307 and 1485. See Joel Rosenthal, *The Purchase of Paradise: Gift-Giving and the Aristocracy, 1307-1485* (London, 1972), 51-52 and passim.

[25] Within York diocese, in 1457, Lady Elena Portyngton left £6 silver to Walter Grymeston for sustaining his children in school for three years. In 1461 Sir John Hedlam, knight, left "my gudis that leves, aftir my dettis paid, to tender my childer ther with, and to helpe to holde tham to the scule with the said gudis, als ferr as thai will suffice, for thai have no nother gudes to keep tham with." Nearly twenty years later Christopher Barton of Qwenby, knight, explained that "for a verray trust that I have to my wiffe trusting that she will se that my said younger childre be honestly keped and put to lernyng I will that she have rewle of the said childre." In 1483 Richard Pigot, esquire, bequeathed eight marks annually for six years to each of three priests "such as be vertuose and lerners of the law of God at Cambridge or at Oxford," while,

The literary and educational concerns of four Yorkshire aristocratic and gentle families (the Roos, Scrope, Plumpton, and Constable families) follow this pattern, exhibiting, initially, an interest in books and only later, toward the end of the fifteenth century, an interest in schooling. The extant Roos wills begin with that of Elizabeth la Zouche, the daughter of William de Roos, whose several book bequests in 1380 have been listed above. John, Lord Roos of Hamlake and Belvoir, who wrote his will in 1392, left only his old breviary, his old missal, and his older large legend of the saints. In the same year Robert de Roos, knight of Ingmanthorp, left four service books to the chapel there; a small psalter to his son Thomas; "unum librum de gallico de Veteribus Historiis" to his daughter-in-law; a French psalter, a Bible, and a French legend of saints to his daughter Eleanor; a small psalter which was his wife's to his daughter Katherine, a nun; and a French book called *Sydrak* to Lady Elizabeth Stapelton. [26] Women dominate the list of legatees. The continuing interest in books which the Roos women had is further exemplified in the 1394 will of Lady Mary Roos, widow of John the fifth Lord Roos of Hamlake and Belvoir mentioned above, who left a French book of the Duke of Lancaster (probably the *Livre de seyntz Medicine*) and her green primer, which had belonged to her father, to Isabella Percy, and a roll of the Passion to Lady Isabella Fauconberge. The 1414 will of Lady Beatrice Roos, widow of Thomas fourth Lord Roos, simply mentioned all her books in the chapel without enumerating further. In 1433 Margaret, widow of Lord Roos, received a book of Gospels in French from Alesia, Lady Deyncourt. [27]

Thomas, son of Robert Roos of Ingmanthorp, in his will of 1399, left his psalter to the rector of Dighton, a *Mandeville* and a *Stimulus Conscienciae* to Lord William Healaugh, a black primer with prayers to William Pynkeston, and a legend of saints to Lady Elizabeth Redeman. In 1413

---

in 1485, Dame Margaret Pigot bequeathed to John, brother of Margaret Copley, twenty marks to find him to school. A final example, which by no means exhausts the evidence, is that of Sir John Pilkington, who, in 1478, gave John Pilkington (his son?) six marks a year "to fynd hym to his lernyng at Oxenforth." BI, Prob. Reg. 2, f. 362, printed in *Test. Ebor.*, 2:211-13; BI, Prob. Reg. 2, f. 451, printed in *Test. Ebor.*, 2:247-48; 5, ff. 186, 231v-32, printed in *Test. Ebor.*, 3:285-86; BI, Prob. Reg. 5, f. 267, printed in *Test. Ebor.*, 4:6-7; BI, Prob. Reg. 5, f. 144, printed in *Test. Ebor.*, 3:238-41. Similar instances of educational gifts occur in the wills of Sir Thomas Markenfeld (1497), Sir Henry Vavasour (1499), Lady Eleanor Laton (1503), Sir Matthew Wentworth (1505), Sir Richard Bassett (1522), Thomas Ryther, esquire (1527), Sir Ninian Markenfeld (1527), John Wickersley, esquire (1528), and Sir Walter Griffith (1530).

[26] Gibbons, *Early Lincoln Wills*, 70-71, 91-92; BI, Prob. Reg. 1, f. 51, printed in *Test. Ebor.*, 1:178-80.

[27] BI, Reg. 14 (Arundel), f. 47v, printed in *Test. Ebor.*, 1:201-203; BI, Reg. 18 (Bowet), f. 357v, printed in *Test. Ebor.*, 1:375-79; Gibbons, *Early Lincoln Wills*, 160.

William, sixth Lord Roos of Hamlake and Belvoir, left £400 to pay the stipends for ten chaplains to celebrate services in his castle at Belvoir, one of whom "in grammatica magis doctum et scientem" was to teach his children. He also left to Thomas Cliff the portable breviary that he always carried with him.[28] Eleanor Roos of York and Ingmanthorp, the daughter to whom Robert de Roos had left several books and to whom Sir William Anthorp, rector of Dighton, had bequeathed all his English books, left a considerable library at her death in 1438, including a psalter, an English book called the first book of Master Walter, a primer of the Holy Spirit, "unum librum de Passione Domini," a book entitled *Credo in Deum*, and a volume called the "Maulde buke." All but two of these books were given to other women; all but two of them were in Latin, and all but one remained within the family.[29]

Hilton [margin annotation]

Although Matilda, Countess of Cambridge and granddaughter of Thomas, Lord Roos, left three primers, a portifor, and two volumes in French called Gyron le Curtasse in 1446, in general the Roos family wills mention fewer and fewer books.[30] The will of Robert Roos, knight and son of William, dated 1448, and the will of John Roos of Routh, knight, dated 1451, contain no book bequests, although we know of two extant volumes, one of French translations of Aegidius Romanus, *De Regimine Principum* and Vegetius, *De Re Militari*, and the other a "livre de linformation des princes" that belonged to Robert.[31] Fewer book bequests, however, do not necessarily suggest literary disinterest. The high level of learning attained by the Roos of this generation is illustrated by Sir Richard Roos, court poet under the Duke and Duchess of Gloucester and subsequently under Henry VI.[32]

Evidence for the literacy of the nobility and gentry of York diocese

[28] BI, Prob. Reg. 3, f. 23v, printed in *Test. Ebor.*, 1:251-53; BI, Reg. 18 (Bowet), f. 363, printed in *Test. Ebor.*, 1:359.

[29] BI, Prob. Reg. 1, f. 51, printed in *Test. Ebor.*, 1:178-80; BI, Prob. Reg. 3, ff. 351, 529. Eleanor Roos's will is printed in *Test. Ebor.*, 2:65-66. The "Maulde buke" may have been an English translation of the *Book of Spiritual Grace* by St. Mechthild.

[30] Exceptions are: 1) the 1503 will of Thomas Roos of Ingmanthorp, who left a *Legenda Aurea*, *Catholicon*, a book called *Dormi Securis*, and a portifor. BI, Prob. Reg. 6, f. 134, printed in *Test. Ebor.*, 4:223-24, and 2) the 1515 will of James Roos of Ingmanthorp who leaves a psalter of Latin and French, a matins book, and a lawbook entitled *Littleton Tenures*. BI, Prob. Reg. 9, f. 23, printed in *Test. Ebor.*, 5:60.

[31] BI, Reg. 19 (Kemp), f. 192, printed in *Test. Ebor.*, 2:118-24; *NCW*, 49-50; BI, Prob. Reg. 2, f. 245, printed in *Test. Ebor.*, 2:159-60. The two volumes which belonged to Robert Roos are: University Library, MS Ee.2.17 and Royal 19.A.xx.

[32] The impressive range of his learning has been documented, in a book of very uneven quality, by Ethel Seaton, *Sir Richard Roos, c. 1410-1482, Lancastrian Poet* (London, 1961).

does not abate in the second half of the fifteenth century, but it does change its character. Mentions of books in wills become less common, and educational abilities and interests are reflected instead in a growing number of bequests for sending sons to the grammar school, university, or Inns of Court and for funding scholars. The Scrope family, with its two branches at Bolton and Upsall-Masham, exemplify this trend. The 1415 and 1419 inventories of Lord Henry Scrope of Masham list more than fifty books, including at least forty-five service books, a copy of Genesis in French, a Bible, *Beda de gestis Anglie*, a book of Dominical Sermons, a legend of saints, and a life of St. Brigit. Thirty-seven books plus all the books of his chapel were mentioned in his will. Altogether Scrope possessed at least eighty volumes, most of which were religious in character. Stephen le Scrope, father of Lord Henry, left a book, the *Pars Oculi*, on his deathbed in 1406, while his brother John left a Bible and two French books, *Tristrem* and *Grace Dieu*. In 1400 Sir Richard Scrope, Lord of Bolton and first cousin of Lord Henry, left 100 shillings for repairing books in St. Agatha Abbey near Richmond, his psalter to his daughter Isabella, and his second-best missal and portable breviary, which he always used for saying his matins and vespers, to his son and heir Roger. Both missal and breviary were subsequently passed on to Roger's son, Richard, as heirlooms.[33]

In 1420 Richard Scrope, third Lord of Bolton, appears to have written his own will (in English) at the siege of Rouen. A few years before, he had left eleven service books to the choir of St. George's chapel, Windsor. In the 1440s Stephen Scrope, grandson of Richard, first Lord of Bolton, translated the *Dicts and Sayings of the Philosophers* and the *Epistle of Othea to Hector* from the French. John, fifth Lord Scrope of Bolton and great-great-grandson of the aforementioned Lord Henry, wrote a codicil to his will in 1498, leaving "my grete Primer . . . my lityll Bibyll that is at Bolton . . . my Bybill inprented, and my book, also inprented, called Cronica Cronicarum . . . my Portose inprented . . . my Masse booke inprented." His third wife, Anne, left "a Masse booke . . . myn embrowdered Sawter . . . a Premer whiche Kynge Edward gauffe me . . . a Frenche book called the Pistill of Othia . . . a French boke . . . my white booke of Prayers . . . a Premer clasped with silver and gylte. . . ."

[33] Charles L. Kingsford, "Two Forfeitures in the Year of Agincourt," *Archaeologia* 60, 2nd ser., 20 (1920):esp. 77-83, 93-94, 98-99. For the text of Lord Henry Scrope's will, see Thomas Rymer, *Foedera*, 3rd ed., (The Hague, 1740), Vol. 4, pt. 2, 131-34. BI, Reg. 5A (Sede vacante), f. 313, printed in *Test. Ebor.*, 3:31-37; YML, D. & C., L 2/4, f. 138, printed in *Test. Ebor.*, 1:338-39. For Richard and Roger Scrope's wills in 1400 and 1403 respectively, see BI, Reg. 16 (Scrope), ff. 142, 143, printed in *Test. Ebor.*, 1:272-78, 328-31.

Both she and her husband signed their wills, as did Lady Elizabeth Scrope in 1514. By 1515 Sir Ralph Scrope, Lord of Upsall-Masham, not only wrote his own will, but also penned some of the paperwork that his various bequests necessitated.[34]

By the 1520s attention was being paid to the education of Scrope children. In 1521 Sir John Cutte, knight, gave his wife Lucy (niece of Elizabeth Scrope) charge of their sons' education, "to fynde my said sonnes John and Henry to theire lernyng to theire profytt and promotion to the tyme that eyther of them be of the age of 24 yeris." A year later, Thomas Wyndam, knight, made the following arrangements for his son by his marriage with Eleanor Scrope. "I will that my sonne Thomas shalbe sent to the universitie of Bonanie in Ytalie assone as it may be conveniently after the warres. And in the meantyme to the Universitie of Loveyn and to contynue his lernyng there . . . till he be of the age of xxi yeres or lengar yf he will after that age at his owne charge . . . also I will that maister Wm Chamberlayn nowe being scolemaister within my house shall goo with him to have the rewle and oversight of my said sonne."[35]

The wills of the Plumpton family are not extant for the earlier period, although Agnes Stapelton's 1448 will, in which she leaves a book with prayers to Sir William Plumpton, a large psalter to William Plumpton, Junior, and a French book to Agnes Plumpton, shows that the family was not bookless.[36] There is, in addition, a fourteenth-century manuscript now at Lincoln's Inn, with various yearbooks and eyre proceedings, which may have belonged to the family.[37] It is the Plumpton correspondence, which covers the last half of the fifteenth century and the first half of the sixteenth, that provides proof of the literacy of the family and shows their concern for education. In 1489/90 Edmund Plumpton wrote to Sir Robert Plumpton, knight, apologetically, "I delivered . . . my poore wrytting therwith, the which was right simple [i.e., unadorned], but I besech you have me excused. Though I wryte not at all tymes, as my dutie is to do, Sir, I had never so great business as I have now for your matters." In a

---

[34] PRO, PCC, Prob. 11/2A and 2B March 49, printed in *Test. Ebor.*, 4:1-3; Cavanaugh, "A Study of Books Privately Owned," 770. See PRO, PCC, Prob. 11/11 Horne 26 for the wills of both John and Anne Scrope. They are printed in *Test. Ebor.*, 4:94-97, 149-54. PRO, PCC, Prob. 11/20 Maynwaring 19; BI, Prob. Reg. 9, f. 29, printed in *Test. Ebor.*, 5:64. John Scrope was also the recipient of several French books from his brother in 1485. *Test. Ebor.*, 3:299. For Stephen Scrope, see Margaret E. Schofield, ed., *The Dicts and Sayings of the Philosophers* (Philadelphia, 1936), 1-23, 35-36.

[35] PRO, PCC, Prob. 11/20 Maynwaring 12; Prob. 11/21 Bodfelde 3. Thomas Wyndam was also heir to his father's Yorkshire estates.

[36] PRO, PCC, Prob. 11/3 Luffenam 35, printed in *NCW*, 48-49.

[37] N. R. Ker, *Medieval Manuscripts in British Libraries*, Vol. 1 (Oxford, 1969), 133.

later letter (c. 1530) Ann Abbot wrote Dame Anne Rokesby, "I pray you, madam, let not my husband know of this letter, and send me word trewly with this bearrer in a little bill of your owne hand, ii or iii words, that he know not of your mind."[38] Additional letters illustrate the writing abilities of Robert Eyre, esquire; German Pole of County Derby, son-in-law to Sir Robert Plumpton; John St. Andrew of Nottinghamshire, esquire; Edith Nevill; and Henry Savill, knight.[39]

In addition to providing these proofs of literacy among the northern gentry, the letters suggest that the Plumpton family valued the education of their children. In a letter from Brian Roucliffe to Sir William Plumpton, in December 1463, Roucliffe boasted that Margaret Plumpton, who had been espoused to John Roucliffe, was speaking French and learning her psalter. In 1506 Isabella Plumpton urged her husband to "remember your chillder bookes." Later on we see Robert Plumpton at the Inner Temple, London, influenced by the new religious currents, sending home the New Testament in English for the edification of his mother.[40]

A growing interest in a grammar, university, and/or legal education is illustrated by the wills of the Constable family from the East Riding, who, before the turn of the sixteenth century, evinced no apparent interest in books outside of a Bible in 1376 and a few service books throughout the fifteenth century.[41] In 1472 there is a bequest of six marks to Stephen Newton, chaplain, for debts incurred in educating the children of Sir John Constable of Halsham.[42] By 1501 the family was sending Marmaduke Constable, heir, to Cambridge for three years until he reached the age of fifteen, and then for three years to an Inn of Chancery, while his younger brother Robert was being prepared in 1505 to attend grammar school.[43] When Marmaduke Constable made out his will in 1518, he gave an exhibition to a poor priest for seven years at Cambridge, and the residue of his goods to support scholars there. By deed in 1527 his executors founded four scholarships at St. John's.[44] Marmaduke Constable of North

[38] *Plumpton Correspondence*, ed. Thomas Stapelton, Camden Society, no. 4 (London, 1839), 92, 229-30.

[39] Ibid., 137, 140, 143-44, 191-93, 196-97, 248.

[40] Ibid., 8, 199, 231-34.

[41] BI, Reg. 12 (A. Neville), f. 59, printed in *Test. Ebor.*, 1:97-99. See also the wills of Marmaduke Constable (1404) and Matilda Constable (1419) in BI, Prob. Reg. 2, f. 214; Reg. 18 (Bowet), ff. 372-72v, printed in *Test. Ebor.*, 1:337-38, 396-97.

[42] BI, Prob. Reg. 4, f. 185(2). The reference is either to an elementary or grammar education.

[43] BI, Prob. Reg. 6, f. 9, printed in *Test. Ebor.*, 4:195-97; BI, Prob. Reg. 6, f. 141, printed in *Test. Ebor.*, 4:236-39.

[44] *Test. Ebor.*, 5:88-93.

Cliffe, esquire, writing his will in 1523, left all his books to his son James and all his lawbooks to Robert, his other son.

> Item I will that my wif kepe my too sones at scolles, there where it shal be devised by my said brother and hir, save that I will not that my sone James be as a fellowe in the Innes of Courte, but under the tuicion of my broder or some other by his advise, onels that he will continue the lawe still . . . and, like wise, I will that my sone, Roberte, by putto hym [my cousin, Sir Robert], if that my sone James die at undre age; and els I will that he shall continue scoles to he be xviii yeres, and than to be theire where my wif and my brother shall thinke best for his advauncement, to that he be brought to socoure and pro-motion.[45]

In 1536 William Constable, Sir Robert's son, was wandering about the country with a schoolmaster from Exeter on his way to Wales when he was arrested in connection with the Pilgrimage of Grace.[46] William had been at grammar school previously at Oxford and at Exeter and was travelling to learn Welsh.

The picture one derives from examining the wills is that the English upper classes were quite literate. The men were capable of reading and writing one, two, and sometimes three languages. The women read English and/or French, with perhaps a smattering of Latin, and some of them were able to write as well. There is no suggestion of a sharp change, of a marked increase in literacy for the aristocracy or gentry throughout the fifteenth century, although with more emphasis upon a university or legal education, knowledge of Latin must have improved. What is most striking in the wills is the shift from an interest in building up libraries of romances, histories, devotional, and service books to an interest in promoting attendance in the schools, universities, and Inns of Court. Perhaps the increasing availability of books made book collecting less the provenance of the nobility and hence less prestigious. Possibly the growing litigation and the increased sophistication of government convinced many members of the upper classes that they needed even more legal or administrative skills.

Before the late fifteenth century, however, the sons of aristocrats and gentry were still not likely to have been educated in the grammar schools, and never in the local parish reading school. Although there are occasional examples of the upper classes of York diocese making use of the grammar

[45] BI, Prob. Reg. 9, f. 352, printed in *Test. Ebor.*, 5:168-69.
[46] *L & P, Henry VIII*, 12:i, no. 30.

schools before about 1450, the majority of the sons and daughters of the noble and gentle classes were educated within their own household, the household of another privileged family, the household of an ecclesiastic, or, in the case of some girls and very young boys, in a nunnery.[47] The education that the gentry and aristocracy received in these household schools was not confined to manners and, for boys, military training; they learned to read and write in the vernacular, and, except in the nunneries, they were supplied with a master who dispensed an education equivalent to that found in the reading and grammar schools. In an exceptional case, that of Belvoir Castle in the 1540s, we have record of three schoolmasters employed simultaneously by the household.

These educational arrangements are difficult to document. In York diocese three of the more prestigious aristocratic household schools were the grammar schools held in Belvoir Castle under Lord Roos; in the household of Lord Percy, Earl of Northumberland; and in the Willoughby family household at Wollaton Hall, Nottinghamshire.[48] Lord Greystock and Sir John Constable may also have had household schools at their residences in Hinderskelfe and Halsham respectively.[49] Rectors, abbots, and other ecclesiastical officials sometimes ran household schools for the well-to-do. Early in the fourteenth century John Boynton, son of Sir Robert Boynton, knight, was described as a young gentleman in the household of the rector of Cottingham. The fact that he had received his first tonsure suggests that he was being educated there.[50] The abbot of Guisborough and the prior of Nostell may have been holding household schools for the sons of the well-born, as were the treasurer and archbishop of York.[51]

[47] Isabella de Fortibus, Countess of Aumale, sent her son to school with the grammarmaster of Hedon in 1271. N. Denholm-Young, "The Yorkshire Estates of Isabella de Fortibus," *YAJ* 31 (1934):392. The accounts of the Countess of Suffolk show that Alexander de la Pole, in 1416, was at school in Ipswich. Thomas Howard, the second Duke of Norfolk, was (c. 1450) "in hys yong age, ofter he had been a sufficient season at the gramer schole, hencheman to Kyng Edward the iiii." McFarlane, *The Nobility of Later Medieval England*, 245.

[48] BI, Reg. 18 (Bowet), f. 363, printed in *Test. Ebor.*, 1:359. Historical Manuscripts Commission, *The MSS of the Duke of Rutland Preserved at Belvoir Castle*, Vol. 4 (London, 1905), 296-97, 308, 345; Thomas Percy, ed., *The Regulations and Establishment of the Household of Henry Algernon Percy, the Fifth Earl of Northumberland at His Castles of Wressle and Leckonfield in Yorkshire, 1512*, new ed. (London, 1905), 311-13, 318; Historical Manuscripts Commission, *Report on the Manuscripts of Lord Middleton Preserved at Wollaton Hall* (London, 1911), 369. See Chapter four above.

[49] BI, Reg. 27 (Wolsey), f. 158, printed in *Test. Ebor.*, 5:204; BI, Prob. Reg. 4, f. 185(2).

[50] W. Brown and A. H. Thompson, eds., *The Register of William Greenfield, Lord Archbishop of York, 1306-1315*, Vol. 3, Surtees Society, no. 151 (Durham, 1936), l, 177, 179-86, 208.

[51] W. Brown and A. H. Thompson, eds., *Cartularium Prioratus de Gyseburne*, Vol. 2, Surtees Society, no. 89 (Durham, 1894), 360-62; BI, Prob. Reg. 4, ff. 185-86, printed in *Test. Ebor.*,

Canons within the cathedral may well have maintained households for young boys,[52] and a number of other household schools are known from the city of York, some conducted by the parsons and vicars choral of the cathedral, others by nonresident or resident rectors or local priests, although it is unlikely that these humbler household schools catered to either gentry or nobility.[53] Finally, both sons and daughters of the nobility might be sent to a convent school, particularly for their elementary education. There is evidence for several such schools within York diocese, and Eileen Power has argued that the numbers were far greater than the surviving evidence suggests.[54]

Because of the popularity of a household education among the nobility, the aristocracy and gentry had little impact on the history of elementary and grammar schools until the end of the fifteenth century. Only after the 1450s, and particularly after 1500, did the upper classes begin to found their own grammar schools, perhaps spurred by the royal foundation at Eton and the ecclesiastical foundations of Winchester, and, within York diocese, Rotherham and Acaster Selby.

Besides Henry VI's patronage of a choristers' grammar school at Bridlington Priory in the middle of the fifteenth century, the first known grammar school in York diocese founded by a member of the upper class was the chantry grammar school at Preston (Lancs.) founded by Helene Houghton in 1448.[55] The next notice is a chantry grammar school founded in 1468 by Richard Hamerton, knight, at Long Preston (West Riding). Thomas, Lord Darcy, founded a grammar school at Whitkirk (West Riding) in 1521, and two years later Edward Stanley, Lord Monteagle, made provision for a chantry and free school at Hornby (Lancs.).[56] Grammar schools were founded at Broughton in Preston in 1527 and St. Mi-

---

3:204; J. Hoeppner Moran, *Education and Learning in the City of York, 1300-1560* (York, 1979), 44 n 44; George Cavendish, "The Life and Death of Cardinal Wolsey," in *Two Early Tudor Lives*, ed. R. S. Sylvester and D. P. Harding (New Haven, 1962), 21.

[52] See Chapter four, p. 107 above.

[53] Moran, *Education and Learning*, 11-12.

[54] Power, *Med. Eng. Nunneries*, 260-84, 579-81. See also Chapter four above.

[55] *VCH, Lancs.*, 2:570-71. For Bridlington, see Appendix B.

[56] Leach, *ESR*, ii:296. For Whitkirk, see YML, Wa (Register of Deeds, etc. I:1508-1543), ff. 19v-27v; *L & P, Henry VIII*, 3: i, 394, no. 1079. For Hornby, see PRO, PCC, Prob. 11/21 Bodefelde 25, printed in *NCW*, 113. Although Stanley provided for the establishment of a free grammar school at Hornby in his will, his executors did not carry out the provisions. In 1548 his heir was supporting a grammarmaster there "of his owne benevolent good will and plesure . . ." Leach, *ESR*, ii:118-19. The Stanleys, through Lady Margaret Beaufort, also founded a grammar school at Wimborne (Dorset). Thomas Stanley, second Earl of Derby, helped endow Blackburn grammar school in 1514. Orme, *ESMA*, 202.

chael's on Wyre in 1528 by Lawrence Stodagh and John Butler respectively, both members of the lower gentry. John Lord Latimer endowed a grammar school at Well (North Riding) in 1542, and Henry Clifford, Earl of Cumberland, endowed Skipton grammar school with a chantry at Kildwike in 1544.[57]

This founding and endowing of grammar schools was accompanied by a change in attitude toward the education provided by these schools, for by the 1460s York diocesan gentlemen were beginning to send their sons to local grammar schools. In 1461 Sir John Hedlam, knight, left "my gudis that leves, aftir my dettis paid, to tender my childer ther with, and to helpe and holde tham to the scule."[58] In 1486 Ralph Gascoigne of Burnby, esquire, put his son in the keeping of John Luffell (of Everingham?) to be "founden to the scole." Another Gascoigne, Sir William of Gawkesthorpe, was attending either a grammar or reading school at Harwood about 1503. Robert Constable was attending a grammar school sometime after 1505, and Thomas Wentworth, son and heir of Matthew Wentworth, esquire, of West Burton Hall, was being sent to the grammar school for two years in 1505.[59] Among several examples from the 1520s,[60] in 1524 Sir William Bulmer, esquire, included among his legacies "certen rekynnynges for my childer bordes where thay were at borde and scole." The grammar school at Macclesfield (Chester), which was just a few miles from the York diocesan border, was founded in 1503 by John Percyvall, knight and mayor of London, as a free grammar school "techyng there Gentilmens Sonnes and other godemennes children of the Towne and contre thereabouts, . . ."[61] By 1540 some grammar schools were considered so much the province of the well-to-do that Archbishop Cranmer had to defend the right of sons of husbandmen to seek entrance. "Where-

---

[57] Francis Gastrell, *Notitia Cestriensis*, ed. J. Raine, Vol. 2, no. 3, Chetham Society, orig. ser., no. 22 (Manchester, 1850), 468; *VCH, Lancs.*, 2:603. For Latimer's will, see PRO, PCC, Prob. 11/29 Spert 17, printed in *Test. Ebor.*, 6:159-63. For Skipton, see A. M. Gibbon, *A History of the Ancient Free Grammar School of Skipton-in-Craven* (Liverpool, 1947) and Leach, *ESR*, ii:295, 301, 306.

[58] BI, Prob. Reg. 2, f. 451, printed in *Test. Ebor.*, 2:247-48.

[59] BI, Prob. Reg. 5, f. 340v, printed in *Test. Ebor.*, 4:16; J. S. Purvis, ed., *Select XVIth Century Causes in Tithe*, YAS rec. ser., no. 114 (York, 1947), 68; BI, Prob. Reg. 6, ff. 141, 192v, printed in *Test. Ebor.*, 4:238, 241.

[60] Additional examples include Sir Richard Basset of Fledborough, knight, who sent his two sons to grammar school in 1522, and Thomas Lacy, gentleman, who sent his son Rauf to the school in 1525. Sir William Meryng, knight, was educated at the grammar school at Kneesall c. 1530. BI, Prob. Reg. 9. ff, 311, 315, printed in *Test. Ebor.*, 5:148-49, 206; Cornelius Brown, *A History of Newark-upon-Trent*, Vol. 2 (Newark, 1907), 178.

[61] BI, Prob. Reg. 9, f. 300; *Test. Ebor.*, 5:190; A. F. Leach, *Educational Charters and Documents, 589 to 1909* (Cambridge, 1911), 436-39.

fore, if the gentlemen's sons by apt of learning, let him be admitted; if not apt, let the poor man's child that is apt, enter his room."[62]

The grammar schools were not the only local educational activities to benefit from the awakened attentions of the upper classes. Around the turn of the sixteenth century one begins to notice that the gentry are, after a conspicuous absence, helping to provide funds for parish scholars. In 1497, for example, James Danby of Thorp and Farneley, knight, left money, meat, and drink to the scholars at Leeds. Dame Jane Chamberleyn, in 1502, left money for "the exhibicion of pure [poor] Chylder apte to learne at scholes," and Geoffrey Frank, esquire, left a bequest to the scholars at Escrick parish church in 1501.[63] The newly generated interest of the aristocracy and gentry in founding grammar schools and, on the part of the gentry, in funding parish scholars must be accounted one factor in promoting the remarkable growth in educational opportunities by the turn of the sixteenth century.

Neither the gentry nor the aristocracy, however, was likely to send its children to a parish elementary school.[64] The people most affected by the growing parochial education were middle-level folk, the less wealthy merchants, artisans, yeomen, and well-to-do husbandmen, many of whom supported parish scholars and sent their children to these schools.

The wills from the York Prerogative and Exchequer Court begin to be preserved in 1389 and almost immediately provide examples of non-noble progeny receiving funds for their schooling from parents, friends, and relatives. In 1391 William de Ulskelf of York, fuller, left 40s., two cows, and a belt with a knife to his son, Richard Walker, in order that he could be sent to school. The same year William Fysche of York, citizen and merchant, bequeathed twenty marks to John and Robert, his grandsons, in order that they would attend school. Two years later another

[62] John Strype, *Memorials of Archbishop Cranmer*, 2 vols. (Oxford, 1812), 1:127. Bishop Latimer made a similar point in a sermon preached before Edward VI in 1549. *Sermons and Remains of Hugh Latimer*, ed. G. E. Corrie, Parker Society, no. 27 (Cambridge, 1844), 102.

[63] BI, Prob. Reg. 5, f. 499v, printed in *Test. Ebor.*, 4:122; BI, Prob. Reg. 6, ff. 5v, 34v. See also the 1452 will of John Lokwod of Parva Broughton in Cleveland, knight; the 1502 will of Elienora Laton, widow of Robert Laton, knight; the 1507/8 will of Robert Lascelles of Brakenburgh, esquire; the 1516 will of Richard Peke of Wakefield, gentleman; and the 1547 will of William Hungate of Saxton, esquire. BI, Prob. Reg. 2, f. 252; 6, f. 64; 7, f. 32; 9, f. 38; 13, f. 379.

[64] The first notice we have is that of Sir John Savile, who came from gentry stock in the chapelry of Elland. Circa 1550 (at the age of four or five) he began to learn the alphabet and English catechism with the curate and parish clerk. J. W. Clay and J. Lister, eds., "Autobiography of Sir John Savile of Methley, Knight, Baron of the Exchequer, 1546-1607," *YAJ* 15 (1900):421-22.

citizen of York, William de York, left 20s. to William, the son of John Junior, to find him to school. The same year Richard de Taunton, citizen and merchant of York, left 20s. to William Westerdale for his schooling, and in 1395 Cecilia de Yharom of York left 13s. 4d. to William de Bliburgh of Heslington in order to find his sons to school. In 1394 John Spaldyng of York, vintner, left 6s. 8d. to Henry Yole for his schooling.[65] As one reads further in the wills the examples multiply and move beyond the city of York.[66] In total, between 1389 and 1530, the collection of wills in the Prerogative and Exchequer Court yields over two hundred such bequests.[67]

In addition to these specific benefactions, the wills provide full and continuous evidence of bequests to parish scholars. The great number of such gifts is evident from even the most cursory look at Appendix B. The testators who left these modest sums were mostly laymen and laywomen from small villages, although townspeople throughout the diocese, and various clergy, especially chaplains, also bestowed small sums on parish scholars in their wills. A few examples will be offered as representative of numerous instances. In 1438 John Bee of Bishopburton, who was to be buried in Bishopburton parish church in the East Riding, left 6d. to each child in the church who was either singing or reading. In 1459 Thomas Dowse of Helperby (N. Riding) left four pennies to the parish

---

[65] BI, Prob. Reg. 1, ff. 35, 47, 58, 63, 67, 92v-93.

[66] In the 1440s, for example, John Farnam of Rufford near Acom left 40s. to his son William to learn grammar, while William Gilliote of Hull, roper, left 20s. to exhibit John, the son of Thomas and Margaret Dysnay, in school. In 1432 John Boythorp of Doncaster, an artisan, left William, his son, ten marks from debts owed to find him in school. Twenty years later Richard Patryngton of Beverley, mercer, left 40s. to Richard Hewlot, the son of his nephew, to sustain him in school. BI, Prob. Reg. 2, ff. 135, 194, 243, 353.

[67] Additional examples of educational benefactions by non-noble laity from volumes 2-6 of the Prerogative and Exchequer Court of York include: Prob. Reg. 2, ff. 58v-59, 61, 158, 180, 185, 238, 277, 281-82, 305(2)-306, 337, 365v, 395, 434, 439, 464, 548, 595, 615, 641; Prob. Reg. 3, ff. 10, 17, 61, 93, 323, 414v-15, 439-41, 481, 488-89; Prob. Reg. 4, ff. 5, 66, 66v-67, 93, 140, 147, 185, 186, 196, 197v-98, 220, 265; Prob. Reg. 5, ff. 38v-39, 49, 100, 119, 244, 261, 264, 318, 319, 331, 355, 385, 392, 402v-403, 418, 447, 457v-59, 483; Prob. Reg. 6, ff. 1v-2, 104, 109, 114. In most cases it is difficult to guess the quality and level of education envisioned by benefactors. The educational aspirations mentioned range from simply learning to read and write to becoming a doctor of theology. In several cases a grammar education is specified. Often a grammar school education is implied by the fact that grammar books were included in the bequest, or from the fact that the value of the gift is in line with the expense of a grammar school education. With bequests which give only 13s. 4d. for finding more than one child to school or 2s. for one child or only request that the scholar learn to read and write, one can presume that an elementary education is being proffered. These, however, are a minority of the cases, and it can generally be assumed that, unless a university education is specified, the testators are thinking of funding a child's grammar education.

clerk and pennies to the other literate youngsters at his funeral. Thirty years later Robert Pynkney left a penny to every learned child at Hornby parish church. In North Grimston parish in the East Riding, two testators named Hall left pennies to the parish scholars at the beginning of the sixteenth century.[68] Generally village wills do not tell us the occupation of testators. It is unusual to find, as one does for Guisborough (N. Riding) in 1426 and 1452, references to two butchers leaving monies for singing boys and for boys in the parish. In another example, Robert Hunter, a yeoman from Scampston (E. Riding), who died about 1510, left 6s. 8d. to be distributed among scholars and poor people in the East Riding parish of Rillington.[69] Mostly the contents of these wills suggest humble folk—the yeomen, husbandmen, and artisans of northern England. Glancing through them, there can be no doubt that many laity of all social classes from northern England were fulfilling William Langland's hopes which he had voiced in his advice to merchants, to "sette scoleres to scole or to somme fode."[70]

In fact, the townspeople and villagers of York diocese followed Langland's advice and went beyond it, not only supporting scholars but also founding schools. The first notice of a school foundation by a non-noble layman is John Gardyner's endowment of Lancaster grammar school. In 1472 Gardyner, a burgess, possibly a miller, of Lancaster, turned over the profits from a mill to support the town school which had already been in existence, probably on a fee-paying basis, from at least the early thirteenth century. His intentions were that a chaplain "instruct the boys coming there in grammar freely, unless perchance something shall be voluntarily offered by their friends to the said chaplain in recompense."[71] From then until 1548 there are notices of at least seventeen other grammar schools founded or endowed throughout the diocese by laity who were not nobility.[72] This is twice the numbers credited to the aristocracy and gentry. In 1512, for example, a longstanding grammar school was endowed at Nottingham by Agnes Mellers, widow of a mayor of Nottingham. There were eighty original subscribers to the foundation, and we have notices

---

[68] BI, Prob. Reg. 3, f. 562v; YML, D. & C., L 2/4, ff. 292, 373; L 2/5a, ff. 105, 136.

[69] BI, Prob. Reg. 2, ff. 258, 269v; 8, f. 36.

[70] *Piers Plowman, The B Version*, ed. George Kane and E. Talbot Donaldson (London, 1975), 26.

[71] *VCH, Lancs.*, 2:562.

[72] The schools are, in Westmorland, at Beetham and Kirkby Kendal; in Lancashire at Kirkby Lonsdale; in Nottinghamshire at Edwinstow, Kneesall, Newark, and Nottingham; and in Yorkshire at Aldborough, Bradford, Gargrave, Halifax, Keighley, Romaldkirk, Wakefield, Wragby, St. William's Chapel, Ousebridge in York, and St. Martin's Coney Street in York.

of several subsequent lay bequests of land to the school.[73] In the same year Harold Staunton, a layman from Newark (Notts.), gave ten marks a year to amortize a chantry priest to be a teacher of grammar. This foundation may have been intended to endow the grammar school that had been in Newark since the thirteenth century, or it may refer to a separate foundation.[74]

At least two schools within the city of York were founded and supported by laity. In 1521 the mayor, aldermen, and council of York appointed Henry Smyth parish clerk of St. William's chapel, Ousebridge. They provided that, at the suitable times and in addition to his regular duties, he should sing in the choir, play the organ, or teach boys. By 1553 the corporation was more heavily committed to supporting schooling when it sought confirmation of a £50 remittance on taxes based largely upon the heavy charge incurred in educating a great number of poor children. In 1555 Robert Morris, priest, was elected by the mayor and aldermen to conduct a school on Ousebridge.[75] A second lay-founded school within the city was in St. Martin parish, Coney Street, where Thomas Drawswerde, an alderman and carver of York, endowed a chantry school in 1528.[76] Outside York, in 1531, Thomas Wilkinson, a draper of Kirkby Kendal, bequeathed 6s. 8d. to the free school just being founded there by Adam Pennington, a merchant of Boston. In 1542 Edmund Person, tanner, left a sum of goods to his parish church of Beetham (Westm.) for supporting a priest to teach a free school.[77] By 1546-1548, at the time of the chantry surveys, there were a number of chantry schools established simply "by the parishioners."[78]

Schools founded by laity were not necessarily governed by laity. The grammar school established at Whitkirk by Lord Darcy was part of a

<hr>

[73] *VCH, Notts.*, 2:216-23; *Records of the Borough of Nottingham*, 4 vols. (London, 1882-1889), 3:396, 453-58; 4:26-31. For additional grants to the school, see BI, Prob. Reg. 8, ff. 106, 120v (printed in *Test. Ebor.*, 5:41-42); 9, ff. 68, 118v, 330v; 11, f. 231 (printed in *Test. Ebor.*, 6:50).

[74] PRO, PCC, Prob. 11/7 Fetiplace 9.

[75] Joyce W. Percy, ed., *York Memorandum Book*, Vol. 3, Surtees Society, no. 186 (Gateshead, 1973), 239; York City Archives, York Corporation Records House Book 21, ff. 20v, 108v; *VCH, Yorkshire: City of York*, 124, 156; *York Civic Rec.*, 5:130.

[76] *Test. Ebor.*, 5:269.

[77] Leeds Central Library, Archives Department, Richmond Archdeaconry, Will Reg. 1, 2, 3 & A, f. 91v; PRO, C142/45, Inquisitions *Post Mortem*, Henry VIII, Chancery Series II, vol. 45, no. 6; Leach, *ESR.*, ii:251, 253; James Raine, ed., *Wills and Inventories from the Registry of the Archdeaconry of Richmond*, Surtees Society, no. 26 (Durham, 1853), 28.

[78] For example, Aldborough, Bradford, Gargrave, Keighley, Romaldkirk, and Wragby in Yorkshire.

larger complex which included a hospital and hermitage, oversight of which was given to St. Oswald's Priory. Darcy also required certification of the schoolmaster by the chancellor of York. Adam Pennington's foundation at Kirkby Kendal was placed in the hands of two executors, one of whom was the warden of the Grey Friars in Boston. Advice of the abbot of Risby was to be sought in connection with the foundation.[79]

In general, however, lay-founded schools were either partially or fully lay-controlled. John Gardyner, for example, did not put his bequest in the hands of the Church. He placed it instead under the control of his executors, both lay and clerical. By 1500 a new ordinance gave the mayor and the chantry priest of the almshouse (which Gardyner also endowed) control over selecting the schoolmaster and oversight of the school.[80] Governance of the Nottingham grammar school before 1512 is nowhere spelled out in the surviving documents, although forty years prior to Agnes Meller's foundation, the grammarmaster had appealed to Southwell Minster against a competing grammarmaster at Wollaton. The borough records suggest, however, that Southwell's supervisory role was a limited one, for most complaints against the schoolmaster seem to have gone to the borough corporation rather than to Southwell. Agnes Mellers's endowment, as well as subsequent gifts of land to the school, were given to the mayor and burgesses, who received a license in mortmain to hold them.[81] The schoolmaster of Preston (Lancs.), endowed by Helene Houghton, was by 1518 appointed by the Earl of Derby. The mayor and burgesses of Preston also exercised some oversight.[82] In the villages it was often the parishioners who set up funds to maintain a schoolmaster. This was the case at Mattersay, Romaldkirk, and Gargrave. The chantry certificates suggest that these funds remained under the control of the parishioners, although they were probably managed by the churchwardens.[83] This manner of sustaining a school may have been a popular one, although the evidence on parish schools is too scant to conclude anything much about their management.

Schools whose founding circumstances are obscure, and whose founders or benefactors may have been churchmen, nonetheless were sometimes

[79] YML, Wa (Register of Deeds, etc., I 1508-1543), ff. 19v-27v, PRO, C142/45, Inquisitions *Post Mortem*, Henry VIII, Chancery Series II, vol. 45, no. 6.

[80] *VCH, Lancs.*, 2:562-63.

[81] *VCH, Notts.*, 2:216-19; *Records of the Borough of Nottingham*, 1:246-49, 262-63; 2:12-13, 122-23, 128-29; 3:396, 453-58; 4:26-31; BI, Prob. Reg. 8, ff. 106, 120v, (printed in *Test. Ebor.*, 5:41-42); 9, ff. 68, 118v, 330v; 11, f. 231 (printed in *Test. Ebor.*, 6:50).

[82] *VCH, Lancs.*, 2:570.

[83] Leach, *ESR.*, ii:161, 288, 302.

governed by laity. The grammar school at Hull, which first emerges in 1347, was endowed by Bishop John Alcock in 1479. It had been controlled by the town corporation before 1479 and, despite its more independent status thereafter, continued to be overseen by the mayor and aldermen. This is similar to the grammar school at East Retford (Notts.). Although it is documented as early as 1318, it led a shadowy life through the fifteenth century, emerging only in 1518 when Parson Thomas Gunthorpe endowed it with a schoolhouse. In the deed setting out the conditions of the gift, it is clear that it is the bailiffs, burgesses, and commonalty who accept the gift and are responsible for providing the schoolmaster.[84] Finally, Richmond's grammar school is an instance of a school that originated under ecclesiastical control and gradually evolved into a lay foundation. At the end of the fourteenth century the school at Richmond was under the control of the archdeacon of Richmond who collated the clerks teaching it. At that time it was apparently supported by several chantries. By about 1486 the burgesses and other laity had gained sufficient say in the appointment of the schoolmaster to refuse the prior of Durham's request for his transfer. At the time of the chantry surveys, the school was completely under lay control, although the schoolmaster continued to be a priest. The stipend of the schoolmaster was paid entirely by the bailiffs and burgesses, and their power was such that they were able to circumvent the chantry commissioners, converting the revenues from at least six chantries into an endowment for the school.[85]

Although it is tempting to see Richmond's evolution as part of a trend, there is too little evidence on governance of schools to argue convincingly that education was moving away from ecclesiastical and toward lay supervision. Evidence for lay involvement in governing schools is suggestive, but it is only when it is reinforced with evidence for growing lay interest in founding schools and funding scholars that one can plausibly posit a gradual laicization of education taking place in York diocese by the beginning of the sixteenth century.

The shifting relationship between lay and clerical involvement in education is apparent from an analysis of bequests to schools and individual scholars. From 1400 to 1530 the wills from the Prerogative and Exchequer Court of York provide 144 instances of lay and 55 of clerical gifts to specified schools and scholars. Although these bequests are no more than

[84] John Lawson, *A Town Grammar School Through Six Centuries* (London, 1963), 12-31; A. D. Grounds, *A History of King Edward VI Grammar School, Retford* (Worksop, 1970), 13-17.

[85] *VCH, Yorks.*, 1:475; L. P. Wenham, "Two Notes on the History of Richmond School, Yorkshire," *YAJ* 37 (1950):369-72.

TABLE 8

LAY AND CLERICAL EDUCATIONAL BEQUESTS IN THE WILLS
OF THE PREROGATIVE AND EXCHEQUER COURT OF
YORK DIOCESE, 1400-1530

Dates	Laity		Clergy		Ratio
1400-1425	4	(57%)	3	(43%)	1.3:1
1426-1450	15	(45.5%)	18	(54.5%)	.8:1
1451-1475	24	(57%)	18	(43%)	1.3:1
1476-1500	27	(67.5%)	13	(32.5%)	2.1:1
1501-1530	74	(96%)	3[a]	(4%)	24.7:1
Total	144		55		

SOURCE: BI, Prob. Reg. 1-10.

[a] The striking decline in clerical benefactions is due, in part, to fewer clerical wills in the probate registers and especially in volume 9.

the tip of an iceberg in terms of charitable gifts,[86] they do produce an interesting ratio between lay and clerical giving. Table 8 displays the number of educational bequests approximately every twenty-five years. They have been broken down into lay and clerical categories.

From 1400 until 1475 the number of testators giving gifts for schooling was forty-three for the laity and thirty-nine for the clergy. Although clerics represented at most 2 percent of the total population, their wills account for 48 percent of the instances of gift-giving.[87] A change takes place in the proportion of gift-giving after 1475. From 1476 to 1500 the number of laity bequeathing educational gifts is up to twenty-seven while that of the clergy is down to thirteen. The result is an increase of 62 percent in the ratio of lay to clerical bequests, with clerical giving to scholars now less than one-half of lay gift-giving, or 32.5 percent of the total number

[86] These do not include educational uses which may have been established by the transfer of titles to trustees before death. They do not include those gifts of funeral pennies to unnamed parish scholars which have been documented in Appendix B. In addition, benefactors who maintained scholars would not ordinarily have waited until on their deathbeds to exercise their charities, and, for many individuals, the monies needed to educate dependents would have been usefully spent long before their deaths.

[87] For the clerical proportion of the population, see below, note 126. It is not possible to compare monetary totals bequeathed to scholars since many of the gifts were in the form of books, clothing, or even, in one instance, a bed. On occasion the amount was left to the discretion of the wife and/or executors.

of bequests. This trend away from clerical educational benefactions would appear to accelerate dramatically in the first three decades of the sixteenth century, but the results are questionable since the ratio of extant lay and clerical wills, which remains steady through the fifteenth century, changes quite noticeably, with far fewer clerical wills being registered in volume 9 of the series. Despite this anomaly the data do suggest growing lay support of scholars.

Lay benefactors often expected that the scholar recipient would pursue a lay career. Although there are some exceptions, laity who bequeathed money or books to their sons or relatives for schooling did not limit these bequests in any way, and there would appear to have been no particular assumption that the child would enter the clergy. Only a few lay wills even make provision for that contingency.[88] One can assume, therefore, that the laity, while not excluding clerical careers for their children, may have had more secular careers in mind. Some of the lay wills specify that the children were being educated to a craft, to go into law, or for court, and these sorts of wills increase in number after 1475.[89] In contrast, the clergy routinely provided funds for schooling until the recipient received holy orders, or books for learning if the scholar promised to become a priest.[90]

If laity, both noble and non-noble, were increasingly interested in founding grammar schools, governing schools, supporting scholars, and promoting lay careers, not only can one legitimately speak of a laicization of education, but one should also expect to find evidence for growing lay literacy. The expansion of educational opportunities and the probability that not all the scholars would enter the ranks of the clergy suggest that lay literacy may have been on the rise. In fact, the evidence for it is there, but much of it is indirect and somewhat speculative.[91]

[88] See BI, Prob. Reg. 4, ff. 135, 140, 185; 6, ff. 115v, 136. In three instances lay testators did not assume that their sons would become priests, but prepared for the contingency by redefining the line of inheritance in the event. Prob. Reg. 5, f. 49; 6, ff. 84, 144.

[89] For example, BI, Prob. Reg. 2, f. 595; 3, ff. 88v-89; 5, ff. 38v-39, 88, 144, 457v-59, 498-99; 6, ff. 9v-10, 123. See also *Wills and Administrations from the Knaresborough Court Rolls*, Vol. 1, ed. F. Collins, Surtees Society, no. 104 (Durham, 1902), 40-41.

[90] A typical example is that of Simon Wenteslaw, rector of Collom on the Wold, who, in 1438, left a portable breviary to Thomas Wenteslaw, son of John, under the condition that Thomas attend school until he entered orders. William Ouresby, a layman (and brewer?) of York, was to have the book in his custody, and if Thomas did not do well or honestly govern himself or did not attend school assiduously, then the breviary was to be sold and the money distributed for the good of the testator's soul. BI, Prob. Reg. 3, f. 563; 4, f. 107. For additional examples, see Prob. Reg. 2, ff. 646, 655; 3, ff. 365, 522; 4, ff. 110-11v; 5, f. 434.

[91] The following analysis is a slightly revised and substantially abbreviated version of an earlier publication. See Moran, "Literacy and Education," 2-17.

The earliest known, reasonably contemporary assessment of the proportion of literate Englishmen, made by Sir Thomas More in 1533 and quoted in Chapter one, suggests that England enjoyed a literacy rate in the first half of the sixteenth century of between 50 and 60 percent.[92] This estimate has been received somewhat skeptically. Carlo M. Cipolla, for example, calls it "a rosy exaggeration," and, in general, Tudor historians of education and literacy have dismissed it. Medievalists have been more sympathetic. Somewhat similar estimates of 30 percent literacy in fifteenth century England and 50 percent male literacy in London by 1470, offered by F.D.R. Du Boulay and Sylvia Thrupp respectively, have been cited in Chapter one.[93] Thrupp's conclusions, which are based on references to literacy in court depositions, provide the only quantifiable documentation heretofore available for the period before 1500, and they tell us only about London.

London was special, however. Beyond its bounds we have only fragmentary evidence for rates of lay literacy. An inquiry in 1466 concerning Sir John Fastolf's will, where one-third of the lay witnesses (including several farmers, a tailor, and a seaman) were described as *literati*, has commonly been cited as an indication of the relatively high rate of Latin literacy throughout the realm. But an even higher proportion of lay literacy is suggested by the depositions of witnesses taken in 1373 in a suit between William of Wykeham and three masters of Holy Cross. Of the twenty-eight witnesses, half were laymen, of whom eleven were described as *literati*. In this instance the very high percentage of lay literacy (presumably in Latin) of 78.5 percent is quite possibly skewed by the presence, in Winchester, of a city grammar school.[94] M. B. Parkes finds the evidence so circumstantial that he is unwilling to provide any estimate of literacy. Nevertheless, he does conclude that the tendency among historians has been to understate the extent to which late medieval Englishmen relied upon the written word.[95]

A number of examples from York diocese suggest not only that literacy was on the increase in the late Middle Ages, but also that it could reach surprisingly far down the social scale. In a will of 1432 John Raventhorp,

[92] *The Complete Works of Sir Thomas More*, Vol. 9, ed. J. B. Trapp (New Haven, 1979), 13.

[93] Carlo M. Cipolla, *Literacy and Development in the West* (Harmondsworth, 1969), 48. See Chapter one, pp. 19-20.

[94] James Gairdner, ed., *The Paston Letters, 1422-1509*, 3 vols. (London, 1872-1875), 2: no. 550; *VCH, Hamps.*, 2:225.

[95] M. B. Parkes, "The Literacy of the Laity," in *Literature and Western Civilization: The Medieval World*, ed. D. Daiches and A. Thorlby (London, 1973), 571-72.

a chaplain from the city of York, left an English book of fables and stories to Agnes of Celayne, his servant for many years.[96] While we cannot be certain that Agnes could read the volume, one suspects that she, or someone in her immediate circle, could. Twenty-six years later, in 1458, Richard Wartere, a citizen of York, asked his executors to give written reminders (presumably in English) in his name to all persons, whether lay or clerical, to whom anything had been left so that they might have the testator in memory and pray for him. Among the beneficiaries of Wartere's will were 100 paupers, both men and women, to whom he had given cloaks and shirts.[97] Although one assumes it unlikely that 100 paupers could read, the distribution of written notices suggests that literacy among the poor might not be unexpected. An inscriptional brass of Thomas Middleton, esquire, written in English in 1500 and referred to above in Chapter two, is significant not only because it spells out the testator's understanding of what it meant to be lettered, but also because it shows his clear expectation that many of the rural parishioners of Spofforth church in the West Riding would be able to read the writing.[98] In 1552 Archbishop Holgate enjoined York Minster to replace the images on its walls with scripture. This was done, of course, more in the interest of the laity than of the clergy. By 1553, when Francis Bigod made an abstract of the Statute of Supremacy, he thought "to nale [it] on a table in my parishe churche [probably Settrington in the East Riding] and delyver all them that can reade a copye of it, to instructe ther famylie therewith at home and then on the holy [day] they sall marke my chaplen's declaration of the same myche more easely."[99] These examples are in sharp contrast to Archbishop Thoresby's expectations in 1357 when he published a lay folks' catechism in English explicitly bidding his clergy, "Enioygne thair parochiens and thaire sugettes That thei *here* [hear] and lere this ilk sex

---

[96] BI, Prob. Reg. 3, f. 358, printed in *Test. Ebor.*, 2:28-29.

[97] BI, Prob. Reg. 4, ff. 115v-16v, printed in *Test. Ebor.*, 2:273-74. "Item volo quod dicti executores mei scribant seu scribi faciant multas sedulas seu billas proprii nominis mei Ricardi Wartere, prefati Willelmi Wartere patris mei et Johannae Wartere matris meae, Aliciae et Aliciae Wartere quondam uxorum mearum, omniumque fratrum atque sororum mearum, sicque animarum omnium fidelium defunctorum, ita ut omnes predicti capellani mei qui pro anima mea—concelebrabunt habeant seu habeat unusquisque eorundem unam billam ad altaria sua, ea intencione, ut habeant me in memoria et specialiter et devote orent. Et volo quod dictae sedulae dentur omnibus aliis personis tam laicis quam clericis cui seu quibus aliquod est legatum—ut et ipsi similiter possint habere me in memoria et devote orent pro anima mea."

[98] *Test. Ebor.*, 3:209.

[99] W. H. Frere and W. M. Kennedy, eds., *Visitation Articles and Injunctions of the Period of the Reformation*, Vol. 2, Alcuin Club Collections, no. 15 (London, 1910), 320; *L & P, Henry VIII*, 8: no. 854.

thinges, And oft sithes reherce tham til that thai kun thaime, And sithen teche tham thair childir, if thai any haue."[100]

Another indicator of growing lay literacy is the anonymous posted bill written in English, which became so common and dangerous a sight by the fifteenth century that a proclamation was issued forbidding the practice.[101] In 1405 Scrope's rebellion in the north produced grievances that were "made by written in English" by the archbishop "and were set on the yatis of the cite [of York], and sent to curatis of the tounes aboute, for to be prechid openli." In 1451 there was the case of two servants of William Tailboys, esquire, who plotted to discredit Lord Cromwell by distributing slanderous bills against him in London, Kent, Lincolnshire, and throughout the north, in towns like Doncaster, York, Hull, Thirsk, and Newcastle. By the time of the Pilgrimage of Grace in 1536 posted bills had become ubiquitous.[102]

The increased propensity to post written bills suggests a broad class of readers. And so does the history of the English translation of the Bible. In 1381/2 the continuator of Knighton's Chronicle complained that Wyclif's translation of the Gospel made it more accessible to laymen and women who knew how to read.[103] Certainly, the history of the spread of Lollardy in the fourteenth and fifteenth centuries provides examples of literacy among the most humble classes. By 1538 a royal injunction admonished the clergy "that none of you discourage any lay person from reading of holy scripture."[104] The reasonable inference to be drawn from these examples is the expansion of literacy among the laity from the middle of the fourteenth century to the eve of the Reformation.

It is not possible to discern the extent to which the growing educational opportunities opened up a world of literacy to the poor layman or lay-

---

[100] *The Lay Folks' Catechism: Archbishop Thoresby's Instruction for the People*, ed. T. F. Simmons and H. E. Nolloth, EETS, orig. ser., 118 (London, 1901), 20-22. (My italics.)

[101] Thomas Rymer, ed., *Foedera*, 3rd ed. (The Hague, 1745), 11:268. For examples of these notices, see V. J. Scattergood, *Politics and Poetry in the Fifteenth Century* (London, 1971), 22 and passim.

[102] *English Chronicle, 1377-1461*, ed. J. S. Davies, Camden Society, no. 64 (London, 1856), 32, cited in Scattergood, *Politics and Poetry*, 119; R. Virgoe, "William Tailboys and Lord Cromwell: Crime and Politics in Lancastrian England," *Bulletin of the John Rylands University Library* 55 (1972):477-82; *L & P, Henry VIII*, 12:i, no. 200. In 1548 the authorities in the city of York were concerned about "dyvers sclaunderous billes that was set upp of dowers and wyndos within the said citie . . ." A. G. Dickens, "Some Popular Reactions to the Edwardian Reformation in Yorkshire," *YAJ* 34 (1939):152.

[103] *Chronicon Henrici Knighton*, Vol. 2, ed. J. R. Lumby, Rolls Series, no. 92, pt. ii (London, 1895), 151-52.

[104] Frere and Kennedy, *Visitation Articles and Injunctions*, 2:46. This is how the injunction was paraphrased in the York registers.

woman. Sons of the poor had traditionally been denied access to a clerical education. Despite this, there are notices scattered throughout fourteenth-century manorial rolls of serfs paying fines for licenses to enable their sons to attend school and occasional examples of serfs refusing to pay at all.[105] After the Statute of Laborers in 1405/6 serfs were to be "free to set their Son or Daughter to take Learning at any manner school that pleaseth them within the Realm."[106] Educational resources were, theoretically, now open to all classes. In reality, it does not appear that simple. With the growth of elementary education at the parish level and the increased demand for clergy in the lower levels of the Church, the opportunities for the poor were there. And the ability of the villein to take advantage of these opportunities may have been augmented by the higher wages and waning seigneurial restraints which characterized fifteenth-century England. In addition, the foundation of tuition-free, endowed schools ought to have resulted in far greater mobility out of the lowest classes. It is far from clear that this did happen. In the first place, the lord of the manor did not always relinquish control over the educational careers of his serfs. As late as 1465 the jurors of the manor of Methley (W. Riding) were fined 1d. "because they have not presented that a certain John Scholes a villein of the Lord, otherwise called John Saxton, was placed at learning without license of the Lord etc."[107] Once free of the restraints of the manor, however, there were expenses for the parish schools (which were rarely endowed) and, at the grammar level, for room and board and sometimes also tuition. Only when a poor scholar was being supported by a charity, either from one of the religious houses or from an individual patron, could he survive. There is little evidence from the wills that the clergy or members of the middle and upper levels of society were explicitly interested in financing poor scholars at the elementary and secondary levels. Most of their educational benefactions seem to have gone to sons and relations; although, in all fairness to the testators, it was not uncommon for them to finance poor university scholars.[108]

---

[105] For some examples from Yorkshire of serfs paying fines, see P. J. Wallis, "Worsborough Grammar School," *YAJ* 39 (1956):147-63 and H. Stanley Darbyshire and George D. Lumb, eds., *The History of Methley*, Thoresby Society, no. 35 (Leeds, 1937), 149. Sylvia Thrupp cites the 1378 case of the Lord of Long Bennington who, when he demanded the names of serfs sending sons to school without license, was met by a refusal on the grounds that the serfs had a right to send their sons to school without permission. Sylvia Thrupp, "The Problem of Replacement-Rates in Late Medieval English Population," *Economic History Review*, 2nd ser., 18 (1965):113.

[106] *The Statutes of the Realm*, Vol. 2 (1816), 157-58.

[107] Darbyshire and Lumb, *History of Methley*, 182.

[108] Only three such instances occur from 1400 to 1500 in the Prerogative and Exchequer Court wills. BI, Prob. Reg. 2, ff. 439, 572; 3, ff. 414v-15.

A particularly poignant example of what could happen to the poor scholar is related in the Norwich corporation records for 1521. There, in an examination of William Green, is the tale of the son of a laboring man from Wantlet, Lincolnshire, who learned his grammar for two years at the village school and then went to work with his father for five or six years, "sometyme in husbondry and other wiles with the longe sawe." Next he moved to Boston where he was living with his aunt, working and going to school for two years, after which time he received "benet and accolet" from one of the Austin friars of Boston. He then dwelt with a merchant of Boston for six months until finally moving on to Cambridge. He had no dependable support at the university, however, and made his way "by the day in berynge of ale and pekynge of saffron, and sometyme going to the Colleges, and gate his mete & drynke of almes." After journeying to Rome unsuccessfully to receive orders, Green returned to Cambridge where he obtained a license to collect subscriptions for one year toward completing his education. Unfortunately, he only collected sufficient funds for eight weeks. Having no other patrons and apparently not wishing to return to labor, Green attempted forgery instead, counterfeiting a new license to collect subscriptions and ordination papers from Rome. As a consequence we find his examination in the records.[109]

Many of the poor like William Green must have depended upon almonry schools, upon charitable homes such as that supported by St. Mary's Abbey for fifty boys attending the York Cathedral grammar school, or upon alms. Although it would be difficult to prove, it may be that the destruction of the monasteries had its greatest educational impact in the ending of alms and almonry education which they had traditionally supplied to the poorer scholars. And, as the wealthier families turned more enthusiastically toward the grammar schools, poorer scholars may have been increasingly shut out by the competition. The sentiments that a board of commissioners expressed in 1540 in support of excluding poor men's children from Canterbury's grammar school may have been echoed by others elsewhere.[110] Hence, the extent to which the expanding educational facilities opened up new channels for the poor must remain an unanswered question. Like William Green, they may still have had to face an arduous and uncertain educational future, made more difficult by the dissolution of the monasteries and, ultimately, the chantries.

On the other hand, lay literacy may have extended into the lower classes, and this, quite possibly, argues for the impact of schooling. The will of

---

[109] *Norfolk Archaeology*, 4 (1885):appendix, 342-44.
[110] Strype, *Memorials of Archbishop Cranmer*, 1:127.

Richard Wartere, inscriptional brass of Thomas Middleton, writing on the walls of York Cathedral, and the abstract prepared by Francis Bigod, all mentioned above, suggest that literacy reached relatively far down the social scale. The maltman of Braughing (Herts.), who learned his grammar from the parish priest in the 1470s, is certainly relevant here.[111] Lansdowne MS 379 in the British Museum tells the story of a literate but poor and troubled husbandman, who benefited from a hundred Pater Noster prayer which had been sent to the Charterhouse of Mount Grace in the north and there circulated in the neighborhood.[112] In her study of benefit of clergy, Leona C. Gabel discovered increasing references to secular trades among those claiming literacy and benefit of clergy. At random from jail delivery rolls dated from 6 Richard II to 1 Edward IV there appear literate "clerks" described as "quondam serviens, mercer, taillour, spicer, fysshmonger, hosyer, smuth, fyssher, shipman, chapman, yoman, bucher, husbandman, masun, walker, webster, couper, vestmentmaker and relatively numerous instances of literate laborers."[113]

Although the level of Latin that enabled laborers to qualify as literate was minimal, these lists nonetheless point to a state of affairs in which the practical distinction between a clerk (a literate individual who was usually, but perhaps decreasingly, at least in minor orders) and a literate layman was in very many cases negligible or even nonexistent. In 1489 benefit of clergy was withdrawn from the literate layman after his first conviction. Thereafter only bona fide clergy, defined as those who could present letters of orders or a certificate from their ordinary, were to be given benefit of clergy.[114] Despite this restriction, however, Margaret Bowker has shown that, of those in the episcopal prisons of Newark or Banbury (Lincoln diocese) in 1509 or later, none was a priest. They were all yeomen and laborers who were first offenders and had been sufficiently instructed to plead benefit of clergy.[115] Examples such as this make it clear that literacy

---

[111] Peter Heath, *The English Parish Clergy on the Eve of the Reformation* (London, 1969), appendix 2b, 208.

[112] British Library, Lansdowne MS 379, ff. 41-54. The monk in Mount Grace Charterhouse had sent "to a deuoute preest of my knowlegge a copy of the Reuelacion aforsaid. . . . And the same preste sent dyuers copies therof to certeyn of hys ffrendes, of whom ther was a good husbond man . . . (who) used hit dayly as deuoutly as he coude." The prayer, in fact, saved his dying ox "And so withyn ii dayes he cam to oure hous of Mountgrace & told me of all hys fortune in this mater and desired Right tendyrly to have a copy in writing of the Reuelacion of this prayer aforesaid which copy I wrotte for hym and he caused others to do the same."

[113] Leona C. Gabel, *Benefit of Clergy in England in the Later Middle Ages* (Northampton, Mass., 1929), 76-85.

[114] *The Statutes of the Realm*, Vol. 2 (1816), 538.

[115] Margaret Bowker, *The Secular Clergy in the Diocese of Lincoln, 1495-1520* (Cambridge, 1968), 122.

was by no means confined to aristocrats and gentlefolk; literacy had become more common at the middle level of lay society and was not altogether absent even among the very poor.

By the fifteenth century the ability to write was also becoming more common, no longer being a skill confined to clergy and professional laymen. An interesting struggle in the city of York from 1487 to 1492 between the textwriters, illuminators et al. and the clergy informs us that it was common for the priests within York and its suburbs to teach writing to children. Apparently various gild members, who also taught writing, were suffering from competition; sufficient numbers of children were being taught to write by the clergy so that the books they produced (which the priests then sold) had become a threat to the livelihood of the gilds.[116] While the evidence from signatures alone is not proof of functional writing ability, it is nonetheless impressive to find the four arbiters (two merchants, a goldsmith, and a grocer) to the textwriters' dispute all signing their names. Further evidence comes from an important financial agreement of 1509 when the corporation of York required "all the sayd presence in recorde herof they that cowthe write hath subscribed thare names with ther owne hands and the resydew hath setto thare marks." Nine aldermen signed and two made marks, while one other member of the corporation signed and four made marks. And in 1558 the twenty-one leading men of the city of Hull all signed their names to an agreement not to force citizens to serve as aldermen. In a more remote corner of York diocese, court records from the Duchy of Lancaster at the beginning of the sixteenth century illustrate the writing abilities of the smaller landowners. In 1514 William Walton of Walton-le-Dale testified that he wrote up two deeds of release by Henry Aynesworth of Preston in Amounderness and saw Henry seal them and sign them with his own hand.[117] These scattered examples strongly suggest that late medieval English laymen below the ranks of the aristocracy and gentry were increasingly capable of reading and writing English and perhaps a little Latin.

In order to move beyond an impressionistic conclusion based on examples which have somewhat haphazardly surfaced in the documents, I have suggested elsewhere using witness lists to wills, in conjunction with signatures and book bequests, as an index, not of any absolute percentage of lay literacy, but rather as a minimal measure of reading literacy among

---

[116] Percy, *York Memorandum Book*, 3:193-97, 206-11.

[117] Ibid., 209-11; D. M. Palliser, *Tudor York* (Oxford, 1979), 174; Hull Corporation Records, Bench Book III, f. 165v; H. Fishwick, ed., *Pleadings and Depositions in the Duchy Court of Lancaster temp. Henry VII and Henry VIII*, Lancashire and Cheshire Record Society, no. 32 (Rochdale, 1896), 54-57.

those laity involved in will-making. The most important question one must address in using these witness lists is whether the witnesses read the wills. The argument derives from the assumption that, when a clergyman is present at the writing of a will, he is listed as a witness. He is, in fact, usually listed first. Thus, lay wills without clerical witnesses were probably drawn up by one of the lay witnesses or perhaps by an unlisted lay scrivener. This and other, rather complex aspects of using witness lists are spelled out in a 1981 article in *Northern History*, and the results are relevant to the concerns of this chapter.[118]

Prior to 1450 the number of wills authenticated with witnesses rather than with seals is insufficient to draw any conclusions. Within the city of York, however, from 1460 to 1500 approximately 34 percent of the lay wills provide evidence of lay literacy, either from witness lists, signatures, booklists, or other evidences of the literacy of a testator. From 1500 to 1506 that proportion drops to 23 percent. This is the result, probably, of an increase in the number of wills proved, which rise from twelve per annum to twenty-five per annum, thereby providing us with a much broader sample of the town's population.[119] By 1530 26 percent of the lay wills from York diocese, excluding Richmond archdeaconry, provide evidence for reading literacy among a wide variety of laity, including gentlemen, merchants, artisans, yeomen, and even husbandmen.[120] And finally, when we turn to the most backward section of York diocese, rural Richmond, an area composed largely of yeomen and husbandmen of modest wealth, we find that, from 1530 to 1548—the earliest years for which substantial numbers of wills are extant in this region—approximately 30 percent yield evidence of lay literacy.[121] These results, while providing no basis for estimating an overall literacy rate, do suggest that a significant number of fifteenth- and sixteenth-century north country laity were indeed literate.

This conclusion is reinforced by applying the data on educational institutions to the problem of literacy. Two indicators of literacy in a society are the number of teachers and the rate of attendance at school in relation to the total population.[122] Population figures for the diocese are highly

---

[118] Moran, "Literacy and Education," 8-13.

[119] BI, Prob. Reg. 4 (entire); 5, ff. 1-110; 6 (entire). A total of 221 wills of York residents have been examined out of a total of approximately 480 from York for the forty years from 1460 to 1499. All 153 wills from the city of York residents registered from 1500 to 1506 have been examined.

[120] Ibid., 10, ff. 1-65. There is a total of 112 wills in these folios.

[121] Leeds Central Library, Archives Department, Richmond Archdeaconry, Will Register, 1, 2, 3 & A. There are approximately 230 wills for the period 1530 to 1548.

[122] Cipolla, *Literacy and Development*, 25-34.

tentative but can be estimated from 1500 to 1530 to have been, at the highest, 250,000.[123] Since we now have an idea of the number of grammar schools throughout the diocese, and we know that the years required to complete the grammar course was, at least in theory, six, the additional information we need is the number of scholars in a typical school and the average life expectancy of a child at age five and beyond. What few figures we have on grammar school attendance range from 30 to 150; an average estimate might be 75.[124] Assuming an average life expectancy of thirty-four years at age five (a low estimate based on the Coale and Demeny Model Life Tables) the result is approximately 26,320 or 10.5 percent of the persons within the diocese by 1530 who may have received a grammar school education.[125] Thus, if 1.6 to 1.8 percent of the population planned to enter the clergy,[126] and entered grammar school to do so, those students receiving a grammar education who would remain laity are the great majority. Since it is clear that some clergy did not receive a grammar school training, the proportion of laity in the grammar schools should be even higher.

Using the same method but taking a figure of ten children per elementary school, each attending for a three-year period, the number of children within the diocese in 1530 who may have received an elementary education would have been approximately 12,211 or 4.8 percent.[127] If we

---

[123] For the considerations which produce this very rough figure of 250,000, see Moran, "Educational Development and Social Change in York Diocese from the Fourteenth Century to 1548" (Ph.D. diss., Brandeis University, 1975), app. d.

[124] For the number of scholars in the grammar schools, see Chapter three above, pp. 87-88. If one takes the instances of numbers of scholars listed at chantry grammar schools (1546-1548), the average is 66, although a chantry school would tend to be smaller than a cathedral or town grammar school. Leach, *ESR*, ii:63, 68, 74, 75, 81, 86, 97, 190, 268, 269, 292, 301.

[125] The totals are calculated using Model Life Table North level 1 in Ansley J. Coale and Paul Demeny, *Regional Model Life Tables and Stable Populations* (Princeton, 1966), pt. ii, 220. This table is the one with the lowest life expectancy for the population of northern Europe. The population at age five is then converted to a base of 1,000, and the declining number of survivors calculated accordingly. The number of schoolchildren in the grammar schools charted in Chapter four would be 5,100 from 1500-1530 and 1,875 from 1450-1500 every six years. This number is then multiplied by the proportion surviving in 1530. All the people schooled over seventy-five years (between 1455 and 1530) and living in the year 1530 were then added up to give the total number of persons who may have received a grammar school education. A similar calculation was done for the elementary schools. Using the number of schools in Chart 1, the number of schoolchildren in elementary schools every three years would be 1,240 from 1500-1530 and 700 from 1450-1500.

[126] The approximately 4,100-4,700 clergy in York diocese in 1500 equal 1.6-1.8 percent of a total estimated population of 250,000. For the numbers of clergy, see Chapter five, p. 126-27.

[127] For the number of scholars in the elementary schools, see Chapter three above, pp. 86-

further assume that many of the grammar school children did not attend separate parish elementary schools but were either tutored privately or instructed in elementary learning at the grammar school, and that some unknown proportion of children would have failed to complete all nine years of schooling, then one could estimate *very* roughly that by 1530 approximately 12 percent of the total population of York dicoese had had some kind of schooling.[128] These figures are highly provisional and tentative, and they are offered here only as a minimal estimate. The total population has been estimated on the generous side, while the average life expectancy is a low estimate. There were undoubtedly some schools (especially monastic schools and short-lived reading schools) that have escaped our attention. And there were certainly rectors, chaplains, and laity who taught in private household schools and about whom we have no information. Considering these factors and all the various informal means of education that have not been considered here, it is likely that an overall literacy rate of 15 percent for northern England is closer to the mark. Of this total, from 1.6 to 1.8 percent would be clergy, resulting in a minimal lay literacy rate of 13-14 percent. Without any information on male-female ratios, either in the total population or among scholars, it is not possible to offer any specific estimates for male and female literacy. The fact that female scholars seem to be associated in small numbers with elementary learning, however, suggests a male literacy rate of between 20 and 25 percent. This rate, calculated on the basis of references to schools,

---

87. This may be a low estimate. For the seventeenth century, John Lawson argues for an average elementary school population of twenty. Lawson, *Primary Education in East Yorkshire, 1560-1902*, East Yorkshire Local History Society, no. 10 (York, 1959), 6.

[128] Another way of going about this would be to estimate that in York diocese in 1530 40 percent of the population was fifteen or younger. Although we have no age structure for the English population at this time, this is typical of developing countries. It assumes a high rather than a low birth rate, which seems typical of northern England in the early sixteenth century if the wills are any indication. See D. Bogue, *Principles of Demography* (New York, 1969), 165-69 and M. G. Powers, "The Effects of Education on Population Structure," in *Education and Population*, ed. H. V. Muhsam (Dolhain, Belgium, 1975), 247. This would result in 100,000 individuals from birth to fifteen years of age. If 50 percent of all children died by age five there would be roughly 50,000 children of school age (from six to fifteen). This is an optimistic estimate given the known death rates in the city of York from 1538 to 1601 which suggest 60 percent mortality by age five and over 70 percent mortality by age fifteen. The mortality rates are similar for both sexes. Ursula M. Cowgill, "Life and Death in the Sixteenth Century in the City of York," *Population Studies*, 21 (1976):53-62. Using this probably too high estimate of 50,000 and calculating 192 elementary and grammar schools, the school population in 1530 would be 6,340 children or 12.7 percent of the school-age population. The percentage would be approximately twice as high for the male school-age population if one assumes that it was not common for girls to attend.

includes a wide range of learning—from song scholars who were only superficially acquainted with Latin and may or may not have been able to read the vernacular to students ready for the university, although clearly the greater proportion are those with a Latin grammar education.

Growing lay initiatives in founding schools, substantial lay support of scholars, and expanding lay literacy combined with significant numbers of laity in the schools suggest that education was being laicized, and that traditional ecclesiastical ties were being eroded. In the final analysis, however, it is important not to overstate the case for laicization. Despite increasing lay involvement in education, there is plenty of evidence that neither the Church nor the clergy abdicated its role in the educational sphere.

Not only were scholars, particularly elementary scholars, being trained in the liturgy and literature of the Church, and not only were schools producing impressively high numbers of priests, but the clergy were also prominent in the movement to found or endow educational institutions. From 1460 to 1548 we have notices of seventeen endowments or foundations of schools within the diocese by members of the Church hierarchy, including Bishop Stillington grammar, song, and writing school at Acaster Selby circa 1475, Archbishop Rotherham's similar school at Rotherham in 1483, Bishop John Alcock's endowment of Hull grammar school in 1479, the dean of Craven's grammar school at Skipton in 1492, Archdeacon Thomas Magnus's endowment at Newark in 1530, and Archbishop Holgate's three grammar schools founded between 1546 and 1548.[129] Nearly half the new foundations were the result of ecclesiastical initiative, and many of them predate the rush of lay foundations. One can conclude that the Church was an active, indeed perhaps a motivating, partner in the educational boom of late medieval and early Tudor northern England.

There are also a number of foundations that appear to be both ecclesiastical and lay in nature. Several of the chantry and stipendiary priests who were teaching grammar were being funded by religious gilds whose funds originally derived from parishioners but which were administered through the ecclesiastical institution of a gild. Such was the case at Middleton, Northallerton, Pickering, and Pontefract. Indeed, it is difficult to find any educational institutions, even those that were lay-founded or endowed, that did not retain some ecclesiastical characteristics. The grammar schools at East Retford, Lancaster, and Nottingham, for example,

[129] See Appendix B. In addition, there were ecclesiastically endowed/founded schools, in Yorkshire, at Bedale, Giggleswick, Hunsingore, Kirkby Ravensworth, Pocklington, Royston, and Sedbergh, and, in Nottinghamshire, at Kneesall. There are no known ecclesiastical foundations for Lancashire and Westmorland/Cumberland within the diocese during this period.

although controlled by the mayor or councils of burgesses, were also subject to the direction of the vicar, chantry priest, or local priory. Most schools founded in the first half of the sixteenth century, whether established by laity or clerics, were founded as chantries. In addition, schoolchildren everywhere were expected to say prayers for the founder's soul and the souls of his family and benefactors.

It was not until 1546, with the foundation of three grammar schools at York, Malton, and Hemsworth, that we find a grammar school whose foundation statutes no longer delineate a specific religious function. Ironically, the founder of these schools was Archbishop Holgate, the most prominent clergyman in the diocese. A corporation sole was set up under royal patent, although the archbishop retained the right to appoint the schoolmaster. The children were expected to begin and end the day with prayers, hymns, and collects and to attend church on Sundays and holidays, but throughout it is clear that the purpose behind Holgate's foundations was primarily educational rather than religious, and that any ecclesiastical involvement was to be highly circumscribed.[130] Even as late as 1551, the grammar school at East Retford (Notts.), which was newly reestablished, fully lay-controlled, and one of the first northern schools to institute a markedly humanistic curriculum, drew up its statutes under the supervision of Archbishop Holgate.[131]

Clearly the Church's responsibility was considerable and continued to be crucial, while religious motivations in education remained strong. Clerical patronage of boys aspiring to the priesthood, ecclesiastical support of schools, and the religious activities that formed part of a schoolchild's day suggest a healthy ecclesiastical investment in pre-university education. There is no doubt, however, that the added input of the laity helped sustain this development and push it to dramatically new heights. Throughout this chapter we have followed in some detail the growth in lay interest in education and the rising lay literacy. Laity not only benefited from the schools but also, to an increasing extent, underwrote their expansion. If a school was not endowed or founded by laity (and many of them were), it might be governed by a council of burgesses or a parochial council, and many of the scholars, again especially in the grammar schools, were being supported increasingly with alms and benefactions from laity. While there is virtually no evidence for concomitant curricular changes (in particular, the impact of humanist learning), the growing lay involvement

[130] York City Archives, Deed of Foundation of the Free School of Robert Holgate, York, ff. 1-8v.

[131] BI, Reg. 29 (Holgate), ff. 53-57v; *VCH, Notts.*, 2:240-42.

in elementary and secondary education surely prepared the ground for curricular changes in the post-Reformation period and for the shifts in school governance which occurred after the dissolution of the chantries.[132] Thus, although a substantial number of schools were founded by clergy or remained under ecclesiastical control, and despite the fact that even those with lay backing usually operated in conjunction with the parish vicar or other priests, there can be no question but that the rise in educational resources, especially toward the end of the fifteenth century, was to a great extent the result of a growing lay interest in education which reinforced but did not supplant an already substantial ecclesiastical commitment to education.

[132] J. Hoeppner Moran, "The Schools of Northern England 1450-1550: Humanist Ideals and Educational Realities" (Paper presented at the Newberry Library Conference on Schooling and the Renaissance, Chicago, 1982).

CHAPTER 7

Literary Interests and Educational Motivations in York Diocese

It is far easier to document educational change than to understand its causes. The previous chapters have advanced several explanations as to why an educational revival in late medieval York diocese should have occurred. First, the growth of elementary education may have been partly in response to demands for more mass priests and singers in the choir. Second, the endowment of schools, generally grammar schools, was due to a large extent to considerable lay investment in addition to some significant ecclesiastical initiatives. Third, lay benefactions to scholars increased just at the time when more and more children of upper-class laity, many without clerical ambitions, were moving into the grammar schools. What motivations spurred the laity to make these educational commitments? Two answers, among others, that have been suggested by historians focusing on the sixteenth century are the religious urge to read the Bible in the vernacular, and the growing popularity of humanism. But Reformation ideas and humanist ideals either did not yet exist or had not yet penetrated to the north of England in time to explain the educational growth documented here. Nor does Lollardy provide much of an answer, because, although it occurred earlier, traces of its influence in the north are slight. Benefit of clergy, which allowed an individual to escape the secular courts for the more lenient jurisdiction of the ecclesiastical courts, was conferred throughout our period on those who demonstrated an ability to read select portions of the Bible. The motivation of gaining benefit of clergy may have made elementary education more attractive, but any connection is hypothetical due to lack of adequate documentation. How, for example, does one explain the interest in education on the part of eighty subscribers to the newly endowed grammar school at Nottingham in 1512, who were unlikely to have been moved by Lollardy, humanism or benefit of clergy, who were ignorant, as yet, of Luther, and most of whom would not have had a Bible (in either Latin or the vernacular) in their possession? What intellectual framework lay behind the awakening interest in education? In order to begin to answer this question, it is useful to look at the intellectual environment in the north and in particular at the books literate laity read. The analysis that emerges stresses the religious concerns of the laity and suggests that investing in education was one response to a growing interest in the literature of the Church. This chapter offers nothing conclusive. It merely follows the leads that result from a study of the will bequests. Any definitive solution to the problem of motivation eludes us and probably always will.

The main obstacle in mapping popular intellectual interests during the late Middle Ages is the sources we have to rely on. There are no sources that provide a wholly satisfying answer to the question of what people read. Until the advent of printing this can only be partially reconstructed from wills, inventories, library catalogs, and extant manuscripts. The most continuous and consistent source for documenting the interests of the reading public is the wills of the period. Despite the fact that they are selective in their information, revealing only those books that a testator wished to bequeath, usually on his deathbed, they are nevertheless sufficiently consistent and informative to provide a basis for comparative analysis from the end of the fourteenth century when they first begin to be preserved with any consistency in the York archives, until 1510, after which date the practice of mentioning titles of books in wills diminishes.[1] By the beginning of the sixteenth century one increasingly finds testators such as a baker of Wakefield, a glazier of York, a widow of Bilburgh, and a dyer of Pontefract bequeathing an entire library or all their books.[2] But, in the absence of the probate inventory, we have no way of knowing the contents of such book collections. Thus, except for Bibles, which have been noted here up to 1530, the following analysis of books bequeathed stops in 1510.

Bibles, however, are of primary importance. The conclusion of Margaret Deanesly, who has done the most extensive analysis of medieval Bibles thus far for England, is that the laity had restricted access to the Bible, which was generally limited to the nobility. She also concludes that it was not common for the secular clergy, other than cathedral priests, to possess a Bible. Deanesly's statistics, compiled mostly from 7,578 printed and manuscript wills, list 110 Vulgate, 9 French, and 17 English Bibles before 1526. Of these it is possible to identify thirty-five of them, including two French and one English Bible, in bequests from the north of England.[3]

---

[1] With the widespread acceptance of printed books after 1510 and their relative cheapness, mention of individual books tended to be relegated to the inventories; even there they are often described in bulk.

[2] BI, Prob. Reg. 5, f. 25v; 6, ff. 71, 92, 239v.

[3] Margaret Deanesly, *The Lollard Bible and Other Medieval Biblical Versions* (Cambridge, 1920).

These totals, however, underestimate the availability of Bibles in late medieval England.[4] The York diocesan wills alone, from 1370 to 1530, mention fifty-nine Bibles. In addition, there are eight Bibles mentioned in wills of Yorkshiremen registered at Canterbury, producing a combined total of sixty-seven Bibles listed in the wills of individuals from York diocese from 1370 to 1530, a small enough total for approximately 15,000 wills but more than has been assumed previously. Another thirty-six Bibles are listed in surviving late medieval library catalogs and inventories from a variety of monasteries, friaries, colleges, parishes, and individuals in the diocese, and in N. R. Ker's compilation of surviving manuscripts from medieval libraries,[5]

---

[4] It is obvious, even from the extant medieval Bibles, that Deanesly's list is an underestimate. Over 230 surviving Wyclifite biblical manuscripts are currently known to historians, of which 23 are whole Bibles. Conrad Lindberg, "The Manuscripts and Versions of the Wycliffite Bible: A Preliminary Survey," *Studia Neophilologica* 42 (1970):333-47. The total number of English medieval Latin Bibles extant is unknown, but it is in the hundreds and must be only a fraction of what once existed.

[5] The following library lists have been searched for references to Bibles: the books noted by John Leland in his *Antiquarii de Rebus Britannicis Collectanea*, 6 vols. (London, 1770), 4:35-46; two fifteenth-century Carthusian booklists from Hull and Mount Grace in E. Margaret Thompson, *The Carthusian Order in England* (London, 1930), 324-26, 330-31; the fifteenth-century catalog of the Cistercian library at Meaux in *Chronica Monasterii de Melsa*, Vol. 3, ed. E. A. Bond, Rolls Series, no. 43 (London, 1868), app., lxxxiii-c; the fourteenth- or fifteenth-century list of manuscripts bequeathed to Swine nunnery in M. R. James, *A Descriptive Catalogue of the Manuscripts in King's College, Cambridge* (Cambridge, 1895), 34-35; the magnificent late fourteenth-century library catalog of the Austin friars in York in M. R. James, "The Catalogue of the Library of the Augustinian Friars at York," in *Fasciculus Joanni Willis Clark dicatus* (Cambridge, 1909), 2-96; books bequeathed by Archbishop Rotherham to Jesus College of Rotherham in 1500 in M. R. James, *A Descriptive Catalogue of the Manuscripts in the Library of Sidney Sussex College, Cambridge* (Cambridge, 1895), 5-8; M. R. James, *A Descriptive Catalogue of Manuscripts in the Library of Jesus College, Cambridge* (London, 1895), 44-55; the 1558 catalog of Monk Bretton Priory in Joseph Hunter, *English Monastic Libraries* (London, 1831), 1-7; a thirteenth-century Bridlington Priory booklist published by H. Omont, "Anciens catalogues de Bibliothèques anglaises XIIᵉ-XIVᵉ siècle," *Zentralblatt für Bibliothekswesen* 9 (1892):203-205 as a *bibliothèque anonyme*; the 1180 library list from Whitby Abbey in George Young, *A History of Whitby*, 2 vols. (Whitby, 1817), 2:918-20; the eleventh-century inventory from Sherburne parish in James Raine, ed., *The Fabric Rolls of York Minster*, Surtees Society, no. 35 (Durham, 1859), 142; original inventories in the BI and the YML; the library of John Vicars, rector of Newton-Kyme c. 1540, in Ralph Thoresby, *Ducatus Leodiensis* (London, 1715), 516; the 1434 inventory of St. Mary's parish church, Scarborough, edited by W. H. St. John Hope in *Archaeologia* 51, no. 2 (1888):66; the 1546 list of books at Brough chantry school in R. L. Storey, "The Chantries of Cumberland and Westmorland, part ii," *Transactions of the Cumberland and Westmorland Antiquarian and Archaeological Society*, new ser., 62 (1962):147; the sixteenth-century inventory of service books at York Minster in James Raine, Jr., *The Historians of the Church of York and Its Archbishops*, Vol. 3, Rolls Series, no. 71 (London, 1894), 387; inventories of the libraries of York cathedral clergy in *Test. Ebor.*, 3:74-77, 110; 4:279-

although some of these may include duplicate references to the same text.[6]

Prior to 1450, the higher-level clergy were the main givers and recipients of Bibles, although officials in the Court of York had Bibles, as did members of the nobility, clerks, and a doctor in York. Thomas Wilton, M.D., received Bibles twice (in 1433 and again in 1436) in payment for services to dying testators.[7] Institutions benefited from the largesse of testators throughout the fourteenth and fifteenth centuries. The York Cathedral Library received two Bibles, as did the Friars Minor of York and St. William's College, York. Bibles went to Gisburn Priory, St. Agatha Abbey in Easby, Drax Priory, Wartre Priory, Valle Dei convent, St. Mary's Abbey, York, and Queen's College, Cambridge.[8] The Austin

---

82; 5:258-59; the 1415 and 1419 inventories of Lord Scrope of Masham edited by Charles L. Kingsford in "Two Forfeitures in the Year of Agincourt," *Archaeologia* 70 (1920):87-99; the post-twelfth-century catalog of books at Welbeck, Notts. in M. R. James, *Descriptive Catalogue of the Manuscripts in St. John's College* (London, 1913), 10-13; and a twelfth-century list of books at Worksop Priory in M. R. James, *Catalogue of the Manuscripts and Early Printed Books from the . . . Library of J. P. Morgan* (London, 1906), 165. A late medieval catalog from Kirkstall Abbey, derived primarily from Ker's *Medieval Libraries*, is in *The Kirkstall Abbey Chronicle*, ed. J. Taylor, Thoresby Society, no. 42 (Leeds, 1952), 30-40. The only booklist I have not seen is the books given by Thomas Colier, a fellow of Michaelhouse, Cambridge, to the Franciscan convent at Richmond in 1506 in Cambridge University Archives, wills 1501-58, ff. 16v-17v.

For Ker's compilation, see N. R. Ker, ed., *Medieval Libraries of Great Britain: A List of Surviving Books*, 2nd ed. (London, 1964).

[6] The two Bibles in Archbishop Bowet's 1421 inventory may be the same Bibles found in the later inventories of Thomas Morton, canon residentiary of York, and William de Melton, chancellor of York, since the prices and descriptions agree. *Test. Ebor.*, 3:71-77, 110; 5:258-59. There may be other duplicates, e.g., the Bible listed in Lord Henry Scrope's 1415 inventory may be the same one bequeathed to him by Sir John Lescrop in 1405. *Test. Ebor.*, 1:339.

[7] For Bibles in the hands of officials of the court, see BI, Prob. Reg. 2, f. 11; YML, D. & C., L 2/4, f. 250, printed in *Test. Ebor.*, 2:79. For nobles with Bibles, see BI, Reg. 12 (Neville), f. 59, printed in *Test. Ebor.*, 1:97-99; BI, Prob. Reg. 1, f. 51, printed in *Test. Ebor.*, 1:178-80; YML, D. & C., L 2/4, f. 138v, printed in *Test. Ebor.*, 1:338-39; Thomas Rymer, ed., *Foedera*, 3rd ed. (The Hague, 1740), 4:pt. ii, 131-34; BI, Prob. Reg. 2, f. 639, printed in *Test. Ebor.*, 2:7. For clerks with Bibles, see BI, Prob. Reg. 1, f. 12; YML, D. & C., L 2/4, ff. 96v-97, 233; BI, Reg. 19 (Kemp), ff. 501-502v. For the bequests to Dr. Wilton, see YML, D. & C., L 2/4, f. 241v; BI, Prob. Reg. 3, f. 473v. It is clear from the wills that Wilton had already either borrowed or appropriated the Bibles before the wills were written.

[8] YML, D. & C., L 2/4, ff. 152, 168v-71, printed in *Test. Ebor.*, 1:364-71; BI, Prob. Reg. 2, ff. 137v-38, printed in *Test. Ebor.*, 2:116-18; BI, Prob. Reg. 2, f. 406; YML, D. & C., L 2/4, ff. 259, 347v; BI, Prob. Reg. 2, f. 639, printed in *Test. Ebor.*, 2:7; PRO, PCC, Prob. 11/11 Horne 26, printed in *Test. Ebor.*, 4:96; YML, D. & C., L 2/4, f. 250, printed in *Test. Ebor.*, 2:79; BI, Reg. 12 (Neville), f. 59, printed in *Test. Ebor.*, 1:97-99; YML, D. & C., L 2/4, f. 287; BI, Prob. Reg. 5, f. 252v, printed in *Test. Ebor.*, 3:256; BI, Prob. Reg. 6, f. 83v, printed in *Test. Ebor.*, 4:220.

Friary at York had at least six Bibles, while Meaux Abbey had three and Rotherham College two. The friars of Nottingham and of Beverley and the monasteries of Bridlington, Newstead, Fountains, Guisborough, and Mount Grace all had at least one Bible in their possession,[9] which is not surprising since, although there is no documentation for most religious houses, it would be inconceivable for a monastery or friary to be without a Vulgate or a Gospel book for the mass.[10] With the exception of three members of the nobility, all the donors to the above religious institutions were members of the higher clergy.[11]

The lower clergy were not, however, without biblical resources. In 1404 William Wilmyncote alias de Coventry, a chaplain in All Saints, Peaseholme (York), gave a small Bible to John Morele, chaplain, on Morele's death to go to Richard de Swayneby, a poor clerk and servant, under the condition that he enter sacred orders. After Richard's death the Bible was to go to other unbeneficed priests, on condition that, should they receive a benefice, they were, within a year, to turn the Bible over to another chaplain. In this manner, many poor priests, from 1404 until the Reformation, may have had the opportunity of possessing a Bible, even if for only a year, and perhaps, in that interval, copying selected passages from it.[12]

In addition to this example, there are a number of other instances among the pre-1450 York diocesan documents of chaplains, clerks, vicars, or rectors receiving or bequeathing Bibles.[13] By the second half of the century the Bible is increasingly found in the hands of the parish clergy. A not untypical example from the post-1450 bequests is that of the vicar of Topcliffe who, in 1463, bequeathed a Bible to William the son of William Ruckshaw, apothecary of York. William was a fellow in Peterhouse, Cambridge. In 1472 he became the vicar of Topcliffe himself, and in 1480, the succentor of York Cathedral.[14]

---

[9] James, "Catalogue of the Augustinian Friars," 19; *Chronica Monasterii de Melsa*, lxxxiv, xcii; James, *Catalogue of MSS in Sidney Sussex College, Cambridge*, 6; H. Omont, "Anciens catalogues," 204; Ker, *Medieval Libraries*, 88 (Fountains), 94 (Guisborough), 132 (Mount Grace), 135 (Newstead), 140 (Nottingham); BI, Reg. 26 (Bainbridge), ff. 136v-37.

[10] Deanesly, *The Lollard Bible*, 168-71.

[11] BI, Reg. 12 (Neville), f. 59, printed in *Test. Ebor.*, 1:97-99; BI, Prob. Reg. 2, f. 639, printed in *Test. Ebor.*, 2:7; PRO, PCC, Prob. 11/11 Horne 26, printed in *Test. Ebor.*, 4:94-97. For the donors to Fountains, Guisborough, Mount Grace, Newstead, and Nottingham, see Ker, *Medieval Libraries*, 263-64, 266, 283, 284, 287.

[12] BI, Prob. Reg. 3, f. 226v.

[13] See, for example, YML, D. & C., L 2/4, ff. 96, 115v, 133v, 168v-71, 233, 241v-42, 255v.

[14] BI, Prob. Reg. 2, f. 483; Emden, *BRUC*, 493.

With one exception,[15] there is no evidence of a Bible being bequeathed to parish churches before 1457, when the rector of Kirkby Ravensworth gave one to the library of Boston (Lincs.) parish church. This does not mean, however, that parish churches lacked Bibles. In 1434, for example, an inventory of St. Mary's parish church in Scarborough noted "unum novum librum vocatum byble." Apparently there could be some doubt as to the security of a Bible in a parish church, for the rector of Saundby (Notts.) in 1467 entailed his Bible to his church with elaborate warnings that it not be removed by the lord of the parish or the rector or sold by the parishioners. It was to be used permanently for better reading in the future—an indication that the Bible was being read in parish church services.[16] Bibles were also left to St. Michael Ousebridge in York, to St. Martin Coney Street in York, to Hornby parish church (N. Riding), and to Hoterton (?) parish church, while a Bible was listed at St. Michael's Spurriergate, York, in the early sixteenth-century churchwarden's accounts.[17]

Non-noble laity with Bibles were uncommon but by no means unheard of in the fifteenth century. In the codicil to his will in 1437 William Ormeshead left an English translation of the scriptures to his nephew, citizen and merchant Nicholas Blackburn, Jr. In 1432 John Raventhorpe, a priest in St. Martin's chapel outside York, left a Bible to John West, who may have been a girdler within the city. In 1446 William Revetour, a chaplain at York who evidently helped supervise the York mystery plays, gave an English book treating of the Bible to Thomas Tutbagg, a merchant and chamberlain of the city, and a large Latin Bible to John Bolton, merchant and former mayor of York. In 1467 the rector of Saundby (mentioned above) left his Bible to his brother William Smyth before entailing it to his parish church. A "biblia picta" was given in 1486 by John Lese, a chaplain at Pontefract, to the brother of his godson. The recipient, William Jene, was probably a student, as he also received some

---

[15] In 1378 Thomas de Farnylawe, chancellor of York Cathedral, left a Bible to be chained in St. Nicholas parish, Newcastle, for common use. YML, D. & C., L 2/4, 69, printed in *Test. Ebor.*, 1:101-103.

[16] YML, D. & C., L 2/4, f. 287; W. H. St. John Hope, "Inventory of the Parish Church of St. Mary Scarborough 1434," *Archaeologia* 51, no. 2 (1888):66; BI, Prob. Reg. 4, f. 52, printed in *Test. Ebor.*, 2:283.

[17] BI, Prob. Reg. 7, f. 25; YML, D. & C., L 2/5a, ff. 127-28; BI, Reg. 27 (Wolsey), f. 145; Ker, *Medieval Libraries*, 224, 325. These Bibles were all devised in the first three decades of the sixteenth century. Earlier, in 1486, Thomas Tutbagg, merchant of York, had bequeathed Peter de Comestor's *Historia Scholastica*, possibly in English, to St. John the Evangelist parish church. BI, Prob. Reg. 5 f. 299. For the Bible at St. Michael's Spurriergate, see BI, PR Y/MS/3, f. 41.

grammar books. In 1479 Thomas Bowes, a gentleman from York and keeper of the exchequer in London, left his Bible to Bartholomew Rede, goldsmith. In 1492 William Poteman, archdeacon of the East Riding, left a small Bible to John Wod, a York scrivener. The rector of Hedon, in 1510, left a Bible to Henry Marshall, a relative, while in 1518 Robert Symkyn, priest, left Cuthbert Symkyn (his brother?) a parchment Bible. Finally, Peter Mydleton, a student, or possibly the schoolmaster at Doncaster, received a Bible in 1528 from the vicar "if he will continue the scole and do well or els not."[18] Thus, although it was not usual to find the Bible in non-noble lay hands, it was by no means improbable after the beginning of the fifteenth century. Nor does there appear to have been any stigma attached to its possession, or surely such gifts would not have been noted so freely for the Church to examine. With the dissolution of the monasteries many of the institutional Bibles came into lay hands. One of the best examples is the library of Henry Savile, esquire, of Banke in Halifax (1568-1617), whose collection consisted of manuscripts from the monastic ruins of Rievaulx, Fountains, and Byland, including a two-volume Wyclifite Bible and several Vulgates.[19] Between 1535 and 1557, with the printing of thirty editions of the entire English Bible and approximately fifty editions of the English New Testament, the Bible had become a regular feature of parish life for both laity and clergy.[20]

In addition to the entire Bible, twenty-five books of the Bible, predominately Gospels and Epistles, were bequeathed prior to 1510, including at least three English Gospels.[21] Library catalogs and inventories, in addition to Ker's compilation of surviving manuscripts from medieval

[18] BI, Prob. Reg. 3, ff. 358, 503-504v. For West, see Prob. Reg. 2, f. 201. Prob. Reg. 2, f. 137v, printed in *Test. Ebor.*, 2:116-18. For Tutbagg, see *Register of the Freemen of the City of York*, Vol. 1, ed. F. Collins, Surtees Society, no. 96 (Durham, 1897), 144, 173, 191; BI, Prob. Reg. 3, f. 526v; 5, f. 299; Prob. Reg. 5, f. 284; PRO, PCC, Prob. 11/7 Logge 12, f. 89; YML, D. & C., L 2/5a, ff. 1-4; BI, Reg. 26 (Bainbridge), f. 138; Prob. Reg. 9, f. 90; Reg. 27 (Wolsey), f. 163.

[19] J. P. Gilson, "The Library of Henry Savile, of Banke," *Transactions of the Bibliographical Society* 9 (1908):127-210.

[20] H. S. Bennett, *English Books and Readers, 1475-1557* (Cambridge, 1952), 26; STC 2063-2092, 2826-2871. In the inventories of church goods for the East Riding in 1552, Bibles were noted in the churches of Foston, Nafferton, Bridlington, Besonby, South Burton, Northcave, Southcliff, and Skipwith. Most other parishes did not provide a list of their books. William Page, ed., *Inventories of Church Goods for the Counties of York, Durham, and Northumberland*, Surtees Society, no. 97 (Durham, 1897), 8-85. Sheriff Hutton had a half Bible in 1538. J. S. Purvis, ed., "The Churchwarden's Book of Sheriff Hutton, A. D. 1524-1568," *YAJ* 36 (1945):181.

[21] For the English Gospels, see BI, Prob. Reg. 1, f. 72v; 2, f. 137v; 3, f. 369v, printed in *Test. Ebor.*, 1:196; 2:34, 117.

libraries, multiply the number, adding one Old Testament and sixty-two separate manuscripts containing Old Testament books (two in French), seven New Testaments, twenty-two Gospels (one of which was in French and three in English) and twenty-four other manuscripts with individual Gospels, thirty Epistles (at least one of which was in English), eight Acts (at least one of which was in English), and eleven Apocalypses.[22]

The higher clergy played a prominent role in the transmission of these books, and institutions of widely varying importance were the recipients.[23] But rectors, vicars, chaplains, and laity were also frequent donors or receivers of books of the Bible as early as 1394. Three English Gospels, all mentioned prior to 1450, passed through the hands of two chaplains and one rector into the possession of Holy Trinity chantry in Goodramgate church, York; and two laymen of York.[24] At the end of the fourteenth century or the beginning of the fifteenth, the vicar of Swine gave a glossed Book of Mark to Swine nunnery. The parson of Rudby had a volume of Gospels, as did a chaplain at St. Michael Belfrey in York. Epistles are noted in the parish church of Leake and Gospels at Scarborough.[25] John Clerk, chaplain, received a book of the Gospels in Latin from the priest in St. Martin's chapel outside York, and a notebook with the Gospels and Epistles from a married layman, William Stanes of Bootham, York. In 1436 the bishop of Durham left a glossed copy of Paul's Epistles to John Radcliff, his guest and a merchant of York.[26] By the latter half of the fifteenth century it became less common for the wills to mention books from the Bible, although in 1479 Master Robert Lythe, a chaplain within York Cathedral, gave a book of Gospels to Robert Tranholm, a layman who may have been a grammarmaster.[27]

[22] See note 5 above.

[23] E.g. YML, D. & C., L 2/4, ff. 115v, 154, 168v, 259; BI, Prob. Reg. 2, f. 399; Reg. 19 (Kemp), ff. 501-502v; Reg. 25 (Savage), f. 163v. Recipients include York Cathedral Library, the Dominican Friary at Spofforth (?), Swine nunnery, Kepier Hospital, the Vicars Choral College at York, the Augustinian Priory at Theisford, St. Michael the Belfrey parish of York, Rotherham College, Leake parish church, and Hull Charterhouse.

[24] See note 21 above.

[25] James, *Catalogue of MSS in King's College, Cambridge*, 34-35; BI, Reg. 18 (Bowet), f. 382v, printed in *Test. Ebor.*, 1:403-405; BI, original inventory of Simon Lastyngham; Ker, *Medieval Libraries*, 221; St. John Hope, "Inventory of St. Mary Scarborough," 66.

[26] BI, Prob. Reg. 3, ff. 358v, 435v. For Clerk, see Prob. Reg. 2, f. 226v. For Stanes see *Register of the Freemen of York*, 128, 138, 144, 157. BI, Reg. 18 (Kemp), ff. 501-502v. For Radcliff, see Prob. Reg. 2, f. 90.

[27] YML, D. & C., L 2/4, ff. 346, 348v. Several of the books which Robert Lythe bequeathed were grammar texts. In 1480 Tranholm also received half the library of Henry Lythe, vicar of Acome.

TABLE 9

CHRONOLOGICAL DISTRIBUTION OF BIBLES AND BOOKS OF
BIBLES BEQUEATHED IN THE WILLS OF INDIVIDUALS FROM
YORK DIOCESE, 1370-1529

Dates	Bibles[a]	Books of Bibles
1370-1399	8	2
1400-1449	31	17
1450-1499	20	3
1500-1529	8	3[b]
Total	67	25

SOURCES: BI, Prob. Reg. 1-10; Reg. 12-27; PRO, PCC,
Prob. 11/1-21; YML, D. & C., L 2/4, L 2/5a.

[a] If a testator bequeathed his best or largest Bible, two Bibles
have been counted.

[b] This covers the years from 1500-1509 only.

Table 9 enumerates, chronologically, both the Bibles and books of Bibles
that were bequeathed in the York diocesan wills between 1370 and the
beginning of the sixteenth century. It draws attention to the dispropor-
tionate number of biblical texts circulating in the first half of the fifteenth
century and raises the question whether Lollardy was not having some
impact in the north.

There is, however, very little to indicate that Bible-reading among the
lower clergy and the laity was anything but orthodox, and nothing to
suggest that it was very widespread. Despite the fact that possession of
biblical texts was clearly not limited to the upper clergy and noble laity,
there is very little evidence of Lollardy in the York archives prior to the
archbishopric of Christopher Bainbridge (1508-1514). And the few fifteenth-century cases from York that show concern for Lollardy did not
involve Bible-reading.[28]

[28] John A. F. Thomson, *The Later Lollards, 1414-1520* (London, 1965), 195-96. Thomson
cites a very few scattered and uncertain references to Lollards from York diocese in the first half
of the fifteenth century and only one (in 1421) whose views were sufficiently extreme to warrant
execution. In addition to these cases, the archbishops' registers describe the instance of William
Cook, "cissor" from Blythe (Notts.), who was brought before Archbishop Bowet in 1410 for
not confessing for two years. Although the marginal note describing the case refers to Cook as
"a certain Lollard," Cook appears orthodox in his beliefs in transubstantiation and proceeded to
make his confession and take communion. BI, Reg. 18 (Bowet), f. 299. Concern with Lollardy
is also manifest in the accusations leveled at Margery Kempe in her visit to York in 1417. *The*

However, it is best to be circumspect, for the increased interest in biblical texts is coincident with the growth of Lollardy in other parts of the country. Although we know very little about the individuals who possessed Bibles, there are hints of Lollard influence here and there. Thomas Wilton, M.D., with whom we are already familiar as the possessor of two Bibles, had been accused of holding heretical opinions as well as of organizing attacks of northerners upon southerners when he was fellow at Oriel College, Oxford, in 1410-1411. Another Bible owner, John Prophet, the dean of York, was a close friend of Lady Cobham, wife of Lollard leader John Oldcastle. Prophet had been at court acting as secretary to Henry IV during the height of Lollard influence there, and he was to be the only dean of York not to gain a bishopric between 1385 and 1436, the years of deepest concern over Lollardy.[29]

By 1428 the possibility of heresy in the north was considered sufficiently disturbing to summon a northern convocation to deal with it, and a fifteenth-century formulary from York contains a (1439?) commission from the archbishop to inquire about Lollards and proceed against them.[30] Considering the official concern, it is even more surprising that no convincing evidence for individual cases of Lollardy has yet been found in the voluminous fifteenth-century records of the diocese. Possibly the heretical influence was sufficiently indirect as to make it difficult to distinguish from the strong vernacular, mystical, and devotional tradition in the north. Or perhaps the evidence of Bible-reading itself was not considered as much a sign of heresy in the north as appears to have been the case in the south. Whatever the reasons, it was not until about 1510 that Lollardy, as a recognizable heretical movement, first emerges in the York diocesan records.

By the second decade of the sixteenth century the archbishops' registers begin to record Lollard cases, and an occasional will begins to exhibit

---

Book of Margery Kempe (1436), ed. W. Butler-Bowdon (New York, 1944), 106-22. See also Charles Kightly. "The Early Lollards. A Survey of Popular Lollard Activity in England, 1382-1428" (Ph.D. diss., University of York, 1975), whose work came to my attention too late to be incorporated into the text. Kightly mentions Davie Gotraie of Pickering, monk of Byland, as a Lollard sympathizer in 1377, Lollard preacher William Thorp's travels in the north from 1387 to 1407, a Lollard community at Nottingham in the 1380s and 1390s, the participation of one Westmorland man and two Yorkshire men in the Oldcastle uprising of 1414, and the 1421 trial of John Taillour, alias Bilton, for heresy in 1421. Kightly, "The Early Lollards," 1-28.

[29] Emden, BRUO, 2055; Test. Ebor., 3:53-55; R. Barrie Dobson, "The Later Middle Ages, 1215-1500," in A History of York Minster, ed. G. E. Aylmer and Reginald Cant (Oxford, 1977), 66.

[30] Thomson, Later Lollards, 196-97.

clearly "Protestant" phraseology.[31] The earliest unmistakable case of Lollardy, that of Roger Gargrave of Wakefield in 1512, illustrates an acquaintance with brief passages of scripture but not necessarily with the written text.

It is not until about 1530 that the growth of heresy and Protestantism begins to bring to light the existence of biblical texts. By 1533 Lambert Sparrow, a Dutchman living in York diocese, abjured a lengthy list of heretical opinions and promised "ne that I woll hereaftre use, reede, teache, kepe, bye or sell any bookes, volumes or quears or any workes callyd Luther's or anye odre mannes bookes of hys hereticall secte or of any oodre, conteighneng heresye in them or prohibyted by the lawes of holy churche."[32] About 1536 Robert Plumpton wrote his mother, "and here I send you a godly New Testament by this bearer. And yf the prologue bee so small ye cannot wel reade them, ther is my fathers books, and they are bothe one, and my fathers book hath the prologue printed in bigger letters. Yf it wil please you to read the introducement, ye shal see marvelous things hyd in it." In 1528 Henry Burnett of Lincolnshire reported to the Lincoln diocesan authorities that Roger Danyell, a sailor from Hull, "had the gospelles in Englyshe, which the Dean of Yorke hath." Later, in 1535, William Senes, the lay teacher of the song school at Rotherham College, was reprimanded by the Earl of Shrewsbury for having the New Testament, while William Rede, the schoolmaster at Dalton (Lancs.) in 1536, was dismissed for preaching against papal authority and teaching from Erasmus's *Paraphrases* of the Bible.[33]

Events quickly overtook the defenders of orthodoxy, however. When the royal injunctions of 1538 were promulgated, they decreed that not only were priests no longer to discourage anyone from reading the English Bible, they were actively to insure that a chained copy was installed in an open place in every parish church.[34] All in all, the evidence for Lollardy in York diocese is too scanty for the earlier period, and too little associated with scriptural reading until too late for it to have had any significant

[31] A. G. Dickens, *Lollards and Protestants in the Diocese of York, 1509-1558* (London, 1959), 16-29. See also the 1514 will of John Topclif of Wodkirk. BI, Prob. Reg. 9, f. 3.

[32] Dickens, *Lollards and Protestants*, 16-17, 19-20. Gargrave may have been related to Thomas Gargrave of Wakefield who died in 1514, left pennies to scholars and signed his will. BI, Prob. Reg. 9, f. 6.

[33] *Plumpton Correspondence*, ed. Thomas Stapleton, Camden Society, no. 4 (London, 1839), 232; Dickens, *Lollards and Protestants*, 25-26, 37-42; Christopher Haigh, *The Last Days of the Lancashire Monasteries and the Pilgrimage of Grace*, Chetham Society, 3rd ser., 17 (Manchester, 1969), 52.

[34] W. H. Frere and W. M. Kennedy, eds., *Visitation Articles and Injunctions of the Period of the Reformation*, Vol. 2, Alcuin Club Collections, no. 15 (London, 1910), 46.

TABLE 10

BIBLES AND SERVICE BOOKS BEQUEATHED IN YORK DIOCESAN WILLS,
1370-1509

Dates	Missals	Portifors	Primers	Psalters	Bibles (or parts thereof)
1370-1399	48 +	77	5	25	10
1400-1449	132	212	73	89	48
1450-1499	99 +	193 +	92	70	23
1500-1509	34	43	12	6	11
Total	313 +	525 +	182	190	92

SOURCES: BI, Prob. Reg. 1-8; Reg. 12-26; YML, D. & C., L 2/4, L 2/5a; PRO, PCC, Prob. 11/1-16.

NOTE: When a testator left his best or largest service book, two books have been counted. When "missalia" or "portiforia" are mentioned, 2 + have been added.

impact upon the clergy and laity of the diocese in their attitudes toward education and the value of learning to read before about 1530. Even though biblical texts were circulating more widely than has been supposed during the height of the Lollard crisis, there is little evidence to connect the two. The mystical, devotional tradition of the north would explain the circulation of such books at least as well and probably better.

Once we turn from our inquiry into Bible-reading and look at the evidence for ownership of other books, we see that by far the greatest number bequeathed were service books, particularly missals (massbooks), portifors (breviaries), primers (books of hours), and psalters. From Table 10 one can gain an idea of the relatively large number of service books bequeathed in comparison to biblical texts. To a certain extent the vagaries in number, e.g., eight missals in the 1370s and forty-five in the 1430s, reflect the number of surviving wills (see Appendix A, Chart 7). However, when one compares the trends in liturgical texts with the findings for biblical texts, some interesting differences occur. Despite a slight decline in their occurrence in the wills of the second half of the fifteenth century, interest in psalters, missals, and portifors remained strong. There is not the significant decline one finds in the bequests of biblical texts. Primers, the basic medieval reading text, were bequeathed in growing numbers, reflecting perhaps the growth in reading schools, or possibly the increased popularity of private devotions during mass. Together, these liturgical books constitute nearly 50 percent of all books bequeathed in York diocesan wills.

Descriptions of missals, portifors, primers, and psalters by testators are generally insufficient to make any determination of the language in which they were written. Only nine liturgical books (seven psalters and two portifors) are described as either in English or French.[35] This is surely an underenumeration of the vernacular service books in circulation. There were several English translations of the psalter available, the most famous of which was Richard Rolle's. With regard to primers, although none is labeled vernacular, more than a dozen extant English versions argue for its relatively common distribution.[36] The wills record such a large proportion of all of these texts in the hands of laity that it is impossible not to assume the existence of a substantial number in the vernacular.

While the ratio of vernacular to Latin texts can probably never be ascertained, it is clear that bequests of service books to and from laity were commonplace and on the increase throughout the fifteenth century. In Archbishop Neville's register (1374-1388), out of thirteen separate bequests of one or more of the above service books, ten (or 77 percent) were given or received by laity.[37] In Archbishop Kemp's register (1426-1452) bequests involving lay benefactors and/or recipients similarly involved 76 percent of the bequests. But by 1480-1500, in Archbishop Rotherham's register, 100 percent of the bequests of these books involved laity. In the Prerogative and Exchequer Court's registered wills for the decades 1420-1429, 1430-1439, 1440-1449, and 1450-1459, the proportion of lay involvement in bequests of service books is 41 percent, 52 percent, 65 percent, and 70 percent respectively.[38] For the 1460s this declines to 58 percent but then climbs up to 72 percent in volume five (1476-1499). Missals, since they, like portifors and unlike primers and psalters, were written primarily for the celebrant,[39] are a good indicator of lay concern with the liturgy. Of the missals bequeathed in volume five, 86 percent were in the hands of laity, who were acting mostly as donors

[35] YML, D. & C., L 2/4, ff. 112v, 261, 331v; BI, Prob. Reg. 1, f. 51; 2, f. 445v; 3, ff. 63v, 570v; Reg. 20 (Wm. Booth), f. 258.

[36] Christopher Wordsworth and Henry Littlehales, *The Old Service-Books of the English Church* (London, 1904), 249.

[37] If the proviso is made that the legate enter holy orders, the recipient has been counted as clergy.

[38] In volume one of the Prerogative and Exchequer wills (1389-1396) the percentage of lay benefactors and/or recipients is 57 percent. These wills represent primarily professional and upper-class laity, while the fifteenth-century wills are more broadly representative.

[39] Andrew Hughes, *Medieval Manuscripts for Mass and Office: A Guide to Their Organization and Terminology* (Toronto, 1982), 122-23.

but also as recipients. Since there is no significant change in the ratio between lay and clerical wills over this period, the evidence strongly suggests that the fifteenth century was one of rising lay ownership of the more popular liturgical texts. In the Dean and Chapter wills, which are overwhelmingly clerical in composition, the percentages of bequests that involved laity is much lower, approximately 23 percent from 1370 to 1449 and 32 percent from 1450 to 1510. Yet among these predominantly clerical wills there is evidence of increased lay ownership of service books.

By the fifteenth century these books, particularly the massbook and the breviary, had evolved to the extent that they included most of what was essential to performing the hours and masses year round. The missal incorporated the calendars, *ordo misse*, common of saints, mass for the dead, antiphons, graduals, Epistles, and Gospels, while the brieviary included antiphons, prayers, lessons, hymns, and the ferial psalter. The primer, as noted above (Chapter two), was both an introductory service book and a schoolbook; it usually included selected psalms. The psalter, of course, whether ferial (choral) or biblical, included that entire book of the Bible.[40] Thus, while the laity only occasionally had access to a non-liturgical biblical text, they were increasingly likely to have had a service book in their possession. Of these, the four most widely distributed included significant portions of scripture.

Two service books, the ordinal and the manual, were books of direction meant for the use of the priest in performing the mass and the office and in administering the sacraments, respectively.[41] They were not as commonly bequeathed as the service books in Table 10, and they rarely ended up in lay hands. While a wealthy layman might include an ordinal or a manual among the books of his chapel, parishioners wishing to bequeath one or the other to the parish church invariably left a sum of money for the purpose. Most of the twenty-four mentions of ordinals and forty-three of manuals were gifts from individual clerics to a particular church to be chained in the choir or in a chantry for the use of the clergy. The importance of these two texts can be ascertained by looking at the York Dean and Chapter visitation records of the fifteenth century. Not only was the sufficiency of ordinals and manuals one of the main questions asked of the parish clergy and their parishioners, but penalties for their lack were costly (usually equivalent to the value of the book).[42]

---

[40] Ibid., 118-21, 157-59, 197-226.

[41] The ordinal gives incipits with rubrics for the performance of mass and office throughout the year. Ibid., 119. The manual contains the forms for the administration of the sacraments. Portions of its text, e.g., the marriage vows, were in English. Wordsworth and Littlehales, *The Old Service-Books*, 52-54.

[42] YML, D. & C., E L2/3a,b,c,d. Visitation Books of the Dean and Chapter, 1408-1550.

About 1455 Clement Maydeston (of Syon) compiled a *Directorium Sacerdotum* or *Pye* (pica), so-called because it was a book in black and white without red letters. It was a twice-removed revision of the older Sarum ordinal, and it was popular among York testators. Between 1469 and 1499 ten *Pyes* were bequeathed. Unlike the older ordinal, the *Pye*, although meant specifically for the guidance of clergy, was given also to laymen.[43] Its popularity probably accounts for its third revision in 1496, this time by W. Clerke of Eton, a married layman in Archbishop Rotherham's household at York. Seven editions issued from the printing press between 1497 and 1509, at which time another revision was undertaken by Roger Avissede, a chaplain in St. Gregory's York and Thomas Hothyrsall, vicar choral of York. It was printed in York by Hugo Goes in 1509/10 despite the fact that Gerard Wandsforth, a York bookseller, already had at least 570 copies on hand.[44]

In addition to the ordinals, *Pyes*, and manuals, the constitutions of the English Church also required that music books be provided within each parish church,[45] and the visitation records show a lively interest in their number and condition. The York diocesan wills record the bequests of forty-two graduals, forty-seven antiphonals, more than thirty-seven processionals, and twenty hymnals.[46] Unlike the manuals and ordinals, church music books, and especially the hymnal, were far more likely to be found in the hands of laity,[47] perhaps because laity were becoming active in the church choirs.[48]

[43] BI, Prob. Reg. 3, f. 318; 4, f. 173v; 5, ff. 30, 207, 440v-41, 455; YML, D. & C., L 2/4, ff. 345, 348v-49; 2, f. 18. Three of these *Pyes* were bequeathed to laity. Two were bequeathed by laity.

[44] Wordsworth and Littlehales, *The Old Service-Books*, 242-43, F. A. Gasquet, "The Bibliography of Some Devotional Books Printed by the Earliest English Printers," *Transactions of the Bibliographical Society* 7 (1902-1904):166; E. Gordon Duff, *The English Provincial Printers, Stationers and Bookbinders to 1557* (Cambridge, 1912), 47-51; Elizabeth Brunskill, "Missals, Portifers and Pyes," *The Ben Johnson Papers* 2 (1974):11.

[45] R. M. Woolley, *The York Provinciale* (1930), Bk. III, tit. xv, 45.

[46] For descriptions of these books, see Hughes, *Medieval Manuscripts*, 124-42, 157-59, 161-97, 236-37, 242-44 and Wordsworth and Littlehales, *The Old Service-Books*, passim.

[47] For example, BI, Prob. Reg. 1, f. 51; 2, ff. 189v, 198v, 510, 589; 3, ff. 8v, 418, 439-41, 598; 4, ff. 6, 16, 67, 173v; 5, ff. 294v, 457v-58; 7, f. 54.

[48] This was the case at York Cathedral by the beginning of the sixteenth century. Frederick Harrison, *Life in a Medieval College* (London, 1952), 238. In 1505 John Reynald left money to the four laymen singing the best at his obit in Stillington parish. YML, D. & C., L 2/5a, f. 71. The song school founded by Thomas Magnus in 1530 was open to "all persons and children that wanted to attend." Perhaps the most famous example of a layman in the church choir comes from Roper's "Life of Sir Thomas More" in *Two Early Tudor Lives*, ed. R. S. Sylvester and D. P. Harding (New Haven, 1962), 225, where Roper describes the Duke of

It was the lay demand for books, especially for service books, that influenced the early book-trade in the diocese. The very first book connected with the history of printing in York was a service book—a breviary for York use—which, although printed abroad, was clearly intended for sale within the diocese. The first printed book intended explicitly for a York bookseller, an *Exposition of the Hymns and Sequences*, was printed in Rouen in 1507 for Gerard Wandsforth and probably reflects the lay interest in church music already apparent from the wills. Demand for printed service books within York diocese was judged by Wandsforth to be sufficiently strong to induce him, in partnership with two other individuals, to purchase at least 252 missals, 399 portable breviaries, and 570 *Pyes*. After Wandsforth's death the major York bookseller for nearly twenty years (1516-1533) was John Gachet, a Frenchman, who depended entirely upon service books for his livelihood.[49]

If, in Wandsforth's judgment, the greatest market for books in York diocese was in service manuals, he had nonetheless stocked up on another type of book which must also have been in demand. Of 300 volumes in his inventory that were not part of a lawsuit upon his death in 1510, the majority were "doctrinalia . . . primaria . . . alphabeta et libri graciarum . . . ," the most basic of the schoolbooks. The rest of the 300 volumes went unnamed, unfortunately, but to judge from the consequent history of printing in York,, they probably included some grammatical texts. Of the three known books printed by Hugo Goes in York about 1510, one was a service book (the *Pye* already mentioned) and the other two were beginning Latin grammar texts, the *Donatus cum Remigio* and the *Accidence* of Stanbridge. Ursyn Mylner, whose press was active in York from 1513 to 1516, published three known texts of which two were service books and one was Whittinton's *Grammar*.[50]

When, however, we turn to the wills, we find that, relative to the number of service books bequeathed, grammar texts and dictionaries were given much less frequently. In the majority of cases in which they were devised, the testators failed to enumerate them, simply passing them on in bulk. Although no conclusions should be drawn from the results, it is nevertheless useful to see which grammar books were bequeathed by name. By far the most common were the *Catholicon* and the *Medulla Grammatice*,

---

Norfolk's dismayed response at finding More "singing in the choir with a surplice on his back." For evidence that girls may have sung in choirs, see Dorothy Gardiner, *English Girlhood at School* (Oxford, 1929), 77-78.

[49] This description is based largely on the discussion in Duff, *The English Provincial Printers*, 42-65.

[50] Ibid., 51-58; Brunskill, "Missals, Portifers and Pyes," 27.

both of which were books of vocabularies.[51] Of the remaining grammar texts, the ones most often named were the *Cato*, which was bequeathed five times between 1429 and 1510; and a grammar of the doubtful vocabulary in scripture, probably William Brito's *Summa Difficiliorum Vocabulorum Biblie*, which was bequeathed six times; two copies of Papias's *Elimentarium* (a glossary); two *Donats*; three copies of John of Garland's *Multorum vocabulorum equivocorum interpretatio*; two bequests of Isidore's *Etymologies*, of Hugucio's *Derivatione* (a glossary), of Everhard of Bethune's literary grammar *Graecismus*; and two books of logic. There is only one mention of the *Doctrinale* of Alexander de Villa Dei. In contrast to these relatively meager findings, there are more than twenty-five bequests of "omnes meos libros grammaticales," "meum librum grammaticalem," or "meum librum vocabulorum."

Although we cannot know much about the content of these books, we do know by whom they were given and to whom they were bequeathed. The overwhelming majority (60 percent) of these grammar texts were given by the clergy to laymen, and more often than not to young boys.[52] In no single case were any of these books given with the proviso, sometimes found in the bequests of service books from clergy to laity, that the legatee was to enter holy orders. Five of the grammar bequests were between laity while 19 percent were from either laity or clergy to clergy. The remaining bequests went to churches and other institutions. Of the twelve instances of clergy receiving grammar texts, only one of the gifts was given with the idea of promoting the cleric's educational status.[53] Although the sample is small, it would appear that the clergy (usually vicars, rectors, or cathedral clergy) were the chief donors of grammar books, and that

---

[51] The *Catholicon* was a comprehensive Latin grammar and dictionary written by John of Genoa, a Dominican friar, about 1285. The title of his book, however, was appropriated by other dictionary writers, and some of these *Catholicons*, especially the later ones, may have been English-Latin vocabularies similar to the *Catholicon Anglicum, an English-Latin Wordbook dated 1483*, ed. S.J.H. Herrtage, EETS, orig. ser., no. 75 (London, 1881), which was written in a Yorkshire dialect. The *Medulla Gramatice* was a Latin to English dictionary compiled at the beginning of the fifteenth century. Fourteen *Catholicons* were bequeathed in the wills between 1375 and 1510. YML, D. & C., L 2/4, ff. 80, 115v, 168v-71, 185; BI, Prob. Reg. 5, f. 486; 6, ff. 113, 133v-34; 7, f. 63; Reg. 18 (Bowet), f. 382; Reg. 20 (Wm. Booth), ff. 258-59, 273; PRO, PCC, Prob. 11/1 Rous 3, 11/3 Luffenam 1, 11/5 Godyn 19. The *Medulla Gramatice* first appears in the wills in the 1430s; there are eight bequests between then and 1512. YML, D. & C., L 2/4, ff. 348v-49; 2, ff. 99v-100; BI, Prob. Reg. 2, ff. 17, 312; 3, f. 318; 4, ff. 18, 67; Reg. 26 (Bainbridge), f. 141.

[52] For example, YML, D. & C., L 2/4, ff. 174, 343; BI, Prob. Reg. 5, ff. 9, 284; 4, ff. 66v-67, 67, 85; 3, ff. 511, 544v-45; 2, ff. 413-14, 469v, 540, 625, 646; Reg. 20 (Wm. Booth), f. 273; PRO, PCC, Prob. 11/5 Godyn 19.

[53] BI, Prob. Reg. 3, f. 266.

they were far more likely to give them to young schoolboys or other laymen, with no apparent expectation that they enter the Church, than they were to give them to clerics who might have used them to brush up on their grammar.

In a few instances the bequests of grammar texts help confirm the existence of a grammar school or suggest its earlier presence. In 1440 William Leventon, the vicar of Thorp Arch, left a grammar book to Roger Lynton. We know that Thorp Arch had a schoolmaster in 1488, and, although evidence is insufficient, it is tempting to conclude that a grammar education was available there at an earlier date. Again, although we only have evidence for scholars at Everingham parish in 1508, the fact that Master Thomas of Anlaby, the rector of Everingham, left a book on logic to John Gillyote, his boy, in 1476 suggests that some kind of education was available in the parish thirty years earlier.[54] In 1465 grammar books were bequeathed to the scholars at Hedon's school, which lets us know, if we had not already discovered it from other sources, that this was a grammar school. In 1515 Thomas Howeden, a chaplain at Hornby (W. Riding), left a copy of Papias to Thomas Caldbeck and the rest of his grammar and music books to various relatives who were attending school. Howeden was teaching the school in Hornby which his relatives may have been attending, and the bequests lend strong support to the conclusion that it was both a grammar and a song school.[55]

The third class of literature that commonly passed between the clergy and laity as a consequence of bequests was, for want of a better label, what we shall call "popular literature," including romances, saints' lives, chronicles, plays and ballads, moral treatises, and devotional literature. Of these, the chronicles, plays and ballads, moral treatises, and many of the romances circulated less extensively through bequests than did the saints' lives and devotional treatises.

Between thirty-five and forty bequests are noted of chronicles (or histories).[56] They generally belonged to the higher clergy, various colleges, and other institutional libraries or to the upper-class laity, although the treasurer of York, in 1375, left several books of history to poor scholars.[57]

[54] BI, Prob. Reg. 2, f. 673; 5, f. 9. See Appendix B for the school at Thorp Arch in 1488 and the scholars at Everingham.

[55] BI, Prob. Reg. 6, f. 66v; YML, D. & C., L 2/5a, f. 218. See Appendix B for more information on Hedon and Hornby.

[56] These bequests include a copy of the chronicle of Walter Gysburn (Hemingbrough), two of Bede's *Historia ecclesiatica*, two of Vincent of Beauvais's *Speculum Historiali*, four copies of the *Brut*, eleven of Ranulf Higden's *Polychronicon*, and three copies of the *Magister Historiarum*. The rest were simply entitled chronicles.

[57] YML, D. & C., L 2/4, f. 60.

Unlike most bequests, we can trace some of these manuscripts over time. In 1391 Master John Percehay, a layman from the noble family of Percehay in Rydall, left a *Brut* in French to Master John de Scardeburgh, notary public, canon of York, and rector of Tickmarsh. At the time of the gift, the book was in the hands of Thomas Slegill (or Skargill), a knight from Leeds. When Scardeburgh died in 1395 the inventory of his study mentions a "Bruyt in Gallico." Thus, within a four-year period, we know of three individuals (two laity and one clergyman) with access to the same historical text.[58] Another chronicle, the "Polychronica (de Latino) ex compilacione Fratris Ranulphi Monachi Cestriae" was left in 1431 by John Morton of York, knight, to Robert Semer, rector of St. Michael's, York. This is probably the "librum vocatum Policronica" that was bequeathed in 1443 by Robert Semer, then vicar of St. Martin's Coney Street, York, to Whitby Abbey.[59]

Interest in historical information among the non-noble and less wealthy laity may have been satisfied in other ways. York Minster, for example, displayed a set of historical tablets which described at some length the political and religious history of England and particularly the north from Roman times into the fourteenth century. The tablets were in Latin and were almost certainly displayed for visitors to the cathedral to read or to hear read. Similar tablets, in abbreviated form, may have been available in other churches, especially the monastic and collegiate churches, throughout York.[60] Several polychronicons were bequeathed to parish churches and, in one case, a parish library, where they would have been available to the laity.[61] And much in the way of religious history could be gained by attending the annual play cycles presented by the gilds in the major northern towns.[62] These plays were enjoyed by hundreds and perhaps even

[58] BI, Reg. 14 (Arundel), f. 27, printed in *Test. Ebor.*, 1:164. For Slegill see BI, Prob. Reg. 3, f. 373, printed in *Test. Ebor.*, 2:35-36. BI, D. & C., inventory of John de Scardeburgh, printed in *Test. Ebor.*, 3:6.

[59] BI, Prob. Reg. 2, f. 653v, printed in *Test. Ebor.*, 2:14; YML, D. & C., L 2/4, f. 254.

[60] J. S. Purvis, "The Tables of the York Vicars Choral," *YAJ*, 41 (1966):741-48. Dobson, "The Later Middle Ages," 108 n. 227; Antonia Gransden, *Historical Writing in England ii, c. 1307 to the Early Sixteenth Century* (Ithaca, N.Y., 1982), app. E. The content of the tables was copied, in 1408, into the *Liber cosmographiae* of John de Foxton, a Yorkshire cleric. John B. Friedman, "John Siferwas and the Mythological Illustration in the *Liber cosmographiae* of John de Foxton," *Speculum* 58 (1983):398-99. There was a *tabula* also on display at Worksop Priory (Notts.). Gransden, *Historical Writing*, 495.

[61] BI, Reg. 18 (Bowet), f. 369; Reg. 19 (Kemp), f. 501; Prob. Reg. 5, f. 194v; YML, D. & C., L 2/4, f. 287.

[62] The major northern towns with play cycles were York, Beverley, Lincoln, Wakefield and Coventry, Chester, Newcastle, Kendal, and probably Lancaster, Louth, and Preston.

thousands from the town and surrounding countryside, and the four brief references to them in the wills in no way suggest their very substantial impact, although they do illustrate the role that the townspeople and the lower clergy had in transmitting and, presumably, directing these plays.[63]

Ballads, particularly those on political themes, circulated widely throughout England by the fifteenth century and were as likely to be encountered in a song school as in the local tavern. In York diocese about 1538 the vicar's chaplain at Wakefield was apparently teaching the song school children slanderous ballads against Cromwell, while there are preserved in the Ripon Minster Library two examples of Tudor political ballads which were sung by the collegiate choir.[64] But ballads, like plays, perhaps because they likewise emerged from a strong oral tradition, were infrequently passed on through wills. When they were, they went into the hands of laymen.[65]

In addition to plays and ballads, other popular literature of the time included romances, saints' lives, moral treatises, and devotional literature. Among these, the book most often bequeathed was the *Golden Legend*, a compilation of lives of saints and short treatises about the Christian festivals which was drawn up by Jacob of Voragine, archbishop of Genoa, in the middle of the thirteenth century.[66] This was followed in popularity by the *Vita Christi*, the early fifteenth-century English translation of pseudo-Bonaventure's *Meditations* by Nicholas Love, prior of Mount Grace Charterhouse; the *Passion of Christ*, an anonymous mid-fourteenth-century English translation of an earlier French poem; and the *Horologium Divinae Sapientiae* of Henry Suso.[67] The works of Richard Rolle are mentioned frequently, although it is difficult to ascertain the extent to which his writings were bequeathed since many of them were commentaries and translations of the service books, especially the psalter and the masses for

[63] YML, D. & C., L 2/4, f. 63 (1376); BI, Prob. Reg. 2, ff. 138-39 (1446), printed in *Test. Ebor.*, 2:116-18; BI, Prob. Reg. 2, ff. 432v-33 (1455); 3, f. 487 (1464), printed in *Test. Ebor.*, 2:268. These references, along with other documents referring to plays and music in York, have been printed in *Records of Early English Drama: York*, ed. A. F. Johnston and M. Rogerson, 2 vols. (Toronto, 1979),

[64] *L & P, Henry VIII*, 13:i, 1054; "Notes," *YAJ* 11 (1890):200-201.

[65] BI, Prob. Reg. 2, ff. 17, 371, printed in *Test. Ebor.*, 2:80, 213; BI, Prob. Reg. 3, f. 546.

[66] The *legenda aurea* or *legenda sanctorum* was bequeathed fifty-six times. At least three of the *legenda* were in English. See BI, Prob. Reg. 2, ff. 137v-38, 594; PRO, PCC, Prob. 11/5 Godyn 19.

[67] There are over fifteen different bequests of pseudo-Bonaventure's *Vita Christi*. The *Horologium* and *Passione Christi* were bequeathed seven and six times respectively. Also bequeathed were, for example, the *Meditations* of (pseudo) Anselm and the *Revelations* of St. Brigid.

the dead, which were passed on without explicit mention of Rolle.[68] Books of prayers were also commonly passed on in wills. There is less frequent mention of romances (those most often given were the *Siege of Troy* and the *Gesta Romanorum*), individual saints' lives (e.g., the *Life of St. Brigid* and the *Life of St. Thomas of Canterbury*), moral treatises (such as the *Speculum ecclesiae* of St. Edmund, various treatises on the vices and virtues, the *Moralia* of Gregory I, and the *Prick of Conscience*), or, for example, in the mystical tradition, the works of Walter Hilton. *Mandeville's Travels* were devised only three times, as were various works of Petrarch. *Piers Plowman* is mentioned twice. Chaucer's *Troilus* and the *Canterbury Tales*, Gower, and Boccaccio are cited only once each among the hundreds of book benefactions.[69] It is quite clear that the literature that the student of today usually associates with late medieval England was in fact the preserve of a very few clergy, or of laity of armigerous or merchant status. Within York diocese, they tended to be concentrated in the city of York. The romances also circulated narrowly, in this case among a few upper-class households such as those of the Hilton, Constable, Dautre, Roos, and Stapilton families. This is in marked contrast to the devotional and liturgical literature which circulated widely among almost all the classes of clergy and laity in all parts of the diocese.

The final class of literature to be considered is the "professional" literature—civil and canon law volumes and the aids to clergy (sermons, homilies, penitentials, and other instructions for parish priests). Books of canon and civil law were bequeathed in impressive numbers. Nearly one hundred separate gifts of law volumes occur in the wills, and each bequest usually provides for several books. Sometimes a whole law library is passed on in a will. Canon law predominates over civil law, but they were frequently devised together. These books circulated among the upper clergy, various institutions (e.g., Balliol College, Oxford; King's College, Cambridge; friaries, several abbeys, and the York Cathedral Library),

---

[68] References to Rolle's work occur in YML, D. & C., L 2/4, ff. 168v-71, 233, 236, 261, 331v, 343; BI, Prob. Reg. 2, ff. 399, 533 and perhaps 3, f. 363. Henry Scrope of Masham had a collection of Rolle's works. See his 1415 will in Rymer, *Foedera* 4:ii, 131-34.

[69] BI, Prob. Reg. 3, ff. 32v-34, 55v-56, 598 (Mandeville's Travels); YML, D. & C., L 2/4, ff. 115v-16; BI, Prob. Reg. 3, ff. 369v-70 (Piers Plowman); YML, D. & C., L 2/4, ff. 168v-71, 250; BI, Prob. Reg. 3, ff. 493v-94 (Petrarch); YML, D. & C., L 2/4, f. 288; BI, Prob. Reg. 4, f. 220 (Chaucer); BI, Prob. Reg. 2, ff. 653v-54 (Gower); 5, f. 480 (Boccaccio). A volume of *St. Albon and Amphiabell* bequeathed by Thomas Chaworth in 1458 is still extant and contains, besides this work of Lydgate's, Chaucer's *Clerk's Tale*, Chaucer's "Truth," *Anelida and Arcite*, and various works of Lydgate. Susan Cavanaugh, "A Study of Books Privately Owned in England: 1300-1450," 2 vols. (Ph.D. diss., University of Pennsylvania, 1980), 1:183.

and the wealthier laity. Although occasionally a chaplain and, more often, an aspiring scholar, were bequeathed a digest or *par decretalium*, lawbooks were clearly of greatest interest to the more elite testators. The most surprising findings from the wills are, first, that references to these legal codices and their commentaries decline rapidly after 1450, and second, that volumes of canon law are found occasionally in the hands of laymen as early as the 1380s.[70]

Even more popular than the law volumes were the aids to clergy, which were the object of approximately 160 bequests over the period 1370-1510. The impetus behind the various aids to clergy came out of the legislation of the Fourth Lateran Council in 1215 and the subsequent program of pastoral instruction outlined in 1281 by Archbishop Peckham. The idea underlying many of these tracts, most of which were written in the fourteenth century, was that parish clergy should be guided in the techniques of teaching the faith to laity through the confessional, from the pulpit, through the divine offices, and in day-to-day advice-giving. Many of the treatises went beyond a program for religious instruction, offering advice in social, moral, and even political spheres.[71] A major contribution to this movement was provided for York diocese in 1357 when Archbishop Thoresby commissioned both a Latin and English catechism to be used for the instruction of parishioners. A copy of both versions was to be sent to every parish church within the diocese.[72]

Discounting service books, these volumes represent approximately 30-40 percent of all named titles bequeathed, rising from about 15 percent at the end of the fourteenth century to 23 percent and 30 percent in the 1430s and 1440s respectively, then dropping to 18 percent in the 1450s but climbing to between 50 and 60 percent by 1480-1510. By far the most common books in this class were the *Pupilla Oculi* and its predecessors, the *Oculus Sacerdotis* and the *Pars Oculi*.[73] Mirk's *Liber Festivalis*

[70] YML, D. & C., L 2/4, ff. 87v-88, 96v-97, 104; BI, Prob. Reg. 1, f. 61; 2, f. 119; 5, f. 271; Reg. 26 (Bainbridge), f. 138.

[71] William A. Pantin, *The English Church in the Fourteenth Century* (Cambridge, 1955), chap. 9.

[72] BI, Reg. 11 (Thoresby), ff. 295-98v, printed as *The Lay Folks's Catechism: Archbishop Thoresby's Instruction for the People*, ed. T. F. Simmons and H. E. Nolloth, EETS, orig. ser., no. 118 (London, 1901).

[73] The *Oculus Sacerdotis* was written in the third decade of the fourteenth century by William of Pagula, a doctor of canon law and vicar of Winkfield (Salisbury) who was originally from Holderness in the East Riding. Although the entire manuscript was bequeathed only seven times, part one (known as *Pars Oculi*) was more popular, being bequeathed sixteen times. The *Pupilla Oculi*, which was bequeathed forty-two times, was a condensation of the *Oculus* written by John de Burgo, chancellor of Cambridge University, in 1385. There are also two bequests of the *Dextra Pars Oculi* and one of the *Sinistra Pars Oculi*.

was also sometimes bequeathed as was his *Manuale Sacerdotis*, the *Speculum Sacerdotis*, *Speculum Christiani*, and the *Manipulus Curatorum* of Guido de Monte Rocherii. In addition to these manuals, a great many collections of sermons and homilies fill the lists of bequeathed books. Many of them are unnamed, although Jacob of Voragine's Sunday sermons are frequently cited, as are the homilies of St. Gregory and the Mary Magdalene sermons. Finally, penitentials, especially the *Summa* of Raymundus and that of Thomas Chebham, were commonly bequeathed. Except for Mirk's treatises, Archbishop Thoresby's instructions, fifteenth-century translations of the *Speculum Christiani* and the *Manipulus* (called the *Doctrinal of Sapience*), and perhaps a few of the sermon collections, most of this literature was in Latin. Many of these works presumed the requisite amount of knowledge on the part of the parish priest, and their major purpose was to promote the role that the parish priest should play in educating his parishioners. These various volumes are so clearly a technical, professional literature for the parish clergy that it is to be expected that they would be bequeathed solely from one cleric to another. It is therefore surprising when we discover that throughout the fifteenth and early sixteenth century there are frequent instances in which instructions to the clergy, canon law collections, homilies, and sermons were being passed between the laity and the clergy. In 1484, for example, Richard Watterhouse, a layman of Warley parish near Halifax, left his *Pars Oculi* to the church of Halifax. Ten years later Brian Roucliffe of Colthorp, one of the barons of the exchequer, left his *Pupilla Oculi* to the rector of Colthorp. Laymen also were on the receiving end. In 1404 Robert de Neuland, chaplain, left his book of homilies to Robert Clerk, a layman, while, in 1469, the rector of Rowley (E. Riding) gave the *Pupilla* to the schoolchildren of John and Isabella Sutton. The wills abound in similar examples,[74] sufficient to show that the literary interests of the laity of York diocese were not only devotional and liturgical, they were also, to a certain extent, clerical. On the basis of this analysis, one can conclude that the average lay individual represented in the wills between 1370 and 1510 might be similar to John Newton, who in 1442 bequeathed a penitential (possibly the *Summa de penitentia* of Thomas Chebham), another book "de dyvynyte qui sequitur regulam a.b.c.d. de Anglico" (possibly the *Alphabet of Tales*, a large

[74] BI, Prob. Reg. 3, ff. 214, 493v-94; 4, f. 138; 5, ff. 248v-49. See also YML, D. & C., L 2/4, ff. 233, 244v; BI, Prob. Reg. 2, ff. 11, 30(?), 71v-72, 312, 673; 3, f. 8v; 4, ff. 127v, 156v; 5, ff. 457v-58, 488; 6, ff. 125, 132, 133v-34; 7, f. 40v; Reg. 15 (Waldby), f. 9; Reg. 19 (Kemp), f. 501; Reg. 20 (Wm. Booth), f. 287; PRO, PCC, Prob. 11/12 Moone 21. See also *Test. Ebor.*, 3:37.

alphabetical compilation of short moral tales and tidbits from saints' lives), a psalter, and another book of prayers.[75]

Accessibility of books, at least in York diocese, does not seem to have stimulated interest in which might be described as an upper-class concern with chronicles and romances, or in a more professional approach through law. Most laity were attracted to the literature of the Church, and one notable feature of the evidence from their wills is the extent to which they had access to what might be thought to have been the parish clergy's intellectual preserve. Not only did the laity manifest a voracious interest in service books, but they were also to be found in possession of the Bible, books of the Bible, psalters, grammar texts, moral treatises, devotional texts, books of prayers, and instructional manuals for priests. This lay interest in both the devotional and practical literature of the Church may have had its origins in any number of circumstances, including the four-teenth-century devotional and mystical tradition in the north, the growing emphasis within the Church hierarchy on a catechetical education for parishioners, the rise of parish schools, and perhaps to a very limited degree, the influence of Lollardy. Undoubtedly a combination of these factors stimulated the increasingly literate laity to educate themselves re-ligiously. It is possible that by the end of the fifteenth century a substantial proportion of lay individuals were as knowledgeable about Church ritual, saints' lives, points of faith, and the devotional tradition as many of the parish clergy. It is quite conceivable, considering their book bequests, that the literate laity of York diocese were, as K. B. McFarlane put it in another context, "taking the clergy's words out of their mouths."[76]

The phraseology of the wills strongly supports such a conclusion. In his study of 148 York diocesan gentry wills dating between 1370 and 1480, M.G.A. Vale remarks at length on the growing devotional and liturgical sophistication exhibited by these testators. Particular saints were being specified by the early fifteenth century. Strict and precise instructions for gifts to churches, liturgical exercises, and the choice of chaplains became more commonplace. By the 1460s sermons were being endowed. "By the later fifteenth century there existed a degree of understanding of

[75] BI, Prob. Reg. 2, ff. 71v-72.

[76] K. B. McFarlane, *Lancastrian Kings and Lollard Knights* (Oxford, 1972), 204, cited in M.G.A. Vale, *Piety, Charity and Literacy among the Yorkshire Gentry, 1370-1480* (York, 1976), 29n. In support of this point, see Janet Coleman, *Medieval Readers and Writers 1350-1400* (New York, 1981), esp. chaps. 4, 5, and Katherine Tachau, "Northern Universities and Ver-nacular Learning in the Fourteenth Century" (paper presented at the annual meeting of the American Historical Association, Washington, D.C., 1982), both of whom argue for the avail-ability of university learning outside the university to the laity by the fourteenth century.

the liturgy, the Scriptures and the lives of the Saints among the gentry which was far less common at the beginning of the century. If it was common at the earlier date, then it does not appear in their wills."[77]

Although the information thus far culled from York wills has given us an impression of strong devotional and liturgical interests among the laity of York, it cannot provide us with a complete picture. The books that have been analyzed above represent an unknown proportion of the total number of bequeathed books, many of which were given either in bulk or unnamed. These, in turn, represent some unknown proportion of the available books. In 1395, for example, John de Scardeburgh, the rector of Tickmarsh and canon of York, left three volumes in his will. The inventory of his study, however, lists twenty-six books, some of which were only notebooks and pamphlets, but many of which were substantial and somewhat uncommon works. Another example is that of Sir Thomas Chaworth of Wiverton (Notts.) who left five very interesting English books and one Latin text besides a number of service books in 1458. Two additional books from his library are, however, extant, although they were not recorded in his will. Chaworth may have neglected to mention them, or they may have been sold or given away before death approached.[78]

a will is not an inventory.

In addition, each individual manuscript most probably contained between its covers a number of works, although testators tended to identify the book by its opening treatise. An individual with one volume to his/her name could, in reality, be the owner of a small library. A typical compilation is a mid-fifteenth century manuscript now in the Cambridge University Library (Ff.2.38). It begins with materials common to a primer, followed by three saints' lives, other moral and devout material, "How the Good Man Taught His Son," "How a Merchaunde Dyd Hys Wyfe Betray," "A Gode Mater of the Marchaund and Hys Sone," and ten romances. M. B. Parkes comments that "between two covers we find a range of reading-matter to satisfy most of the practical and intellectual requirements of a 15th-century middle-class family."[79] With the possible exception of the romances, this compilation could easily have been found in the hands of any number of non-armigerous laity within fifteenth-century York diocese.

[77] Vale, *Piety, Charity and Literacy*, 15-18.

[78] YML, D. & C., L 2/4, f. 112v; BI, D. & C., inventory of John de Scardeburgh. Both are printed in *Test. Ebor.*, 3:1-8. On Chaworth see *Test. Ebor.*, 2:220-29 and Cavanaugh, "A Study of Books Privately Owned," 2:181-83. On the disposition of books before death, see George R. Keiser, "Lincoln Cathedral Library MS 91: Life and Milieu of the Scribe," *Studies in Bibliography* 32 (1979):167.

[79] M. B. Parkes, "The Literacy of the Laity," in *Literature and Western Civilization: The Medieval World*, ed. D. Daiches and A. Thorlby (London, 1973), 569.

A more famous example of the single-volume library is that of Robert Thornton's manuscripts. Thornton, a member of a gentry family from East Newton, compiled two extant, largely English manuscripts of miscellaneous items. The Lincoln Cathedral manuscript (MS A.i. 17), written about the year 1440, contains, among other things, a *Life of Alexander the Great*, the *Morte Arthure*, the *Romance off Syr Percyvelle of Gales* and other romances, several charms, Latin prayers, works by Richard Rolle, the *Vita Sancti Christofori*, two moral poems, various hymns and collects, the Latin psalter, and the *Liber de diversis medicinis*.[80]

For those laity without bookish resources or desiring to expand their reading, there were other alternatives. Parish libraries were developing throughout this period. One of the largest and best documented is the library at Boston parish (Lincs.), but York diocesan parishes also had respectable libraries. In 1434 the book collection of St. Mary's Scarborough included a large breviary, ten antiphonals, two portable breviaries, four legends, eight processionals, six graduals, a troper, a collect, four manuals, a martyrology, two ordinals, a funeral massbook, a hymnal, a book called the "Venite" book, a Gospel and a Bible, a *Huguycion*, a glossed psalter and a psalter of Richard Rolle's, a *Magister Historiarum*, Isidore's *Summa* (sic), a small book of confessions, and a verse book.[81] About 1535 the vicar of Ecclesfield donated his library of the Fathers and of medieval commentators to his parish church,[82] and testators throughout this period left books of lives of saints to parish churches "for the good of the parishioners there."

Monastic libraries sometimes lent their books to neighboring laity. In 1397 the Priory of Newstead (Notts.) went to law to get their volume of the *Stimulus Conscientiae*, which they had lent to one John Ravensfield, returned. In 1440 Henry Kipping of Wistow willed three books, which they had lent him, to the abbot and convent of Whitby. William Banks, a gentleman of York, left 20s. to Mountgrace Charterhouse in 1458 under the condition that they make no claim to a book entitled *Florarium Bartholomei*. He may have originally borrowed the volume from their library.[83] In this regard, the libraries of the Charterhouses would probably have had most appeal to the laity since they included a large proportion

---

[80] J. O. Halliwell, ed., *The Thornton Romances*, Camden Society, no. 30 (London, 1844).

[81] St. John Hope, "Inventory of St. Mary Scarborough," 66.

[82] A. H. Thompson and C. T. Clay, eds., *Fasti Parochiales*, Vol. 1, YAS rec. ser., no. 85 (Wakefield, 1933), 105; Jonathan Eastwood, *History of the Parish of Ecclesfield* (London, 1862), 175.

[83] *Records of the Borough of Nottingham*, Vol. 1 (London, 1882), 334-37; BI, Prob. Reg. 2, ff. 449v-50; YML, D. & C., L 2/4, f. 288, printed in *Test. Ebor.*, 2:218.

of devotional literature, much of which was in English.[84] Lending of books was also very common among individuals as is evidenced by the frequency with which testators devised books to friends and relatives who already had them in their possession.

Given all these circumstances, the question is whether the corpus of works that was actually in the hands of fourteenth- and fifteenth-century individuals is mirrored by the literary tastes reflected in the surviving bequests. How representative is our sample? Unfortunately, this is a question that cannot be satisfactorily answered before the advent of the printed book, since the extant manuscripts may not themselves be representative, and surviving inventories of individual holdings are too uncommon to be of any comparative use. The best way to measure the accuracy of our findings from wills is to compare them with the output of the printing press. Here, however, it is more difficult to pinpoint regional trends.

The impact of printing in York diocese occurred relatively late. The earliest bookseller in York surfaces in 1493,[85] but printed books remained scarce until about 1509/10 when the existence of a printing press in York is first known to historians. As late as 1498 one testator bequeathed a printed mass-book to a chapel "if it can be gotten."[86] The largest concentration of printed books may have been in the library of the cathedral treasurer, whose incomplete 1509 inventory lists 54 printed books out of a total of 147 volumes. Earlier, in 1498, the library of John, Lord le Scrope, also contained significant numbers of printed books, but the way in which three clerical wills from 1508 single out service books as printed suggests that they were still unusual.[87] Indeed, among the Prerogative and Exchequer and Dean and Chapter wills from 1500 to 1509 there are only nine references to printed books, although one testator divided his library into printed paper and written parchment books.[88]

One can conclude from this analysis that the earliest printed books began to be found in appreciable quantities within the diocese only after 1510. At this point the output of the presses, especially the London presses,

[84] Thompson, *Carthusian Order in England*, chap. 9.

[85] In 1493 Frederick Egmont, a York stationer, commissioned a breviary for York use from Johannes Hertzog in Venice. Colin Clair, *A History of Printing in Britain* (Oxford, 1965), 115.

[86] BI, Prob. Reg. 5, ff. 518v-19.

[87] *Test. Ebor.*, 4:96-97, 279-82; D. M. Palliser and D. G. Selwyn, "The Stock of a York Stationer, 1538," *The Library*, 5th ser., 27 (1972):208-209; *Test. Ebor.*, 278; YML, D. & C., L 2/5a, ff. 73, 75v.

[88] BI, Prob. Reg. 6, ff. 67, 113; 7, ff. 17-19, 32-35; YML, D. & C., L 2/5a, ff. 31, 56, 73, 75, 84-85.

only partially reflects the interests described in this chapter on the basis of wills. The wills and the printed editions both testify to the popularity of devotional literature. Between 40 and 45 percent of the publications of Caxton, Worde, Pynson, and Berthelet were religious or moral in nature (including approximately 5 percent that were service books), and the most popular of these were books with which we are already familiar—the *Golden Legend*, Mirk's *Liber Festivalis*, the *Manipulus Curatorum*, and pseudo-Bonaventure's *Life of Christ*. As for the service books, they were in such great demand that the domestic printers were unable to satisfy the need, and 60 percent of all breviaries, primers, manuals, and missals came from Continental presses.[89]

Despite these similarities, there are important differences between the bequests of manuscript books and the catalogs of printed editions. While service books and devotional literature retained their preeminent popularity well into the sixteenth century, the other popular class of manuscripts in the York diocesan wills, the instructions and sermons for parish clergy, failed to attract the attention of early English printers. This may be an instance of what Elizabeth Eisenstein describes as the inability of early printers always to gauge their market correctly.[90] In this case the distance between London and the north may have contributed, and interest in clerical literature may not have been as strong in southern England. Among the combined output of Wynkyn de Worde, Richard Pynson, and Thomas Berthelet, for example, books of instruction for clergy and collections of homilies and sermons account for less than 10 percent of the total, excluding service books.[91] And not one of these three major English printers produced a single edition of the *Pupilla Oculi*, the *Oculus Sacerdotis*, or the *Pars Oculi*, the most popular clerical texts bequeathed among York testators.[92] Although the printers chose to publish relatively few books for the parish clergy, the demand for such literature in York diocese remained high. The 1538 inventory of Neville Mores, a York stationer, illustrates this. Excluding the service books inventoried (e.g., three dozen missals, twenty-five portifors, etc.), there are fifty-eight named books on the list and roughly 29 percent of those are aids to the clergy.[93]

[89] Bennett, *English Books and Readers*, 17, 66; E. Gordon Duff, *Hand-List of English Printers 1501-1556*, 2 vols. (London, 1895).

[90] Elizabeth Eisenstein, *The Printing Press as an Agent of Change*, 2 vols. (Cambridge, 1979).

[91] Duff, *Hand-List of English Printers 1501-1556*.

[92] The *Oculus Sacerdotis* and *Pars Oculi* were never printed, but the *Pupilla Oculi* was printed once in London in 1510 and twice more shortly thereafter in Paris and Rouen. Leonard E. Boyle, "The *Oculus Sacerdotis* and Some Other Works of William of Pagula," *TRHS*, 5th ser., 5 (1955):94-95.

[93] Palliser and Selwyn, "The Stock of a York Stationer," 207-19. Twenty-six percent of the

On the other hand, while we can document only about fifty or sixty bequests of grammar books within the diocese between 1370 and 1510, the production of grammar texts from the printing press was remarkable. The two most popular grammatical treatises, those of Stanbridge and Whittinton, have survived in over two hundred editions, and they were supplemented by frequent printings of the grammar texts of Colet and Lily and the grammatical treatise *De Ratione Studii* of Erasmus.[94] This nationwide interest in Latin grammar is reflected in the history of York printing and bookselling. As has been noted above, primers and *Doctrinales*, as well as copies of *Donatus cum Remigio*, Stanbridge's *Accidence*, and Whittinton's *Grammar*, were among the first books sold or printed in the city of York. Approximately 20 percent of Mores's inventory, excluding the service books, were schooltexts, including two primers, the *Logica* of Johann Reuchlin, a *Liber synonymorum*, a *Copia verborum* (of Cicero?), an *Expositio Donati*, the *Ars versificatoria* of Johannes Despauterius, an *Expositio hymnorum*, and the "bounshe of doctorinalez." Most of these books were available for only 1 or 2d. The group of *Doctrinales*, for example, were inventoried at only 2d. for the total.[95]

Whereas hitherto, on the basis of our information from wills, we have limited evidence of lower clergy's possessing grammatical texts (the bequests suggest, for example, that scholars benefited more from gifts of grammars than did the lower clergy), the existence of cheaply printed grammar books must have put their possession within the means of even the poorest parish priest. While this makes common sense, there is no proof. The wills and inventories of the poorer clergy survive less frequently and rarely mention books after the turn of the sixteenth century. As Elizabeth Eisenstein puts it, "The effect produced by printing on medieval curricula and academic institutions usually has to be inferred by reading between the lines."[96] The explosion of grammar texts must have had an impact, and it should therefore not be surprising that the sixteenth century saw an expansion in grammar instruction by chantry priests. Whether the chantry chaplain charged his grammar pupils or received an endowment, it was clearly in his economic interest to teach as much grammar as he was capable of understanding himself. With the decline

---

books were law volumes. Conspicuously absent were the devotional tracts popular among the laity (a fact which the editors attribute to Mores's clientele, chiefly clergy and ecclesiastical lawyers), and the works of any of the new Reformation or humanist thinkers.

[94] Bennett, *English Books and Readers*, 86-87.

[95] Palliser and Selwyn, "The Stock of a York Stationer," 213-19.

[96] Eisenstein, *The Printing Press*, 134.

in interest in chantries by the 1530s,[97] the income from teaching may have been increasingly welcome, and the investment in self-education a far more sensible proposal, economically, than it had ever been in the fifteenth century.

While the sudden availability of inexpensive grammar texts in York diocese after 1510 may have helped stimulate an expansion in the ranks of grammar teachers, it does not explain the developing educational interests of the laity. Lay involvement in education, as described in Chapter six, began by the middle of the fifteenth century and had already expanded significantly before 1510. While the printing press may have further spurred the expansion of education, its impact postdates the initial stages of educational growth and the subsequent lay involvement.

The question of grammar texts raises the issue of humanism.[98] While English presses in the south were publishing works of Erasmus and Cicero, the only "humanist" texts printed by the York presses were the grammars of Stanbridge and Whittinton. Even as late as 1538 Neville Mores's inventory gives very little indication of humanist influence, although Erasmus's translation of Lucian's *Dialogues* is listed. The wills from the diocese provide few hints of humanism.[99] This impression is corroborated when one looks at the founders of schools and the evidence for humanist curricula within the diocese. It is particularly interesting to look at those northern schools that were most closely associated with humanist developments in the south. Sedbergh grammar school was founded between 1525 and 1528 by Roger Lupton, a lawyer-cleric who was a canon at Windsor, provost of Eton, and a friend of Bishop Fisher. He was obviously aware of the new educational currents in the south of England. His schoolmaster was, however, to be a chantry priest "sufficiently learned and instruct to fulfill

---

[97] Alan Kreider, *English Chantries: The Road to Dissolution* (Cambridge, Mass., 1979), chap. 6.

[98] Humanism, besides being concerned with the introduction of classical learning (both Christian and pagan), was profoundly didactic. The value of education was extolled in the works of More, Erasmus, Vives, and Colet, all of whom flourished in England simultaneously with the expansion in grammar education which took place in York diocese between 1500 and 1548.

[99] The wills and inventories from 1500 to 1530 yield only two exceptions: the 1509 inventory of Martin Colyns, treasurer of York, which includes a number of Cicero's writings, and that of William de Melton, the York chancellor who died in 1528. YML, original inventories, printed in *Test. Ebor.*, 4:279-82; 5:258-59. The wills from 1530 to 1548 have not been read in full. Among a selection of clerical wills for this period edited by Claire Cross (University of York, forthcoming), one, that of Richard Oliver, the vicar of All Saints, North Street in York, shows an acquaintance with the new learning. BI, Reg. 28 (Lee), ff. 168-69; D. & C., original inventory. See also Claire Cross, "Priests into Ministers: The Establishment of Protestant Practice in the City of York, 1530-1630," in *Reformation Principles and Practice: Essays in Honour of Arthur Geoffrey Dickens*, ed. P. N. Brooks (London, 1980), 208-209.

the chantry duties and able to teach a grammar school." Nothing was specified with regard to the curriculum. The scholars were given careful directions for school prayers and the annual obit of the founder.[100]

Thomas Magnus's foundation of a grammar and song school at Newark in 1530 shows a similar preoccupation with religious over educational concerns, and a similar lack of any apparent humanist goals or curriculum. Magnus, like Lupton, was a canon at Windsor, and in 1530 he was, in fact, renting Lupton's town house at Eton. He was a royal chaplain and a member of the Privy Council. He was also a pluralist of some magnitude, and most of his benefices were institutions with grammar and song schools attached, e.g., St. Leonard's Hospital, York; the rectorships of Kirby in Cleveland and of Bedale; the vicarage of Kendal; and Sibthorpe College. Nevertheless, he seems not to have become involved in any discernible way with these schools except to surrender both St. Leonard's and Sibthorpe to the Crown in 1539 and 1545 respectively. His enormous income of £743 13s. 8d. in 1535 was put to educational use only at Newark, his place of birth, where he endowed a song and grammar school in 1530. The endowment was given over to the rector of Guiseley, a lawyer from Newark, and twenty-one others. It was these feoffees, in conjunction with the vicar of Newark and four aldermen from various religious gilds, who appointed the schoolmasters. Two priests were to be found, one to teach grammar and the other to teach plainsong, prick song, and descant. They were to help maintain divine service at Newark parish church and to pray for the souls of various benefactors including, of course, Magnus himself. The children were bound to attend church either nightly or weekly, and elaborate directions for the psalms, collects, and prayers were set down. The only faint echoes of humanism at Magnus's foundation consist of the oath required of the schoolmaster, which was similar to that used at Colet's school in St. Paul's, and the inclusion of rhetoric in the curriculum, which might as easily be attributed to medieval curricular models as to the new learning. The rest of the demands in the curriculum were certainly traditional: grammar, the Ten Commandments, the Apostles' Creed, the psalms, and hymns.[101]

The impression of traditional medieval religiosity that one gets from looking at Magnus's foundation is confirmed by looking at his will. Written in 1551, it shows no trace of humanism. He asks "that a sermond be

[100] *EYS*, 2:286-381; *VCH*, *Yorks.*, 1:467; H. L. Clarke and W. N. Weech, *History of Sedbergh School 1525-1925* (Sedbergh, 1925), 18-31.

[101] N. G. Jackson, *Newark Magnus: The Story of a Gift* (Nottingham, 1964); Cornelius Brown, *A History of Newark-upon-Trent*, Vol. 2 (Newark, 1904), 181-92; *VCH*, *Notts.*, 2:199-209.

maide to the people to exorte them to lerne to die, and soo to leve that they maye all ways be redie to die"—scarcely a humanist sentiment.[102]

Another example is that of Lord Thomas Darcy, who was the founder of Whitkirk grammar school, a member of the circle that surrounded Thomas More, and, by 1531, the godfather of More's grandchild.[103] Darcy's grammar school was established as part of his hospital and hermitage, with oversight given to St. Oswald's Priory and certification of the schoolmaster required by the chancellor of York. The schoolmaster was specifically allowed to discipline with a stick (not an especially humanist directive), and the boys were expected to be in chapel at dawn. The statutes that describe the grammar school devote most of their attention to the hymns, psalms, and collects which the students were to say or sing. No curriculum is specified, and in fact the hospital receives far more detailed attention than does the school.[104]

One of the ways in which humanism could have reached the schools of northern England would have been through the many connections between York diocesan grammar schools and the universities of Cambridge and Oxford, and especially with two colleges usually closely associated with humanism—St. John's College, Cambridge and Magdalen College, Oxford. John Dowman, the founder of Pocklington grammar school in 1514, was a law graduate of Cambridge and a canon of St. Paul's. He was a close associate of Bishop Fisher and had at one time housed the executors of Lady Margaret Beaufort's will. Perhaps as a consequence of these connections, Dowman tied Pocklington to St. John's. Five scholarships were established at St. John's for those Pocklington boys who had proven themselves the best grammarians. There is no hint, however, of a humanist curriculum. The school was founded "for the zeal and love that he had to his country, and to the education and bringing up of youth in virtue and learning." It was to be governed by a religious gild, with advice from St. John's, and it would appear that at the time of the chantry surveys no schoolteacher was in fact in residence. Dowman's 1526 will leaves his lawbooks and books of theology to the Cambridge University Library and to St. John's and his books of sermons to his godchildren. There is no mention of his school.[105]

---

[102] Brown, *History of Newark*, 2:210-11.

[103] Francis E. Zapatka, "Thomas More and Thomas Darcy," *Moreana* 18 (1981):16-19; Orme, *ESMA*, 202-203.

[104] YML, Wa, ff. 19v-27v.

[105] A. F. Leach, "The Foundation and Refoundation of Pocklington Grammar School," *Transactions of the East Riding Antiquarian Society* 5 (1897):63-114; P. C. Sands and Christopher M. Haworth, *A History of Pocklington School, East Yorkshire, 1514-1950* (Hull, 1951), 8-22; A.D.H. Leadman, "Pocklington School," *YAJ* 14 (1896):142-45.

Sedbergh, mentioned earlier, sent eight of its scholars to St. John's on scholarship. In 1548 St. John's actively intervened to protect the school from the effects of the chantry dissolution, and in 1550 Sedbergh was the subject of a special plea by the master of St. John's before Edward VI to save its endowment. Through all of this there is no hint of any humanist influence. Lupton's statutes provided that the schoolmaster "shall rule and order the grammar school . . . and teach freely grammar after the manner, form and use of some laudably notable and famous school of England." Since Lupton was provost of Eton, it has been assumed that he was referring to Eton, but his failure to specify a model is significant, and the schoolmaster could as easily have chosen St. Peter's at York Cathedral for a model.[106] It is likewise interesting that the arguments raised in defense of Sedbergh between 1548 and 1550 mention nothing regarding the curriculum. St. John's argued in 1548 that "if the schools are abolished the University will perish," while Dr. Lever, in his 1550 sermon, noted the needs of ignorant youths in those parts as well as the needs of the university.[107]

Other efforts to link northern schools with the universities were less successful. Bishop Alcock, who endowed Hull's grammar school in 1479 and also founded Jesus College, Cambridge, did not attempt to link the two, deciding instead to establish a grammar school within Jesus College.[108] John Haldsworth, father of the vicar of Halifax, bequeathed sums to set up a grammar school at Halifax in 1497 and to endow scholarships at Oxford. His son (and executor) never carried out his father's intentions. A similar circumstance occurred at Appleby (Westmorland—just beyond the York diocesan borders) when Robert Langton, archdeacon of Dorset from 1486 to 1514, a member of London's Charterhouse from 1514 to 1524, and a friend to Colet and More, left £200 to Queen's College, Oxford to purchase land for a grammar school at Appleby. One of the executors appears to have held the bequest in trust until his own death in 1569.[109]

---

[106] Lupton may have been expecting that the northern convocation of clergy would consider a single grammar just as, from 1525-1529, was being considered by the southern convocation for the province of Canterbury. T. W. Baldwin, *William Shakspere's Small Latine & Lesse Greeke*, 2 vols. (Urbana, Ill., 1944), 1:123.

[107] *EYS*, 2:286-381; Clarke and Weech, *History of Sedbergh School*, 18-31. Another grammar school with connections to St. John's was Southwell Minster, where John Keton, canon of Salisbury, founded two scholarships in 1530. *VCH, Notts.*, 2:187.

[108] John Lawson, *A Town Grammar School Through Six Centuries* (Oxford, 1963), 22-34. See esp. p. 23 for Alcock's other educational activities.

[109] M. W. Garside, "Halifax Schools prior to 1700 A.D.," in *Papers, Reports, etc. Read before the Halifax Antiquarian Society* (Halifax, 1924), 186-88; Edgar Hinchcliffe, *Appleby Grammar School—from Chantry to Comprehensive* (Appleby, 1974), 22-23.

Several schools had connections with Magdalen College, Oxford. In 1502 John Forman, M.A. Magdalen 1449/50, a benefactor of Magdalen, and someone who left considerable monies for loans to poor scholars, helped to establish a grammar school at Royston in the West Riding. There is nothing to suggest a humanist foundation and, indeed, this would probably be too early.[110] Between 1528 and 1536 Thomas Knolles was president of Magdalen College. He was vicar of Wakefield from 1502 until his death in 1546. Wakefield's grammar school already had a long history, and there is nothing to suggest that Knolles felt called upon to endow it or enhance it in any way during his tenure. Knolles's will, written in 1546, shows him to have been a traditionally oriented cleric with a strong interest in masses for the dead. Although the will shows some interest in scholars, the books he passes on, his sermons and the works of St. Augustine, are medieval-minded.[111] After Knolles, another Yorkshireman, Owen Oglethorp, became president of Magdalen College (from 1535 until 1554, with a brief hiatus in 1552-1553). But it was not until 1558 that he established a grammar school at Tadcaster, his place of birth, to "improve scollers in the art of grammar."[112]

In theory classical grammar, which began to dominate the grammar curriculum at Oxford and Cambridge by 1510,[113] could have been brought north by the two grammarmasters (William Beaumont at Halifax in 1515-1516 and Christopher Holdsworth at York in 1531) we know of with B. Gram.'s from Oxford. In actuality, however, the first clear evidence of humanism in the schools of York diocese comes from the 1547 grammar foundations of Archbishop Holgate at York, Malton, and Hemsworth. According to Holgate's statutes, "the said scolemaister shalbe convenientlie scene and have understandinge in the Hebrue, Greke and Latyne tonges, and shall teache . . . the same to suche scolers in the said scole as shalbe moste mete and apte for the same."[114] Holgate's foundation deed emphasizes Latin learning, the reading of good authors in the Latin tongue, and the writing of Latin and lessons in the children's own hand. Holgate's concern with the schools is uppermost, and he spends much time insuring

---

[110] Joseph Hunter, *South Yorkshire*, Vol. 2 (London, 1831), 381.

[111] See Chapter three above; W. D. Macray, *A Register of . . . Magdalen College, Oxford*, new ser., 1 (London, 1894), 130-32.

[112] H. D. Eshelby, ed., "The Episcopal Visitations of the Yorkshire Deaneries of the Archdeaconry of Richmond in 1548 and 1554," *YAJ*, 14 (1898):402-403; S. J. Curtis, "Tadcaster Grammar School," *Leeds Institute of Education Researches and Studies*, no. 6 (1952):69-81.

[113] Damian Leader, "Grammar in Late-Medieval Oxford and Cambridge," *History of Education* 12 (1983):11-13.

[114] York City Archives, Deed of Foundation of Archbishop Holgate's School at York, f. 3.

their continuity. At York a corporation sole was set up separate from the cathedral and under royal patent. No specific religious function was delineated in the foundation deed, although the children were expected to begin and end the days with prayers and to attend church on Sundays and holidays.

More clearly humanist is the 1551 foundation deed for East Retford which is recorded in Holgate's register and was composed under his direction.[115] It specifies the following curriculum: first form: Cicero's Letters "for the more prone natures"; second form: Erasmus's *Colloquies*, the more difficult of Cicero's Letters, the Old and New Testament, Sallust and Justinian's *Institutes*; third form: the King's Latin Grammar, Virgil, Ovid, Cicero's Letters, and Erasmus's *Copia*; fourth form: Latin verse, Latin letter-writing, Greek, and Hebrew. Examples of humanism in the schools accumulate throughout the 1550s, but the history of its development in the north is a story that moves beyond the chronological bounds of this study.

The foregoing analysis has told us a good deal about book ownership and literary interests in the north. To a certain extent the results from examining book bequests have been corroborated by the history of early printed works, the religious interests of testators exhibited elsewhere in their wills, and the motivations behind some of the more prominent school foundations of the early sixteenth century. Despite the incompleteness of the data, it is probably true that the tastes of York testators were primarily religious, and that they were slow to respond to humanist influences. By the fifteenth century these religious tastes were being fueled by a growing literacy and increased access to education. As a result, lay interests were quite possibly beginning to encroach on the clerical sphere, not only in the choice of reading materials but also in other areas of religious activity—the choir, the liturgy, and, especially, the founding and support of education.

Considering the growing number of laity receiving some kind of education, and their increasingly sophisticated religious and devotional interests, many lay persons may no longer have considered education solely to be the concern of the clergy. It is therefore hardly surprising that, when churchmen began to found and endow schools in the fifteenth century, the laity should have quickly followed suit. Endowed schools provided free education for their children and at the same time assured the benefactors of countless prayers. Other factors may have come into play, including perhaps the declining power of the various ecclesiastical juris-

---

[115] BI, Reg. 29 (Holgate), ff. 53-57v.

dictions to enforce educational monopolies, but it is unlikely that the laity of York diocese would have ventured into the educational arena to the extent that they did if, throughout the fifteenth century, their growing acquaintance with devotional tracts and religious guides had not prepared them to take on a role that had traditionally been a function of the Church.

CONCLUSION

There are a number of conclusions to be drawn from this study which have a marked impact on the debates outlined in Chapter one. Among other findings, the documentation gathered in Appendix B and analyzed in the first four chapters of the book details an early sixteenth-century explosion in grammar education. After centuries of slow growth, grammar schools within York diocese nearly tripled in number (from twenty-five to sixty-eight) in the relatively short period between 1500 and 1548. How sophisticated the curriculum of these newer grammar schools was must remain problematic. Roger Ascham's reminiscences of the rote learning at Kirby Wiske may have been more typical than not. In many cases, however, the quality of grammar education must have been enhanced by the expanding resources northern English people were putting into their schools.

Beginning with the first endowment of a grammar school at Preston (Lancs.) in 1448 by Helene Houghton, the number of documented endowments and foundations of schools within the diocese was to reach thirty-eight by 1548. One significant factor behind this development was the number of clergy, ranging from archbishops to parish priests, who provided many of the resources for founding, endowing, and teaching grammar schools and supporting scholars. But ecclesiastical involvement in education was not new and may not have been much more remarkable on the eve of the Reformation than it was in the twelfth and thirteenth centuries. Nor can the ecclesiastical foundations alone account for such a dramatic increase after 1500. Of the known grants to grammar schools in York diocese before 1548, the laity ultimately contributed the greater share—endowing or founding twenty-one grammar schools in comparison with the seventeen that benefited from clerical largesse. In fact, it is the expanding lay interest in schooling that is crucial to an understanding of the growing momentum in education which northern England experienced in the fifteenth and early sixteenth centuries. Laity of all social classes—nobles, gentry, townspeople, and villagers—were turning their attention to the schools in a new and dramatic way. Not only were they founding, financing, and governing grammar schools, they were also sending their children to them and leaving bequests to scholars in greater numbers than ever before.

Besides the growth in grammar education, however, there was another dynamic at work in northern England, namely, the accelerating access of the people in the diocese to elementary learning in reading, song, and, to a certain extent, writing. Not only in the cities such as York, where references to elementary schooling increase from five in the fourteenth century to nearly a dozen by the end of the fifteenth century, but also in outlying towns and rural areas, these schools were proliferating throughout the fifteenth century and possibly earlier (although the relative dearth of documents for the fourteenth century leaves this an open question). By 1500 there are notices for seventy such schools within the diocese. In all between 1300 and 1548 there are references to over two hundred elementary schools within York diocese. Together with the documentation on grammar schools, the combined evidence for educational opportunities emerging from this survey is nearly equivalent to the totals A. F. Leach and Nicholas Orme discovered for all of England. Keeping in mind that many of the more elementary schools were transitory, offering at most a reading and writing education and sometimes less than that, it is nevertheless beyond dispute that the availability of schooling in late medieval England has been previously underestimated rather than exaggerated. The results from York diocese suggest that late medieval England was a period expansive in educational opportunities and productive in numbers of pre-university scholars.

In York diocese many, although not most, of these scholars went into the priesthood. By 1510 the rate of clerical recruitment within the diocese had more than doubled since the first half of the fifteenth century, and the clerical population had grown 60-90 percent greater than the already impressively high numbers recorded in the 1377 poll tax returns. The reasons for such an enormous influx of clergy has little to do with plague or the ease of ordination, although both factors are relevant for explaining clerical recruitment patterns in the fourteenth century. Reasons for the growth in clerical ranks on the eve of the Reformation have much more to do with the expanding opportunities for clergy (as mass priests and private chaplains, for example) and increasing educational opportunities which enabled more candidates to acquire the sometimes minimal learning required for ordination. Behind this development was a history of ecclesiastical legislation that had long promoted education at the parish level for parishioners, parish scholars, and potential priests. By the 1460s the success of the Church in recruiting clergy was apparent, at least in York diocese, although many new ordinands came from rural areas where they may have absorbed little more than the elementary learning typical of a parish education. The cumulative effect of ordaining large numbers of clergy, many without a Latin grammar education, can scarcely have been beneficial for the Church in the long run as the laity turned toward education in an increasingly impressive fashion.

Lay interest in education is documented on many fronts—in the foundations and endowments of schools, governance of schools, benefactions to scholars, and career plans and schooling choices for their children. The result is a gradual laicization of education throughout the fifteenth and early sixteenth centuries, although the religious purpose of education is never entirely lost sight of, and lay involvement develops in tandem with the Church and not, apparently, in opposition to it. By 1548 most schools were governed in part or in whole by laity; laity of all classes within the diocese outnumbered clergy in foundations and endowments of schools and benefactions to scholars; and children attending school were more likely to pursue lay careers than to enter orders. Indeed, by 1530 the proportion of laity receiving an education of some kind or another was approaching 15 percent while the proportion of clergy within the diocese, whose educational experience would have been, of course, similar, was a mere 1.6-1.8 percent.

The results of this laicization of education ought to have been obvious in an increase in lay literacy by the end of the period under study here. Lay literacy, however, is not easy to measure where signatures are rarely required and writing, taught separately from reading, cannot be used as an index. This study has looked at lay literacy in three ways, all of which reflect a reading literacy. First, there are numerous indirect developments that suggest growing lay literacy. The increased prevalence of posted bills, the rise of Lollardy, the occasional contemporary comment describing literate laity, the abuse of benefit of clergy—all suggest expanding lay literacy. These indirect pieces of evidence have been supplemented with the evidence from wills. Lay testators whose wills show no sign of the presence of clergy at the will-making or whose references to books or writing skills testify to their literacy are increasingly abundant. By the sixteenth century 20-30 percent of the extant wills from the city of York, where one might expect it, and those from the archdeaconry of Richmond, where one might not expect it, appear to be the product of lay, not clerical, willmakers. Finally, added to this is the evidence for lay literacy derived from school attendance estimates. Calculated on the basis of an estimated population of 250,000 for the diocese by 1530, the schools, in theory, would have been educating roughly 12-13 percent of the population on the eve of the Reformation. Considering the schools about which we know nothing and the various informal modes of education that have left no documents, an estimated reading literacy of just slightly less than 15 percent of the lay population seems reasonable.

The chronology of change in terms of schooling, rates of clerical recruitment, and growth of lay literacy are easier to establish than an understanding of the motivations behind these changes. The arguments explaining educational change have traditionally focused on the sixteenth century. They have been succinctly delineated by Lawrence Stone and elaborated on by Joan Simon and include factors such as Bible-reading, humanism, the role of Edward VI's government, and puritan educational impulses. None of these factors has any relevance to the educational changes taking place in York diocese on the eve of the Reformation. In an effort to obtain some insight into the minds of York diocesan laity in the late Middle Ages, it has been enlightening to look at their book bequests. The survey of literary interests undertaken in Chapter seven suggests that York diocesan testators were preoccupied with devotional and liturgical, if not clerical, matters, and that their concerns were quite traditional, neither heretical nor reform-minded. In terms of education, however, this combination of traditional religiosity, aided by the Church's own interest in parish and grammar education, resulted in the developing educational opportunities and increased involvement of the laity that has been documented throughout this study. Traditional and devotional as the motivations may have been, they had begun to produce profound changes in the relationship between clergy and laity on the eve of the Reformation.

It is now time to turn to the debates delineated in Chapter one in light of the evidence presented above. The disagreements over education and literacy which have separated medieval from Tudor historians have been fueled too often by insufficient evidence and fanned by the fact that the available evidence has not always seemed consistent. Lawrence Stone, Joan Simon, and others have noted a remarkable growth in the number of grammar schools by the early seventeenth century. Their estimate of the revolutionary importance of the post-Reformation phase of that development rests to a large degree (with some reservations on both Stone's and Simon's part) upon the work of W. K. Jordan, whose estimates of grammar schools for pre-1548 York diocese, at any rate, have been shown to be very wide of the mark. The educational data from York, taken together with the recent work of Nicholas Orme, suggest that the sixteenth-century educational revolution had significant medieval roots and, particularly with regard to the grammar schools, may need to be pushed back by fifty to sixty years.

One reason the idea of a sixteenth-century educational revolution has been so readily accepted is the numerous sixteenth-century references to elementary learning as well as the publication of late sixteenth-century educational treatises devoted to the subject. In contrast, the medieval educational scene has seemed relatively barren, although various scholars, citing scattered references, have assumed the existence of widespread medieval elementary education. Not only have medievalists been hard put to document such schools, they have been unable to clearly differentiate them from grammar institutions. For all these reasons no history of medieval elementary schools has been attempted or has, indeed, seemed possible. This study is the first to detail the widespread existence of elementary education. It has argued from the data in Appendix B that the late Middle Ages was a period of expanding elementary educational opportunities. Perhaps in the fourteenth, and certainly in the fifteenth century, elementary schooling in reading, song, and also writing was becoming available to such an extent that the sixteenth century can no longer be assumed to be revolutionary in this respect.

Problems similar to those in the educational field face the historian attempting to reconcile pre-Reformation and post-Reformation assessments of literacy. Medievalists have stressed the growth of lay literacy as early as the twelfth century, while a few scholars have ventured to provide estimates of literacy from the fifteenth century. Except for the London court depositions, from which Sylvia Thrupp extracted a 50 percent male literacy rate, no very substantial data base has been available. The estimate of nearly 15 percent lay literacy (20-25 percent male literacy) in York diocese by 1530 is the result of the more comprehensive educational data developed throughout this study, combined with the evidence from wills. These quantified and more broadly based conclusions, which take parts of rural England into account for the first time, move the pre-Reformation historian away from dependence upon literary sources, chance contemporary observations, and singular examples and enable him or her to compare results with the data available for the later Tudor and Stuart periods. These estimates for York diocese at the beginning of the sixteenth century coincide not at all with estimates for early Tudor England presented in David Cressy's 1980 study of reading and writing in Tudor and Stuart England. The differences reflect the measurement of different types of literacy. Cressy is using signature literacy as the basis for his more pessimistic statistics, while the percentages developed here measure a reading literacy. Combined, the statistics from Cressy's research and the results reached here offer a richer picture of literacy in the period just before the Reformation and reinforce the idea of an evolutionary rather than a revolutionary development of educational resources and literate skills.

The evidence of expanding late medieval elementary education, the growth of grammar schools in the early sixteenth century, and the extent of lay literacy on the eve of Reformation support an evolutionary view of educational history, a view that suggests the need for Tudor historians to look back to the late Middle Ages to lengthen their perspective and deepen their understanding of the educational changes of the sixteenth century. But such an evolutionary view of England's educational history also raises a question that has not hitherto been asked: Did the growth in education prepare the way for the Reformation? Late medieval northerners harbored few heretical sentiments, and Protestant beliefs only gradually made their way into the north. Nevertheless, long-term changes in the relationship between clergy and laity had been evolving over a century or more before the Reformation. With the Church producing more and more clergy, many with only a few years of education to recommend them, and the laity showing increasing support for and reaping more and more benefits from education, it is clear that the late medieval clergy no longer dominated the educational sphere or even the educated elite. As a result, the changes that have been documented throughout this study may have ultimately worked to the disadvantage of the Church. As any educational superiority the clergy may have once had over the laity disappeared, the stage may have been very gradually being set for the final transference of power, within the Church itself, from ecclesiastical to lay control.

APPENDIX A

The Testamentary Sources Used in this Study

York diocese is particularly rich in late medieval probate materials. Although there are very few original wills remaining from the period of this study,[1] there is a substantial collection of registered copies of wills in the archiepiscopal Prerogative and Exchequer Court.[2] The first ten volumes, which form the basis for this study, cover the years 1389-1530 and comprise over 10,500 wills.[3] There are an additional 7,400 wills from 1530 to 1548 (volumes 11-13) which have not been systematically searched, in part because of the bulk and in part because the sixteenth-

[1] Original wills were not regularly retained by the archbishop's courts before 1559 and are not extant in any bulk before 1591. After being registered and proved original wills were usually returned to the rural deans. There is a partial act book of these wills available from Harthill deanery for the years 1502-1505, but the only significant number of original wills extant before 1530 comes from the deaneries of the archdeaconry of Richmond and the court of the Dean and Chapter of York. An index of original wills 1427-1858 (the earliest of these being from the Exchequer Court) is printed in the YAS rec. ser., no. 73 (Leeds, 1928), where they are mistakenly attributed to the archbishop's Consistory Court.

[2] The medieval Exchequer Court of the archbishop concerned itself with probates within York diocese, excluding almost eighty peculiar jurisdictions, the archdeaconry of Richmond, the chapelries of Saddleworth and Whitewell, and the beneficed clergy. It had no jurisdiction where the deceased had *bona notabilia* (goods valued at over £5) in more than one diocese or peculiar. Even during metropolitan visitations, when other jurisdictions in the province were inhibited, the probates were a function of the visitors then appointed, rather than of the Exchequer. The prerogative jurisdiction of the Exchequer was not established until 1577, after which time the archbishop's Prerogative and Exchequer Court had jurisdiction over any person having goods either in more than one jurisdiction within the diocese of York, in more than one diocese in the northern province, or in both northern and southern provinces. In these courts, as in other probate courts, if a person died within a court's jurisdiction but had no goods there, the will was subject to its control.

[3] A 1397 inventory in the *sede vacante* register records nine volumes of registered wills. Except possibly for BI, Prob. Reg. 1 (1389-1397), these have not survived. We do not know how early such registers were being kept, although there is a reference to them in 1362. David M. Smith, "Lost Archiepiscopal Registers of York: The Evidence of Five Medieval Inventories," *Borthwick Institute Bulletin* 1, (1975):37. An index to the Prerogative and Exchequer wills has been printed by the YAS rec. ser., no. 6 (Leeds, 1888) and no. 11 (Leeds, 1891).

century wills are briefer and less informative than the earlier documents. References to schools which may have been missed in volumes 11-13 are partially compensated for by the retrospective coverage of schools provided in the chantry surveys of 1546 and 1548. In addition to the Prerogative and Exchequer Court wills, wills have survived from the Chancery Court of the Archbishop (written into the archbishops' registers),[4] from the Prerogative Court of Canterbury (where York diocesan individuals with properties worth over £5 in one or more diocese outside York registered their wills),[5] from the peculiar court of the Dean and Chapter of York Cathedral,[6] and from the archdeaconry of Richmond and its eight deaneries.[7] Except for the peculiars of Southwell; Durham; St. Leonard's Hospital,

[4] These consist of an additional 991 wills from 1340-1549. For the index, see YAS rec. ser., no. 93 (Leeds, 1937). The Chancery court had jurisdiction over testamentary causes concerning the estates of the clergy beneficed in the diocese, and of those beneficed in the diocese who had goods or chattels in more than one diocese or peculiar jurisdiction, together with estates of the deceased of peculiar jurisdictions who died during the regular diocesan visitations.

[5] This consists of another 230 wills, most of them of considerable length and interest. A few of these wills have been printed in NCW. For an index, see Index of Wills Proved in the Prerogative Court of Canterbury 1383-1558, 2 vols., British Records Society Index Library (London, 1893-1895).

[6] This is a particularly important body of registered wills, since it includes a large proportion of clerical wills. The total number of extant registered wills from this court between 1340 and 1549 is 1,253. An index of these wills has been published by the YAS rec. ser., no. 38 (Leeds, 1907). There are some original wills from this court before 1660. Thirty-seven wills are also enrolled in the Chapter Act Books, 1336-1429 (YML, D. & C., H 1/4, H 2/1) and in the Registrum Antiquum de Testamentis, 1336-1343 (YML, D. & C., M 2/4). For an index to both collections, see Wills in the York Registry, YAS rec. ser., no. 60 (Leeds, 1920), 189-90.

[7] There are several volumes of registered copies of wills from the eastern deaneries which were proved in the Consistory Court of Richmond. These are labeled volumes 1, 2, 3 & A. They are bound together and are now in the Leeds Archives Department. Registers 1, 2, and A are in very poor condition and include only about a dozen wills from the 1470s and 1480s. Volume 3 begins in 1529 and contains about 230 wills before 1548. See the Northern Genealogist 2 (1896) and 3 (1897), supplement, for a partial index. There are seven fifteenth-century wills which were included in one of the early registers of the archdeacon of Richmond. These, plus a selection of the others, have been edited by James Raine, Wills and Inventories from the Registry of the Archdeaconry of Richmond, Surtees Society, no. 26 (Durham, 1853). The registers for the archdeaconry have been edited by A. Hamilton Thompson in the YAJ 25 (1919); 129-268; 30 (1930):1-132; 32 (1935):111-46. In addition to the registered copies of wills, there are a few early original wills which were deposited in the courts of the western deaneries. These are on deposit in the Lancashire Record Office, Preston, Lancs. For an index to the Lancashire wills proved within the archdeaconry of Richmond, see A List of the Lancashire Wills Proved within the Archdeaconry of Richmond . . . 1457 to 1680, ed. H. Fishwick, Lancashire and Cheshire Record Society, no. 10 (Manchester, 1884) and A Collection of Lancashire and Cheshire Wills not now to be found in any Probate Registry 1301-1752, ed. W. F. Irvine, Lancashire and Cheshire Record Society, 30 (Manchester, 1896). British Library Additional MS 32115 is a volume of abstracts of wills from the western deanery of Amounderness which was made by Christopher

York; Beverley; and the Honour of Knaresborough,[8] the other smaller peculiar, manorial, and prebendal courts with wills extant before 1548 are insignificant for the purposes of this study.[9] There are several wills preserved in the Hull Corporation records. Wills devising lands and houses in York were sometimes enrolled in the York city records, and occasionally wills were recorded in manor court rolls.[10]

Adding these together, the number of wills that have been examined for this study is close to 15,000, the vast majority of which are unprinted.[11]

Towneley in the seventeenth century. The originals have since disappeared. Out of 2,279 abstracts perhaps half a dozen date from 1505 to 1556. For an index to these abstracts, see *A List of the Lancashire Wills*, passim.

[8] Thirty-four wills from the peculiar of Southwell have been published in A. F. Leach, ed., *Visitations and Memorials of Southwell Minster*, Camden Society, new ser., no. 48 (London, 1891), 96-145. Original wills after 1521 from the peculiar court of the Dean and Chapter of Durham within the jurisdiction of Howden and Howdenshire are on deposit at the Borthwick Institute (BI, Prob. Reg. E 6). There are 100 pre-Reformation wills from St. Leonard's Hospital, York deposited in York Minster Library [M 2/6e]. An index to these wills is printed in the YAS rec. ser., no. 60 (1920):191-93. Ninety-five registered wills from the peculiar court of the provost of the collegiate church of St. John, Beverley for the years 1539-1548 are in the Borthwick Institute (Prob. Reg. E 4). The index is printed along with those from St. Leonard's Hospital in YAS rec. ser., 60 (1920):182-84. Ninety wills are recorded in the *Acts of Chapter of the Collegiate Church of SS Peter and Wilfrid, Ripon A.D. 1452 to A.D. 1506*, ed. J. T. Fowler, Surtees Society, 64 (Durham, 1874). There are seventy-two wills from the court rolls of the Honour of Knaresborough from 1507 to 1548. See *Wills and Administrations from the Knaresborough Court Rolls*, Vol. 1, ed. F. Collins, Surtees Society, no. 104 (Durham, 1902), 1-51.

[9] These include Acomb peculiar with wills dating from 1456, Ampleforth peculiar with wills from 1528, Alne and Tollerton peculiar with wills from 1458, Bishop Wilton peculiar with wills from 1531, Bole prebend with wills from 1546, Bugthorp prebend with wills from 1544, Fenton prebend with wills from 1528, Langtoft prebendal with wills from 1520, North Newbald prebendal with wills from 1496, Salton peculiar with wills from 1531, Strensall prebend with wills from 1528, Stillington prebend with wills from 1515, Weighton prebend with wills from 1502, and Wetwang prebend with wills from 1458, housed at the Borthwick Institute. See David M. Smith, *A Guide to the Archive Collections in the Borthwick Institute of Historical Research* (York, 1973), 164-73.

[10] For Hull, see L. M. Stanewell, ed., *Calendar of Ancient Deeds, etc. in the Archives of the Corporation* (1951) and *Northern Genealogist* 2 (1896), 181-83. For York see Maud Sellers, ed., *York Memorandum Book*, 2 vols., Surtees Society, nos. 120, 125 (Durham, 1912-1915), 1:xvii, lxiv, 13; 2:vii-viii, 251-54; Joyce W. Percy, ed., *York Memorandum Book*, Vol. 3, Surtees Society, no. 186 (Gateshead, 1973), passim. There is a reference at the end of the fourteenth century to a separate register of deeds and wills for the city which is not now extant. Ibid., 79. For wills in manor court rolls, see H. Stanley Darbyshire and George D. Lumb, eds., *The History of Methley*, Thoresby Society, no. 35 (Leeds, 1937), 177; Michael M. Sheehan, *The Will in Medieval England* (Toronto, 1963), 210-11; and an essay on wills in manor court rolls by E. A. Levett in *Studies in Manorial History*, eds. Cam, Coate and Sutherland (Oxford, 1938), 208-34.

[11] Many of the more interesting wills from the archbishops' court and a small number of wills

Chart 7

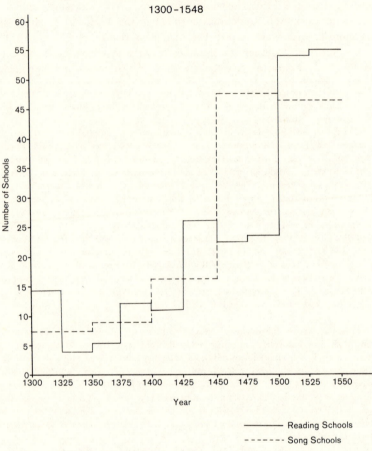

READING AND SONG SCHOOLS IN YORK DIOCESE
1300–1548

——————— Reading Schools

– – – – – – Song Schools

Source: Chapter four, tables 4,5.

Chart 8 provides a breakdown by decades of the testamentary materials from the three largest probate collections (that of the Prerogative and Exchequer Court, the archbishop's Chancery Court, and the peculiar court of the Dean and Chapter). The loss of the pre-1389 volumes from the

from the Dean and Chapter's peculiar court have been printed fully or in part in *Test. Ebor.* Unfortunately the editors often abstracted the wills without so indicating, and it is therefore best to continue to rely on the manuscript materials.

230

Chart 8

REGISTERED WILLS PROVED IN THE
ARCHBISHOP'S COURTS AND THE
PECULIAR COURT OF THE YORK
DEAN AND CHAPTER

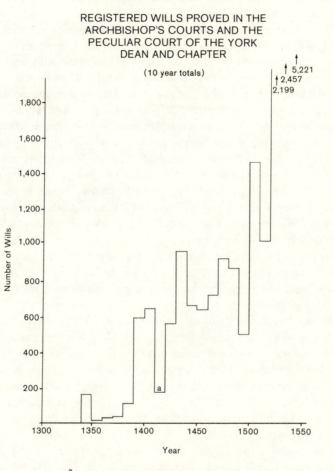

(10 year totals)

↑
↑ 5,221
↑ 2,457
2,199

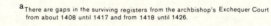

[a]There are gaps in the surviving registers from the archbishop's Exchequer Court
from about 1408 until 1417 and from 1418 until 1426.

Sources: Wills in the York Registry, YAS rec. ser., nos. 6, 9, 38, 93 (Leeds, 1888–1937).

Prerogative and Exchequer Court means that the wills extant before 1390 are relatively few in number, and this raises the question of whether the increase in schooling is related more to the increased availability of the testamentary sources than to any real expansion in education. It is a question relevant only for the analysis of elementary education since documentation of the grammar schools is largely independent of the wills.

In order to compare the growth in references to elementary education with the increased availability of wills, Chart 7, which graphs the census of song schools every fifty years and reading schools every twenty-five years, should be superimposed on Chart 8.

We will begin with the song school evidence because it accords relatively poorly with the availability of testamentary sources. Chart 7 shows a very slight increase in references to song schools just as the wills begin to be preserved. In the first half of the fifteenth century, when the testamentary materials are readily available, there is a relatively low number of song schools in comparison with the enormous jump in song schools in the second half of the fifteenth century (from sixteen to fifty, an increase of over 200 percent) at which time the available wills climb by only 21 percent. The first half of the sixteenth century sees a decline in the number of existing song schools although the wills continue to increase substantially. The chronology of references to song schools appears to have little to do with the availability of sources, but it does coincide nicely with the history of the introduction of liturgical polyphony with choirs into English parishes and the fifteenth-century investments in parish churches.[12] The comparison of song school references with the testamentary data suggests that, however much we are dependent on the wills for information on song schools, the chronology of change for these schools is not controlled by the availability of these sources.

We need to keep this firmly in mind as we turn to the evidence for reading schools, for here the growth in schooling is more consistent with the charted will evidence. The fact that there are relatively few wills extant before 1390 may, in part, explain the absence of references to reading schools in the fourteenth century, especially when the documentation on convent schools disappears after 1325. Of the thirteen references to reading schools in the period 1376-1400, six depend upon the will evidence and all derive from the 1390s. Since four of those come from the bequests of a single testator, only 3 wills out of 600 in the 1390s actually provide evidence for parish schools. It is therefore likely that were the missing fourteenth-century wills available, some additional schools, although perhaps not very many, would surface. It is suggestive that among the over four hundred wills extant before 1390, not one testator mentions parish scholars, whereas in the fifteenth-century wills parish scholars are mentioned far more frequently than once every four hundred wills. Such silence argues that parish scholars may not have been around to participate in the liturgy and receive the usual financial rewards for funeral masses which are so common in the fourteenth, fifteenth, and early sixteenth

---

[12] Frank Ll. Harrison, *Music in Medieval Britain* (London, 1958), chap. 4; Colin Platt, *The Parish Churches of Medieval England* (London, 1981).

centuries. Certainly such silence suggests that references to education in the missing wills would not be as plentiful as they become in the fifteenth and early sixteenth centuries.

In the fifteenth century the rise in reading schools outpaces the growth in testamentary materials. While the number of wills increases by 21 percent between 1450 and 1500, the number of reading schools rises from thirty-one in 1400-1450 to forty-two in 1450-1500 (a growth of 35 percent).[13] More dramatically, from the first quarter to the last quarter of the fifteenth century the number of reading schools rises 100 percent while the number of wills increases by only 60 percent. Similarly, between 1500 and 1530 the will evidence increases by only 27 percent while the number of reading schools climbs from 42 to 65, a growth of 55 percent.[14] Although the rise in reading schools in the fifteenth and sixteenth centuries may be, in part, a function of the availability of data, the schools consistently outrun the data, suggesting that the fifteenth and early sixteenth centuries were a period of growth in reading schools and that the references to schools in wills are not simply a function of the availability of sources but also of the very real and increasing presence of scholars.

The major question with which the source problem leaves us is whether, were more wills available for the fourteenth century, the origins of the educational development in reading schools might be dated somewhat earlier. If so, the fifteenth-century developments would appear somewhat less dramatic. It is extremely unlikely that the educational resources documented here could be pushed back any earlier than the fourteenth century. This is especially true in the north of England where recovery from the late eleventh-century destruction of William the Conqueror was slow,[15] the ecclesiastical hierarchy was still being consolidated as late as the thirteenth century,[16] and no other indirect indicators (such as lay literacy or clerical learning) point toward such a development.[17] In addition, schooling of any kind, although spreading in the twelfth and thirteenth centuries, seems to have been confined largely to the towns and monasteries, while

[13] The number of reading schools graphed in Chart 7 is based on existing schools every twenty-five years. Since some schools are continued over two quarters, the total number of schools in any fifty-year period will be less than the total for two quarters combined.

[14] The wills from 1530 to 1548 were not systematically examined and have therefore been excluded from the analysis.

[15] William Kapelle, *The Norman Conquest of the North* (Chapel Hill, N.C., 1979).

[16] *VCH, Yorks.*, III, 80-81.

[17] G.W.S. Barrow, "Northern English Society in the Twelfth and Thirteenth Centuries," *Northern History* 4 (1969):1-28; Donald Nicoll, *Thurstan, Archbishop of York 1114-1140* (York, 1964); Barbara English, *The Lords of Holderness 1086-1260* (Oxford, 1979); *VCH, Yorks.*, Vol. 3, passim.

most of the reading schools documented here are found in rural villages.[18]
In the final analysis the argument for a fifteenth-century growth in elementary education will stand or fall to the degree that it is consistent with
other developments such as the growth of chantries as educational institutions, the endowment of schools, increases in lay literacy and benefactions
to scholars, availability of books, recruitment of clergy, and growth in
grammar education. It is helpful to have discovered, for example, that
large numbers of scholars apply for letters dismissory at the end of the
fifteenth and beginning of the sixteenth century, whereas they are only
occasionally noted in the archbishop's registers of the fourteenth century.[19]
But whether the expansion in elementary schools is largely a fifteenth-
century phenomenon or, in part, a development of the fourteenth century,
it clearly belongs to the late Middle Ages in York diocese. Although the
uneven availability of sources renders the exact chronology of educational
change somewhat tentative, the fact of educational growth is unmistakable.

Apart from the difficulty of having to depend upon a source with varying
rates of survivability, using wills has other drawbacks. Wills do not
normally make for exciting reading. One must wade through many standard and uninformative documents in search of individuality or significant
patterns. The wealthier and more educated the testator, the more likely
he or she would be to enumerate bequests. Consequently, wills are most
satisfactory for studying the upper classes (merchants, gentry, aristocracy,
and upper clergy), although there is much useful information on chaplains,
artisans, yeomen, and husbandmen. Almost every class of north country-
man or woman might leave a will, including a few wills that are the
product of laborers.[20]

The women who left wills were most often widows. Unmarried women
infrequently did so, and married women were not supposed to leave a
will without their husband's permission, although some seem to have done
so. Even when women did leave written testaments, the survival rate of
these documents was not high. Among the nine wills of women mentioned
in the account books of the gild of St. George in Nottingham between
1459 and 1499, none can now be found either in the original or as a
registered copy. In contrast, 38 percent of the male testators' wills have

[18] Orme, *ESMA*, chap. 6. Michael Clanchy, however, argues for the availability of instruction
in the villages throughout England in the thirteenth century. M. T. Clanchy, *From Memory to
Written Record: England, 1066-1307* (Cambridge, Mass., 1979), 192-93.

[19] See above, Chapter five.

[20] E.g., BI, Prob. Reg. 2, f. 177 (will of Richard Johnson, laborer of York) and 10, f. 38v
(will of John Mawpas of Bilton in Holderness, laborer).

survived.[21] Consequently, women are underrepresented in the existing testamentary collections. Only 12 percent of the wills from the Prerogative and Exchequer Court belong to women.

No will was necessary for a person with goods worth less than £5, although the Church preferred that no one die intestate. Those persons with goods valued at over £5 within only one archdeaconry would be most likely to have their wills proved at that level, thus decreasing the likelihood of their survival. Those who had *bona notabilia* (goods worth over £5) in more than one archdeaconry went to the episcopal court for probate, although it was not uncommon for testators in four of the archdeaconries (excluding Richmond) to have their wills proved at the archbishop's Exchequer Court even if they had goods in only one archdeaconry.

In order for the executors to prove a will and gain administration of a testator's estate, the executors paid a fee to the probate courts and to the rural dean who often handled the transaction. Already by the thirteenth century, however, complaints were being heard against excessive fees.[22] Obviously the poorer testators would have been less likely to have had their wills registered. This does not mean, however, that they did not leave wills. One such example surfaced in 1409, during the visitation of the Dean and Chapter of York to the parish of St. Maurice outside the walls of York. The visitors discovered the will of Agnes Melscryp written in Latin in a missal belonging to the church. Although they copied it into the visitation record, there is no record that it was ever proved in the Dean and Chapter's peculiar court or anywhere else.[23]

We have no way of knowing what proportion of the people left wills like Agnes Melscryp. Information is too scanty on this score. In the town of Rotherham in 1492, two out of ten deceased within the parish left wills, but we cannot determine how typical this was.[24] And because of the destruction of most archdeaconal and deanery records, the number of extant wills is much less than the number of wills that was originally written. In the account books of the gild of St. George, mentioned above, only twelve out of forty-one wills recorded (or 24 percent) are now extant.

For all these reasons (the failure of most women to leave wills, the lack of sufficient goods to warrant the writing of a will, the expense of probate, and the unknown proportion of records that have not survived) only a

---

[21] *The Account Books of the Gilds of St. George and of St. Mary in the Church of St. Peter, Nottingham*, Thoroton Society record series, no. 7 (1939).

[22] B. L. Woodcock, *Medieval Ecclesiastical Courts in the Diocese of Canterbury* (Oxford, 1952), 22-23.

[23] YML, D. & C., E L 2/3a, f. 17.

[24] *EYS*, 2:102, quoted by Leach from British Library, Harl. 2374, f. 30,6.

very small percentage of the population is represented by the extant wills. There is, however, one consolation. The extant wills represent a sample that has selected out wills proved or otherwise recorded at the local level. Consequently, they speak for those individuals with the greater goods to bequeath, and hence, for the purposes of analyzing monetary and book bequests to schools and scholars, the surviving wills are probably more informative than the lost wills would have been.

Schools within the Diocese of York

Below is a listing of every notice of a school within York diocese that has come to my attention. All major sources have been listed, and every effort has been made to arrive at the original documentation. In a few cases this has not been possible, and the ascription of a school rests on secondary material. It has been assumed throughout Appendix B that children singing in the choirs or reading in the parish church must have received some training, however informal. These schools should not be understood to be institutionalized, although in a number of cases there was continuity. In those instances where it is difficult to judge the nature or date of a school, I have included my reasoning or presented the documentation. As new information is gathered and our knowledge of medieval education becomes more refined, these conclusions will be revised accordingly.

ABERFORD (W. Riding)   song school, 1476
John Pykhard of Hillum, who was to be buried in St. Recarius of Aberford, mentioned children with surplices attending the funeral. BI, Prob. Reg. 4, f. 89v.

ACASTER MALBIS (W. Riding)   song school, 1492/3; reading school, 1499
John Bowmer of Acaster Malbis, who was to be buried in Holy Trinity of Acaster Malbis, willed one penny "to every child that canne syng" (Jan. 4, 1492). BI, Prob. Reg. 5, f. 428. In 1499 Roger Radclif left pennies to the five scholars of this village of Acaster (Malbis) on the day that his funeral was to be celebrated in Holy Trinity. Prob. Reg. 3, f. 339.

ACASTER SELBY (W. Riding)   grammar, writing, and song schools, circa 1470-1548
EYS, 2:xxi-xxii, 89-100; Orme, ESMA, 295. The college of St. Andrew at Acaster Selby in Stillingfleet parish was founded by Robert Stillington, a Yorkshireman who became bishop of Bath and Wells, probably between 1467 and 1475. No license in mortmain can be found, but a private act passed in the first Parliament of Richard III (1483) over a dispute between the college of Acaster Selby and the inhabitants of Nether

Acaster recites the foundation of a free school but not its date. *Rot. Parl*, 5:256. We know from the will of Walter Cawdry, vicar of Stillingfleet, that boys were ministering in his church in 1470. BI, Prob. Reg. 4, f. 156. It may be that these were children from Acaster Selby college, which would place its foundation prior to 1470. Note also the will of Robert Beckwith of Stillingfleet (June 19, 1529) which leaves "every scolar a penny," although Beckwith does not specify where his funeral was to be held. Prob. Reg. 9, f. 460; *Test. Ebor.*, 5:273; Leach, *ESR*, ii:298-99, 304-305.

ADWICK LE STREET (W. Riding)   reading school, 1525/6
In 1525/6 Richard Cusworth was buried at Adwick and left every scholar at his burial two pennies. BI, Prob. Reg. 9, f. 337. In 1563-1564 a schoolmaster from Adwick, George Myller, was examined. BI, Chanc. A.B. 8a, f. 86.

ALDBOROUGH (W. Riding)   song school, 1473; grammar school, pre-1548
In 1473 Sir John Marston, chaplain of Our Lady Chantry in Aldborough, asked to be buried in Aldborough parish church where he bequeathed each boy wearing a surplice one penny. YML, D. & C., L 2/4, f. 336; Leach, *ESR*, ii, 297, 308.

ALDINGHAM (Lancs.)   reading school, 1543
John Cowper requested that he be buried in St. Cuthbert's parish church of Aldingham, leaving a penny to every scholar there. James Raine, ed., *Wills and Inventories from the Registry of the Archdeaconry of Richmond*, Surtees Society, no. 26 (Durham, 1853), 50.

ARDEN NUNNERY (N. Riding)   reading school, 1306
See Power, *Med. Eng. Nunneries*, 260-84 for her argument that the presence of young girls and sometimes boys in a nunnery connotes a school. BI, Reg. 7 (Greenfield), f. 86v; Power, *Med. Eng. Nunneries*, 579.

ARTHINGTON NUNNERY (W. Riding)   reading school, 1315-1318
See ARDEN above. BI, Reg. 8 (Greenfield), f. 58v; Reg. 9 (Melton), f. 132; Power, *Med. Eng. Nunneries*, 579.

ASKHAM (Notts.)   reading and song school, 1474
Thomas Smyth of Askham, who was to be buried at Askham, mentions the clerks who know how to sing and other children who know the psalms and *De Profundis*. BI, Prob. Reg. 4, f. 1.

ASLOCKTON (Notts.)   grammar school, circa 1503
John Gough Nichols, ed., *Narratives of the Days of the Reformation*,
Camden Society, orig. ser., no. 77 (London, 1859), 218, 238-40.

BAINTON (E. Riding)   possible reading school, 1375-1429; song school,
1450; reading school, 1509
There is an inscription, slightly mutilated, in Bainton church which
reads:

> Subjacet hic stratus Rogerus Godeale vocitatus
> Ecclesie gratus rector baynton peramatus
> Hic [coluit multos] pueros pietatis amore
> Ordinibus cultos quos fecit laudis honore . . .

Mill Stephenson, "Monumental Brasses in the East Riding," *YAJ* 12
(1893):198; 14 (1898):507 for corrections and additions. Roger Godeale
was instituted May 25, 1375. He died May 1, 1429, still in possession
of the rectorship. Angelo Raine notes that Godeale sent boys from his
village to St. Peter's, but provides no source for this statement. Angelo
Raine, *History of St. Peter's School, York, A.D. 627 to the Present Day*
(London, 1926?), 57-58.

John Kynnyowe of Bainton, in his 1450 will, gave a penny to each
child with a surplice at his funeral. In 1509 Sir William Costayn gave
a penny to each holy water carrier and each scholar. BI, Prob. Reg. 2,
f. 206; 8, f. 25.

BARNSLEY (W. Riding)   grammar or reading school, 1370
E. Hoyle, "The History of Barnsley and District," xxxvi, 12 in the
Barnsley Chronicle, Sept. 10, 1904; Orme, *ESMA*, 295.

BATLEY (W. Riding)   reading and song school, 1493
Richard Cokson, vicar of Batley, left a penny to each scholar having a
surplice at his funeral. BI, Prob. Reg. 5, f. 442. See also D.N.R. Lester,
The History of Batley Grammar School (Batley, 1962).

BAWTRY (W. Riding)   song school, 1504
William Darlington of Bawtry gave a penny to every child with a
rochet. BI, Prob. Reg. 6, f. 111.

BEDALE (N. Riding)   song and grammar school, pre-1541; grammar
school, 1548
Leach states (*VCH, Yorks.*, 1:477) that a chantry grammar school at
Bedale was founded by a scholar of Magdalen College in 1502. The source

is W. D. Macray, *Register of . . . Magdalen College, Oxford*, new ser., 1 (London, 1894), 84, where the reference is to Royston, not Bedale. Robert Wardropp, who was to be buried at Bedale, willed in 1541 "yt the preastes and scolars shall synge dirige and masse for my soule and therfore to be paid as [ ] ben accustomed." Leeds Central Library, Archives Department, Richmond Archdeaconry Will Register 1, 2, 3 & A, f. 204. The chantry commissioners recorded a grammar school at Bedale in 1548. Leach, *ESR*, ii:286, 288-89.

BEEFORD (E. Riding)   possible reading school, 1431-1472
An inscription from the brass of Thomas Tonge, LL.B. and rector of Beeford, notes: ". . . clericos ffovebat, illos gratanter habebat, Pauperes pascebat, honestos et diligebat." Tonge was instituted to the rectory on Nov. 6, 1431; his will is dated July 16, 1472 and was proved at York that year. Mill Stephenson, "Monumental Brasses in the East Riding," *YAJ* 12 (1893):198; *Yorkshire Church Notes 1619-1631 by Roger Dodsworth*, YAS rec. ser., no. 34 (Leeds, 1904), 217. Sir Thomas's reputation, as described on his brass, is confirmed by his will and his bequests of two portable breviaries, two other necessary books, and 20s. to William Thursby to exhibit him in school. BI, Prob. Reg. 4, f. 179.

BEETHAM (Westm.)   grammar or reading school, circa 1542
James Raine, ed., *Wills and Inventories from the Registry of the Archdeaconry of Richmond*, Surtees Society, no. 26 (Durham, 1853), 28.

BELVOIR CASTLE (Notts.-Leics border)   household grammar school, 1412/13; household grammar and other schools, 1539-1544.
Test. Ebor., 1:359. See also E. F. Jacob, ed., *The Register of Henry Chichele, Archbishop of Canterbury, 1414-1443*, Vol. 2 (Oxford, 1938), 22 and BI, Reg. 18 (Bowet), f. 363; Orme, *ESMA*, 322; Historical MSS Commission, *The MSS of the Duke of Rutland Preserved at Belvoir Castle*, Vol. 4 (London, 1905), 296-97, 308, 345. The schoolmaster, Matthew Watson, had his own chamber, while a separate schoolhouse is mentioned in a 1544 inventory. In 1540 three schoolmasters are recorded.

BEMPTON (E. Riding)   song school, 1462
Sir William Bempton of York, chaplain, requested burial at Bempton and left a penny to each small boy of that church who attended his funeral wearing a surplice. BI, Prob. Reg. 2, f. 474.

BEVERCOTES (Notts.)   possible reading school, 1513
William Bevercotes of Retford requested that he be buried in the choir of St. Egidius chapel in Bevercotes; he left one penny for every scholar

at his funeral. It is possible that these scholars would have come from the school at East Retford rather than from Bevercotes. BI, Prob. Reg. 8, f. 114v.

BEVERLEY (E. Riding)   grammar and song school, 12th c.-1548

Nicholas Orme lists only those years in which there is specific mention of either a song or grammar school. Orme, *ESMA*, 296; *EYS*, 1:xxxix-li, 80c-109. There is an additional reference in 1251 to the schoolmaster of Beverley and in 1457 to thirty-three scholars of St. John's, Beverley saying psalms at the funeral of Stephen Wilton, canon of York. Janet E. Burton, ed., *The Cartulary of the Treasurer of York Minster and Related Documents* (York, 1978), 3; BI, Prob. Reg. 2, f. 353v. There is, in fact, little doubt that both song and grammar schools had continuous existences at least from the twelfth century until the time of the Reformation. John Lawson, "Beverley Minster Grammar School in the Middle Ages," *University of Hull Studies In Education* 2 (May 1954):151-67.

BILBOROUGH (Notts.)   grammar school, 1505-1513
VCH, Notts., 2:221-22; Orme, *ESMA*, 296.

BINGLEY (W. Riding)   possible grammar school, 1529-1548

E. E. Dodd, *A History of the Bingley Grammar School, 1529-1929* (Bradford, 1930?), 1-12; Dodd, "Bingley Chantry Endowments," *Bradford Antiquary*, new ser., 8 (Oct. 1954):xxxvii, 91-99; Dodd, "Two Bingley Postscripts," *Bradford Antiquary*, new ser., 8 (Apr. 1958):xxxix, 194-96.

BIRDFORTH (N. Riding)   reading school, 1477

Robert Douse of Birdforth left a penny to each of the scholars at the parish church of Birdforth. BI, Prob. Reg. 5, f. 24.

BISHOPBURTON (E. Riding)   reading and song school, 1438

John Bee of Bishopburton, who asked to be buried in All Saints of Bishopburton, left 6d. to each child in the church who was either singing or reading. BI, Prob. Reg. 3, f. 562v.

BLYTH (Notts. and W. Riding)   petty school, 1481; possible pre-Reformation reading or grammar school

Robert Wilson of Blyth, to be buried at Blyth, left a penny to each child "qui scit dicere hunc psalmum de profundis." BI, Prob. Reg. 5, f. 64. See Samuel Corner, "Education in the Middle Ages," *Transactions of the Thoroton Society* 18 (1914), 78 for reference to an endowed pre-Reformation school. He provides no source for his statement.

BOLTON UPON DEARNE (W. Riding)   grammar school, 1548
Leach, *ESR*, ii:308.

BOLTON PERCY (W. Riding)   petty school, 1505
Thomas Beswyght, who desired to be buried in All Hallows parish church of Bolton Percy, bequeathed one penny to every child that could say *De Profundis*. BI, Prob. Reg. 6, f. 201.

BOROUGHBRIDGE (W. Riding)   possible grammar school, 1548
Leach, *ESR*, ii:307. W. Tate and P. J. Wallis suggest that the continuation warrant for a grammar school in Boroughbridge chapel (Aldborough parish) refers to the school at Aldborough and "that the reference is to one school, not, as appears on the surface, two." "A Register of Old Yorkshire Grammar Schools," *The University of Leeds Institute of Education, Researches and Studies*, no. 13 (1956), 73, 101. However, a continuation warrant for the Aldborough school follows, and it is possible, although it seems unlikely, that there were two grammar schools within the parish. Two separate grammarmasters are named.

BRADFORD (W. Riding)   grammar school, 1548
VCH, Yorks., 1:471-72.

BRANDSBY (N. Riding)   reading and song school, 1512; reading school, 1528
In 1512 Thomas Otterburne, yeoman of Brandsby, left one penny to "every scoler that beres sorples or rochet." BI, Prob. Reg. 8, f. 103v. In 1528 Anne Constable of Brandsby left a penny to every scholar. BI, Prob. Reg. 9, f. 402v.

BRAYTON (GATEFORD) (W. Riding)   grammar school, 1548
Leach, *ESR*, ii:300.

BRETTANBY (N. Riding)   possible reading school, 1545
The will of Matthew Wytham of Brettanby leaves 1d. to every scholar at his funeral. However, he was to be buried where it should please God and not necessarily at Brettanby. James Raine, ed., *Wills and Inventories from the Registry of the Archdeaconry of Richmond*, Surtees Society, no. 26 (Durham, 1853), 57.

BROTTON (N. Riding)   song school, 1501
John Jonson of Brotton, priest, bequeathed two pennies to each child having a surplice. BI, Prob. Reg. 6, f. 19.

BRIDLINGTON PRIORY (E. Riding)   possible reading or grammar school, circa 1130; song and grammar school, circa 1450; possible reading or grammar school, 1530s

Gilbert de Gant, earl of Lincoln and son of the founder of Bridlington Priory, was raised at the priory in the 1120s and 1130s. *Early Yorkshire Charters*, vol. 2, ed. W. Farrer (Edinburgh, 1915), 429-30. J. S. Purvis prints a 1447 (?) charter with various grants and exemptions from Henry VI in which six (sic) boy choristers are mentioned. *Bridlington Charters, Court Rolls and Papers, XVI-XIX Century* (London, 1926), 9. In 1450 the recent privileges of the Bridlington canons were declared unaffected by the Parliamentary Act of Resumption on condition that they continue to keep twelve choristers with a master to teach them grammar and song. *VCH, East Riding*, 2:78; *Rot. Parl.*, 5:188 (1450). See also John Lawson, *The Endowed Grammar Schools of East Yorkshire*, East Yorkshire Local History Society, no. 14 (York, 1962), 7-8. There may have been a school at Bridlington, perhaps at the priory, which served the parish before the dissolution. In 34 Elizabeth I an anonymous petitioner requested the Lord Chancellor to provide the parish with a more adequate stipend for the maintenance of "a Compotent minister or supplie of a Scholmaster unto wch nothinge hath byn applied since the suppression." Purvis, *Bridlington Charters*, 34.

BROUGHTON (Lancs.)   grammar school, 1527-1548
Francis Gastrell, *Notitia Cestriensis*, ed. J. Raine, Chetham Society, orig. ser., no. 22 (Manchester, 1850), 468.

BUBWITH (E. Riding)   reading school, 1521/2
The will of Agnes Wright, who asked to be buried at Bubwith, left a penny to every scholar at her burial. BI, Prob. Reg. 9, f. 224.

BULMER (N. Riding)   possible reading school, circa 1503
In 1556 Sir Robert Scalinge, priest, vicar of Langtoft, aged seventy-two, deposed that he "was borne in Bulmer and contynued ther till he was maid prest and a yere after which is by the space of XXV yeres . . . aboutes liii yeres sence [1503] as he nowe remembreth he did use sometymes to say mattyns with Parson Jakson then Parson of Bulmer." J. S. Purvis, ed., *Select XVIth Century Causes in Tithe*, YAS rec. ser., no. 114 (Leeds, 1949), 93. We do not know whether Scalinge was tutored on his own or was a member of a parish school, but it is clear that some education was available at Bulmer parish at the opening of the sixteenth century.

BURNSALL (W. Riding)   reading school, 1535
In his will Henry Young of Burnsall left a penny for every scholar at his funeral. BI, Prob. Reg. 11, f. 142.

BURTON AGNES (E. Riding)   reading school, 1497; song school, 1519; possible grammar or reading school, 1540

In his will of 1497 Robert Dynse, chaplain of Burton Agnes, left one or two pennies to the rest of the children at his funeral who were literate. BI, Prob. Reg. 6, f. 37. For the song school, see Prob. Reg. 9, f. 84. In 1540 a Burton Agnes man left money for a boy "to find him at the school." BI, Prob. Reg. 11, f. 462. Earlier, in 1481, a Master Walter Barr, M.A., from Burton Agnes, was ordained acolyte. His presence could suggest a grammar school there. BI, Reg. 23 (Rotherham), f. 380.

BUTTERCRAMBE (N. Riding)   reading and song school, 1525
In 1525 William Mason left a penny to every scholar that sang in the choir. BI, Prob. Reg. 9, f. 311v.

CATTON (E. Riding)   song school, 1505
Thomas Floure of Stamfordbridge, yeoman, who was to be buried at All Hallows, Catton, provided one penny "to every chylde that can syng." BI, Prob. Reg. 6, f. 207.

CATTON (N. Riding)   grammar school, 1547/8
An inventory for 1547/8 notes that "Goods were also sold at Catton for the building of a school." William Page, ed., *Inventories of Church Goods for the Counties of Yorkshire, Durham, and Northumberland*, Surtees Society, no. 97 (Durham, 1897), xi.

CAWOOD (W. Riding)   reading and song school, 1458
John Holme of Cawood, weber, left "cuilibet clerico 2d. Et omnibus aliis pueris cantant' cuilibet 1d." BI, Prob. Reg. 2, f. 398.

CAWTHORNE (W. Riding)   grammar school, 1535?-1548
In 1548 a grammar school there was taught by Richard Wigfall, the chantry priest in the Boswell chantry. Leach, *ESR*, ii:308-309. Wigfall had been the chantry priest since at least 1535. *Valor Ecclesiasticus* (1825), 5:56. There is no evidence that the school was maintained from the first foundation of the chantry, as Leach supposed. *VCH Yorks.*, 1:477.

CHURCH FENTON (W. Riding)   reading school, 1447
Sir Robert Wryght, vicar of Church Fenton, gave 2d. to each little clerk at his funeral. YML, D.&C., L2/4, f. 262.

COCKERMOUTH (Cumberland)   grammar or reading school, second half of 13th c.; grammar school, 1530-1548
The Register of the Priory of St. Bees, ed. James Wilson, Surtees Society, no. 126 (Durham, 1915), 560-61; Orme, *ESMA*, 300; Leach, *ESR*, ii:44. See also Barbara English, *The Lords of Holderness, 1086-1260* (Oxford, 1979), 93-94 for references to clerks who may have been ed-

ucated at Cockermouth. The 1530 reference comes from the will of Henry Chaloner, who requested to be buried at Cockermouth and bequeathed [one] penny to every scholar present at his funeral. Leeds Central Library, Archives Department, Richmond Archdeaconry Will Register 1, 2, 3 & A, f. 87. Since the school had a history and the chantry certificate labels it grammar, these were probably grammar scholars at the funeral.

COTTINGHAM (E. Riding)   possible reading or grammar school, circa 1310; reading school, 1501/2; song school, 1528

About 1310 John Boynton, son of Sir Robert Boynton, knight, who had already received his first clerical tonsure, was described as a young gentleman in the household of John Bygot, rector of Cottingham. W. Brown and A. H. Thompson, eds., *The Register of William Greenfield Lord Archbishop of York 1306-1315*, Vol. 3, Surtees Society, no. 151 (Durham, 1936), l, 208. He was undoubtedly receiving an education there, but there is no evidence that this was a school. In 1501/2 William Stakhouse of Cottingham, yeoman, left 1d. to every scholar who was present on the day of his burial. BI, Prob. Reg. 6, f. 33. In 1528 Richard Tonne, chaplain, left a penny to every child in the choir. BI, Prob. Reg. 9, f. 470v.

COXWOLD (N. Riding)   song school, 1508

John Bell of Ulneston, who requested to be buried in Coxwold parish church, left one penny "to each boy singing." BI, Prob. Reg. 7, f. 51.

CROFT (N. Riding)   reading school, 1532, 1536

William Clarnaux of Maulevere in 1532 and Robert Patyson of Jolbye in 1536, both being buried in Croft parish church, left a penny to every scholar at the funeral. Leeds Central Library, Archives Department, Richmond Archdeaconry Will Register 1, 2, 3 & A, ff. 148, 173.

CROFTON (W. Riding)   grammar school, 1372

John of Gaunt's Register, 1371-1375, Vol. 1, ed. S. Armitage-Smith, Camden Society, 3rd ser., 20 (London, 1911), 111; Orme, *ESMA*, 300.

CROMWELL (Notts.)   reading school, 1465

Robert Gawsell, rector of St. Egidius parish church, Cromwell, left one penny to "aliis parvis clericis." BI, Prob. Reg. 4, f. 259.

DALTON, SOUTH (E. Riding)   grammar school, 1304-1306

In 1304 and 1306 the grammarmaster of Beverley Minster complained of the activities of Robert of Dalton, *clericus* (possibly Robert de Offinton, the rector of Dalton), who kept a school in South Dalton. The conclusion that this was a grammar school rests upon the supposition that the grammarmaster of Beverley would not have been given any competition (and thus cause to complain) if the school had taught either song or reading. That the teacher may have been the rector also argues for a grammar school. A. F. Leach, ed., *Memorials of Beverley Minster: The Chapter Act Book*, Vol. 1, Surtees Society, no. 98 (Durham, 1898), 42-43, 114, 169; *EYS*, 1:80m-81, 92; Orme, *ESMA*, 316; W. Brown, ed., *The Register of Henry of Newark, Lord Archbishop of York, 1296-1299*, Surtees Society, no. 128 (Durham, 1916), 324.

DALTON-IN-FURNESS (Lancs.) grammar school, 1533-1536

William Rede, a local priest, was dismissed from keeping the school at Dalton in 1536 for preaching against the authority of the Pope and teaching from Erasmus's *Paraphrases*. The use of the *Paraphrases* suggests a curriculum of Latin grammar. Christopher Haigh, *The Last Days of the Lancashire Monasteries and the Pilgrimage of Grace*, Chetham Society, 3rd ser., 17 (Manchester, 1969), 52.

DARFIELD (W. Riding) reading school, 1427

William Stevyn, the vicar *medietatis* of Darfield, bequeathed "cuilibet clerico aquebanilo 2d. et ceteris clericulis cuilibet 1d." BI, Prob. Reg. 2, f. 516v.

DONCASTER (W. Riding) grammar school, 1351; grammar or reading school, 1436-1468?, 1524?, 1528?

EYS, 1:22; Orme, *ESMA*, 301. In 1436 John Thomson of Dewsbury (near Doncaster), ironmaker, left 12d. and 4d. to William Herryson for his son, whom Herryson was teaching. This may have been William Herryson, chantry chaplain of St. Katherine's chantry within St. George's, whose will is dated 1468. On July 19, 1447 Sir William Stokbrig, chaplain of Doncaster, wrote his will asking that he be buried in St. George's and that each small clerk attending his funeral receive a penny. BI, Prob. Reg. 2, f. 169; 3, f. 481; 4, f. 63. In 1524 John Jacson of Bentley, living "at brig end of Doncastre" bequeathed 40s. a year to his nephew "to fynd hym at the scole . . . during XVth yeres," and in 1528 Simon Robinson, vicar of Doncaster, left 10s. to Roger Robynson "to fynd him to the scole and it to be paid as he haith neede upon it" and to Peter Mydleton "the hoole bible, if he will continue the scole and do well, or els not." BI, Prob. Reg. 9, f. 335; *Test. Ebor.*, 5:176-77; BI, Reg. 27 (Wolsey), f. 163. It is likely that they are referring to a school at Doncaster of which Mydleton might possibly be the master. See also *A Short History of the Doncaster Grammar School 1350-1950* (Doncaster, 1950).

DUFFIELD, SOUTH (E. Riding)   reading school, 1540

BI, original will of James Blanschard, vicar of South Duffield; also Reg. 29 (Holgate/Heath), f. 74. Vicar Blanschard left "to . . . evere one of my scholers that lernit w^t me 6d. Also to Thomas Blanchard my brother son the scoler 40s."

DUNHAM (Notts.)   grammar school, pre-1351
   VCH, Notts., 2:179; Orme, *ESMA*, 301.

EASINGTON (E. Riding)   reading school, 1529?, 1538

The will of John Swift of Easington, dated April 28, 1529, requests that "the rest of my rayment, I will that my uncle Prior (of the Charterhouse of Hull) dispose amonges oure poore scholars as he thinks most expedient for the health of my sall." BI, Prob. Reg. 9, f. 440; *Test. Ebor.*, 5:272. The testator may have been referring to scholars at the Charterhouse, Hull, although we have no additional information which would lead one to conclude that the Charterhouse had a school and specific reasons for supposing it did not. (See HULL below.) John Lawson suggests that these were scholars from Hull's town school who may have been receiving charity from the Charterhouse. Lawson, *A Town Grammar School Through Six Centuries* (Oxford, 1963), 38-39. There was, however, a school at Easington in 1538. The will of Margarie Lutton of Easington asks that she be buried in All Hallows, Easington and that a penny be left to every scholar at her funeral. BI, Prob. Reg. 11, f. 367; *Test. Ebor.*, 6:79.

EAST BRIDGFORD (Notts.)   possible reading school, 1514

Robert Wryght of East Bridgford, buried there, left 12d. to William Thomson, "scholastico," 8d. to John Cheke, "scholastico," and a similar amount to Adam Jonson, "scholastico." BI, Prob. Reg. 9, f. 12. It is possible that these were scholars from Nottingham, eight miles away.

EAST RETFORD (Notts.)   grammar school, 1318, 1393; reading and song school, 1431; song school, 1521; grammar school, 1518, 1538-1548

While a 1318 quitclaim refers only to Master Henry, the schoolmaster, a 1393 writ specifies that this was a grammar school. A. D. Grounds, *A History of King Edward VI Grammar School, Retford* (Worksop, 1970). Grounds states that there is no single mention of the school in the fifteenth century. However, the will of Agnes, wife of John Sherwynde of East Retford, written in 1431, left one penny to every small clerk having a surplice within the chancel of St. Smithin's. BI, Prob. Reg. 2, f. 608v. The grammar school may have degenerated into a reading school, but the educational facilities did not disappear altogether. The monies provided in 1518 by Master Thomas Gunthorpe, parson of Babworth, to build a schoolhouse (the school to be held in the parlor and garden) and the efforts made to endow the schoolmaster in the 1540s suggest that grammar was taught in the sixteenth-century school, although the chantry certificates, along with other sixteenth-century documents, refer only to the bringing up of children in godly learning. Grounds suggests that Sir Charles Weste, schoolmaster in 1548, was Charles West, B.A. from Cambridge in 1528. If the identification is correct, it would argue for a grammar school. Leach, *ESR*, ii:160-61, 164-66; Grounds, *History*, 21. For the song school in 1521, see BI, Prob. Reg. 9, f. 205v.

ECCLESFIELD (W. Riding)   probable reading or grammar school, 1478, 1510, 1529-1548

Thomas Parker of Whitley, in his will dated August 20, 1510, asked to be buried within the parish church of Ecclesfield and left "to the vicar . . . 5d., to the clerc for v mynnyngs, 2d., the residue of the mese i.e. 2s. 4d. my childer 1d. and the residue to poore folkes having most nede." Considering the formula used throughout the wills, this reference to children occurs where the testator often left a penny or two to the scholars or choristers of the parish. The testator would not be speaking of his own children. If he had been speaking of his godchildren this would have been specified. It is more likely that he was either the choir- or schoolmaster and was speaking of the children he taught. There is supporting evidence for a reading or grammar school. In 1478 Master Thomas Swyft, the vicar of Ecclesfield, left 40s. for the making of a book for the children. BI, Prob. Reg. 5, ff. 128v-29. And Edward Hatfield, vicar of Ecclesfield from at least 1534-1535 until 1544, donated a chained library to the church. *Fasti Parochiales*, Vol. 1, ed. A. H. Thompson and Charles T. Clay, YAS rec. ser., no. 85 (Leeds, 1933), 105.

Wallis and Tate identify a grammar school at Ecclesfield in 1529 and base their assumption upon the fact that Richard Cowper, probably B.A. Cambridge, received payments as chantry priest of the stipendiary service of Our Lady from 1529 and was "curatus et ludimagister" in 1564. Wallis and Tate, "A Register of Old Yorkshire Grammar Schools," *The University of Leeds Institute of Education, Researches and Studies*, no. 13 (1956), 78, 102 n 97; BI, Chanc. AB 8a, f. 85v. There is no proof that he was teaching a school in 1529, but together with the evidence just cited, it does not appear improbable.

EDWINSTOWE (Notts.)   possible reading school, 15th c.

In the fifteenth century one John Waterall gave a house to the clerk of the parish of Edwinstowe, rent free, to teach children in. Cornelius Brown, *A History of Newark-upon-Trent*, 2 vols. (Newark, 1904-1907), 2:178. No source is cited for this statement.

ESCRICK (E. Riding)   reading school, 1474, 1501
In 1474 Thomas Jakeson of Escrick, yeoman, requested to be buried in St. Helen's church of Escrick and left 1d. to each "clericulo" attending his funeral. In the will of Geoffrey Frank, esquire, dated July 20, 1501, the testator asked to be buried in the parish church of St. Helen's in Escrick and left a bequest to the little scholars according to the discretion of his executors. BI, Prob. Reg. 4, f. 5v; 6, f. 5v.

ESHOLT NUNNERY (W. Riding)   reading school, 1315, 1318, 1537
See ARDEN above. BI, Reg. 8 (Greenfield), f. 89; Reg. 9 (Melton), f. 231v; *YAJ* 9 (1888):321n; Power, *Med. Eng. Nunneries*, 579.

ESTRONWICK (E. Riding)   reading school, 1391
John Frankys of Hedon left four pennies to each child saying his psalter in Estronwick parish church. BI, Reg. 14 (Arundel), ff. 29v-30.

EVERINGHAM (E. Riding)   reading and song school, 1508
In the will of John Barde of Everingham, the testator left 1d. to each scholar with a surplice. BI, Prob. Reg. 8, f. 2.

FAIRBURN (W. Riding)   grammar or reading school, 1348
PRO, JUST 2/213, m. 1; *Select Cases from the Coroners' Rolls, 1265-1413*, ed. C. Gross, Selden Society, no. 9 (London, 1896), 111; Orme, *ESMA*, 303.

FLAWFORTH (Notts.)   petty school, 1515
Sir William Jowkyn, vicar of Rodington, asked to be buried in the chapel of Flawforth and left two pennies to every child that could say *De profundis*. BI, Reg. 27 (Wolsey), f. 141; *Test. Ebor.*, 5:71.

FLINTHAM (Notts.)   reading school, 1480
In 1480 Henry Huse of Flintham desired to be buried within St. Augustine's parish church of Flintham and bequeathed 2d. to every child reading the lesson and 1d. to every literate child. BI, Prob. Reg. 5, f. 89.

FOSTON (N. Riding)   reading school, 1444
The will of John Brynsall, vicar of Foston, left one penny to the little clerks at his funeral. BI, Prob. Reg. 2, f. 83.

FOSTON-ON-THE-WOLDS (E. Riding)   song school, 1475

The will of Sir Thomas Crosse, vicar of St. Andrews, Foston, left 2d. to each child singing at his funeral and 1d. to each child there who was not singing. BI, Prob. Reg. 4, f. 90.

FOUNTAINS ABBEY (Lancs.)   possible song school, 15th c.

"Fragment from Fountains Abbey," British Library, Add MS 40011B; described by Percy M. Young, *A History of British Music* (New York, 1967), 61.

FRYSTON (W. Riding)   reading school, 1489, 1532; song school, 1489

In the will of Robert Nelson of Wheldale, dated 1489, the testator requested to be buried in the parish church of Fryston and left one penny to each scholar with a surplice. BI, Prob. Reg. 5, f. 366. The will of John Meryng of Fryston is dated Jan. 1, 1532. He asked to be buried in Water Fryston church and left "to every other prest 4d, and every clarke 1d. unto Sir John Robinson, prest, to teach my children John, Robert and Nicholas 10s." John Robinson witnessed the will. BI, Prob. Reg. 11, f. 48; *Test. Ebor*, 6:34.

FURNESS ABBEY (Lancs.)   grammar and reading school, circa 1450-1536

A witness in an Exchequer suit under Elizabeth I in 1582 said that at Furness Abbey, where the abbot ruled almost a principality of his own, some children of the tenants, of whom he was one, had been educated in the abbey. Thomas West, *The Antiquities of Furness*, new ed. (Ulverston, 1805), 195. One of the children educated in the abbey's school was Christopher Urswick (1448-1522), chaplain to Margaret Beaufort and Henry VIII, whose parents were lay brother and sister of the abbey and tenants of the monastery. Urswick went on to Cambridge, as did Edwin Sandys, archbishop of York, who was born of humble parents at Hawkeshead, in Furness Fells, and was educated at Furness Abbey in the beginning of the sixteenth century. T. A. Urwick, *Records of the Family of Urswyk, Urswick, or Urwick*, ed. W. Urwick (St. Albans, 1893), 83; W. K. Jordan, *The Social Institutions of Lancashire, 1480-1660*, Chetham Society, 3rd ser., 11 (Manchester, 1962), 48. In 1536 the monks ignored the injunctions of Legh and Layton to keep a schoolmaster there. The lack of a schoolmaster must have been recent since, in 1535, Furness still supported its own scholar at Oxford. Christopher Haigh, *The Last Days of the Lancashire Monasteries and the Pilgrimage of Grace*, Chetham Society, 3rd ser., 17 (Manchester, 1969), 57.

The fact that its scholars went directly from the abbey's school to the

University argues that the school was a grammar school, although a reading education must also have been available.

GANTON (E. Riding)   reading and song school, 1510
Henry Stevynson of Potter Brompton desired to be buried in St. Nicholas parish church of Ganton and left one penny to each scholar wearing a surplice. BI, Prob. Reg. 8, f. 39.

GARFORTH (W. Riding)   reading school, 1519
Robert Hymesworth, buried at Garforth, left one penny to each scholar at his funeral. BI, Prob. Reg. 9, f. 82.

GARGRAVE-IN-CRAVEN (W. Riding)   reading school, 1548
The chantry certificate for 1548 notes "One preist, founde by the parochiners there, as well to teache theyre children as to assist the vicar in serving the cure." Leach, ESR, ii:302. There are a number of reasons for thinking this was only a reading school. In addition to not specifying a grammar school and speaking of children rather than youths, the chantry certificate describes the chantry priest, Nicholas Cleveland, as indifferently learned. Nor is the school mentioned among the continuation warrants for grammar schools.

GIGGLESWICK (W. Riding)   grammar school, 1499?-1548; reading school, 1512-1548; reading school, 1545-1548
Although a 1507 building lease is the first knowledge we have of the grammar school, Leach argues, plausibly, that the school was conducted as early as 1499. VCH, Yorks., 1:460. The school building was erected in 1512. Leach provides the inscription from it: "For priests and little clerks this house was made in the year 1512," implying perhaps that several priests taught there. Gentleman's Magazine for 1786 has a description of the original building, which was low, small, and irregular, with two stages, one for the elementary school and another for the advanced students. By 1516 it was a boarding school. Edward A. Bell, A History of Giggleswick School from Its Foundation: 1499-1912 (Leeds, 1912), 1-19. EYS, 2:232-40; Orme, ESMA, 303.
In 1545 two men bequeathed £24 13s. 4d. for the maintenance of a schoolmaster. Leach, ESR, ii:296, 302-303, 306; PRO, E 301, 103 (74), f. 3v.

GILLING IN RYDALL (N. Riding)   reading and song school, 1516
The 1516 will of Robert Druer of Dalton, gentleman, to be buried at Gilling, left "every scoller havyng a rochett id. and every poor scoller

havyng no Rotchitt to have after the discrecion of myn executores." BI, Prob. Reg. 9, f. 50.

GOOSNARGH (Lancs.)   reading and song school, 1541

Roger Barnys, who was to be buried at Goosnargh, left a penny to every scholar that sang and one-half penny to the other scholars. Leeds Central Library, Archives Department, Richmond Archdeaconry Will Register, 1, 2, 3 & A, f. 201.

GRANBY (Notts.)   reading school, 1482

Sir John Shipman, vicar of Granby, left "cuilibet alio clerico adulto 3d. Item ceteris minoribus 2d. Item omnibus aliis 1d." Although this is somewhat obscure, it implies that there were both men and boy clerks at his funeral. BI, Prob. Reg. 5, f. 25.

GRIMSTON, NORTH (E. Riding)   reading school, 1513, 1523

In the will of Adam Hall, dated 6 Ides of June, 1513, the testator wished to be buried in St. Nicholas parish church and to leave 1d. to each scholar there. Thomas Hall of North Grimston, probably a relative of Adam Hall, left 1d. to "ever scolar" on May 31, 1523. YML, D. & C., L 2/5a ff. 105, 136.

GUISBOROUGH (N. Riding)   reading and song school, 1426, 1452, 1461?

The will of John Coke of Guisborough in Cleveland, butcher, who was to be buried in St. Nicholas church of Guisborough, provided for 2d. apiece to the ten boys singing at the funeral (Sept. 18, 1452). The will of John How of Guisborough, butcher, is also dated in 1452. He asked to be buried in St. Nicholas church of Guisborough in Cleveland and left 2s. 6d. to thirty boys. The will of Robert Fyschman of Guisborough, dated Sept. 26, 1426, leaves "cuilibet puero cantanti et ministranti circa corpus meum 4d." at St. Nicholas. The will of Agnes Bywell of Guisborough in Cleveland, widow, dated July 13, 1461, mentions three chaplains, sixteen clerks, and a parish clerk. BI, Prob. Reg. 2, ff. 258, 269v, 497; 4, f. 166.

GUISBOROUGH PRIORY (N. Riding)   grammar school, 1266-1268, 1280

C. R. Cheney, "Letters of William Wickwane, Chancellor of York, 1266-1268," *EHR* 47 (1932):629, 633; Orme, *ESMA*, 248, 304; W. Brown and A. H. Thompson, eds., *Cartularium Prioratus de Gyseburne*, Vol. 2, Surtees Society, no. 89 (Durham, 1894), 360-62. This was a boarding school and therefore, most likely, a grammar school. There is no later mention of a school at the priory and it may have been discontinued after the priory church was destroyed by fire in 1289.

GUISELEY (W. Riding)   song school, 1496
Richard Browne, rector of Guiseley, bequeathed two pennies to each small boy in a surplice at his funeral. BI, Prob. Reg. 5, f. 482.

HALIFAX (W. Riding)   projected grammar school, 1497; grammar school, 1516-1517
M. W. Garside, "Halifax Schools prior to 1700 A.D." in *Papers, Reports, etc. Read before the Halifax Antiquarian Society* (Halifax, 1924), 186-88.

HALSHAM (E. Riding)   reading or grammar school, pre-1472
In 1472 Sir John Constable of Halsham, knight, left 6 marks to Stephen Newton, chaplain, to celebrate masses in the parish church of Halsham. The payment was for debts owed to Newton for educating Constable's children. BI, Prob. Reg. 4, f. 185(2).

HAMPOLE NUNNERY (W. Riding)   reading school, 1313-1314
See ARDEN above. BI, Reg. 8 (Greenfield), ff. 30, 58, 730; Reg. 9 (Melton), f. 231; Power, *Med. Eng. Nunneries*, 579.

HAMPSTHWAIT (W. Riding)   reading school, 1527
The will of Thomas Wickley states that he wishes to be buried in Hampsthwait parish church and devises 1d. to "evrie scolar." *Wills and Administrations from Knaresborough Court Rolls*, Vol. 1, ed. F. Collins, Surtees Society, no. 104 (Durham, 1902), 20-21.

HAREWOOD (W. Riding)   reading or grammar school, circa 1505; possible reading and song school, 1532
Richard Robynson, yeoman aged sixty and over, testified in 1554/5 that "fiftie yeres since he lerned at scole at Harwode with one Sir Robert Huddleston wher Sir William Gascoigne also lerned." J. S. Purvis, ed., *Select XVIth Century Causes in Tithe*, YAS rec. ser., no. 114 (Leeds, 1949), 68. Orme, *ESMA*, 304. In 1532 Richard Ryley of Harewood left monies to the scholars helping to sing mass at his funeral. However, he did not expect to be buried at Harewood but rather at whatever parish God was pleased to choose. BI, Prob. Reg. 9, f. 82.

HARSLEY (N. Riding)   reading school, 1527
In 1527 William Sanderson of Harlesay left two pennies to every parish clerk and one penny to the other scholars. BI, Prob. Reg. 9, f. 371.

HAWKSHEAD (Lancs.)   reading school, circa 1536
John Henshaw, priest, suspected of Protestant heresy in 1533 at Dalton, was schoolmaster at Hawkshead by 1536 where he was teaching that images

were of no value. Christopher Haigh, *Reformation and Resistance in Tudor Lancashire* (Cambridge, 1975), 42, 83. PRO, SP 1/75, f. 63; PL 25/15, m. 19v; BI, Reg. 28 (Lee), ff. 195, 196v.

HEDON (E. Riding)   grammar school, 1271-1465; reading school, 1391

N. Denholm-Young, "The Yorkshire Estates of Isabella de Fortibus," *YAJ* 31 (1934):392; J. Robert Boyle, *Early History of the Town and Port of Hedon in the East Riding of York* (Hull, 1895), cxxiv, clxxxv, cxc, 92, 169-71; *Test. Ebor.*, 2:270. In 1271 Stephen, a son of the late William de Fortibus, Earl of Aumale, was at the grammar school. In subsequent references several schoolmasters are mentioned, one (in 1335) appointed by Edward III in letters patent. A building and messuage given to the schoolmaster and his clerks is described in the Hedon church records, and in 1465 John Elwyn of Hedon devised his grammar books "pro doctrina et reformacione puerorum ibidem addiscentium in scola grammaticali ibidem." In 1391, John Frankys of Hedon left 4d. to each child saying his psalter. BI, Reg. 14 (Arundel), ff. 29v-30. Orme, *ESMA*, 305.

HELMSLEY (N. Riding)   grammar or reading school, 13th c.; reading and song school, 1471

Historical Manuscripts Commission, *The MSS of the Duke of Rutland*, Vol. 4 (London, 1905), 91; Orme, *ESMA*, 305. In 1471 John Dawy, chaplain of Harom, asked to be buried in All Saints, Helmsley, and left a penny to each surpliced "clericulo" who participated in the mass. BI, Prob. Reg. 4, f. 163.

HELPERBY (N. Riding)   reading and song school, 1458-1459

On Apr. 17, 1458 Johanna Atkynson, a widow of Helperby, left 1d. to each child who sang at her funeral. The will of Thomas Dowse of Helperby, dated Nov. 9, 1459, left 4d. to the parish clerk and 1d. to the other young literates. YML, D. & C., L 2/4, ff. 287, 292.

HEMINGBROUGH (E. Riding)   school, probably grammar, 1397

Liber Presentationum et Literarum Ecclesie Dunelmensis, British Library, MS Cotton Faustina A VI, f. 71v. In 1397 the prior of Durham appointed John, son of Walter of Hemingbrough, priest and B.A., to the school of Hemingbrough. Since the school is not labelled grammar, and since similar appointments to Howden and Northallerton do specify the schools, it cannot be certain that this was a grammar school. John's B.A. would suggest that it was. Orme, *ESMA*, 305.

HEMSWORTH (W. Riding)   reading school, 1435, 1541, 1548; grammar school, 1548

In 1435 Sir Adam Erghom of Hemsworth left a penny to each small clerk present at his funeral. Over a century later, when Lady Elizabeth Savile of Tankersley wrote her will, it was witnessed by Edmunde Ashton, "scole-maister of Hemesworth." BI, Prob. Reg. 3, f. 423; 11, f. 591; *Test. Ebor.*, 6:139. For Archbishop Holgate's 1548 foundation, see *VCH, Yorks.*, 1:474 and Nicholas Carlisle, *A Concise Description of the Endowed Grammar Schools in England and Wales*, 2 vols. (London, 1818), 2:821-22.

HINDERSKELFE (N. Riding)   reading school, 1525
Richard Willoughby, a priest attached to the household of Lord Greystock, left 2d. to the scholars attending his funeral. There was probably a household school, although it is possible that these were parish scholars. BI, Reg. 27 (Wolsey), f. 158; *Test. Ebor.*, 6:139.

HOLME-UPON-SPALDING-MOOR (E. Riding)   reading school, 1407
Sir John Wryght, rector of Holme, left 4d. to "cuilibet clericulo de mea parochia." BI, Prob. Reg. 3, f. 285.

HORNBY (N. Riding)   grammar school, 1439, 1489, 1515; song school, 1515
Sir John Orre, vicar of Hornby within Richmond liberty, left a large breviary to the choir of the church with the stipulation that the boys or clerks learning and learned (*addiscentes et erudientes*) in the church would not injure or soil it (Mar. 24, 1439). On Aug. 7, 1489 Robert Pynkney gave 1d. "to every chyld lernyd . . . in ye parish church of Hornby." In 1515 Thomas Howeden of Hornby, chaplain, gave 1d. to every scholar [ ] knowing how to sing and one-half penny to all other scholars present. Howeden also left a Papias (a grammar text) to one Thomas Caldbek and the rest of his grammar books plus his music books to his relatives attending school. Howeden was probably the schoolmaster (both song and grammar) at Hornby. YML, D. & C., L 2/4, ff. 251, 373; L 2/5a, f. 128.

HORNBY (Lancs.)   grammar school, 1524?-1548
PRO, PCC, Prob. 11/21 Bodfelde, 25; printed in Surtees Society, no. 116, 113. BI, Reg. 5a Sede vacante, f. 644v; Leach, *ESR*, ii:118-19. The 1523 will of Edward Stanley, Lord Monteagle, provided for the establishment of a free grammar school at Hornby. After his death in 1524 his executors did not carry out the provisions, but his heir was supporting a grammarmaster there "of his own benevolent good will and plesure" in 1548. See also W. K. Jordan, *The Social Institutions of Lancashire, 1480-1660*, Chetham Society, 3rd ser., 11 (Manchester, 1962), 37-38; Orme, *ESMA*, 306.

HOVINGHAM (N. Riding) possible grammar or reading school, circa 1310; reading school, 1538

A school is mentioned here by Sir George R. Sitwell, *The Hurts of Haldworth* (Oxford, 1930), xxii and by Nicholas Orme, *ESMA*, 306. The reference is to *Calendar of Inquisitions Post Mortem*, vol. 5 (1908), 192, where I can find no mention of a school. In 1538 Lancelot Stapilton of Wath asked to be buried at Hovingham, requesting "all scolers to have a penny." BI., Prob. Reg. 11, f. 350; *Test. Ebor.*, 6:84.

HOWDEN (E. Riding) grammar or reading school, 1378/9; grammar, reading, and song schools, pre-1393-1456; 1456-1465?; another reading school, 1397-1401; grammar school, 1548

Charles Cox, "Poll Tax Returns of the East Riding with Some Account of the Peasant Revolt of 1381," *Transactions of the East Riding Antiquarian Society*, 15 (1909):26; *EYS*, 2:84-87; *VCH, Yorks.*, 1:439-40; Orme, *ESMA*, 306. For John Lowyk's privilege of teaching an additional reading school for twelve (1397) and then eighteen children (1401), see British Library, MS. Cotton Faustina A VI, ff. 97v, 100v. C. J. Kitching, "The Chantries of the East Riding of Yorkshire at the Dissolution in 1548," *YAJ* 44 (1972):182.

HULL (E. Riding) school (probably grammar) 1347; grammar and reading school, 1431-1548; song school, 1479-1548

The first evidences for the school occur in deeds from the town records which refer to School Street and School Lane in 1347. *VCH, Yorkshire, East Riding*, 1:348. From 1431 to 1487 entries in the Chamberlains' Accounts and the town Bench Books show that the town appointed the grammarmaster, regulated his fees and at times supplied his house, clothing, and salary. When the grammarmaster was given a monopoly in 1454 (which suggests existing competing schools), an exception was made for the little ones learning their alphabets and graces and the elements of English spelling and reading. Corporation of Hull, Bench Book IIIa, f. 38. John Lawson, *A Town Grammar School Through Six Centuries* (Oxford, 1963), 17. Leland described the school's location in his *Itinerary*, 1:49. See also Leach, *ESR*, ii:290-1; Orme, *ESMA*, 306.

There is an unlikely possibility that the Charterhouse of Hull also had a school. The will of John Swift of Easington, written at Hull in 1529, requests his uncle, the prior of the Charterhouse, to dispose of the rest of his clothes "amongst oure poore scholars." Only one Charterhouse, that at Coventry, is known to have held a school. It educated twelve poor boys aged seven to seventeen, but this was done at the royal command and contravened the statutes and practices of the order. The reference could be to scholars at Hull's endowed school or to parish scholars at Easington. BI, Prob. Reg. 9, f. 440; *Test. Ebor.*, 5:272; E. Margaret Thompson, *The Carthusian Order in England* (London, 1930), 213.

HUMBLETON (E. Riding)   reading school, 1391
John Frankys of Hedon gave 4d. to every child saying his psalter at Humbleton parish church. BI, Reg. 14 (Arundel), ff. 29v-30.

HUNMANBY (E. Riding)   reading school, 1401, 1429, 1432, 1480; song school, 1480
In 1401 John Paulyn of Hunmanby gave 2d. to each scholar at his funeral. The will of Stephan Grysacre of Hunmanby, dated June 10, 1429, gave 2d. to each scholar or clerk of Hunmanby. Sir Thomas Coke, vicar of Hunmanby, gave 2d. to each small scholar attending his funeral in 1432, and about fifty years later Sir John Ramage of Malton, chaplain, was buried at Hunmanby and left 1d. to every scholar wearing a surplice. BI., Prob. Reg. 2, ff. 557, 615; 3, f. 84; 5, f. 113.

HUNSINGORE (W. Riding)   reading school, 1539
John Acaster, late abbot of Topholme, appointed Sir William Kyngston "assone as he shalbe able to teache a scoole [to] synge at hongsynger in Yorkshyre & teache & brynge up children in vertue & lernyng." PRO, PCC, Prob. 11/26 19 Crumwell.

HUTTON BUSCEL (N. Riding)   reading school, 1503
Thomas King, vicar of Hutton Buscel, left discretionary bequests to the priests, clerks, and scholars at his funeral. BI., Prob. Reg. 6, f. 101.

HUTTON-ON-THE-HILL (N. Riding)   reading school, 1505
Thomas Welburn's will requests that he be buried at Hutton on the Hill and that a penny be left to every scholar. BI, Prob. Reg. 6, f. 162.

KAYINGHAM (E. Riding)   reading school, 1391
John Frankys left 4d. to every child saying his psalter at Kayingham parish church. BI, Reg. 14 (Arundel), ff. 29v-30.

KEIGHLEY (W. Riding)   reading school, 1548
Leach, *ESR*, ii:303.

KELDHOLME NUNNERY (N. Riding)   reading school, 1318
See ARDEN above. D. Robinson, ed., *The Register of William Melton, Archbishop of York, 1317-1340*, Vol. 2, Canterbury and York Society, no. 71 (Torquay, 1978), 50.

KELK (E. Riding)   grammar school, 1304/5

This was an unlicensed school, competing with Beverley's grammar school. A. F. Leach, ed., *Memorials of Beverley Minster: The Chapter Act Book*, Vol. 1, Surtees Society, no. 98 (Durham, 1898), 48; Orme, *ESMA*, 306.

KINOULTON (Notts.)   grammar school, 1289

Notice of a school here arises from the circumstance that the grammarmaster at Nottingham felt that a school at Kinoulton infringed his rights by drawing from beyond its parish boundaries. W. Brown, ed., *The Register of John le Romeyn, Lord Archbishop of York, 1286-1296*, Vol. 1, Surtees Society, no. 123 (Durham, 1913), 285-86; Orme, *ESMA*, 307.

KIPPAX (W. Riding)   reading school, 1521; possible school, probably grammar, 1545-1548

In 1521 Matilda Freman of Allerton, buried at Kippax, left a penny to every scholar at the dirge and mass. BI, Prob. Reg. 9, f. 217. In an inquisition taken in 1638 it appears that, in 1545, George Goldsmith left cottages and a close to five trustees. The Charity Commissioners judged, in 1826, that since the gift was being used for the free school in the 1570s, it was likely that the original gift had been for the use of a free school. *Parliamentary Papers, Charity Commissioners' Reports* (London, 1826), 13:659; (London, 1898), 68:242-43.

KIRBY GRINDALYTHE (E. Riding)   reading school, 1525

In 1525 John Pacoke, to be buried in Kirby Grindalyth, left a penny to the scholars there. BI, Prob. Reg. 9, f. 393.

KIRBY MISPERTON (N. Riding)   reading school, 1520

In 1520 Rollande Vicars of Kirby Misperton left money to every scholar at his burial. BI, Prob. Reg. 9, f. 152.

KIRBY UNDERDALE (E. Riding)   possible reading and song school, 1531

Roger Wilberfosse of Garraby, who asked to be buried where it please God best, left "my parishe kirke of Kirkby Hundelfdale 6s. 8d . . . and every scholar that synges 1d." BI, Prob. Reg. 11, f. 12; *Test. Ebor.*, 6:26-27.

KIRBY WISKE (N. Riding)   song school, 1507/8; grammar and reading school, circa 1520

Robert Lascelles of Brakenburgh, esquire, whose will is dated 1507/8, asked to be buried at St. John Baptist at Kirby upon Wiske and gave to "every childe yt cometh and synges at my messe and derige 1d." BI,

Prob. Reg. 7, f. 32; extracts in *Test. Ebor.*, 4:270. Roger Ascham, who began his elementary education in the parish school, later referred to the grammar school at Kirby. Ascham, *The Schoolmaster* (1570), ed. L. V. Ryan (Ithaca, N.Y., 1967), xiii, 79.

KIRKBY IN CLEVELAND (N. Riding)   reading school, 1438, 1452, 1462; song school, 1452

In 1438 John Lokwood, being buried in St. Augustine parish church of Kirkby, provided 2d. to each small clerk. The 1452 will of another John Lokwood, knight, asked that the testator be buried in St. Augustine church and gave 2d. to each clerk wearing a surplice and 1d. to each boy scholar not having a surplice. Ten years later Sir Richard Driffeld, rector of Kirkby, left 1d. to each small clerk who attended and ministered at his funeral. BI, Prob. Reg. 2, ff. 252, 468; 3, f. 558.

KIRKBY KENDAL (Westm.)   grammar school, 1521-1548

Leeds Central Library, Archives Department, Richmond Archdeaconry, Will Register 1, 2, 3 & A, f. 91v; PRO, C 142/45, Inquisitions *Post Mortem*, Henry VIII, Chanc. Ser. 2, vol. 45, no. 6; R. L. Storey, ed., "The Chantries of Cumberland and Westmorland, part 2," *Transactions of the Cumberland and Westmorland Antiquarian and Archaeological Society*, new ser., 62 (1962):169-70.

KIRKBY LONSDALE (Westm.)   petty school, 1529; grammar school, pre-1542

The 1529 will of Bryan Mansargh requests that the testator be buried at Kirkby Lonsdale and gives "unto every scholer that day beyng yer present that can and wyll say that day de Profundis for my soule 1d." Leeds Central Library, Archives Department, Richmond Archdeaconry Will Register, 1, 2, 3 & A, f. 78. The 1542 will of Wilfrid Borrowe grants land (with appurtenances), books, and money to the free grammar school at Kirkby Lonsdale. Preston Record Office, Archdeaconry of Richmond, Lonsdale, Original Wills, Box 300 B 1532-1610.

KIRKBYMOORSIDE (N. Riding)   reading and song school, 1433, 1525-1526

The 1433 will of John Westeby of Kirkbymoorside requests that he be buried in the parish church there and leaves 2d. to each small clerk with a surplice. The 1526 will of Sir Robert Wildon, parish chaplain of Kirkbymoorside and dean of Buckrose, left 1d. to "every scolar with rochett." BI, Prob. Reg. 3, f. 389; 9, f. 366v; *Test. Ebor.*, 5:218. The will of Thomas Marcer (1525) also refers to scholars and scholars with surplices. BI, Prob. Reg. 9, ff. 321v.

KIRKHAM (Lancs.)   grammar school, 1537?-1548

P. J. Wallis, "A Preliminary Register of Old Schools in Lancashire and Cheshire," *Transactions of the Historic Society of Lancashire and Cheshire* 120 (1968):13 (table 2). No source is given for the 1537 date. For a school circa 1548, see *VCH, Lancs.*, 2:604.

KIRKHAM PRIORY (N. Riding)   grammar or reading school, circa 1465

J. S. Purvis, *Educational Records* (York, 1959), 10-11.

KNARESBOROUGH (W. Riding)   reading school, 1522, 1526?

Katherine Boundell, in her will of 1522, asked to be buried at Knaresborough parish church and mentioned nine scholars of the parish. In 1526, the will of John Busby (Kent?) requested that his son follow the school until he was twenty-three and be succored by the vicar of Knaresborough and others. *Wills and Administrations from Knaresborough Court Rolls*, Vol. 1, ed. F. Collins, Surtees Society, no. 104 (Durham, 1902), 14-15, 20.

KNEESALL (Notts.)   grammar school, 1527?-1548

Cornelius Brown, *A History of Newark-upon-Trent*, 2 vols. (Newark, 1904-1907), 2:178; *VCH, Notts.*, 2:180. No documentation is offered, although the reference is very full.

LANCASTER (Lancs.)   grammar or reading school, 13th c.; grammar school, circa 1470-1548

W. O. Roper, ed., *Materials for the History of the Church of Lancaster*, Vol. 2, Chetham Society, new ser., no. 31 (Manchester, 1894), 316; *A Calendar of the Lancashire Assize Rolls*, ed. J. Parker, Vol. 2, Lancashire and Cheshire Record Society, 49 (Manchester, 1905), 183-85; Edward Baines, *The History of the County Palatine and Duchy of Lancaster*, 2 vols., rev. ed. (London, 1868-1870), 2:567-68; *VCH, Lancs.*, 2:561-64; Leach, *ESR*, ii:123. See also W. K. Jordan, *The Social Institutions of Lancashire, 1480-1660*, Chetham Society, 3rd ser., 11 (Manchester, 1962), 30-31, who notes Christopher Urswick's gift to the schoolhouse in 1521. Orme, *ESMA*, 307.

LECONFIELD (AND WRESSLE) (E. Riding)   grammar, reading, and song household school, 1512

Thomas Percy, ed., *The Regulations and Establishment of the Household of Henry Algernon Percy, the Fifth Earl of Northumberland at His Castles of Wressle and Leckonfield in Yorkshire, 1512*, new ed. (London, 1905), 311-13, 318. It is unclear whether two separate households are involved and hence separate educational facilities at each place.

LEEDS (W. Riding)   grammar or reading school, early 14th c.-1400; song school, 1490-1503; reading school, 1496/7; possible reading and writing school, 1517

J. Le Patourel, *Documents Relating to the Manor and Borough of Leeds, 1066-1400*, Thoresby Society, no. 45 (Leeds, 1956), intro., 41, 44, 74; Orme, *ESMA*, 307. Between 1490 and 1502 three testators left pennies to children singing or wearing a surplice at their funerals in Leeds parish church. BI, Prob. Reg. 5, f. 382; 6, ff. 39, 68v. The will of Sir James Danby, knight, dated March 6, 1496/7, directed that he was to be buried in the parish church "if it fortune me to decesse in the parish of Ledes" and willed "that all maner of expenses as well as almose to pore folkes, rewardes to prestes, clarkes, and scolers, in money and also in mete and drinke . . . be doone after the discrecion of myn executors." BI, Prob. Reg. 5, f. 499v; *Test. Ebor.*, 4:122. In 1517 Brian Baynes of Leeds left 26s. 8d. to Thomas Wynffelde "and he to be kepte at the scolle unto suche tyme as he can writt and redde." It is not clear that Baynes is referring to a school at Leeds, although it is possible that he was. A free grammar school appears to have been functioning in Leeds by 1555. *Parliamentary Papers, Charity Commissioners' Reports* (London, 1826), 13:662.

LONG PRESTON (W. Riding)   grammar and song school, 1468-1548
    Leach, *ESR*, ii:296.

MALTON, OLD (N. Riding)   school (probably grammar, possibly at the priory), 1245, 1391, 1517-1520?; reading and grammar school, 1547-1548
    Bodleian, MS Laud misc. 642, ff. 4v-6; BI, Reg. 14 (Arundel), ff. 27-27v; *Test. Ebor.*, 1:164. The continuity of references to scholars suggests a long-standing grammar school, perhaps associated with the Gilbertine Priory. It is possible that some of the references to scholars in the wills of 1517 and 1520 refer to this school. BI, Prob. Reg. 9, ff. 127, 173. For Archbishop Holgate's foundation on the priory grounds in 1547, see Nicholas Carlisle, *A Concise Description of the Endowed Grammar Schools in England and Wales*, 2 vols. (London, 1818), 858-59, and Leach, *ESR*, ii:287. See also David J. Lloyd, *The History of Malton Grammar School* (Malton, 1966), 6-7; Orme, *ESMA*, 310.

MALTON, NEW (N. Riding)   reading and song school, 1489-1522
    Surpliced scholars were attached to St. Leonard's chapel and St. Michael Archangel chapel in New Malton. BI, Prob. Reg. 5, ff. 360, 456, 467; 6, ff. 82v, 128; 7, ff. 4, 54. See also BI, Prob. Reg. 9, ff. 110, 120, 123, 241.

MARRICK NUNNERY (N. Riding)   reading school, 1252
See ARDEN above. *VCH, Yorks.*, 3:117.

MARSKE (N. Riding)   possible reading school, 1521
John Blakewell of Redcar, fisherman, in a will written by the curate of Marske, requested his "sone go to the scole duringe his childhod." "The Fallow Papers," *YAJ*, 21 (1911):236.

MARTON-IN-CRAVEN (W. Riding)   song and reading school, 1521; reading school, 1548
In 1521 John Smyth of Marton left pennies to the scholars with surplices at his funeral. BI, Prob. Reg. 9, f. 153. In 1548 Thomas Hever of West Marton asked to be buried in St. Peter's, Marton and that there be given "to every scholer 1d. to praye for my soull." BI, Prob. Reg. 13, f. 449; *Test. Ebor.*, 6:269.

MATTERSAY (Notts.)   reading school, 1546-1548
Leach, *ESR*, ii:161, 170-71. All three chantry certificates refer to a priest helping to teach children, with no foundation for a school.

MEAUX ABBEY (E. Riding)   possible song school, 15th c.
G. S. McPeek, ed., *The British Museum Manuscript Egerton 3307: The Music, Except for the Carols* (London, 1963). The music required *pueri* as one of the three grades in the choir. McPeek favors Windsor rather than Meaux, however, as the place of origin of the manuscript.

MIDDLEHAM (N. Riding)   song school, 1478-*temp*. Henry VII
James Raine, "The Statutes for the College of Middleham," *Archaeological Journal* 14 (1857):163; *The Itinerary of John Leland 1535-1543*, ed. L. T. Smith, 5 vols. (London, 1906-1910), 4:25. Orme, *ESMA*, 311.

MIDDLETON (N. Riding)   grammar school, 1548
Leach, *ESR*, ii:307-309

MIDDLETON TEESDALE (N. Riding-Durham border)   reading school, 1501, 1543; song school, 1501
In 1501 Henry Richardson of Egleston asked to be buried at St. Mary's Middleton Teesdale and left 2d. to each scholar with a surplice and 1d. to each scholar without a surplice. BI, Reg. 25 (Savage), f. 158. The 1543 will of Tomes Smythson in Middleton parish left "to evere paryche clerk 2d. and to all oither scollers and poor people as my freynds thynks gud." James Raine, ed., *Wills and Inventories from the Registry of the Archdeaconry of Richmond*, Surtees Society, no. 26 (Durham, 1853), 49.

MONK BRETTON PRIORY (W. Riding)   grammar and reading school, 1513-1536

In 1513 John Holme of Felkyrk made provision for his two sons to go to school and to board in the priory until they reached lawful age. BI, Prob. Reg. 9, f. 23; extract in *Test. Ebor.*, 5:44-45. In 1574 a sixty-year-old husbandman recalled the seven or eight years of education he had received at the Priory circa 1520-1530. J. S. Purvis, "New Light on the Chartularies of Monk Bretton Priory," *YAJ* 37 (1948):68.

MOXBY NUNNERY (N. Riding)   reading school, 1314

See ARDEN above. BI, Reg. 8 (Greenfield), f. 100v; Power, *Med. Eng. Nunneries*, 580.

NAFFERTON (E. Riding)   song school, 1521

Sir William Swattock, chantry priest of Wandesford, asked to be buried at Nafferton and left 2d. to every child that sang. BI, Reg. 27 (Wolsey), f. 153.

NEWARK (Notts.)   grammar school, pre-1238, 1333-1499, 1512; grammar, reading, and song school, 1531-1548

A. F. Leach, ed., *Visitations and Memorials of Southwell Minster*, Camden Society, new ser., no. 48 (London, 1891), xli-xlii, 13, 52, 125-28; BI, Reg. 9A (Melton), ff. 44v, 61v; Reg. 9B (Melton), f. 427v; *VCH, Notts.*, 2:199-209; Cornelius Brown, *A History of Newark-upon-Trent*, 2 vols. (Newark 1904-1907), 2: chap. 8; BI, Prob. Reg. 3, ff. 316-18. In 1512 the archdeacon of York bequeathed 20s. to Master Haryson, the learned man. He is possibly the same as Magister Haryson, *Informator Grammaticorum* of Newark in 1541. BI, Prob. Reg. 8, f. 123; *Test. Ebor.*, 5:32. That reading was taught in Thomas Magnus's foundation of 1531 is clear from his deed, which describes the children's functions in church and makes special provision for those as yet unable to sing or read well. Brown, *History of Newark*, 2:188.

There may have been another grammar school at Newark. The 1512 will of Harold Staunton requests amortization of a chantry priest, singing in Our Lady chapel, to be a teacher of grammar. PRO, PCC, Prob. 11/17, 9 Fetiplace. Since, however, there is no reference to the other grammar school between 1500 and 1531, it may have lapsed; Staunton's benefaction would have filled the gap. Orme, *ESMA*, 311.

NEWBALD (E. Riding)   reading school, 1457, 1509

In 1457 the vicar of Newbald left 1d. to each boy clerk. Later (1509) another vicar (Sir Richard Walker) left 1d. to every scholar and "to William John ye sone of John Johnson and he keip the scooll 40s. and it to ly in John Wilson handes to thay see whether he wooll keipe the scooll or nay and if he wooll keep the scoole he to have it and he wooll not keip the scooll it to be disposed as I have commanddit it." YML, D. & C., L 2/4, f. 291; L 2/5a, f. 90.

NEWBURGH ABBEY (N. Riding)   song school, 1492; grammar school, circa 1517

In 1492 John Waterhouse of Newburgh wished to be buried in St. Mary's, Newburgh, and to leave a penny to each child singing at the funeral mass. BI, Prob. Reg. 5, f. 413. In 1538 Thomas Grey, priest, described his three years with a schoolmaster at the "farmarye" of Newburgh Abbey, after which he went to Oxford. *L & P, Henry VIII*, 13:ii, 403 (2).

NORMANTON (W. Riding)   grammar and writing school, 1548
    Leach, *ESR*, ii:307-309

NORTHALLERTON (N. Riding)   grammar and song school, 1322-1445; reading school, 1426-1445; grammar school, 1548
    EYS, 2:60-74; *VCH, Yorks.*, 1:445-46; British Library, MS. Cotton Faustina A VI, ff. 81, 84v, 104, 106-107; Orme, *ESMA*, 311.

NOSTELL PRIORY (W. Riding)   grammar school, 1472
    The will of Ralph Snaith of Pomfret directs his wife to "putt John and George my sons, att the age of x yere, into the abbay of Seynt Oswaldis, and agree with the Priour for their burds and lernyng." BI, Prob. Reg. 4, ff. 185-86; *Test. Ebor.*, 3:204.

NOTTINGHAM (Notts.)   grammar and possible reading school, 1289, 1382-1548; reading school, 15th c., 1512; song school, 1523; writing, 1532
    W. Brown, ed., *The Register of John le Romeyn, Lord Archbishop of York, 1286-1296*, Vol. 1, Surtees Society, no. 123 (Durham, 1913), 285-86. See KINOULTON above. A. F. Leach, ed., *Visitations and Memorials of Southwell Minster*, Camden Society, new ser., no. 48 (London, 1891), xli-xlii, 13, 31; *VCH, Notts.*, 2:216-23; *Records of the Borough of Nottingham*, 4 vols. (London, 1882-1889), 1:246-49, 262-63; 2:12, 122, 128, 406; 3:48, 140, 372, 396, 402, 443, 453-59; 4:26-31, 106, 108; Leach, *ESR*, ii: 164, 171; Orme, *ESMA*, 312. For grants to the grammar school, see also BI, Prob. Reg. 8, ff. 106, 120v (1512); 9, ff. 68 (1517), 118v (1520), 330v (1525); 11, f. 231 (1535); *Test. Ebor.*, 5:41-42. In 1424 and 1512 there is mention of an usher or ushers of the grammar school, which indicates that the school was large and probably

accommodated elementary pupils. In 1433 George Mortymer is found suing two fathers for debts of 4d. for schooling their sons. This was at a time when Thomas Ridley was the grammarmaster. Additional evidence for reading schools comes from the mention of little clerks at both St. Mary's and St. Peter's in 1467 and 1474 respectively, and scholars saying *De profundis* at St. Mary's in 1525. BI, Prob. Reg. 4, ff. 188v, 123; 9, f. 309v. While, in 1512, the corporation paid for repairs to a lean-to in which the children learned. *Borough Records*, 3:402-403. In 1523 six children singing the versicles are mentioned. BI, Prob. Reg. 9, f. 280v.

In 1532 a writing education was available in Nottingham. A bill of that year includes costs for twenty-five weeks of training in writing with three different writing teachers. *VCH, Notts.*, 2:222.

NUN APPLETON NUNNERY (W. Riding)   reading school, 1489
See ARDEN above. BI, Reg. 23 (Rotherham), f. 245; Power, *Med. Eng. Nunneries*, 580.

NUNBURNHOLME NUNNERY (E. Riding)   reading school, 1318
See ARDEN above. BI, Reg. 9 (Melton), f. 275; Power, *Med. Eng. Nunneries*, 580.

NUNKEELING NUNNERY (E. Riding)   reading school, 1314
See ARDEN above. BI, Reg. 8 (Greenfield), f. 123v; Power, *Med. Eng. Nunneries*, 580.

ORSTON (Notts.)   reading school, 1522-1524
Hugh Kirchisall's will, proved in 1522, left £10 to a priest to sing at Orston church and "to enforme childer." BI, Prob. Reg. 9, f. 246v.

OTTERINGTON, SOUTH (N. Riding)   possible reading school, 1435
Sir William Fyngall, rector *medietatis* of South Otterington, left 1d. to one small clerk. BI, Prob. Reg. 3, f. 446.

OWSTON (W. Riding)   grammar school, circa 1520-1548
Robert Parkyn, curate of Aldwick-le-Street from 1540 until 1570, learned his Latin (c. 1520-1530) in the chantry school of Owston village. A. G. Dickens, "Aspects of Intellectual Transition among the English Parish Clergy of the Reformation Period: A Regional Example," *Archiv für Reformationsgeschichte* 43 (1952):55-58. Leach, *ESR*, ii:308-309.

PENISTONE (W. Riding)   reading school, 1543
The 1543 will of Robert Wattes bequeaths "unto everie childe that commithe in forme of a scoler 1d." BI, Reg. 29 (Holgate/Heath), f. 97.

John Addy, "Penistone Grammar School 1392-1700," *YAJ* 39 (1959):508-14 is full of errors.

PICKERING (N. Riding)   grammar school, 1548
Leach, *ESR*, ii:307-308.

POCKLINGTON (E. Riding)   grammar school, 1514-pre 1548
A. F. Leach, "The Foundation and Refoundation of Pocklington Grammar School," *Transactions of the East Riding Antiquarian Society* 5 (1897):63-114. There does not seem to have been a schoolmaster there in 1548. C. J. Kitching, "The Chantries of the East Riding of Yorkshire at the Dissolution of 1548," *YAJ* 44 (1972):187. Orme, *ESMA*, 313, although Dowman scholars from Pocklington are to be found yearly in the College Register of St. John's from 1545.

PONTEFRACT (W. Riding)   grammar school, c. 1086, 1267, 1437-1464, 1480, 1548; song school at Pontefract Castle, 1381; song school, 1494-1499
EYS, 2:vii-xiii, 1-15; *Early Yorkshire Charters*, ed. W. Farrer, Vol. 3 (Edinburgh, 1916), 185-86. The Ralph Grammaticus mentioned may have been a schoolmaster, but by the twelfth century Grammaticus or Gramary was a family name, the head of whose fee was at Knottingley (W. Riding). *Early Yorkshire Families*, ed. Charles Clay and Diana E. Greenway, YAS rec. ser., no. 135 (Leeds, 1973), 35-36. *VCH, Yorks.*, 1:436-37; BI, Prob. Reg. 5, f. 90; Leach, *ESR*, ii:308-309. The grammar school, by the thirteenth century and perhaps before, was housed at St. Clement's in Pontefract Castle. In 1381 the Duke of Lancaster moved the personnel of his chapel, including boy choristers, to Pontefract Castle. *John of Gaunt's Register, 1379-83*, eds. E. C. Lodge and R. Somerville, 2 vols., Camden Society, 3rd ser., 56, 57 (London, 1937), 1:41, 90, 177; 2:278. In the fifteenth century there was a song school at Knolles almshouse, where two boys who sang well were granted £20 for five years in 1494. BI, Prob. Reg. 5, f. 446; *Test. Ebor.*, 4:93-94. Orme, *ESMA*, 313.

PRESTON (E. Riding)   reading school, 1474
The will of William Paynter, chantry chaplain of St. Mary's chantry in Preston, left 1d. to each little clerk. YML, D. & C., L 2/4, f. 330.

PRESTON (Lancs.)   grammar school, 1327-1358, 1400-1414, 1460s?-1518, circa 1528-1548
Rosalind M. T. Hill, ed., *The Register of William Melton: Archbishop of York, 1317-1340*, Vol. 1, Canterbury and York Society, no. 70 (Tor-

quay, 1977), cviii; *VCH, Lancs.*, 2:570-71; W. A. Abram, *Memorials of the Preston Guilds* (Preston, 1882), 14; BI, Reg. 21 (Neville), f. 165; A. H. Thompson, ed., "The Registers of the Archdeaconry of Richmond, 1361-1442," *YAJ* 25 (1919):200; Leach, *ESR*, ii:117-18, 122, 124-25; Orme, *ESMA*, 313.

RICCALL (E. Riding)   song school, 1509
Sir Raufe Newham, vicar of Riccall, left "to every child at Ricall yt hath a surples 2d." YML, D. & C., L 2/5a, f. 88.

RICHMOND (N. Riding)   grammar school, 1392-1548; song school, 1530-1545
L. P. Wenham, "Two Notes on the History of Richmond School, Yorkshire," *YAJ* 37 (1950):369-72; Wenham, *The History of Richmond School, Yorkshire* (Arbroath, 1958); Wenham, "The Chantries, Guilds, Obits and Lights of Richmond, Yorkshire," *YAJ* 38 (1953): 188-89, 214; Leach, *ESR*, ii:285, 287; Orme, *ESMA*, 314. In 1530 Ralph Foster, chantry priest of Richmond, left 12d. to the parish clerk and 1d. to the other scholars who were in surplices. In 1537 Margaret Ashe left a penny to "every scholar of the sayd towne [Richmond] y' hayff a surples for their dewty doyn at messe and dirige," and in 1542 James Allen of Snason who asked to be buried at Richmond, left one penny to scholars. Leeds Central Library, Archives Dept., Richmond Archdeaconry, Will Register 1, 2, 3 & A, ff. 1v-2, 194, 210. Foster's will is transcribed in Wenham, "Chantries, Guilds, Obits," appendix D and the original is at the Borthwick Institute, York. See also the wills of Henry Wallar (1541), Margaret Cowling (1545), and John Brokhole, the last chantry priest (1558) in James Raine, ed., *Wills and Inventories from the Registry of the Archdeaconry of Richmond*, Surtees Society, no. 26 (Durham, 1853), 24, 59, 112-13.

RILLINGTON (E. Riding)   reading school, 1509-1515?
Robert Hunter, a yeoman from Scampston, asked to be buried in Rillington church and "yerely during vi yeres be expended and delt to the preists, scolars and poor people ther beyng present and within the same parish 6s. 8d." BI, Prob. Reg. 8, f. 36.

RIPON (W. Riding)   grammar and song school, pre-1300-1548; reading school, 1391-1394; possible grammar school, 1468-1477
There is no evidence to support Leach's conviction that there was an Anglo-Saxon school in Ripon, although it is probable that there was one. The first secure notice, in the Ingilby MS at Ripon Cathedral Library, contains an undated entry from the early fourteenth century consisting of

"ancient statutes confirmed" in which the "rector scolarum" is regularly mentioned. A "rector chori" is also mentioned. In addition, the Hospital of St. John the Baptist at Ripon, whose endowment dates from 1109-1114, later (probably by the end of the thirteenth century) offered support to four or five poor boys attending the school. J. T. Fowler, ed., *Memorials of the Church of SS Peter and Wilfrid, Ripon*, Vol. 1, Surtees Society, no. 74 (Durham, 1882), 217; *VCH, Yorks.*, 1:430-34; Philip W. Rogers, *A History of Ripon Grammar School* (Ripon, 1954), 9-48. For additional fourteenth- and fifteenth-century references, see BI, Reg. 11 (Thoresby), ff. 72-72v; Cons. AB 1 (1416/17-1420), f. 177v; Fowler, *Memorials of Ripon*, Vol. 3, Surtees Society, no. 81 (Durham, 1888), 110, 127-29, 140, 143-45, 148-51, 154; Fowler, ed., *Acts of Chapter of the Collegiate Church of SS Peter and Wilfrid, Ripon*, Surtees Society, no. 64 (Durham, 1874), 41, 53-4, 64-5, 115, 181, 216; *EYS*, 1:141-57, 236-37. See also Leach, *ESR*, ii:295 and Orme, *ESMA*, 314. At one point in the fifteenth century (1468-1477) there appear to have been two grammar schoolmasters. Fowler, *Acts of Chapter*, 115, 181, 216.

ROMALDKIRK (N. Riding)   grammar school, 1548
Leach, *ESR*, ii:286, 288.

ROSEDALE NUNNERY (N. Riding)   reading school, 1315
See ARDEN above. BI, Reg. 7 (Greenfield), f. 107v.

ROTHERHAM (W. Riding)   grammar school, circa 1430; grammar, writing, and song schools, 1483-1548
EYS, 2:101-231; J. S. Purvis, *Educational Records* (York, 1959), 24-25; Orme, *ESMA*, 314; Leach, *ESR*, ii:292-94, 299-300, 305. For some wills with relevant information, see YML, D. & C., L 2/5a, f. 23 (Rotherham's will), printed in *Test. Ebor.*, 4:138-48; BI, Reg. 27 (Wolsey), f. 157, printed in *Test. Ebor.*, 5:198; Prob. Reg. 5, f. 88, referred to in *Test. Ebor.*, 4:141n; Prob. Reg. 8, f. 123, printed in *Test. Ebor.*, 5:32.

ROTHWELL (W. Riding)   reading school, 1408-1440
John, priest and schoolmaster of Rothwell parish, witnessed a 1408 will. BI, Prob. Reg. 2, f. 586. In 1414 John Bryge of Rothwell left 3d. to each child saying his psalter and 2d. to each child saying the seven penitential psalms. BI, Reg. 18 (Bowet), f. 356. In 1440 Gilbert Lee, buried at Rothwell, left 2d. to each scholar not yet a priest. BI, Prob. Reg. 2, f. 38.

ROYSTON (W. Riding)   grammar school, 1503-1548

Joseph Hunter, *South Yorkshire*, 2 vols. (London, 1828-1831), 2:381; Leach, *ESR*, ii:292, 308-309; Orme, *ESMA*, 314. The school appears to have been endowed both by the vicar of Royston, John Forman, and by the prior of Monk Bretton; unless, although it is unlikely, two schools were involved.

RUDBY (N. Riding)   reading and writing school, 1402; song school, 1474-1502; reading school, 1502

In 1402 Sir John Depeden, Lord of Healaugh, left £20 to John, son of John Fitz Richard, so that he might be placed either in the custody of Master John de Newton, treasurer of York, or of Sir Robert Wyclif, parson of Rudby, until he learned "aliqualiter intelligere et scribere." *Test. Ebor.*, 1:296. The will of Alicia Midelton of Estrington, dated 1474, asked that she be buried in Rudby parish church and leaves 1d. to each child with a surplice. In 1480 Richard Lyndley of Scotershelf, also to be buried at Rudby, left a similar bequest. In the same year Robert Laton of Saxhowe, knight, did the same, and in 1502 Elienora Laton, his widow, asked to be buried in Rudby parish church and left 1d. to each scholar with a surplice. BI, Prob. Reg. 4, f. 121; 5, ff. 100, 175v; 6, f. 64.

RYLSTONE (W. Riding)   song and petty school, 1524

George Burton of Rylstone left monies to the children with surplices and to those saying *De profundis*. BI, Prob. Reg. 9, f. 304.

ST. MICHAEL'S ON WYRE (Lancs.)   grammar school, 1528-1548

VCH, Lancs., 2:603; Leach, *ESR*, ii:118, 122, 124-25; W. K. Jordan, *The Social Institutions of Lancashire, 1480-1660*, Chetham Society, 3rd ser., 11 (Manchester, 1962), 39-40; Henry Fishwick, *History of the Parish of St. Michael's on Wye*, Chetham Society, new ser., 25 (Manchester, 1891), 54-55; Orme, *ESMA*, 315.

SAXTON (W. Riding)   reading school, 1547

William Hungate of Saxton, esquire, buried at Saxton, left every scholar being present a penny. BI, Prob. Reg. 13, f. 379; *Test. Ebor.*, 6:257.

SAXWELL (?)   reading school, 1541

Thomas Smyth of Saxwell, who was to be buried there, left two pennies to every clerk and one penny to the other scholars at his funeral. Leeds Central Library, Archives Department, Archdeaconry of Richmond, Will Register 1, 2, 3 & A, f. 202.

SCARBOROUGH (N. Riding)   grammar school, pre-1407-1444

BI, Reg. 18 (Bowet), f. 6v, where Hugo Rasen, the schoolmaster, is named executor. For his status in the community and as a teacher of grammar see BI, Prob. Reg. 2, ff. 356, 516; *Test. Ebor.*, 2:209; Arthur Rowntree, ed., *The History of Scarborough* (London, 1931), 139n. In 1444 the corporation of the town of Hull invited the grammarmaster of Scarborough to fill the vacant position at Hull. John Lawson, *A Town Grammar School Through Six Centuries* (London, 1963), 16; Orme, *ESMA*, 315.

SEDBERGH (W. Riding)   grammar, reading, and song school, 1525-1548

EYS, 2:xli ff., 286-381; H. L. Clarke and W. N. Weech, *History of Sedbergh School 1525-1925* (Sedbergh, 1925), 18-31; Leach, *ESR*, ii:303, 307, 309-11; Orme, *ESMA*, 315. The foundation deed, with the statutes of the school, is extant in English from March 9, 1527/8. The endowment ensured that the grammar school was free, but the statutes make it clear that the grammarmaster or his scholars could teach reading only if they were paid for it. The statutes also refer to a song school. At the obit of the founder, some of the children in surplices were expected to sing the dirge and mass while other children of the school were to say the dirge.

SESSAY (N. Riding)   reading school, 1521

Robert Johnson's 1521 will mentions the scholars "of my parishe of Cesay." BI, Prob. Reg. 9, f. 211v.

SHEFFIELD (W. Riding)   probable reading or grammar school, circa 1297

About 1297 Thomas de Boys of Sheffield, then about nine years old, left his school to visit his father at Whiston, a few miles outside Sheffield. His father, Adam de Boys, was server to Sir Thomas de Furnyvaus who resided in Sheffield castle, and it is probable that Thomas was attending school in the castle or town of Sheffield. PRO, C 133/82 m. 13; *Calendar of Inquisitions Post Mortem, 1216-1384* (London, 1912) 3:336.

SHELFORD (Notts.)   possible reading school, 1502

John Kneton, buried at Shelford church, left "to clarkes that be men 2d. et to children 1d." The language is ambiguous, but it implies that some of the clerks were children. BI, Prob. Reg. 6, f. 79.

SHERBURN (E. Riding)   reading and song school, 1504

Richard Fawethere, buried in St. Hilda parish church of Sherburn, left 1d. to each scholar in a surplice. BI, Prob. Reg. 6, f. 197.

SHERBURN IN ELMET (W. Riding)   grammar or reading school, 1321;
probable grammar school, 1435-1452, 1506-1545; song school, 1545

W. Wheater, *The History of the Parishes of Sherburn and Cawood*, 2nd
ed. (London, 1882), 34; Orme, *ESMA*, 316. In 1435 Christopher Mil-
ner, who wished to be buried in the parish church of Sherburn in Elmet,
left a penny to each boy clerk present. John Mews of Milforth, in 1452,
left two pennies to each little clerk present. Fifty-four years later Henry
Whitacre of Barston, being buried in Sherburn church, left 1d. to each
poor scholar coming to his funeral. In 1517-1518 John Barnaby, M.A.,
born at Sherburn, bequeathed 40s. a year for three years to five Oxford
scholars "born yn to the town of Sherburn." Emden, *BRUO, 1501-1540*,
27. In 1525/6 the schoolmaster, John Boswell, witnessed a will. BI, Prob.
Reg. 2, f. 288v; 3, f. 434v; 6, f. 214; 9, f. 344; *Test. Ebor.*, 5:216.
The school at Sherburn is mentioned in a 1534 will and the two scholars
who usually sing prick song are mentioned in 1546. BI, Prob. Reg. 11,
f. 116; 13, f. 194v. The long history suggests a grammar school.

SHERIFF HUTTON (N. Riding)   reading school, 1523-1528
Scholars are mentioned at Sheriff Hutton in 1523 and 1528. BI, Prob.
Reg. 9, ff. 283, 431.

SIBTHORPE (Notts.)   reading and song school, 1342-1540?
A. H. Thompson, "Song Schools in the Middle Ages," *Church-Music
Society Occasional Papers*, no. 14 (1942):22-23. Thompson, "The Chantry
Certificate Rolls for the County of Nottingham," *Transactions of the Thoroton Society* 16 (1912):108-19. The 1342 statutes contain directions for
the choice by the warden of a clerk sufficiently instructed in reading and
song. He was required every day, whenever he could find time, to teach
small children of the parish and others who wanted to learn their letters
for a reasonable sum to be agreed upon between him and the several
parents. The college at Sibthorpe was surrendered in 1540, but it is
unlikely that the schools were still functioning by then. Orme, *ESMA*,
316.

SINNINGTHWAITE NUNNERY (W. Riding)   reading school, 1315, 1319
See ARDEN above. BI, Reg. 8 (Greenfield), f. 83v; Reg. 9 (Melton),
f. 134; Power, *Med. Eng. Nunneries*, 580.

SKEFFLING (E. Riding)   reading school, 1391; reading and song school,
1509
In 1391 John Frankys of Hedon left 4d. to each child saying his psalter
at Skeffling parish church. The 1509 will of Christofer Sharp, vicar of

Skeffling, left two pennies to each scholar with a surplice. BI, Reg. 14 (Arundel), ff. 29v-30; Reg. 26 (Bainbridge), ff. 137v-38.

SKIPTON (W. Riding)   grammar school, ?pre-1492-1548

The earliest date for the school is debatable. See A. M. Gibbon, *The Ancient Free Grammar School of Skipton-in-Craven* (Liverpool, 1947) for evidence supporting the pre-1492 date. By the time of the chantry surveys in 1548 the grammar school had 120 scholars; it cannot therefore have been a very recent foundation. The incumbent had been teaching there at least since 1543, at which time the school had been further endowed with a chantry at Kildwick. Leach, *ESR*, ii:295, 301, 306.

SLEDMERE (E. Riding)   reading school, 1408; song school, 1484

William Ledes of Sledmere, buried in Sledmere chapel in 1408, left 4d. to each child saying his psalter. The will of Thomas Smyth of Sledmere, dated June 6, 1484, left 1d. to each child with a surplice at his burial in Sledmere chapel. BI, Prob. Reg. 2, f. 577; 5, f. 266.

SOUTH CLIFFE (E. Riding)   reading school, circa 1540

In 1552 a bequest was made to Cliffe chapel where the donor "sometimes went to school." *VCH, Yorkshire, East Riding*, 4:36.

SOUTHWELL (Notts.)   grammar and song school, 13th c.-1548; reading school, 1499; projected grammar school, 1512

See especially A. F. Leach, ed., *Visitations and Memorials of Southwell Minster*, Camden Society, new ser., no. 48 (London, 1891), passim. For additional references to the grammar and song schools, see W. Brown and A. H. Thompson, eds., *The Register of William Greenfield, Lord Archbishop of York 1306-1315*, Vol. 4, Surtees Society, no. 152 (Durham, 1938), 137; A. Hamilton Thompson, ed., "The Certificates of the Chantry Commissioners for the College of Southwell in 1546 and 1548," *Transactions of the Thoroton Society* 15 (1911):63-158; Historical Manuscripts Commission, *Report on the Manuscripts of Lord Middleton Preserved at Wollaton Hall* (London, 1911), 383, 385; A. F. Pollard, *Thomas Cranmer*, new ed. (London, 1926), 9; BI, Reg. 20 (Booth), f. 272; *Test. Ebor.*, 2:209; BI, Prob. Reg. 13, f. 570v; *Test. Ebor.*, 6:289-90; *VCH, Notts.*, 2:183-89; Orme, *ESMA*, 316. In 1499 one of the vicars choral, who was neither the grammarmaster nor his usher, taught young boys in his chantry. Leach, *Visitations and Memorials*, 67. In 1512 Robert Batemanson bequeathed land for the establishment of a free grammar school in Southwell. Leach, *Visitations and Memorials*, 117. There is no evidence that the school was ever founded.

SPOFFORTH (W. Riding)   reading school, 1404, 1408, 1522; song school, 1473

In 1404 Sir William Wodrove, the rector of Spofforth, gave 12d. to each "parvulo" ministering in the church at the time of his funeral. Four years later Ralph Kylstern, chaplain in Spofforth, left unspecified amounts to each small clerk ministering at his funeral. In 1522 Isabel Ward of North Kighton requested burial at Spofforth church and left a penny to every scholar there. BI, Prob. Reg. 2, f. 576; 3, f. 223; 9, f. 267; *Test. Ebor.*, 5:148. Sir Thomas Lematon, rector of Spofforth, left 1d. to each child with a surplice in 1473. BI, Prob. Reg. 4, f. 212.

STANWICK (N. Riding)   reading school, 1542

Isabell Lynschall of Stanwick bequeathed a penny to every scholar who came to her funeral. James Raine, ed., *Wills and Inventories from the Registry of the Archdeaconry of Richmond*, Surtees Society, no. 26 (Durham, 1853), 26.

STILLINGTON (N. Riding)   song school, 1505

John Reynald, the archdeacon of Cleveland and prebendary of Stillington, left 2d. to the four laymen of Stillington parish who sang the best on the anniversary of the testator's obit, and 1d. to each of the ten children singing in the choir. YML, D. & C., L 2/5a, f. 71.

STRENSALL (N. Riding)   song school, 1493

John Gray of Strensall left 1d. to each child singing at his funeral. YML, D. & C., L 2/4, f. 380.

SUTTON-IN-GALTRES (W. Riding)   song school, 1447, 1476, 1502; reading school, 1488, 1527

Brother William Sutton, vicar of All Saints in Sutton, left 2d. to each small child in Sutton church who was singing exequies and mass the day of his funeral, 1447. In 1476 John Fenton of Huby, wishing to be buried at All Saints, Sutton-in-Galtres, left 1d. to each child who was singing. Thomas Birtby, vicar of Sutton-in-Galtres, left a similar bequest in 1502. BI, Prob. Reg. 2, f. 172; 5, f. 187; 6, f. 51. In 1488 Richard Tarte of Sutton-in-Galtres left 1d. to the small clerks of the parish. BI, Prob. Reg. 5, f. 356. Two wills in 1527 mention the parish scholars. BI, Prob. Reg. 9, ff. 372, 394.

SUTTON DERWENT (E. Riding)   petty school, 1505

Thomas Helton, clerk and "prepositus" of St. Andrews College, Acaster Selby, was to be buried in St. Michael Archangel, Sutton-on-Derwent, where he left a penny to every scholar who knew how to say *De profundis*. BI, Reg. 16 (Scrope), 164.

SWINE NUNNERY (E. Riding)   reading school, 15th c.
J. E. Thorold Rogers, *Six Centuries of Work and Wages*, 8th ed. (London, 1906), 166; Power, *Med. Eng. Nunneries*, 581.

TADCASTER (W. Riding)   reading school, 1446
William Nunwyk of Tadcaster asked to be buried at Tadcaster and left "to each boy cleric at the funeral 1d." BI, Prob. Reg. 2, f. 136v.

TERRINGTON (N. Riding)   reading school, 1528
Scholars at Terrington are mentioned in the will of Edmund Bentley. BI, Prob. Reg. 9, f. 399v.

THIRSK (N. Riding)   grammar school, 1521-1548; song school, 1521
Leach, *ESR*, ii:285; twenty-four scholars were to sing at an obit in 1521. BI, Prob. Reg. 9, f. 174.

THORNER (W. Riding)   reading school, 1541
In 1541 William Morres left pennies to the scholars at Thorner. BI, Prob. Reg. 11, f. 573.

THORNHILL (W. Riding)   grammar school, circa 1361
A Wakefield man testified that, about 1361, he sent his son away to school at Thornhill (presumably a boarding school, since Thornhill is a good five miles from Wakefield) and placed the date of his going in the psalter in Wakefield's parish church. *Calendar of Inquisitions Post Mortem, 1216-1384*, Vol. 14 (London, 1952), 182. Orme, *ESMA*, 318.

THORP ARCH (W. Riding)   reading school, 1488
In 1488 William Scolemaister witnessed a will from Thorp Arch. BI, Prob. Reg. 5, f. 355.

TICKHILL (W. Riding)   song school, 1460-1480; grammar school, 1548
Evidence from the wills indicates that a song school was kept at the parish church in the 1460s and 70s. See BI, Prob. Reg. 4, f. 13v (will of Robert Dugmanton of Tickhill); 4, f. 228 (will of Sir Richard Grene, chaplain of Thirsk, buried at Tickhill); 4, f. 79 (will of Master William Lame [or Lawe] of Tickhill). For the grammar school, see Leach, *ESR*, ii:308-309.

TICKHILL FRIARY (W. Riding)   probable reading and grammar school, circa 1503-1524
In the 1560s, two witnesses, a yeoman and a husbandman, testified that

they had spent seven and ten years respectively in the friary school. J. S. Purvis, *Select XVIth Century Causes in Tithe*, YAS rec. ser., no. 114 (Leeds, 1949), 107-108.

TOPCLIFFE (N. Riding)   reading school, circa 1430, 1463; circa 1513-1517, 1539-1549; song school, 1517, 1548.

The will of Henry, son of Walter Clerk, vicar of Topcliffe, is undated but proved in 1430. In it he left 2d. to the minor clerks and 1d. to the "petites" of the parish. In 1463 Thomas Covell, the vicar of Topcliffe, left 2d. to each little clerk at his funeral. BI, Prob. Reg. 2, ff. 483, 657. In 1538 Sir Thomas Grey, priest, testified that he spent his first four years of schooling at Topcliffe, under the tuition of Sir Henry Osgoodby, steward to the Earl of Northumberland. *L & P, Henry VIII*, 13:ii:403(2). This coincides with the mention of scholars there in 1517. BI, Prob. Reg. 9, f. 63v. In 1539 Robert Busse of Disfarthe left 6d. to the six scholars of Our Lady's Gild of Topcliffe. And in 1540 Thomas Toppan of Dis-farthe left another 6d. to the six Lady children. Leeds Central Library, Archives Department, Archdeaconry of Richmond, Will Register 1, 2, 3 & A, ff. 175, 187. The will of Rycharde Grene of Newbie near Topcliffe, dated 1549, left a penny to every scholar in Topcliffe church. BI, Prob. Reg. 12a, f. 20; *Test. Ebor.*, 6:191-92. For the song school, see BI, Prob. Reg. 9, f. 63v and Leach, *ESR*, ii:284. Orme, *ESMA*, 318.

WAKEFIELD (W. Riding)   grammar school, 1275-1338, 1427-1548; song school, 1514-1548

See above, chap. 3, for the grammar school. With regard to the song school, scholars with surplices are mentioned in 1514, 1524 and 1527. BI, Prob. Reg. 9, ff. 6, 299v, 404. About 1530 the vicar's chaplain in Wakefield taught the boys slanderous songs against Cromwell. *L & P, Henry VIII*, 13:i:1054. In 1530 Margaret Dymong of Wakefield, buried at All Hallows, Wakefield, left a penny to "every scolar belongyng to the quere." BI, Prob. Reg. 10, f. 47. In 1548 Thomas Knolles, vicar of Wakefield, left 2d. to scholars with rochets there. W. D. Macray, *A Register of . . . Magdalen College, Oxford*, new ser., 1 (London, 1894), 130. Orme, *ESMA*, 318.

WAWME (E. Riding)   reading school, 1440

Alicia Person of Sutton-in-Holderness asked to be buried at St. Peter's, Wawme, and left 1d. to the small clerks of the parish. BI, Prob. Reg. 2, f. 166; printed in *Transactions of the East Riding Antiquarian Society* 10 (1903):12.

WEAVERTHORPE (E. Riding)   reading school, 1539
In 1539 Robert Awnewike of Weaverthorpe and Thomas Holme, vicar of Helperthorpe, both of them buried in Weaverthorpe church, bequeathed pennies to the parish scholars. YML, D. & C., L 2/5a, ff. 185, 186.

WELL (N. Riding)   grammar school, 1542-1548; song school, 1532?-1548
PRO, PCC, Prob. 11/29, 17 Spert; *Test. Ebor.*, 6:163; William Page, ed., *Inventories of Church Goods for Yorkshire, Durham, and Northumberland*, Surtees Society, no. 97 (Durham, 1897), xi; Leach, *ESR*, ii:286, 288; Page, *The Certificates of the Commissioners Appointed to Survey the Chantries, Guilds, Hospitals, etc., in the County of York* , Vol. 2, Surtees Society, no. 92 (Durham, 1895), 496.

WEST TANFIELD (N. Riding)   reading school, 1538
Nicholas Sanderson of West Tanfield, who was to be buried there, left a penny to every scholar at his funeral. Leeds Central Library, Archives Department, Archdeaconry of Richmond, Will Register 1, 2, 3 & A, f. 156.

WETWANG (E. Riding)   reading and song school, 1530
William Batty, vicar of Wetwang, referred to the thirteen children that "beres serges" and the other scholars who can sing plainsong. YML, D. & C., L 2/5a, f. 155.

WHARRAM LE STREET (E. Riding)   reading school, 1452
Richard Dogleby, the vicar of Wharram le Street, left a penny to each "clericulo" at his funeral. YML, D. & C., L 2/4, f. 270.

WHARRAM PERCY (E. Riding)   reading school, 1526
Richard Richardsone mentions parish scholars at Wharram Percy in 1526. BI, Prob. Reg. 9, f. 354.

WHITBY ABBEY (N. Riding)   reading school, 1366, 1446?
W. A. Pantin, *Documents Illustrating the Activities of the General and Provincial Chapters of the Black Monks*, 3 vols. (London, 1931-1937), 3:281. The poor scholars which the Abbey was scarcely maintaining were probably attending an almonry school. In 1446, small children are noted as ministering during a funeral. They may have been from the almonry school. BI, Prob. Reg. 2, f. 145.

WHITKIRK (W. Riding)   grammar and song school, 1521-1538 or 1546-1548

YML, Wa (Register of Deeds, etc. I 1508-1543), ff. 19v-27v gives the foundation deed of the hospital, grammar and song school. An abstract is in YML, Torre MSS L 1/8, 166. See also *L & P, Henry VIII*, 3:i:394; PRO, SP 1/21, 128v; G. E. Kirk, *A History of the Parish Church of St. Mary, Whitkirk, Leeds* (Leeds, 1935), 244-47; G. M. Platt and J. W. Morkill, *Records of the Parish of Whitkirk* (Leeds, 1892), 42-43. We have no record of the fate of the hospital and school, but it must have fallen under the attainder of its founder, Lord Darcy, in 1538 or been suppressed in 1546-1548.

WILBERFOSS (E. Riding)   reading school, 1484
William Bargeman of Newton, buried in St. John the Baptist church of Wilberfoss, left 1d. to each small clerk. BI, Prob. Reg. 5, f. 222.

WILFORTH (Notts.)   reading or grammar school, 1466
William Wright of Wilforth left 40s. to his son, Robert, with the intention that he attend school under the governance of Sir Henry Pynson, rector of the parish church. The cost of education and role of the rector suggest that this was a grammar school. BI, Prob. Reg. 4, f. 66.

WINTRINGHAM (E. Riding)   reading school, 1505
James Dryng, chaplain, requested burial in St. Peter's parish church of Wintringham and left 1d. to each scholar attending his funeral. BI, Prob. Reg. 6, f. 205.

WOLLATON (Notts.)   grammar school, pre-1473-1475; song school, 1489; grammar or reading school, 1524; household song school, 1526
For the grammar school in 1473, see A. F. Leach ed., *Visitations and Memorials of Southwell Minster*, Camden Society, new ser., no. 48 (London, 1891), 13. William Cowper, the grammarmaster, died in 1475. BI, Prob. Reg. 4, f. 128. In 1489 Master Robert Ilkston left two pennies to every child that sang in the choir of St. Leonard's, Wollaton. BI, Reg. 23 (Rotherham), f. 339. For a brief reference to the scholars of Wollaton in 1524, see Historical Manuscripts Commission, *Report on the Manuscripts of Lord Middleton Preserved at Wollaton Hall* (London, 1911), 369. There was a household song school at Wollaton Hall. Ibid., 382-86. Orme, *ESMA*, 320.

WORSBOROUGH (W. Riding)   possible grammar school, *temp*. Henry VIII
Peter Wallis argues from the Worsborough court rolls, which made note of the fines levied on bondsmen for sending their children to school, that a school existed in Worsborough prior to 1406. This is questionable,

as the children could have been sent away to school. P. J. Wallis, "Worsborough Grammar School," *YAJ* 39 (1956):147-63. At an inquisition of charitable uses September 28, 1614, it was found that a stipend of £5 6s. 8d. had been paid since the time of Henry VIII for provision of a free school there. Leach, *SME*, 243.

WRAGBY (W. Riding)   grammar school, 1546-1548
    Leach, *ESR*, ii:297, 308-309.

YAFFORD (N. Riding)   reading school, 1540
    Margery Rockeby asked to be buried in Yafford chapel and left 2d. to every scholar that could say dirge the day of her burial. James Raine, ed., *Wills and Inventories from the Registry of the Archdeaconry of Richmond*, Surtees Society, no. 26 (Durham, 1853), 17-19.

YARM (N. Riding)   reading school, 1139-1140; grammar or reading school, 1383-1390?; grammar school, 1520
    Reginaldi Dunelmensis Libellus, ed. James Raine, Surtees Society, no. 1 (Durham, 1835), 34; Joyce W. Percy, ed., *York Memorandum Book*, Vol. 3, Surtees Society, no. 186 (Gateshead, 1973), 13, 20-22. A grammar school was taught there in 1520, when Friar Clement Guadel of the Dominican convent of Yarm was allowed to attend it after divine service. L. M. Goldthorpe, "The Franciscans and Dominicans in Yorkshire," *YAJ* 32 (1936):418-19, and A. G. Little, "Educational Organization of the Mendicant Friars in England," *TRHS*, new ser., 8 (1894):51. Orme, *ESMA*, 321.

CITY OF YORK
    Documentation for the following schools can be found in J. Hoeppner Moran, *Education and Learning in the City of York, 1300-1560* (York, 1979).
    York Minster, theological school, 12th-15th c.
    York Minster, grammar and song schools, 13th c.-1548
    Hebrew *schola*, 12th-13th c.
    St. Leonard's Hospital, grammar, reading, and song schools, pre-14th c.-1539
    Archbishop Holgate's grammar and reading school, 1546-1548
    St. Mary's Abbey, school, 13th c.
    Franciscan Friary, theology school, 1433, 1483
    Dominican Friary, school, (possibly theological), pre-1546
    Augustinian Friary, schools of philosophy, theology, song, grammar, and logic, second half of the 14th c.
    St. Clement's Nunnery, reading school, 1310, circa 1312, 1317

Holy Trinity Priory, reading school, 1439

possible grammar school taught by Nicholas de Ferriby, 1375

reading school taught by William Akers, priest, possibly under the auspices of St. John's Gild, 1480

St. John's Gild, grammar school, 1531-1548?

All Saints, North Street, possible song school, 1438; reading school, 1535

St. Martin's, Coney Street, reading school, 1408, 1452; probable grammar school, 1528-1548

St. Michael le Belfrey, reading school, 1508

St. Mary's, Castlegate, reading school, 1394, 1447; song school, 1447, 1453

St. Sampson's, reading school, 1508

St. William's chapel, Ouse Bridge, reading and song school, 1521-1541

St. Michael's, Spurriergate, song school, 1489-1548

Holy Trinity, King's Court, reading school, 1430s; song school, 1463

St. Martin, Mickelgate, reading and song school, 1435

St. John del Pyke, possible song school, 1546-1548

Treasurer's household school, 15th c.

various schools (grammar and reading) held in the households of rectors living in York and in the households or chantries of Cathedral personnel, 14th-15th c.

writing taught by various parish priests, 15th c.

song schools held in parish churches, houses, and other places in York, 1367

In addition, D. M. Palliser, *Tudor York* (Oxford, 1979), 175, mentions a school at Merchants' Hall in 1546.

BIBLIOGRAPHY

There are a number of citations throughout the book, and especially in Appendix B, to documents and books that were not read in full, in which there may have been only a single reference to a school or schoolmaster. As far as possible I have excluded those sources from the bibliography.

Manuscript Sources

Public Record Office, London
    DL 38 Duchy of Lancaster, Certificates, etc. of Colleges and Chantries
    E 301 Exchequer, Augmentations Office, Certificates of College and Chantries
    Prob. 11/1-32 PCC, Registered Copy Wills, 1389-1548
    SP 1 State Papers, Henry VIII
British Library, London
    Lansdowne MSS
    MS Cotton Faustina A VI
    Additional MS 32115
    Additional MS 32466
Borthwick Institute, York
    Cons. AB 1-11 (1417-1530) Archbishops' Consistory Court Books
    Chanc. AB 1 and 8a Archbishops' Chancery and Audience Court Books
    Reg. 9-29 Archbishops' Registers
    Reg. 5A Sede vacante Register
    E and F Cause Papers
    D/C AB 2-3 Dean and Chapter of York Court Books
    Exchequer and Prerogative Courts of York: Original Wills and Inventories, Prob. Reg. 1-10 Registered Copy Wills, 1389-1530
    Chancery Court of York: Original Wills and Inventories
    Court of Dean and Chapter of York: Original Wills and Inventories
    Probate Register, Peculiar Court of St. John, Beverley, 1539-1552
    PR Y/MS/3 Churchwarden's Draft Account Book, St. Michael's Spurriergate, 1537-1548
York Minster Library, Dean and Chapter, York
    E 3/12-41 Fabric Accounts
    Chapter Acts: Registrum Antiquum M 2/4f 1339-1343, H 1/1a 1343-1353, H 1/2a 1343-1368, H 1/3a 1352-1386, H 2/1a 1401-

281

1429, H 2/2a 1468-1480, L 2/3a 1410-1427, H 2/3a 1427-1504, H 3/1a 1504-1543

Visitation Books: E L 2/3a 1408-1417, L 2/3b 1426, L 2/3c 1472-1550, L 2/3d 1523-1526

Probate Registers: L 2/4 1321-1493, L 2/5a 1472-1550

L 1/17 Inventories

Ms Add 220/2 Churchwarden's Draft Account Book, St. Michael's Spurriergate, 1518-1528

M 2/6e Register of Wills, Peculiar of St. Leonard's Hospital, 1410-1533

Wa Register of Deeds, etc. I 1508-1543

Torre MSS L 1/8

City Archives, York

Foundation Deed of Archbishop Holgate's School

Corporation Archives, Hull

Bench Books I-IIIa

D, Original Wills

Leeds Central Library, Archives Department

Richmond Archdeaconry, Will Register 1, 2, 3 & A, Late 15th century-1548 (Mormon Genealogical Library film #98914), Will Register C 1544-1564 (Morman Genealogical Library film #98915)

Preston Record Office

Lonsdale, Archdeaconry of Richmond, Original Wills: Box 300 B 1532-1610 (Mormon Genealogical Library film #98824), Box 320 F 1537-1660 (Mormon Genealogical Library film #098846), Box 323 G 1480-1620 (Mormon Genealogical Library film #0098849)

Printed Primary Sources

Abstracts of the Inquisitions Post Mortem relating to Nottinghamshire. Edited by W.P.W. Phillimore, John Standish, Thomas M. Blagg, K.S.S. Train, and Mary A. Renshaw. Thoroton Society Record Series, vols. 3, 4, 6, 12, 17. Nottingham, 1905-1956.

The Account Books of the Gilds of St. George and of St. Mary in the Church of St. Peter, Nottingham. Translated by R.F.B. Hodgkinson, Thoroton Society Record Series, no. 7. Nottingham, 1939.

Allnut, W. H. *An Early Sixteenth-Century A B C in Latin after the Use of Sarum*. Oxford, 1891.

Allot, Stephen, ed. *Alcuin of York—His Life and Letters*. York, 1974.

Anwykyll, John. *Compendium* (1483). STC 695.

The Ars Minor of Donatus. Edited and translated by W. J. Chase. Madison, 1926.

Ascham, Roger. *The English Works of Roger Ascham*. Edited by W. A. Wright. Cambridge, 1904.

———. *The Schoolmaster* (1570). Edited by L. V. Ryan. Ithaca, N.Y., 1967.

Babington, C. and Lumby, J. R., eds. *Polychronicon Ranulphi Higden*. 9 vols. Rolls Series, no. 41. London, 1865-1886.

Barker, E. E., ed. *The Register of Thomas Rotherham, Archbishop, 1480-1500*. Vol. 1. Canterbury and York Society, no. 69. Torquay, 1976.

Breviarum ad Usum Insignis Ecclesiae Eboracensis. 2 vols. Surtees Society, nos. 71, 75. Durham, 1871-1883.

Brown, Carleton F. *A Register of Middle English Religious and Didactic Verse*. 2 vols. Oxford, 1916-1920.

Brown, W., ed. *The Registers of John le Romeyn, Lord Archbishop of York, 1286-1296, and of Henry of Newark, Lord Archbishop of York, 1296-1299*. 2 vols. Surtees Society, nos. 123, 128. Durham, 1913-1916.

———. *The Register of Thomas of Corbridge, Lord Archbishop of York, 1300-1304*. 2 vols. Surtees Society, no. 138. Durham, 1925-1928.

———. *The Register of Walter Giffard, Lord Archbishop of York, 1266-1279*. Surtees Society, no. 109. Durham, 1904.

Brown, W. and Thompson, A. H., eds. *Cartularium Prioratus de Gyseburne*. Vol. 2. Surtees Society, no. 89. Durham, 1894.

———. *The Register of William Greenfield, Lord Archbishop of York, 1306-1315*. 5 vols. Surtees Society, nos. 145, 149, 151, 152, 153. Durham, 1931-1938.

———. *Yorkshire Inquisitions*. Vol. 4. YAS rec. ser., no. 37. Leeds, 1906.

Burton, Edward, ed. *Three Primers Put Forth in the Reign of Henry VIII*. Oxford, 1834.

Burton, Janet E. *The Cartulary of the Treasurer of York Minster and Related Documents*. York, 1978.

Bury, Richard de. *Philobiblon: The Text and Translation of E. C. Thomas*. Edited by M. Maclagan. Oxford, 1960.

Calendar of Inquisitions Post Mortem, 1216-1392. 16 vols. London, 1904-1974.

Calendar of Inquisitions Post Mortem, Henry VII. 3 vols. London, 1898-1955.

Cardwell, Edward, ed. *Documentary Annals of the Reformed Church of England*. Vol. 1. Oxford, 1844.

Catholicon Anglicum, an English-Latin Wordbook dated 1483. Edited by S.J.H. Herrtage. EETS, orig. ser., no. 75. London, 1881.

Chronicon Domini Walteri de Hemingburgh. Vol. 2. Edited by H. C. Hamilton. London, 1849.

Clay, J. W., ed. *Yorkshire Church Notes 1619-1631 by Roger Dodsworth,* YAS rec. ser., no. 34. Leeds, 1904.

————. *North Country Wills: Abstracts of Wills at Somerset House and Lambeth Palace, 1383-1558.* Surtees Society, no. 116. Durham, 1908.

Clay, J. W. and Lister, John, eds. "Autobiography of Sir John Savile, of Methley, Knight, Baron of the Exchequer, 1546-1607." *YAJ* 15 (1900):420-27.

Colet, John. *Aeditio* (1527). STC 5542.

Corbett, James A., ed. *The De instructione puerorum of William of Tournai, O.P.* Notre Dame, Ind., 1955.

Corpus Juris Canonici. Edited by E. Friedberg. 2 vols. Leipzig, 1879-1881.

Councils and Synods I, 871-1204. Edited by D. Whitelock, M. Brett, and C. Brooke. Oxford, 1981.

Councils and Synods II, 1205-1313. Edited by F. M. Powicke and C. R. Cheney. Oxford, 1964.

Cressy, David, ed. *Education in Tudor and Stuart England.* New York, 1976.

Darbyshire, H. Stanley and Lumb, George D., eds. *The History of Methley.* Thoresby Society, no. 35. Leeds, 1937.

Davis, Norman, ed. *Paston Letters and Papers of the Fifteenth Century.* 2 vols. Oxford, 1971-1976.

Dickens, A. G., ed. *The Clifford Letters of the Sixteenth Century.* Surtees Society, no. 172. Durham, 1962.

The Distichs of Cato. Edited by W. J. Chase. Madison, 1922.

Dugdale, William, *Monasticon Anglicanum.* Vol. 6. New ed. London, 1830.

Early Yorkshire Charters. Edited by William Farrer and C. T. Clay. 12 vols. Edinburgh and Wakefield, 1914-1965.

Elyot, Sir Thomas. *The Boke Named the Governour.* Edited by H. S. Croft. 2 vols. New York, 1967.

Erasmus. *The Colloquies of Erasmus.* Translated by C. R. Thompson. Chicago. 1965.

Eshelby, H. D., ed. "The Episcopal Visitations of the Yorkshire Deaneries of the Archdeaconry of Richmond in 1548 and 1554." *YAJ* 14 (1898):390-421.

Fallow, T. M. "The East Riding Clergy in 1525-6." Edited by W. Brown. *YAJ* 24 (1916):62-80.

"The Fallow Papers." *YAJ* 21 (1911):234-52.

Fishwick, H., ed. *Pleadings and Depositions in the Duchy Court of Lancaster temp. Henry VII and Henry VIII.* 2 vols. Lancashire and Cheshire Record Society, nos. 32, 35. Rochdale, 1896-1897.

———. *Pleadings and Depositions in the Duchy Court of Lancaster time of Edward VI and Philip and Mary.* Lancashire and Cheshire Record Society, no. 40. Rochdale, 1899.

Flynn, Vincent J., ed. *A Shorte Introduction of Grammar by William Lily.* New York, 1945.

Fowler, J. T., ed. *Acts of Chapter of the Collegiate Church of SS Peter and Wilfrid, Ripon A.D. 1452 to A.D. 1506.* Surtees Society, no. 64. Durham, 1874.

———. *Memorials of the Church of SS Peter and Wilfrid, Ripon.* 4 vols. Surtees Society, nos. 74, 78, 81, 115. Durham, 1882-1908.

———. *Rites of Durham.* Surtees Society, no. 107. Durham, 1903.

Frere, W. H. and Kennedy, W. M., eds. *Visitation Articles and Injunctions of the Period of the Reformation.* 3 vols. Alcuin Club Collections, nos. 14-16. London, 1910.

Furnivall, F. J., ed. *Early English Meals and Manners.* EETS, orig. ser., no. 32. London, 1868.

———. "The Mirror of the Periods of Man's Life." In *Hymns to the Virgin.* EETS, orig. ser., no. 24. London, 1867.

Gairdner, James, ed. *The Paston Letters, 1422-1509.* 3 vols. London, 1872-1875.

Gascoigne, Thomas. *Loci e Libro Veritatum.* Edited by J. Thorold Rogers. Oxford, 1881.

Gastrell, Francis. *Notitia Cestriensis.* Edited by J. Raine. Vol. 2, nos. 1-3. Chetham Society, orig. ser., nos. 19, 21, 22. Manchester, 1849-1850.

Gibbons, A., ed. *Early Lincoln Wills.* Lincoln Record Series, no. 1. Lincoln, 1888.

Halliwell, J. O., ed. *The Thornton Romances.* Camden Society, no. 30. London, 1844.

Hill, Rosalind M. T., ed. *The Register of William Melton: Archbishop of York, 1317-1340.* Vol. 1. Canterbury and York Society, no. 70. Torquay, 1977.

Historical Manuscripts Commission. *The MSS of the Duke of Rutland Preserved at Belvoir Castle.* Vols. 1 and 4. London, 1888, 1905.

———. *Ninth Report.* London, 1883.

Historical Manuscripts Commission. *Report on the Manuscripts of Lord Middleton Preserved at Wollaton Hall*. London, 1911.

Holt, John. *Lac Puerorum* (1510?). STC 13604.

Horae Eboracensis, The Prymer or Hours of the Blessed Virgin Mary. Surtees Society, no. 132. Durham, 1920.

Horman, William. *Vulgaria*. Edited by M. R. James. Oxford, 1926.

Hoskins, Edgar. *Horae Beatae Mariae Virginis or Sarum and York Primers with Kindred Books and Primers of the Reformed and Roman Use*. London, 1901.

Irvine, W. F., ed. *A Collection of Lancashire and Cheshire Wills Not Now to Be Found in Any Probate Registry 1301-1752*. Lancashire and Cheshire Record Society, no. 30. Manchester, 1896.

Jacob, E. F., ed. *The Register of Henry Chichele, Archbishop of Canterbury, 1414-1443*. Vol. 2. Oxford, 1938.

James, M. R., ed. "The Catalogue of the Library of the Augustinian Friars at York." In *Fasciculus Joanni Willis Clark dicatus*, 2-96. Cambridge, 1909.

John of Gaunt's Register, 1371-1375. Edited by S. Armitage-Smith. 2 vols. Camden Society, 3rd ser., nos. 20, 21. London, 1911.

John of Gaunt's Register, 1379-83. Edited by E. C. Lodge and R. Somerville. 2 vols. Camden Society, 3rd ser., nos. 56, 57. London, 1937.

Johnston, A. F. and Rogerson, M., eds. *Records of Early English Drama: York*. 2 vols. Toronto, 1979.

Kennedy, P. A., ed. *Nottingham Household Inventories*. Thoroton Society Record Series, no. 22. Nottingham, 1963.

The Lay Folk's Catechism: Archbishop Thoresby's Instruction for the People. Edited by T. E. Simmons and H. E. Nolloth. EETS, orig. ser., no. 118. London, 1901.

Leach, A. F., ed. *Early Yorkshire Schools*. 2 vols. YAS rec. ser., nos. 27, 33. Leeds, 1898-1903.

―――. *Educational Charters and Documents, 589 to 1909*. Cambridge, 1911.

―――. *Memorials of Beverley Minster: The Chapter Act Book of the Collegiate Church of St. John of Beverley 1286-1347*. 2 vols. Surtees Society, nos. 98, 108. Durham, 1898-1903.

―――. *Visitations and Memorials of Southwell Minster*. Camden Society, new ser., no. 48. London, 1891.

Legg, J. Wickham, ed. *The Clerk's Book of 1549*. Henry Bradshaw Society, no. 25. London, 1903.

Leland, John. *Antiquarii de Rebus Britannicis Collectanea*. 6 vols. London, 1770.

———. *Itinerary*. Edited by L. T. Smith. 5 vols. London, 1906-1910.

Le Patourel, J. *Documents Relating to the Manor and Borough of Leeds, 1066-1400*. Thoresby Society, no. 45. Leeds, 1956.

Letters and Papers, Foreign and Domestic, of the Reign of Henry VIII. Edited by J. S. Brewer, J. H. Gairdner, and R. H. Brodie. 21 vols. London, 1860-1920.

Littlehales, Henry, ed. *Pages in Facsimile from a Layman's Prayer Book in English c. 1400 A.D.* London, 1890.

———. *The Prymer or Lay Folks Prayer Book*. 2 vols. EETS, orig. ser., nos. 105, 109. London, 1895-1897.

———. *The Prymer, or Prayer-Book of the Lay People in the Middle Ages*. 2 vols. London, 1891-1892.

Lyndwood, William. *Provinciale*. Oxford, 1679.

McPeek, G. S., ed. *The British Museum Manuscript Egerton 3307: The Music, Except for the Carols*. London, 1964.

Madan, Falconer, ed. "Day Book of John Dorne, Bookseller in Oxford, A.D. 1520." *Collectanea*, 1st ser., part 3, 71-177; 2nd ser., appendix, Oxford Historical Society, nos. 5, 16. Oxford, 1885, 1890.

The Manual of Prayers, or the Prymer in Englyshe and Latin. STC 16009-16010.

Manuale et Processionale ad Usum Insignis Ecclesiae Eboracensis. Surtees Society, no. 63. Durham, 1875.

Maskell, William. *Monumenta Ritualia Ecclesiae Anglicanae*. Vol. 3. 2nd ed. Oxford, 1882.

Meech, Sanford B. "Early Application of Latin Grammar to English." *PMLA* 50 (1935):1012-32.

———. "An Early Treatise in English Concerning Latin Grammar." *University of Michigan Publications in Language and Literature*, no. 13, 81-125. Ann Arbor, Mich., 1935.

———. "John Drury and His English Writings." *Speculum* 9 (1934):70-83.

Melton, William de. *Sermo exhortatorius cancellarii Eboracensis hiis qui ad sacros ordines petunt promoueri*. STC 17806.

Missale ad Usum Insignis Ecclesiae Eboracensis. 2 vols. Surtees Society, nos. 59, 60. Durham, 1874.

More, Thomas. *The Apology*. Edited by J. B. Trapp. *The Complete Works of St. Thomas More*, Vol. 9. New Haven, 1979.

———. *The Confutation of Tyndale's Answer*. Edited by Louis A. Shuster,

Richard C. Marius, James P. Lusardi, and Richard J. Schoeck. *The Complete Works of St. Thomas More*, Vol. 8. New Haven, 1973.

———. *A Dialogue Concerning Heresies*. Edited by Thomas M. C. Lawler, Germain Marc'hadour, and Richard C. Marius. *The Complete Works of St. Thomas More*, Vol. 6. New Haven, 1981.

Myrc, John. *Instructions for Parish Priests*. Edited by E. Peacock. EETS, no. 31. London, 1868.

Nelson, W., ed. *A Fifteenth-Century School Book*. Oxford, 1956.

Nève, Joseph. *Catonis Disticha; Facsimiles, notes, liste des éditions du XVe siècle*. Liège, 1926.

Nichols, John Gough, ed. *Narratives of the Days of the Reformation*. Camden Society, orig. ser., no. 77. London, 1859.

The Nun's Rule; Being the Ancren Riwle Modernized. Edited by James Morton. London, 1924.

Orme, Nicholas. "An Early-Tudor Oxford Schoolbook." *Renaissance Quarterly* 34 (1981):11-39.

———. "A Grammatical Miscellany of 1427-1465 from Bristol and Wiltshire," *Traditio* 38 (1982):301-26.

Page, William, ed. *The Certificates of the Commissioners Appointed to Survey the Chantries, Guilds, Hospitals, etc. in the County of York*. 2 vols. Surtees Society, nos. 91, 92. Durham, 1894-1895.

———. *Inventories of Church Goods for the Counties of Yorkshire, Durham, and Northumberland*. Surtees Society, no. 97. Durham, 1897.

Percy, Joyce W., ed. *York Memorandum Book*. Vol. 3. Surtees Society, no. 186. Gateshead, 1973.

Percy, Thomas, ed. *The Regulations and Establishment of the Household of Henry Algernon Percy, the Fifth Earl of Northumberland at His Castles of Wressle and Leckonfield in Yorkshire, 1512*. New ed. London, 1905.

Piccope, G. J., ed. *Lancashire and Cheshire Wills and Inventories from the Ecclesiastical Court, Chester*. Vol. 1. Chetham Society, old ser., no. 33. Manchester, 1857.

Piers Plowman: The B Version. Edited by George Kane and E. Talbot Donaldson. London, 1975.

Piers Plowman, Selections from the C Text. Edited by Elizabeth Salter and Derek Pearsall. Evanston, Ill., 1967.

Plimpton, George A. *The Education of Chaucer*. Oxford, 1935.

Plumpton Correspondence. Edited by Thomas Stapleton. Camden Society, no. 4. London, 1839.

The Primer in Englishe moste necessary for the educacyon of chyldren abstracted oute of the Manuall of prayers or primer in Englishe and laten, set forth by Jhon, laet byshop of Rochester (1539?). STC 16011.

Promptorium Parvulorum sive Clericorum, lexicon anglo-latinum princeps. Edited by A. Way. 3 vols. Camden Society, nos. 25, 54, 89. London, 1843-1865.

Promptorium Parvulorum: The First English-Latin Dictionary. Edited by A. L. Mayhew. Camden Society, extra ser., no. 102. London, 1908.

Purvis, J. S. *Bridlington Charters, Court Rolls and Papers, XVI-XIX Century.* London, 1926.

———. "The Churchwarden's Book of Sheriff Hutton, 1524-1568." *YAJ* 36 (1945):178-89.

———. *Educational Records.* York, 1959.

———. *A Medieval Act Book with Some Account of Ecclesiastical Jurisdiction at York.* York, 1943.

———. *Select XVth Century Causes in Tithe.* YAS rec. ser., no. 114. Leeds, 1949.

———. *Tudor Parish Documents of the Diocese of York.* Cambridge, 1948.

Raine, Angelo, ed. *York Civic Records.* 5 vols. YAS rec. ser., nos. 98, 103, 106, 108, 110. Leeds, 1939-1946.

Raine, James, ed. *The Fabric Rolls of York Minster.* Surtees Society, no. 35. Durham, 1859.

———. "The Statutes Ordained by Richard Duke of Gloucester, for the College of Middleham." *Archaeological Journal* 14 (1857):160-70.

———. *Wills and Inventories from the Registry of the Archdeaconry of Richmond.* Surtees Society, no. 26. Durham, 1853.

———. *Wills and Inventories . . . of the Northern Counties of England.* Surtees Society, no. 2. London, 1835.

Raine, James et al. *Testamenta Eboracensia.* 6 vols., Surtees Society, nos. 4, 30, 45, 53, 79, 106. Durham, 1836-1902.

Raine, James, Jr. *The Historians of the Church of York and Its Archbishops.* Vol. 3. Rolls Series, no. 71. London, 1894.

Raines, F. R., ed. *A History of the Chantries within the County Palatine of Lancaster.* Chetham Society, orig. ser., nos. 59, 60. Manchester, 1862.

Records of the Borough of Nottingham. 4 vols. London, 1882-1889.

Records of the Northern Convocation. Surtees Society, no. 113. Durham, 1906.

Register of the Freemen of the City of York. Vol. 1. Edited by F. Collins. Surtees Society, no. 96. Durham, 1897.

Robinson, D., ed. *The Register of William Melton, Archbishop of York,*

1317-1340. Vol. 2. Canterbury and York Society, no. 71. Torquay, 1978.

Roper, W. O., ed. *Materials for the History of the Church of Lancaster.* 2 vols. Chetham Society, new ser., nos. 26, 31. Manchester, 1892-1894.

Rotuli Parliamentorum. Edited by J. Strachey. 6 vols. London, 1767-1777.

Rous, John. *Historia Regum Angliae*. Edited by T. Hearne. Oxford, 1716.

Rymer, Thomas, ed. *Foedera, conventiones, literae et cujuscunque generis acta publica*. 10 vols., 3rd ed. The Hague, 1740.

Sellers, Maud, ed. *York Memorandum Book*. 2 vols. Surtees Society, nos. 120, 125. Durham, 1912-1915.

Sermons and Remains of Hugh Latimer. Parker Society, no. 27. Cambridge, 1844.

Seymour, M. C., ed. *On the Properties of Things: John Trevisa's Translation of Bartholomaeus Anglicus De Proprietatibus Rerum*. 2 vols. Oxford, 1975.

Shuckburgh, Evelyn S., ed. *The ABC Both in Latyn and Englysche*. London, 1889.

Smith, David M. *A Calendar of the Register of Robert Waldby, Archbishop of York, 1397*. York, 1974.

Stanbridge, John. *Accidence* (1505?). STC 23140.

Starkey, Thomas. *A Dialogue between Reginald Pole and Thomas Lupset*. Edited by K. M. Burton. London, 1948.

The Statutes, etc. of the Cathedral Church of York. 2nd ed. Leeds, 1900.

Statutes of the Realm, 1235-1624. 4 vols. London, 1810-1819.

Storey, R. L., ed. "The Chantries of Cumberland and Westmorland." *Transactions of the Cumberland and Westmorland Antiquarian and Archaeological Society*, new ser., 60 (1960):66-96; 62 (1962):145-70.

Stow, John. *A Survey of London* (1598). Edited by Henry Morley. London, 1890.

Strype, John. *Memorials of Archbishop Cranmer*. 2 vols. Oxford, 1812.

Swanson, R. N., *A Calendar of the Register of Richard Scrope Archbishop of York, 1398-1405*. Part i. York, 1981.

Sylvester, R. S. and Harding, D. P., eds. *Two Early Tudor Lives*. New Haven, 1962.

Tanner, Norman P., ed. *Heresy Trials in the Diocese of Norwich, 1428-31*. Camden Society, 4th ser., no. 20. London, 1977.

"Testamenta Leodiensia." Edited by W. Brigg and G. D. Lumb. *Publications of the Thoresby Society*, no. 2, 98-110, 205-14; no. 4, 1-16,

139-47; no. 9, 81-96, 161-92, 246-77; no. 11, 37-68, 289-320; no. 15, 10-25; no. 19, entire. Leeds, 1891-1913.

Thompson, A. Hamilton, ed. "The Certificates of the Chantry Commissioners for the College of Southwell in 1546 and 1548." *Transactions of the Thoroton Society* 15 (1911):63-158.

————. "The Chantry Certificate Rolls for the County of Nottingham," *Transactions of the Thoroton Society* 16 (1912):91-133; 17 (1913):59-119; 18 (1914):83-184.

————. "Documents Relating to Diocesan and Provincial Visitations from the Registers of Henry Bowet . . . and John Kempe. . . ." In *Miscellanea, II*. Surtees Society, no. 127, 131-302. Durham, 1916.

————. "The Register of the Archdeacons of Richmond, 1442-1477, part i." *YAJ* 30 (1930):1-132; part ii, *YAJ* 32 (1935):111-45.

————. "The Registers of the Archdeaconry of Richmond, 1361-1442." *YAJ* 25 (1919):129-268.

————. *Visitations of Religious Houses in the Diocese of Lincoln, 1420-1449*. 3 vols. Lincoln Record Society, nos. 7, 14, 21. Horncastle, 1914-1929.

Thurot, Charles. *Notices et extraits de divers manuscrits latins pour servir à l'histoire des doctrines grammaticales au moyen âge*. Vol. 22, part ii of *Notices et extraits des manuscrits de la bibliothèque impériale et autres bibliothèques, publiées par l'institut impérial de France*. Paris, 1868.

Topham, John. "Subsidy Roll of 51 Edward III." *Archaeologia* 7 (1785):337-47.

Tudor School-Boy Life: The Dialogues of Juan Luis Vives. Translated by Foster Watson. London, 1970.

Valor Ecclesiasticus temp. Henr. VIII auctoritate regia instituta. Vol. 5. London, 1825.

The Vulgaria of John Stanbridge and the Vulgaria of Robert Whittinton. Edited by Beatrice White. EETS, orig. ser., no. 187. London, 1932.

Watkin, A., ed. *Dean Cosyn and Wells Cathedral Miscellanea*. Somerset Record Society, no. 56. London, 1941.

Welch, Mary A. ed. "Willoughby Letters of the First Half of the Sixteenth Century," *Nottinghamshire Miscellany*, no. 4, Thoroton Society Record Series, no. 24, 1-98. Nottingham, 1967.

Wilkins, David, ed. *Concilia Magnae Britanniae et Hiberniae*. 4 vols. London, 1737.

Williams, C. H., ed. *English Historical Documents*. Vol. 5. London, 1967.

Wills and Administrations from the Knaresborough Court Rolls. Vol. 1. Edited by F. Collins. Surtees Society, no. 104. Durham, 1902.

Woolley, R. M. *The York Provinciale*. N.p., 1930.

Wright, T. and Halliwell, J. O., eds. *Reliquiae Antiquae*. 2 vols. London, 1845.

Wordsworth, Christopher, ed. *Statuta Ecclesiae Cathedralis Lincolniensis*. London, 1873.

York Cathedral Statutes. Leeds, 1900.

Yorkshire Church Notes 1619-1631 by Roger Dodsworth. YAS rec. ser., no. 34. Leeds, 1904.

SELECTED SECONDARY SOURCES

Abram, W. A. *Memorials of the Preston Guilds*. Preston, 1882.

Adamson, John William. "Education." In *The Legacy of the Middle Ages*, edited by C. G. Crump and E. F. Jacob, 255-85. Oxford, 1926.

———. *"The Illiterate Anglo-Saxon" and Other Essays on Education, Medieval and Modern*. Cambridge, 1946.

———. *A Short History of Education*. Cambridge, 1919.

Allen, C. G. "The Sources of 'Lily's Latin Grammar.' " *The Library*, 5th ser., 9 (1954):85-100.

Anglin, Jay P. "The Expansion of Literacy: Opportunities for the Study of the Three Rs in the London Diocese of Elizabeth I." *Guildhall Studies in London History* 4 (1980):63-74.

Aston, Margaret. "Lollard Women Priests?" *J. Eccl. Hist.* 31 (1980):441-61.

———. "Lollardy and Literacy," *History* 62 (1977), 347-71.

Atchley, E. G. Cuthbert F. "The Halleway Chauntry at the Parish Church of All Saints, Bristol, and the Halleway Family." *Bristol and Gloucestershire Archaeological Society* 24 (1901):74-125.

———. *The Parish Clerk and His Right to Read the Liturgical Epistle*. Alcuin Club Tracts, no. 4. London, 1903.

Aylmer, G. E. and Cant, Reginald, eds. *A History of York Minster*. Oxford, 1977.

Baines, Edward. *The History of the County Palatine and Duchy of Lancaster*. 2 vols. Rev. ed. London, 1868-1870.

Baldwin, T. W. *William Shakspere's Petty School*. Urbana, Ill., 1943.

———. *William Shakspere's Small Latine & Lesse Greeke*. 2 vols. Urbana, Ill., 1944.

Barrow, G.W.S. "Northern English Society in the Twelfth and Thirteenth Centuries." *Northern History* 4 (1969):1-28.

Bartlett, J. N. "The Expansion and Decline of York in the Later Middle Ages." *Economic History Review*, 2nd ser., 12 (1959-1960):17-33.

Bartlett, Kenneth. "The Decline and Abolition of the Master of Grammar: An Early Victory of Humanism at the University of Cambridge." *History of Education* 6 (1977):1-8.

Bauml, F. H. "Varieties and Consequences of Medieval Literacy and Illiteracy." *Speculum* 55 (1980):237-65.

Beckingsale, B. W. "The Characteristics of the Tudor North." *Northern History* 4 (1969):67-83.

Bell, Edward A. *A History of Giggleswick School from Its Foundation: 1499-1912*. Leeds, 1912.

Bell, H. E. "The Price of Books in Medieval England." *The Library*, 4th ser., 17 (1936-1937):312-32.

Bell, Susan Groag, "Medieval Women Book Owners: Arbiters of Lay Piety and Ambassadors of Culture." *Signs* 7 (1982):742-67.

Bennett, H. S. "A Check-List of Robert Whittinton's Grammars." *The Library*, 5th ser., 7 (1952):1-14.

————. *English Books and Readers, 1475-1557*. Cambridge, 1952.

————. "Medieval Ordination Lists in the English Episcopal Registers." In *Studies Presented to Sir Hilary Jenkinson*, edited by J. C. Davies, 20-34. Oxford, 1957.

————. "The Production and Dissemination of Vernacular Manuscripts in the Fifteenth Century." *The Library*, 5th ser., 1 (1946-1947):167-78.

Birchenough, Edwyn. "The Prymer in English." *The Library*, 4th ser., 18 (1937-1938):177-94.

Bischoff, B. "The Study of Foreign Languages in the Middle Ages." *Speculum* 36 (1961):209-24.

Bowen, James. *A History of Western Education*. Vol. 2. London, 1975.

Bowers, Roger. "Obligation, Agency and *Laissez-faire*: The Promotion of Polyphonic Composition for the Church in Fifteenth-Century England," In *Music in Medieval and Early Modern England*, edited by Iain Fenlon, 1-19. Cambridge, 1981.

Bowker, Margaret. *The Secular Clergy in the Diocese of Lincoln, 1495-1520*. Cambridge, 1968.

Boyle, J. Robert. *Early History of the Town and Port of Hedon in the East Riding of York*. Hull, 1895.

Boyle, Leonard E. "Aspects of Clerical Education in Fourteenth-Century England." *Acta of the Center for Medieval and Early Renaissance Studies, Binghamton* 4 (1977):19-32.

————. "The Constitution 'Cum ex eo' of Boniface VIII." *Mediaeval Studies* 24 (1962):263-302.

293

Boyle, Leonard E. "The *Oculus Sacerdotis* and Some Other Works of William of Pagula." *TRHS*, 5th ser., 5 (1955):81-110.

Bramble, J. R. "Ancient Bristol Documents, Nos. II and III." *Proceedings of the Clifton Antiquarian Club 1884-8*, 1, pt. ii (1888):136-50.

Brown, Cornelius. *A History of Newark-upon-Trent*. 2 vols. Newark, 1904-1907.

Brunskill, Elizabeth. "Missals, Portifers and Pyes." *The Ben Johnson Papers* 2 (1974):1-34.

Buhler, C. F. *The Fifteenth-Century Book*. Philadelphia, 1960.

Bursill-Hall, G. L., "Medieval Donatus Commentaries." *Historiographia Linguistica* 8 (1981):69-97.

———. "Medieval Grammatical Theories." *Canadian Journal of Linguistics* 9 (1963-1964):40-54.

———. "Teaching Grammars of the Middle Ages: Notes on the Manuscript Tradition." *Historiographia Linguistica* 4(1977):1-29.

Butler, L. H. "Archbishop Melton, His Neighbors and His Kinsmen, 1317-1340." *J. Eccl. Hist.* 2 (1951):54-68.

Butterworth, Charles C. "Early Primers for the Use of Children." *Papers of the Bibliographical Society of America* 43 (1949):374-82.

———. *The English Primers (1529-1545)*. Philadelphia, 1953.

Camp, Anthony J. *Wills and Their Whereabouts*. 3rd ed. Canterbury, 1963.

Carlisle, Nicholas. *A Concise Description of the Endowed Grammar Schools in England and Wales*. 2 vols. London, 1818.

Chaplin, W. N. "A. F. Leach: A Re-appraisal," *BJES* 11 (1962-1963):99-124.

———. "A. F. Leach: Agreement and Difference," *BJES* 12 (1963-1964):173-83.

Charlton, Kenneth. "Ages of Admission to Educational Institutions in Tudor and Stuart England: A Comment." *History of Education* 5 (1976):221-26.

———. *Education in Renaissance England*. London, 1965.

Cheney, C. R. "Letters of William Wickwane, Chancellor of York, 1266-1268." *EHR* 47 (1932):626-42.

Cipolla, Carlo M. *Literacy and Development in the West*. Harmondsworth, 1969.

Clanchy, M. T. *From Memory to Written Record: England, 1066-1307*. Cambridge, Mass., 1979.

Clair, Colin. *A History of Printing in Britain*. Oxford, 1965.

Clarke, H. L. and Weech, W. N. *History of Sedbergh School 1525-1925*. Sedbergh, 1925.

Clay, Rotha Mary. *The Medieval Hospitals of England.* London, 1909.

Coale, Ansley J. and Demeny, Paul. *Regional Model Life Tables and Stable Populations.* Princeton, 1966.

Coleman, Janet. *Medieval Readers and Writers 1350-1400.* New York, 1981.

————. *Piers Plowman and the 'Moderni.'* Rome, 1981.

Corner, Samuel. "Education in the Middle Ages." *Transactions of the Thoroton Society* 18 (1914):66-81.

Cottle, Basil. *The Triumph of English 1350-1400.* London, 1969.

Coulton, G. G. "Religious Education before the Reformation." In *Medieval Studies*, edited by G. G. Coulton, 69-78. 2nd rev. ed. London, 1915.

Courtenay, William J. *Adam Wodeham: An Introduction to His Life and Writings.* Leiden, 1978.

————. "The Effect of the Black Death on English Higher Education." *Speculum* 55 (1980):696-714.

Cressy, David. "Educational Opportunity in Tudor and Stuart England." *History of Education Quarterly* 16 (1976):301-20.

————. "Levels of Illiteracy in England, 1530-1730." *Historical Journal* 20 (1977):1-23.

————. *Literacy and the Social Order: Reading and Writing in Tudor and Stuart England.* Cambridge, 1980.

————. "Literacy in Pre-Industrial England." *Societas* 4 (1974):229-40.

————. "Social Status and Literacy in North-East England, 1560-1630." *Local Population Studies*, no. 21 (1978):19-23.

Cross, Claire. "Lay Literacy and Clerical Misconduct in a York Parish during the Reign of Mary Tudor." *York Historian* 3 (1980):10-15.

————. "Priests into Ministers: The Establishment of Protestant Practice in the City of York, 1530-1630." In *Reformation Principles and Practice: Essays in Honour of Arthur Geoffrey Dickens*, edited by P. N. Brooks, 203-25. London, 1980.

————. "York Clerical Piety and St. Peter's School on the Eve of the Reformation." *York Historian* 2 (1978):17-20.

Curtis, S. J. "The Ancient Schools of Yorkshire." *The University of Leeds Institute of Education, Researches and Studies*, no. 8 (1953):25-39; no. 9 (1954):13-19.

————. "Ripon Grammar School." *The University of Leeds Institute of Education, Researches and Studies*, no. 4 (1951):73-80.

————. "Tadcaster Grammar School." *The University of Leeds Institute of Education, Researches and Studies*, no. 6 (1952):69-81.

Danhieux, Luc. "Literate or Semi-Literate?" *Local Population Studies*, no. 18 (1977):52-53.

Davies, William J. Frank. *Teaching Reading in Early England*. London, 1973.

Deanesly, Margaret. *The Lollard Bible and Other Medieval Biblical Versions*. Cambridge, 1920.

————. "Vernacular Books in England in the Fourteenth and Fifteenth Centuries." *Modern Language Review* 15 (1920):349-58.

De Molen, Richard, "Ages of Admission to Educational Institutions in Tudor and Stuart England." *History of Education* 5 (1976):207-19.

De Montmorency, J.E.G. *State Intervention in English Education*. Cambridge, 1902.

Denholme-Young, N. *The Country Gentry in the Fourteenth Century*. Oxford, 1969.

————. "The Yorkshire Estates of Isabella de Fortibus." *YAJ* 31 (1934):389-420.

Dickens, A. G. "Aspects of Intellectual Transition among the English Parish Clergy of the Reformation Period: A Regional Example." *Archiv für Reformationsgeschichte* 43 (1952):51-69.

————. *Lollards and Protestants in the Diocese of York, 1509-1558*. London, 1959.

————. "Robert Parkyn's Narrative of the Reformation." *EHR* 62 (1947):58-83.

————. "Sedition and Conspiracy in Yorkshire during the Later Years of Henry VIII." *YAJ* 34 (1939):379-98.

————. "Some Popular Reactions to the Edwardian Reformation in Yorkshire." *YAJ* 34 (1939):151-69.

————. "South Yorkshire Letters, 1555." *Transactions of the Hunter Archaeological Society* 6 (1949):278-84.

————. "The Writers of Tudor Yorkshire." *TRHS*, 5th ser., 13 (1963):49-76.

Ditchfield, P. H. *The Parish Clerk*. London, 1907.

Dobson, R. Barrie. *Durham Priory 1400-1450*. Cambridge, 1973.

————. "The Foundation of Perpetual Chantries by the Citizens of Medieval York." In *Studies in Church History*, Vol. 4, edited by G. J. Cuming, 22-38. Leiden, 1967.

————. *The Jews of Medieval York and the Massacre of March 1190*. York, 1974.

————. "The Residentiary Canons of York in the Fifteenth Century." *J. Eccl. Hist.* 30 (1979):145-74.

————. "Urban Decline in Late Medieval England." *TRHS*, 5th ser., 27 (1977):1-22.

Dodd, E. E. "Bingley Chantry Endowments." *Bradford Antiquary*, new ser., 8, pt. xxxvii (Oct. 1954):91-99.

————. *A History of the Bingley Grammar School, 1529-1929*. Bradford, 1930?

————. "Two Bingley Postscripts" *Bradford Antiquary*, new ser., 8, pt. xxxix (Apr. 1958):194-96.

Drake, Francis. *Eboracum*. 2 vols. York, 1788.

Du Boulay, F.R.H. *An Age of Ambition: English Society in the Late Middle Ages*. New York, 1970.

Duby, Georges. "The Culture of the Knightly Class: Audience and Patronage." In *Renaissance and Renewal in the Twelfth Century*, edited by R. L. Benson and G. Constable, 248-62. Cambridge, Mass., 1982.

Duff, E. Gordon. *The English Provincial Printers, Stationers and Bookbinders to 1557*. Cambridge, 1912.

————. *Fifteenth-Century English Books*. Oxford, 1917.

————. *Hand-List of English Printers 1501-1556*. 2 vols. London, 1895.

Edwards, Kathleen. *The English Secular Cathedrals in the Middle Ages*. 2nd ed. Manchester, 1967.

Eisenstein, Elizabeth L. *The Printing Press as an Agent of Change: Communications and Cultural Transformations in Early-Modern Europe*. 2 vols. Cambridge, 1979.

Emden. A. B. *A Biographical Register of the University of Cambridge to 1500*. Cambridge, 1963.

————. *A Biographical Register of the University of Oxford to 1500*. 3 vols. Oxford, 1957-1959.

————. *A Biographical Register of the University of Oxford 1501-1540*. Oxford, 1974.

English, Barbara. *The Lords of Holderness, 1086-1260*. Oxford, 1979.

Evans. N. R. "Testators, Literacy, Education and Religious Belief." *Local Population Studies* 25 (1980):48-50.

Evans, Seiriol. "Ely Almonry Boys and Choristers in the Later Middle Ages." In *Studies Presented to Sir Hilary Jenkinson*, edited by J. C. Davies, 155-63. Oxford, 1957.

Fasti Parochiales. Edited by A. H. Thompson, C. T. Clay, N.A.H. Lawrence, and Norah K. M. Gurney. 4 vols. YAS rec. ser., nos. 85, 107, 129, 133. Wakefield and Leeds, 1933-1971.

Feingold, Mordechai. "Jordan Revisited: Patterns of Charitable Giving in Sixteenth and Seventeenth Century England." *History of Education* 8 (1979):257-73.

Firth, C. B. "Benefit of Clergy in the Time of Edward IV." *EHR* 32 (1917):175-91.

Fisher, R. M. "Thomas Cromwell, Humanism and Educational Reform, 1530-40." *Bulletin of the Institute of Historical Research* 50 (1977):151-63.

Fishwick, Henry, ed. *A List of the Lancashire Wills Proved within the Archdeaconry of Richmond . . . 1457 to 1680.* Lancashire and Cheshire Record Society, no. 10. Manchester, 1884.

Fletcher, A. J. "The Expansion of Education in Berkshire and Oxfordshire, 1500-1670." *BJES* 15 (1967):51-59.

Flynn, Vincent J. "The Grammatical Writings of William Lily,?1468-?1523." *Papers of the Bibliographical Society of America* 37 (1943):85-113.

Friedman, John B. "John Siferwas and the Mythological Illustrations in the *Liber cosmographiae* of John de Foxton." *Speculum* 58 (1983):391-418.

Froude, J. A. *Life and Letters of Erasmus.* New York, 1895.

Furet, François and Ozouf, Jacques. "L'alphabétisation." *Annales* 32 (1977):488-502.

———. *Lire et écrire: l'alphabétisation des français de Calvin à Jules Ferry.* 2 vols. Paris, 1977.

Gabel, Leona. *Benefit of Clergy in England in the Later Middle Ages.* Northampton, Mass., 1929.

Galbraith, V. H. "The Literacy of the Medieval English Kings." *Proceedings of the British Academy*, 5th ser., 21 (1935):201-38.

Gardiner, Dorothy. *English Girlhood at School.* Oxford, 1929.

Garside, M. W. "Halifax Schools prior to 1700 A.D." In *Papers, Reports, etc. Read before the Halifax Antiquarian Society*, 183-205. Halifax, 1924.

Garton, Charles. "A Fifteenth Century Headmaster's Library." *Lincolnshire History and Archaeology* 15 (1980):29-38.

Gasquet, F. A. "The Bibliography of Some Devotional Books Printed by the Earliest English Printers." *Transactions of the Bibliographical Society* 7 (1902-1904):163-89.

Gibbon, A. M. *The Ancient Free Grammar School of Skipton-in-Craven.* Liverpool, 1947.

Gibson, J.S.W. *Wills and Where to Find Them.* Chichester, 1974.

Gillett, Edward and MacMahon, Kenneth A. *A History of Hull.* Oxford, 1980.

Gilson, J. P. "The Library of Henry Savile, of Banke." *Transactions of the Bibliographical Society* 9 (1908):127-210.

Goldthorp, L. M. "The Franciscans and Dominicans in Yorkshire." *YAJ* 32 (1935-1936):264-320, 365-428.

Gottfried, Robert S. *Bury St. Edmunds and the Urban Crisis 1290-1539.* Princeton, 1982.

———. *Epidemic Disease in Fifteenth-Century England.* New Brunswick, N.J., 1978.

Graff, Harvey J. *Literacy in History.* New York, 1981.

Grassi, J. L. "Royal Clerks from the Archdiocese of York in the Fourteenth Century." *Northern History* 5 (1970):12-33.

Grounds, A. D. *A History of King Edward VI Grammar School, Retford.* Worksop, 1970.

Grundmann, H. "Litteratus-illiteratus: Der Wandel einer Bildungsnorm vom Altertum zum Mittelalter." *Archiv für Kulturgeschichte* 40 (1958):1-65.

Gunner, W. H. "Catalogue of Books Belonging to the College of St. Mary, Winchester, in the Reign of Henry VI." *Archaeological Journal* 15 (1858):59-74.

Haigh, Christopher. *The Last Days of the Lancashire Monasteries and the Pilgrimage of Grace.* Chetham Society, 3rd ser., 17. Manchester, 1969.

———. *Reformation and Resistance in Tudor Lancashire.* Cambridge, 1975.

Haines, Roy M. "Education in English Ecclesiastical Legislation of the Later Middle Ages." In *Studies in Church History*, Vol. 7, edited by G. J. Cuming and D. Baker, 161-75. Cambridge, 1971.

———. "The Education of the English Clergy during the Later Middle Ages: Some Observations on the Operation of Pope Boniface VIII's Constitution *Cum ex eo* (1298)." *Canadian Journal of History* 4 (1969):1-22.

Hamilton, D. H., ed. *A History of St. Peter's School.* York, 1977.

Hamilton, George L. "Theodulus: A Medieval Textbook." *Modern Philology* 7 (1909):1-17.

Harrison, Frank Ll. *Music in Medieval Britain.* London, 1958.

Harrison, Frederick. *Life in a Medieval College.* London, 1952.

Hatcher, John. *Plague, Population and the English Economy, 1348-1530.* London, 1977.

Heath, Peter. *The English Parish Clergy on the Eve of the Reformation.* London, 1969.

Hexter, J. H. "The Education of the Aristocracy in the Renaissance." In *Reappraisals in History*, 45-70. London, 1961.

Hill, Rosalind M. T. *The Labourer in the Vineyard: The Visitations of Archbishop Melton in the Archdeaconry of Richmond*. York, 1968.

Hinchcliffe, Edgar. *Appleby Grammar School—from Chantry to Comprehensive*. Appleby, 1974.

———. *A History of King James's Grammar School in Almondbury*. Huddersfield, 1963.

Hinnebusch, William. *The History of the Dominican Order*. 2 vols. New York, 1966-1973.

Hollingsworth, T. H. *Historical Demography*, Ithaca, N.Y., 1969.

Hoppin, Richard H. *Medieval Music*. New York, 1978.

Hoyle, E. "The History of Barnsley and District." *Barnsley Chronicle*, Sept. 10, 1904.

Hughes, Andrew. *Medieval Manuscripts for Mass and Office: A Guide to Their Organization and Terminology*. Toronto, 1982.

Hughes, Philip. *The Reformation in England*. 3 vols. London, 1950-1954.

Hunt, R. W. "English Learning in the Late Twelfth Century." In *Essays in Medieval History: Selected from the TRHS on the Occasion of Its Centenary*, 106-28. London, 1968.

———. *The History of Grammar in the Middle Ages: Collected Papers*. Edited by G. L. Bursill-Hall. Amsterdam, 1980.

———. "The History of Grammar in the Middle Ages: Additions and Corrections." Edited by M. T. Gibson and S. P. Hall. *Bodleian Library Record* 11 (1982):9-19.

Hunter, Joseph. *English Monastic Libraries*. London, 1831.

———. *South Yorkshire*. 2 vols. London, 1828-1831.

Index of Wills, etc. from the Dean and Chapter's Court at York, 1321-1636. YAS rec. ser., no. 38. Leeds, 1907.

Index of Wills, Adminstrations, and Probate Acts in the York Registry 1666 to 1672 and also of the Wills, etc. in Certain Peculiars. YAS rec. ser., no. 60. Leeds, 1920.

Index of the Original Documents of the Consistory Court of York 1427 to 1658. YAS rec. ser., no. 73. Leeds, 1928.

Index of the Wills and Administrations Entered in the Registers of the Archbishops at York, Being Consistory Wills, etc. 1316 to 1822. YAS rec. ser., no. 93. Leeds, 1936.

An Index of Wills Proved in the Prerogative Court of Canterbury 1383-1558. 2 vols. London, 1893-1895.

Jackson, N. G. *Newark Magnus: The Story of a Gift*. Nottingham, 1964.

Jarrett, Bede. *The English Dominicans*. London, 1921.

Jewell, Helen M. " 'The Bringing Up of Children in Good Learning and Manners': A Survey of Secular Educational Provision in the North of England, c. 1350-1550." *Northern History* 18 (1982):1-25.

Jewels, E. N. *A.History of Archbishop Holgate's Grammar School, York, 1546-1946.* York, 1963.

Jordan, W. K. *The Charities of Rural England, 1480-1660.* London, 1961.

————. *Philanthropy in England, 1480-1660.* London, 1959.

————. *The Social Institutions of Lancashire, 1480-1660.* Chetham Society, 3rd ser., 11. Manchester, 1962.

Keiser, George R. "Lincoln Cathedral Library MS 91: Life and Milieu of the Scribe." *Studies in Bibliography* 32 (1979):158-79.

Ker, N. R. *Medieval Libraries of Great Britain: A List of Surviving Books.* 2nd ed. London, 1964.

————. *Medieval Manuscripts in British Libraries.* 2 vols. Oxford, 1969-1971.

Kermode, Jennifer I. "The Merchants of Three Northern English Towns." In *Profession, Vocation and Culture in Later Medieval England*, edited by C. H. Clough, 7-48. Liverpool, 1982.

Kingsford, Charles L. *English Historical Literature in the Fifteenth Century.* Oxford, 1913.

————. "Two Forfeitures in the Year of Agincourt." *Archaeologia* 70, 2nd ser., 20 (1920):71-100.

————. *Prejudice and Promise in Fifteenth Century England.* Oxford, 1925.

Kitching, C. J. "The Chantries of the East Riding of Yorkshire at the Dissolution in 1548." *YAJ* 44 (1972):178-94.

Knight, C. B. *A History of the City of York.* York, 1944.

Kreider, Alan. *English Chantries: The Road to Dissolution.* Cambridge, Mass., 1979.

Lawson, John. "Beverley Minster Grammar School in the Middle Ages." *University of Hull Studies in Education* 2 (May 1954):151-67.

————. *The Endowed Grammar Schools of East Yorkshire.* East Yorkshire Local History Society, no. 14. York, 1962.

————. *Medieval Education and the Reformation.* London, 1967.

————. *Primary Education in East Yorkshire, 1560-1902.* East Yorkshire Local History Society, no. 10. York, 1959.

————. *A Town Grammar School Through Six Centuries.* London, 1963.

Lawson, John and Silver, Harold, eds. *A Social History of Education in England.* London, 1973.

Leach, A. F. "Edward VI: Spoiler of Schools." *Contemporary Review* 62 (Sept. 1892):368-84.

————. *English Schools at the Reformation, 1546-8*. Westminster 1896.

————. "The Foundation and Refoundation of Pocklington Grammar School." *Transactions of the East Riding Antiquarian Society* 5 (1897):63-114.

————. *History of Warwick School*. London, 1906.

————. "Lincoln Grammar School, 1090-1906." *The Journal of Education* (Aug. 1906):524-25.

————. "School Supply in the Middle Ages." *The Contemporary Review* 66 (Nov. 1894):674-84.

————. *The Schools of Medieval England*. London, 1915.

————. "Some Results of Research in the History of Education in England; with Suggestions for Its Continuance and Extension." *Proceedings of the British Academy* 6 (1913-1914):433-80.

Leader, Damian. "Grammar in Late-Medieval Oxford and Cambridge." *History of Education* 12 (1983):9-14.

Leadman, A.D.H. "Pocklington School." *YAJ* 14 (1896):133-46.

Lester, D.N.R. *The History of Batley Grammar School*. Batley, 1962.

Lindberg, Conrad. "The Manuscripts and Versions of the Wycliffite Bible: A Preliminary Survey." *Studia Neophilologica* 42 (1970): 333-47.

Lister, John. "The Old Free Chapels in the Parish of Halifax." In *Papers, Reports, etc. Read before the Halifax Antiquarian Society*, 29-54. Halifax, 1909.

Little, A. G. "Educational Organization of the Mendicant Friars in England." *TRHS*, new ser., 8 (1894):49-70.

————. "Review of A. F. Leach, *The Schools of Medieval England*." *EHR* 30 (1915):525-29.

————. *Studies in English Franciscan History*. Manchester, 1917.

————. "Theological Schools in Medieval England." *EHR* 55 (1940):624-30.

Lloyd, David J. *The History of Malton Grammar School*. Malton, 1966.

Lupton, J. H. *A Life of John Colet*. 2nd ed. London, 1909.

McConica, James. *English Humanists and Reformation Politics under Henry VIII and Edward VI*. Oxford, 1965.

McFarlane, K. B. *The Nobility of Later Medieval England*. Oxford, 1973.

McMahon, Clara P. *Education in Fifteenth-Century England*. Baltimore, 1947.

McNulty, Joseph. "William of Rymyngton, Prior of Salley Abbey, Chancellor of Oxford, 1372-3." *YAJ* 30 (1931):231-47.

Marchant, R. A. *The Church under the Law: Justice, Administration and Discipline in the Diocese of York 1560-1640.* Cambridge, 1969.

Martin, C. T. "Clerical Life in the Fifteenth Century." *Archaeologia* 60, pt. 2 (1907):353-78.

Mead, H. R. "Fifteenth-Century Schoolbooks." *Huntington Library Quarterly* 3 (1939):37-42.

Miner, J. N. (Br. Bonaventure). "Schools and Literacy in Later Medieval England." *BJES* 11 (1962):16-27.

———. "The Teaching of Latin in Later Medieval England." *Mediaeval Studies* 23 (1961):1-20.

Moorman, J.R.H. *Church Life in England in the Thirteenth Century.* Cambridge, 1945.

Moran, J. Hoeppner. "Clerical Recruitment in the Diocese of York, 1340-1530: Data and Commentary." *J. Eccl. Hist.* 34 (1983):19-54.

———. *Education and Learning in the City of York, 1300-1560.* York, 1979.

———. "Literacy and Education in Northern England, 1350-1550: A Methodological Inquiry." *Northern History* 17 (1981):1-23.

Munden, A. F. *Eight Centuries of Education in Faversham.* Faversham Papers, no. 9. Kent, 1972.

Murray, A. *Reason and Society in the Middle Ages.* Oxford, 1978.

Murray, Athol Laverick. *The Royal Grammar School, Lancaster.* Cambridge, 1951.

Noakes, Susan. "The Fifteen Oes, The *Disticha Catonis*, Marculfius, and Dick, Jane and Sally." *The University of Chicago Library Society Bulletin* 2 (1977):2-15.

O'Carroll, Maura. "The Educational Organization of the Dominicans in England and Wales 1221-1348: A Multidisciplinary Approach." *Archivum Fratrum Praedicatorum* 50 (1980):23-62.

O'Day, Rosemary. *Education and Society 1500-1800.* London, 1982.

Orme, Nicholas. "Chaucer and Education." *Chaucer Review* 16 (1981):38-59.

———. "The Early Musicians of Exeter Cathedral." *Music and Letters* 59 (1978):395-410.

———. "Education and Learning at a Medieval English Cathedral: Exeter 1380-1548." *J. Eccl. Hist.* 32 (1981):265-83.

———. *Education in the West of England 1066-1548.* Exeter, 1976.

———. "Education in the West of England, 1066-1548: Additions and Corrections." *Devon and Cornwall Notes & Queries* 34 (1978):22-25.

Orme, Nicholas. *English Schools in the Middle Ages*. London, 1973.
———. "Langland and Education." *History of Education* 11 (1982):251-66.
———. "The Medieval Schools of Worcestershire." *Transactions of the Worcestershire Archaeological Society*, 3rd. ser., 6 (1978):43-51.
———. "Schoolmasters, 1307-1509." In *Profession, Vocation and Culture in Later Medieval England*, edited by C. H. Clough, 218-41. Liverpool, 1982.
Owst, G. R. *Literature and Pulpit in Medieval England*. Cambridge, 1933.
———. *Preaching in Medieval England*. Cambridge, 1926.
Pafort, Eloise. "A Group of Early Tudor School Books." *The Library*, 4th ser., 26 (1946):227-61.
Page, Rolph B. *The Letters of Alcuin*. New York, 1909.
Palliser, D. M. "Civic Mentality and the Environment in Tudor York." *Northern History* 18 (1982):78-115.
———. *The Reformation in York 1534-1553*. York, 1971.
———. *Tudor York*. Oxford, 1979.
Palliser, D. M. and Selwyn, D. G. "The Stock of a York Stationer, 1538." *The Library*, 5th ser., 27 (1972):207-19.
Pantin, William A. *The English Church in the Fourteenth Century*. Cambridge, 1955.
Parkes, M. B. *English Cursive Book Hands 1250-1500*. Oxford, 1969.
———. "The Literacy of the Laity." In *Literature and Western Civilization: The Medieval World*, edited by D. Daiches and A. Thorlby, 555-77. London, 1973.
Picard, Jean-Charles. "L'Education dans le haut moyen âge." *Histoire de l'éducation*, no. 6 (1980):1-8.
Platt, Colin. *The Parish Churches of Medieval England*. London, 1981.
Potter, G. R. "Education in the Fourteenth and Fifteenth Centuries." In *The Cambridge Medieval History*, Vol. 8, edited by C. W. Previté-Orton and Z. N. Brooke, 688-717. Cambridge, 1936.
Power, Eileen. *Medieval English Nunneries c. 1275 to 1535*. Cambridge, 1922.
Purvis, J. S. "The Literacy of the Later Tudor Clergy in Yorkshire." In *Studies in Church History*, Vol. 5, edited by G. J. Cuming, 147-65. Leiden, 1969.
———. "New Light on the Chartularies of Monk Bretton Priory." *YAJ* 37 (1948):67-71.
———. "Notes from the Diocesan Registry at York." *YAJ* 35 (1943):393-403.

————. "The Tables of the York Vicars Choral." *YAJ* 41 (1966):741-48.

Putnam, Bertha H. "Maximum Wage-Laws for Priests after the Black Death, 1348-1381." *American Historical Review* 21 (1915):12-32.

Raine, Angelo. *History of St. Peter's School, York, A.D. 627 to the Present Day.* London, 1926?

Rashdall, Hastings. *The Universities of Europe in the Middle Ages.* 3 vols. Rev. ed. Oxford, 1936.

Richardson, H. G. "The Parish Clergy of the Thirteenth and Fourteenth Centuries." *TRHS*, 3rd ser., 6 (1912):89-128.

Richardson, R. C. "Wills and Will-Makers in the Sixteenth and Seventeenth Centuries: Some Lancashire Evidences." *Local Population Studies* 9 (1972):33-42.

Riché, Pierre. *Les Ecoles et l'enseignment dans l'Occident chrétien de la fin du Vᵉ siècle au milieu du XIᵉ siècle.* Paris, 1979.

————. *Education and Culture in the Barbarian West from the Sixth through the Eighth Century.* Translated by J. J. Contreni. Columbia, S.C., 1976.

————. "L'Instruction des laïcs au XIIᵉ siècle." *Mélanges Saint Bernard.* XXIV Congrès de l'association bourguignonne des sociétés savantes, 212-17. Dijon, 1953.

————. "Recherches sur l'instruction des laïcs du IXᵉ au XIIᵉ siècle." *Cahiers de civilisation médiévale* 5 (1962):175-82.

"Richmondshire Wills (Eastern Deaneries), Being a Calendar to the Probate Records formerly in the Custody of the Archdeacon of Richmond." *Northern Genealogist* 2 (1896) and 3 (1897): supplement, 1-48.

Richter, Michael. "A Socio-Linguistic Approach to the Latin Middle Ages." In *Studies in Church History*, Vol. 11, edited by D. Baker, 69-82. Oxford, 1975.

Rickert, Edith, "Chaucer at School." *Modern Philology* 29 (1932):257-74.

Riley, Marjorie A. "The Foundation of Chantries in the Counties of Nottingham and York, 1350-1400" *YAJ* 33 (1937):122-65; 237-85.

Ritchie, C.I.A. *The Ecclesiastical Courts of York.* Arbroath, 1956.

Robins, R. H. *Ancient and Medieval Grammatical Theory in Europe.* London, 1951.

Robinson, David. *Beneficed Clergy in Cleveland and the East Riding 1306-1340.* York, 1969.

Rogers, Philip W. *A History of Ripon Grammar School.* Ripon, 1954.

Rosenthal, Joel T. "Aristocratic Cultural Patronage and Book Bequests, 1350-1550. "*Bulletin of the John Rylands University Library* 64 (1982):522-48.

————. *The Purchase of Paradise: Gift-Giving and the Aristocracy, 1307-1485.* London, 1972.

————. "The Yorkshire Chantry Certificates of 1546: An Analysis." *Northern History* 9 (1974):26-47.

Roth, Francis. *The English Austin Friars.* 2 vols. New York, 1966.

Rothwell, W. "The Role of French in Thirteenth-Century England." *Bulletin of the John Rylands University Library* 58 (1976):458-64.

Rowntree, Arthur, ed. *The History of Scarborough.* London, 1931.

Russell, J. C. *British Medieval Population.* Albuquerque, N.M., 1948.

————. "The Clerical Population of Medieval England." *Traditio* 2 (1944):177-212.

Saenger, Paul. "Silent Reading: Its Impact on Late Medieval Script and Society." *Viator* 13 (1982):367-414.

St. John Hope, W. H. "Inventory of the Parish Church of St. Mary Scarborough 1434." *Archaeologia* 51, pt. ii (1888):61-72.

Sands, P. C. and Haworth, Christopher M. *A History of Pocklington School, East Yorkshire, 1514-1950.* Hull, 1951.

Saul, Nigel. "The Religious Sympathies of the Gentry in Gloucestershire, 1200-1500." *Bristol and Gloucestershire Archaeological Society Transactions* 98 (1980):99-112.

Scattergood, V. J. *Politics and Poetry in the Fifteenth Century.* London, 1971.

Schofield, R. S. "The Measurement of Literacy." In *Literacy in Traditional Society,* edited by J. Goody, 311-25. Cambridge, 1968.

Seaborne, Malcolm. *The English School: Its Architecture and Organization 1370-1870.* London, 1971.

Seaton, Ethel. *Sir Richard Roos, c. 1410-1482: Lancastrian Poet.* London, 1961.

Sessions, William K and Sessions, E. Margaret. *Printing in York.* York, 1976.

Shaw, A. E. "The Earliest Latin Grammars in English." *Transactions of the Bibliographical Society* 5 (1898-1900):39-65.

Sheehan, Michael M. *The Will in Medieval England from the Conversion of the Anglo-Saxons to the End of the Thirteenth Century.* Toronto, 1963.

Shelby, Lon R. "The Education of Medieval English Master Masons." *Mediaeval Studies* 32 (1970):1-6.

A Short History of the Doncaster Grammar School 1350-1950. Doncaster, 1950.

Simon, Joan. "A. F. Leach on the Reformation." *BJES* 3 (1954-1955):128-43; 4 (1955-1956):32-48.

————. "A. F. Leach: A Reply." *BJES* 12 (1963-1964):41-50.

————. "Education." In *The New Cambridge Bibliography of English Literature*, Vol. 1, edited by George Watson, 627-39, 2381-2418. Cambridge, 1974.

————. *Education and Society in Tudor England.* Cambridge, 1966.

————. "The Reformation and English Education." *Past and Present*, no. 11 (1957):48-65.

————. *The Social Origins of English Education.* London, 1972.

————. "Town Estates and Schools in the Sixteenth and Early Seventeenth Centuries." In *Education in Leicestershire 1540-1940*, edited by Brian Simon, 3-26. Leicester, 1968.

Sisson, Charles. "Marks as Signatures." *The Library*, 4th ser., 9 (1928):1-37.

Smalley, Beryl. *English Friars and Antiquity in the Early Fourteenth Century.* Oxford, 1960.

Smith, David M. *A Guide to the Archive Collections in the Borthwick Institute of Historical Research.* York, 1973.

————. "Lost Archiepiscopal Registers of York: The Evidence of Five Medieval Inventories." *Borthwick Institute Bulletin* 1, no. 1 (1975):31-37.

Smith, R. B. *Land and Politics in the England of Henry VIII.* Oxford, 1970.

Spufford, Margaret. *Contrasting Communities: English Villages in the Sixteenth and Seventeenth Centuries.* Cambridge, 1974.

————. "The Scribes of Villagers' Wills in the Sixteenth and Seventeenth Centuries and Their Influence." *Local Population Studies* 7 (1971):28-43.

————. "Wills and Their Scribes." *Local Population Studies* 8 (1972):55-57.

Stanewell, L. M., ed. *Calendar of Ancient Deeds, etc. in the Archives of the Corporation.* Hull, 1951.

Stephenson, Mill. "Monumental Brasses in the East Riding." *YAJ* 12 (1893):195-229; 14 (1898):507-13.

Stevens, John. *Music & Poetry in the Early Tudor Court.* London, 1961.

Stevenson, W. H. "The Introduction of English as the Vehicle of Instruction in English Schools." In *An English Miscellany Presented to*

Dr. Furnivall, edited by W. P. Ker, A. S. Napier, and W. W. Skeat, 421-29. Oxford, 1901.

Stock, Brian. *The Implications of Literacy: Written Language and Models of Interpretation in the Eleventh and Twelfth Centuries*. Princeton, 1983.

Stone, Lawrence. "Ages of Admission to Educational Institutions in Tudor and Stuart England: A Comment." *History of Education* 6 (1977):9.

―――. "The Educational Revolution in England, 1560-1640." *Past and Present*, no. 28 (1964):41-80.

―――, ed. *Schooling and Society*. Baltimore, 1976.

―――, ed. *The University in Society*. 2 vols. Princeton, 1974.

Storey, R. L. *Diocesan Administration in Fifteenth-Century England*. 2nd ed. York, 1972.

―――. *The End of the House of Lancaster*. London, 1966.

―――. Review of *A Calendar of the Register of Henry Wakefield*. *EHR* 89 (1974):378-80.

Suggett, Helen. "The Use of French in England in the Middle Ages." *TRHS*, 4th ser., 28 (1946):61-83.

Tate, W. E. *A. F. Leach as a Historian of Yorkshire Education*. York, 1963.

―――. "Some Sources for the History of English Grammar Schools." *BJES* 1 (1952-1953):164-75; 2 (1953-1954):67-81, 145-65.

Temperley, Nicholas. *The Music of the English Parish Church*. 2 vols. Cambridge, 1979.

Thompson, A. Hamilton. *The English Clergy and Their Organization in the Later Middle Ages*. Oxford, 1947.

―――. "English Colleges of Chantry Priests." *Transactions of the Ecclesiological Society*, new ser. 1, pt. ii (1943):92-108.

―――. "Notes on Colleges of Secular Canons in England." *The Archaeological Journal* 74 (1917):139-98.

―――. "The Pestilences of the Fourteenth Century in the Diocese of York." *The Archaeological Journal* 71 (1914):97-154.

―――. "The Registers of the Archbishop of York." *YAJ* 32 (1935):245-63.

―――. "Song Schools in the Middle Ages." *Church-Music Society Occasional Papers*, no. 14, 3-29. London, 1942.

―――. "The Village Churches of Yorkshire." In *Memorials of Old Yorkshire*, edited by T. M. Fallow, 106-64. London, 1909.

Thompson, E. Margaret. *The Carthusian Order in England*. London, 1930.

Thompson, J. W. *The Literacy of the Laity in the Middle Ages.* Berkeley, 1939.

Thomson, David. *A Descriptive Catalogue of Middle English Grammatical Texts.* New York, 1979.

———. "The Oxford Grammar Masters Revisited." *Mediaeval Studies* 45 (1983):298-310.

Thomson, John A. F. *The Later Lollards, 1414-1520.* London, 1965.

———. "Piety and Charity in Late Medieval London." *J. Eccl. Hist.* 16 (1965):178-95.

Thorndike, Lynn. "Elementary and Secondary Education in the Middle Ages." *Speculum* 15 (1940):400-408.

Thrupp, Sylvia. *The Merchant Class of Medieval London, 1300-1500.* Ann Arbor, Mich., 1948.

Tuer, Andrew W. *The History of the Hornbook.* 2 vols. London, 1897.

Turner, Ralph V. "The *Miles Literatus* in Twelfth- and Thirteenth-Century England: How Rare a Phenomenon?" *American Historical Review* 83 (1978):928-45.

Vale, M.G.A. *Piety, Charity and Literacy among the Yorkshire Gentry, 1370-1480.* York, 1976.

Victoria History of the Counties of England. (For a list of all the articles on medieval schools, see Orme, *ESMA*, 339.)

Virgoe, R. "William Tailboys and Lord Cromwell: Crime and Politics in Lancastrian England." *Bulletin of the John Rylands University Library* 55 (1972):477-82.

Walker, John W. *Wakefield, Its History and People.* 2 vols. 2nd ed. Wakefield, 1939.

Wallis, P. J. *Histories of Old Schools: A Revised List for England and Wales.* Newcastle-upon-Tyne, 1966.

———. "Leach—Past, Present, and Future." *BJES* 12 (1963-1964):184-94.

———. "A Preliminary Register of Old Schools in Lancashire and Cheshire." *Transactions of the Historic Society of Lancashire and Cheshire* 120 (1968):1-21.

———. "Worsborough Grammar School." *YAJ* 39 (1956):147-63.

Wallis, P. J. and Tate, W. E. "A Register of Old Yorkshire Grammar Schools." *The University of Leeds Institute of Education, Researches and Studies*, no. 13 (1956):64-104.

Watson, Foster. *The Old Grammar Schools.* Cambridge, 1916.

Wenham, L. P. "The Chantries, Guilds, Obits and Lights of Richmond, Yorkshire." *YAJ* 38 (1952-1955):96-111, 185-214, 310-32.

———. *The History of Richmond School, Yorkshire.* Arbroath, 1958.

Wenham, L. P. "Two Notes on the History of Richmond School, York-shire." *YAJ* 37 (1950):369-75.

West, Thomas. *The Antiquities of Furness*. New ed. Ulverston, 1805.

Williams, J. F. "Ordination in the Norwich Diocese during the Fifteenth Century." *Norfolk Archaeology* 31 (1956):347-58.

Wills in the York Registry 1389 to 1514. YAS rec. ser., no. 6. Leeds, 1888.

Wills in the York Registry 1514 to 1553. YAS rec. ser., no. 11. Leeds, 1891.

Witty, J. R. "The History of Beverley Grammar School." *Beverley Guardian*, nos. 2-42 (1930-1931).

Wood, N. *The Reformation and English Education*. London, 1931.

Wood-Legh, K. L. *Perpetual Chantries in Britain*. Cambridge, 1965.

Woodcock, B. L. *Medieval Ecclesiastical Courts in the Diocese of Canterbury*. Oxford, 1952.

Wordsworth, Christopher and Littlehales, Henry. *The Old Service-Books of the English Church*. London, 1904.

Yardley, Edward. *Menevia Sacra*. Edited by F. Green. Cambrian Archaeological Association, supplementary vol. London, 1927.

York Minster Fasti. Edited by C. T. Clay. YAS rec. ser., nos. 123, 124. Wakefield, 1958-1959.

Young, Percy M. *A History of British Music*. New York, 1967.

Zapatka, Francis E. "Thomas More and Thomas Darcy." *Moreana* 18 (1981):15-27.

Zell, Michael L., "Fifteenth- and Sixteenth-Century Wills as Historical Sources." *Archives* 14 (1979):67-74.

DISSERTATIONS AND UNPUBLISHED PAPERS

Bowers, Roger. "Choral Institutions within the English Church: Their Constitution and Development 1340-1500." Ph.D. diss., University of East Anglia, 1975.

Burns, K. F. "The Administrative System of the Ecclesiastical Courts in the Diocese and Province of York: The Medieval Courts." Borthwick Institute, 1962. Typescript.

Cavanaugh, Susan. "A Study of Books Privately Owned in England: 1300-1450." 2 vols. Ph.D. diss., University of Pennsylvania, 1980.

Crawford, Karis. "Prymers in England: An Untapped Source for Fifteenth-Century Studies." Paper presented at the International Congress on Medieval Studies, Kalamazoo, Mich., 1977.

Kightly, Charles. "The Early Lollards: A Survey of Popular Lollard

Activity in England, 1382-1428." Ph.D. diss., University of York, 1975.

Miner, J. N. (Br. Bonaventure). "The Teaching of Grammar in England in the Later Middle Ages." Ph.D. diss., University of London, 1959.

———. "The Use of the Disputation in England's Medieval Grammar Schools." Paper presented at the International Congress on Medieval Studies, Kalamazoo, Mich., 1982.

Moran, J. Hoeppner. "Educational Development and Social Change in York Diocese from the Fourteenth Century to 1548." Ph.D. diss., Brandeis University, 1975.

———. "The Schools of Northern England 1450-1550: Humanist Ideals and Educational Realities." Paper presented at the Newberry Library Conference on Schooling and the Renaissance, Chicago, 1982.

Tachau, Katherine. "Northern Universities and Vernacular Learning in the Fourteenth Century." Paper presented at the annual meeting of the American Historical Association, Washington, D.C., 1982.

INDEX

A B Cs, 40-41
academic degrees, *see* degrees
Acaster Malbis, 94
Acaster Selby, 51, 84
accessibility of books, schools, etc., 208, 222
Accidence (Donatus's *Ars Minor*), 28
acolyte (minor orders), 125, 131, 140
Adam, precentor of York, 57, 86, 112
Adam de Boys, 270
Adamson, John William, 24
Aelfric ("Grammaticus"), 143
age of students, 22, 64, 86n, 180, 181n
Agnes of Celayne, 173
Akers, William, 86, 110n, 279
Alcock, John (bishop), 169, 182, 217
Alcuin (*Albinus*), 22
Alexander de Villa, Dei, 27, 29
Alexander of Neckham, 27
Allen, James, 267
Allen, William (cardinal), 147
almonry schools, 65, 82n, 115, 176
Alnwick, William (bishop), 58
alphabet, learning of, 40-41
antiphonals, 217
Ardern, Peter, 151, 153-54
aristocracy, 116, 151, 152, 156-57, 162, 164, 186, 189
Arundel, Thomas (archbishop), 32, 38, 44
Ascham, Roger, 31, 34, 36, 58-59n, 94, 221, 259
Ashe, Margaret, 267
Atkinson, Thomas, 133, 140
Atkynson, Johanna, 254
Augustinians, 113
Avissede, Roger, 199
Awnewike, Robert, 276
Aynesworth, Henry, 178

B.A. (bachelor of art degree), 71, 81
Babthorp, John, 55
Bagley, J. J., 33n
Bainbridge, Christopher (archbishop), 141, 192
Balbi, John, 18n. *See also* John of Genoa
ballads (popular songs), 204

Banks, William, 210
Barboure, William, 70, 87
Barde, John, 249
Bargeman, William, 277
Barnby, John, 271
Barnys, Roger, 252
Barr, Walter, 244
Barre, John, 55
Barton, Christopher, 154n
Basset, Sir Richard, 69
"bastard Latin," 39
Batemanson, Robert, 272
Bath and Wells (diocese), 138
Batty, William, 276
Baxter (schoolmaster of Kneesall), 76-77
Baynes, Brian, 261
Beaufort, Lady Margaret, 162n
Beaumont, William, 72, 218
Beckington, 78
Beckwith, Robert, 238
Bee, John, 56, 165, 241
Beetham, 167
Bell, John, 245
Bell, Roger, 86
Belton, Robert, 109
Belvoir Castle, 97, 116, 161
Bempton, Sir William, 240
Benedictine monasteries, 83n, 119
benefices, *see* ecclesiastical benefices
benefit of clergy, 16
Bennett, H. S., 144
Bentley, Edmund, 274
bequests, *see* wills
Berkowitz, David, xvii
Best, Richard, 119
Bevercotes, William, 240-41
Beverley, 58, 73, 74, 93n, 148, 165n, 229n
Bewchampe, Robert (brother), 113
Bible: O.T. Psalms, 53; study & teaching, 19, 22-23, 32, 44, 174, 185, 186, 206; translations, 190
Bigod, Francis, 173
Bilborough, 73, 76
Birthby, Thomas, 273

313

Library of Congress Cataloging in Publication Data

Moran, Jo Ann Hoeppner
The growth of English schooling, 1340-1548.

Bibliography: p.
Includes index.
1. Education, Elementary—England—Yorkshire—
History. 2. English language—Grammar—Study and
teaching—England—Yorkshire—History. 3. Literacy—
England—Yorkshire—History. 4. Education, Medieval.
5. Church of England. Diocese of York—History.
I. Title.
LA638.Y6M67 1984   372.9428'1   84-42570
ISBN 0-691-05430-4

Jo Ann Hoeppner Moran is Associate Professor of History at Georgetown University. She is the author of *Education and Learning in the City of York* (1979).